THE PACIFIC BASIN SINCE 1945

The Postwar World
General Editors: A.J. Nicholls and Martin S. Alexander

As distance puts events into perspective, and as evidence accumulates, it begins to be possible to form an objective historical view of our recent past. *The Postwar World* is an ambitious new series providing a scholarly but readable account of the way our world has been shaped in the crowded years since the Second World War. Some volumes will deal with regions, or even single nations, others with important themes; all will be written by expert historians drawing on the latest scholarship as well as their own research and judgements. The series should be particularly welcome to students, but it is designed also for the general reader with an interest in contemporary history.

The Pacific Basin since 1945

A History of the Foreign Relations
of the Asian, Australasian and
American Rim States and the Pacific Islands

Roger C. Thompson

Longman
London and New York

LONGMAN GROUP LIMITED,
Longman House, Burnt Mill,
Harlow, Essex CM20 2JE, England
and Associated Companies throughout the world.

*Published in the United States of America
by Longman Publishing, New York*

© Longman Group Limited 1994

First published 1994

ISBN 0 582 02128 6 CSD
ISBN 0 582 02127 8 PPR

British Library Cataloguing-in-Publication Data

A catalogue record for this book is
available from the British Library

Library of Congress Cataloging-in-Publication Data

Thompson, Roger C., 1941–
    The Pacific Basin since 1945: a history of the foreign relations
of the Asian, Australian, and American rim states and the Pacific
islands / Roger C. Thompson.
      p. cm. — (The Postwar world)
    Includes bibliographical references and index.
    ISBN 0–582–02128–6. — ISBN 0–582–02127–8 (pbk.)
    1. Pacific Area—Politics and government. 2. United States–
–Foreign relations—Pacific Area. 3. Pacific Area—Foreign
relations—United States. I. Title. II. Series.
DU29.T48 1994
909′.09823′09045—dc20
                                           93–44480
                                              CIP

Set by 5B in 10pt Bembo
Produced by Longman Singapore Publishers (Pte) Ltd.
Printed in Singapore

Contents

List of Maps

Abbreviations

AMG	American Military Government in South Korea
ANCOM	Andean Common Market
ANZUS	Australia, New Zealand, United States Security Treaty
APEC	Asia-Pacific Economic Conference
ARENA	*Alianza Republicana Nacionalista*
ARVN	Army of the Republic of Vietnam
ASEAN	Association of Southeast Asian Nations
BMA	British Military Administration in Malaya
BRA	Bougainville Revolutionary Army
CCP	Chinese Communist Party
CDGK	Coalition Government of Democratic Kampuchea
CDP	Christian Democratic Party of Chile
CEP	*Centre d'Expérimentation du Pacifique*
CIA	United States Central Intelligence Agency
COSVN	Central Committee Directorate for South Vietnam
CSR	Colonial Sugar Refining Company
DPRK	Democratic People's Republic of Korea
DRV	Democratic Republic of Vietnam
EEC	European Economic Community
FI	*Front Indépendantist*
FLNKS	*Front de Libération Nationale Kanak et Socialiste*
FMLN	*Farabundo Martí Frente de Libearción Nacional*
FNSC	*Fédération pour une Nouvelle Société Calédonienne*
FSM	Federated States of Micronesia
GDP	Gross Domestic Product
GNP	Gross National Product
GVN	Government of the Republic of South Vietnam
JCS	United States Joint Chiefs of Staff

KMM	*Kesatuan Malaya Muda*
KPA	Korean People's Army
KPMP	*Kalipunan Pambansa ng mga Magsaska sa Pilipinas*
KPNLF	Khmer People's National Liberation Front
LDP	Liberal Democratic Party
MAAG	Military Assistance and Advisory Group in Vietnam
MACV	Military Assistance Command Vietnam
MCP	Malayan Communist Party
MNP	Malay Nationalist Party
MPAJA	Malayan People's Anti-Japanese Army
MRLA	Malayan Races Liberation Army
MRP	*Mouvement Républicain Populaire*
MSC	Malaysian Solidarity Convention
NATO	North Atlantic Treaty Organization
NEI	Netherlands East Indies
NIC	newly industrializing countries
NFP	National Federation Party
NHNP	New Hebrides National Party
NLF	National Front for the Liberation of South Vietnam
NSC	United States National Security Council
OAS	Organization of American States
OPM	*Organisasi Papua Merdeka*
PALIKA	*Parti de Libération Kanak*
PAP	People's Action Party
PAVN	People's Army of Vietnam
PECC	Pacific Economic Cooperation Conference
PKI	Indonesian Communist Party
PKM	National Peasants' Union
PKP	Philippines Communist Party
PLA	Chinese People's Liberation Army
PLAF	Vietnamese People's Liberation Armed Force
PNI	Indonesian Nationalist Party
PRG	People's Revolutionary Government of South Vietnam
PRK	People's Republic of Kampuchea
RDPT	*Rassemblement Démocratique des Populations Tahitiennes*
ROK	Republic of Korea
ROKA	Republic of Korea Army
RPCR	*Rassemblement pour la Calédonie dans la République*
RVN	Republic of Vietnam
SCAP	Supreme Commander of the Allied Powers in Japan
SDF	Self Defence Force of Japan
SEAC	South East Asia Command

SEATO	South East Asia Treaty Organization
SLN	*Société le Nickel*
UC	*Union Calédonienne*
UDT	Timorese Democratic Union
UFC	United Fruit Company
UMNC	*Union Multiracial de Nouvelle Calédonie*
UMNO	United Malay National Organization
UN	United Nations
UNA	United Nations army
UNO	*Unión Nacional de Opositora*
UNTCOK	United Nations Temporary Commission on Korea
UPM	*Union Progressiste Mélanesienne*
US	United States of America
USI	United States of Indonesia
USSR	Union of Soviet Socialist Republics
VCP	Vietnamese Communist Party

ABBREVIATIONS USED IN FOOTNOTES

ASDSC	Australian National University Strategic and Defence Studies Centre
CIDM	*Commission Internationale D'Histoire Militaire: ACTA No. 14 Montreal, 16–19 viii 1988*
CO	Colonial Office
FEA	*The Far East and Australasia: A Survey and Directory of Asia and the Pacific*
FRUS	*Foreign Relations of the United States*
PIYB	*Pacific Islands Yearbook*
PP	*The Pentagon Papers* (Senator Gravel Edition)
PRO	Public Record Office
UGVW	*The U.S. Government and the Vietnam War: Executive and Legislative Roles and Relationships*
YITS	*Yearbook of International Trade Statistics*

Preface

There are numerous people I wish to thank for their assistance in writing this book. Professor Peter Dennis recommended me as the author to the editors of the series and arranged special study leave for me at a crucial stage in the writing process. The staff of the well stocked library of the Australian Defence Force Academy showed commendable patience as I borrowed an enormous number of books and journals. Mrs Elizabeth Greenhalgh provided valuable service in proof-reading the manuscript and compiling the index. I received useful information from Dr Jeffrey Grey. Dr Stewart Lone read most of the book and gave me extremely valuable advice, especially from his expertise in East Asian history. Dr Stephen Henningham generously lent me a pre-publication copy of his good book on France and the postwar Pacific Islands. My children, Ian and Susan, who are recent university graduates, benefited me with advice from students' perspectives. My wife, Sheila, provided me with excellent support while I was immersed in the final writing process.

Editorial Foreword

The aim of this series is to describe and analyse the history of the World since 1945. History, like time, does not stand still. What seemed to many of us only recently to be 'current affairs', or the stuff of political speculation, has now become material for historians. The editors feel that it is time for a series of books which will offer the public judicious and scholarly, but at the same time readable, accounts of the way in which our present-day world was shaped by the years after the end of the Second World War. The period since 1945 has seen political events and socio-economic developments of enormous significance for the human race, as important as anything which happened before Hitler's death or the bombing of Hiroshima. Ideologies have waxed and waned, the industrialized economies have boomed and bust, empires have collapsed, new nations have emerged and sometimes themselves fallen into decline. While we can be thankful that no major armed conflict has occurred between the so-called superpowers, there have been many other wars, and terrorism has become an international plague. Although the position of ethnic minorities has dramatically improved in some countries, it has worsened in others. Nearly everywhere the status of women has become an issue which politicians have been unable to avoid. These are only some of the developments we hope will be illuminated by this series as it unfolds.

The books in the series will not follow any set pattern; they will vary in length according to the needs of the subject. Some will deal with regions, or even single nations, and others with themes. Not all of them will begin in 1945, and the terminal date may similarly vary; once again, the time-span chosen will be appropriate to the question under discussion. All the books, however, will be written by expert historians drawing on the latest fruits of scholarship, as well as their own expertise and judgement. The series should be particularly welcome to students, but it is designed also for the general reader with an interest in contemporary history. We hope that the books will stimulate scholarly discussion and encourage specialists to look beyond their own particular interests to engage in wider controversies. History, and particularly the history of the recent past, is neither 'bunk' nor an intellectual form of stamp-collecting, but an indispensable part of an educated person's approach to life. If it is not written by historians it will be written by others of a less discriminating and more polemical disposition. The editors are confident that this series will help to ensure the victory of the historical approach, with consequential benefits for its readers.

A.J. Nicholls
Martin S. Alexander

Introduction

If we continue the war, Japan will be altogether destroyed. Although some of you are of opinion that we cannot completely trust the Allies, I believe an immediate and peaceful end to the war is preferable to seeing Japan annihilated. As things stand now the nation still has a chance to recover.[1]

Thus spoke Emperor Hirohito on 8 August 1945, in making the pronouncement which persuaded his evenly divided Cabinet to seek the peace that came with Japan's surrender six days later to the United States (US). His analysis was correct. Japan was saved from further destruction by fire and atomic bombs and from Russia's eleventh hour entry into the Pacific war by the belief that Japan could trust the US to support its reconstruction. Indeed, when Hirohito died in 1989, Japan had achieved peacefully, with American assistance, an economic dominance in the Pacific Basin far greater than that acquired by military conquest in the years to 1945.

Japan's re-emergence after World War II as an economic power in the Pacific Basin is an important theme of this book. Another major theme is the way the US became involved after the war in contesting the expansion of communism in the Pacific Basin, which involved the US in two major Asian wars. The profound influences of these wars on other Pacific Basin countries are analyzed. The struggles by former colonies in Asia to achieve independence and the ways in which these contests became intertwined with US fears of communism are discussed. The efforts by the US to combat imagined and real threats of communism in Latin America and the relationships of those

1. The Pacific War Research Society, *Japan's Longest Day* (London 1968) 70.

struggles to the maintenance of US hegemonic control are explored in terms of the Pacific rim nations of the Western hemisphere. Attempts by the new nations of Asia, the Pacific Islands and the Pacific rim republics of Latin America to cooperate together are considered. The emphasis of the book is on international relations rather than internal histories of the various nations, although attention is paid to the latter where necessary for a full understanding of the relevant issues. More information is provided about internal developments in Pacific Islands in two separate chapters, since these islands are not part of any other book in the Postwar World series.

The series explains the starting date of this book. However, attention is given to some developments before 1945 where necessary to explain postwar events. The year 1991 has been chosen as the terminating date to bring the book as close as possible to the present, it being the year in which most of the book has been written. That was also the year after the end of the Cold War between the US and the USSR, which started in 1945.

The Pacific Basin is defined as those countries on the rim of the Pacific Ocean and its subsidiary seas, such as the Sea of Japan and the Gulf of Thailand, and the islands within those waters. At times the definition is arbitrary. The Timor Sea adjoins the Indian Ocean, but Timor is included in the book because it is part of Indonesia. Only a small portion of Honduras touches the Pacific Ocean, but its inclusion makes Central America an entity for the book. The arbitrary nature of the geographic division is indicated by the exclusion of Laos, though it is part of the former French colonies of Indochina, except for its influence on the Vietnam War. Bolivia, though one of the Andean nations, is also excluded because, like Laos, it is landlocked. Canada faces the Atlantic in its international affairs much more than the Pacific and therefore is not extensively treated.

In citation of names modern-day local usage is preferred, except where westernized versions have dominated in English language literature. An example of the latter is citing two of the Vietnamese Ngo brothers by their first names: Diem and Nhu. It should be noted that in Asian languages family name comes first and that in Latin America the principal family name is usually placed second as in Salvador Allende Gossens.

Great emphasis in this book is given to US policies in the Pacific Basin. This is partly because of the pervasive impact of the US on the region. This aspect of the book also is influenced by the English language sources on which it is based and the fact that much more has been revealed to historians from archives, private papers, congressional hearings and memoirs about the making of American foreign policy than about the foreign policies of the other great powers in the Pacific, especially China and the Soviet Union. However, the book has been able to use some recent memoirs and records of conversations with decision makers of those two communist powers.

The book is based principally on published works. Its main value is as a synthesis of the many, especially recent, publications about aspects of Pacific Basin history. The aim is to provide the reader with the most up to date interpretations, to indicate major differences of opinion among historians and to provide an interpretation that should not be regarded as the only explanation of events. Some published primary source material has been used plus recently opened files in the British Public Record Office. The author also has drawn on some of his own experiences of relevant historical events and the memories of other participants.

The author does not claim complete objectivity, for such an ideal is an impossibility. He writes from a liberal political perspective. He is a citizen of a Pacific Basin nation, Australia, that has had some wider regional influence, though often as a supporter of a greater power, Britain or the US. He has travelled extensively in the Pacific Islands and to some of the rim countries and writes from knowledge gained from many years of teaching US, Pacific and Southeast Asian history. He acknowledges the assistance of colleagues with greater knowledge of other parts of the Pacific Basin.

CHAPTER ONE

Postwar Asian Reconstruction and Political Changes, 1945–1949

Before 1941 the East and Southeast Asia had been dominated by the imperial powers: Britain, France, the Netherlands, Japan and the United States (US). Japan forced these nations out of their Pacific Basin colonies during the Second World War, which stimulated indigenous nationalist groups, some working with Japan to gain independence, others assisting the allies against Japan. As a result, the situation in East and Southeast Asia at the time of Japan's surrender in 1945 was inevitably complex. Major questions were whether the western colonists could hope to regain control of their former colonies; what was to be the future of defeated Japan; and how far would the head of the victorious coalition, the US, remain involved in the area in the face of new threats of communist expansion? This chapter takes up these questions for each of the main trouble spots of East and Southeast Asia, starting with Japan under US-dominated allied occupation.

RECONSTRUCTING JAPAN

Japan's surrender on 14 August 1945 presented the US with a unique opportunity to shape the future of its former rival in the Pacific. Since 1943 planning had been carried out by experts on Japan in the American State Department for a demilitarized democracy that would threaten no more its neighbours or world peace. They approached the subject comprehensively, and they knew that reform would need the cooperation of new or previously suppressed leadership groups in Japan.[1]

Control of detailed planning and implementation of policies for Japan's future, however, was left to an army general, Douglas MacArthur. Before the war he had been politically exiled to organize the defence of the Philippines so as to remove a threat to President Franklin Roosevelt's re-election chances. But MacArthur had generated great self-publicity and popularity from his command of the American army in the Pacific which, with allied assistance, had rolled back the Japanese military tide. Roosevelt's successor, Harry Truman, dared not dismiss MacArthur. So he received the Japanese surrender and was in a natural position to head the occupation force in Japan. Furthermore, Truman was keen to keep a potentially strong political rival well outside the US. MacArthur, in turn, saw an opportunity to write his name in history as the creator of democracy for seventy million Japanese, which also might serve future political ambitions in the US.[2]

In Japan MacArthur became the Supreme Commander of the Allied Powers (SCAP), an acronym applying also to the planning organization he headed, and which was American in almost all but name. He acted as a grand proconsul. He hardly ever strayed outside his daily journeys in Tokyo from the American Embassy to his official headquarters. Only his chief confidant, his prewar attorney, Courtney Whitney, could see him without an appointment. The only real constraints placed on MacArthur by Washington before 1948 resulted from the wartime planning, especially the State-War-Navy Coordinating Committee's document SWNCC-228 which was cabled to him in October 1945. It outlined major features of a proposed democratic government with the emperor as a constitutional monarch, and it stressed that the government's ultimate form should be determined by the freely expressed will of the Japanese people. While it did indicate the final shape of the new Japanese constitution, MacArthur was determined to maintain freedom of control in implementation of the reforms. Indeed, until 1948 this was permitted

---

1. Robert E. Ward, 'Presurrender Planning: Treatment of the Emperor and Constitutional Changes' in Robert E. Ward and Sakamoto Yoshikazu (eds), *Democratizing Japan: The Allied Occupation* (Honolulu 1987) 1–41.

2. Michael Schaller, *Douglas MacArthur* (New York 1989) chs 2, 9–10; Michael Schaller, *The American Occupation of Japan: The Origins of the Cold War in Asia* (New York 1985) ch. 2; and Theodore Cohen, *Remaking Japan: The American Occupation As New Deal* (New York 1987) ch. 4.

by the administration in Washington, whose foreign policy attention was directed much more to European than to Asian affairs.

MacArthur established a broad policy agenda for his staff. It was summed up in his statement on 11 October 1945: 'The emancipation of women; the encouragement of the unionization of labor; the opening of schools to more liberal education; the abolishment (*sic.*) of systems which through secret inquisition and abuse have held people in constant fear; the democratization of Japanese economic institutions to the end that monopolistic industrial controls be revised'.[3] Detailed planning for the implementation of these principles was left to SCAP personnel.

By 25 April 1946, 1,550 American military personnel and civilians had been engaged for SCAP operations. They were a disparate set of people usually appointed with minimal or no screening. But they included many qualified people recruited from the large number of American soldiers in Japan, many of whom were former civilians, and from expert teams that MacArthur requested from the US. Few SCAP members had previous knowledge of Japan, including the trio at the head of the organizational pyramid: Whitney and Major Generals William Marquat and Charles Willoughby.[4]

Some more junior members of SCAP, who did have prior knowledge of Japan, had important influence because the separate planning sections enjoyed significant autonomy. An example was twenty-two-year-old American college graduate Beate Sirota, whose prewar childhood in Japan had made her fluent in Japanese. She was given by SCAP's Civil Rights Committee the task of drafting measures to improve the status of Japanese women. She collected information in Tokyo libraries about women's rights in European constitutions and contacted liberal-minded Japanese women. Consequently, the Japanese constitution not only outlawed in article fourteen any 'discrimination in political, economic or social relations because of race, creed, sex, social status or family origin', but also article twenty-four made marriage dependent 'on the mutual consent of both sexes' and declared 'the essential equality of the sexes' in all respects. As well as being revolutionary in a society in which women were

---

3. Quoted in Carol Gluck, 'Entangling Illusions – Japanese and American Views of the Occupation' in Warren I. Cohen (ed.), *New Frontiers in American East Asian Relations: Essays Presented to Dorothy Borg* (New York 1983) 198.
4. Cohen, *Remaking Japan* ch. 4.

subordinate to men, these clauses were more progressive than legal rights in the US.[5]

There were other radical clauses in the Japanese constitution of 1947, the final draft of which was made public on 6 March 1946. It extended Anglo-American human rights, in a Westminster-style government with a constitutional emperor, by including 'the right to maintain the minimum standard of wholesome and cultural living', 'academic freedom', and the right of workers to collective bargaining. Article nine also declared Japan's renunciation of war and the maintenance of armed forces.

SCAP's reforming arm stretched further into Japanese society. All land held by absentee landlords and other property above ten acres was bought by the government and sold to tenant farmers on easy credit terms. This reform, established on Australian advice, aimed to reduce the large class of tenant farmers who might become the seed-bed for radical revolution, as well as to break the power of Japanese landowners. Its success was measured by a reduction in the land worked by tenant farmers from 46 to 10 per cent by the end of the allied occupation. The Home Ministry, the central pillar of the prewar national bureaucracy, was abolished and local government became elective. Compulsory education was extended from six to nine years, and greater emphasis was given to individual skills and learning. New rights for workers allowed rapid unionization. Eighty-three *zaibatsu* companies, which had dominated the prewar economy, were targeted to be broken up, and anti-trust laws were passed. Another major programme to break the power of the prewar leadership was the purging of over 200,000 former military officers and high officials of government and business. Twenty-five were tried for war crimes, most receiving long jail sentences; seven of them were executed in December 1948.

Japanese reaction to these reforms was mixed. Though Emperor Hirohito's command had impelled Japanese armies to lay down arms and the people to accept peace, the first postwar Japanese Cabinet resigned on 16 October 1945 when faced with SCAP's directive to free political prisoners and to start the purge of military and civilian officials. With MacArthur's agreement former foreign minister Shidehara Kijurō, who had resigned over the Manchuria incident of 1931, became prime minister. His Cabinet worked on

5. Susan J. Pharr, 'The Politics of Women's Rights' in Ward and Sakamoto (eds), *Democratizing Japan* ch. 8.

a draft of constitutional reform, which retained much of the Meiji constitution. But SCAP insisted on its own version. Japanese Cabinet members were shocked, particularly about the status of the emperor and the renunciation of war. But Hirohito accepted the change in his position, telling the Cabinet: 'If that is what they want, I see no reason not to accept it'.[6] MacArthur also had clearly stated that the constitution was non-negotiable. The Japanese Government duly approved the SCAP constitution, though one Cabinet official wrote: 'thus the draft Constitution, reeking of defeat was born. Unable to contain my feelings of rage, I secretly wept'.[7]

Though the constitution was certainly not the free expression of the Japanese people, there was significant public support for SCAP's policies. Former Japanese liberals, educated women, union leaders and others saw the American occupation as an opportunity to create a new Japan freed from the militarism and despotism of the recent past. Many of the reforms, especially of land and labour, had been proposed in Japan prior to the war but had been blocked by the dominance over the government of the military and the socio-economic elite. General public acceptance of SCAP's sweeping constitutional changes was assisted by the way the Japanese population, initially very fearful that the occupying American army's treatment of civilians might match that of the Japanese army in China, welcomed the generous and easygoing attitude of most American soldiers. There was some freezing of this goodwill when puritanical military officers closed down the brothels provided for American servicemen and banned overnight visits to Japanese homes. But soldiers found other ways to enjoy the company of Japanese women. On balance, wrote Theodore Cohen, one of the SCAP officials who married a Japanese woman, relations between the occupying Americans and the Japanese generally encouraged public acceptance of the radical reforms.[8]

In fact MacArthur was idolized by many Japanese like another god emperor. Little more than a year after his arrival in the country, a booklet in Japanese outlining his biography had sold 800,000 copies. Noting this phenomenon, Japanese newspaper editor Itakura Takuzō commented: 'The Japanese people have long been plagued by the

6. Quoted in Masumi Junnosuke, *Postwar Politics in Japan, 1945–1955* (Berkeley 1985) 61.

7. Shirasu Jiroō, quoted in ibid. 66.

8. Makote Iokibe, 'Japan Meets the United States for the Second Time' and Herbert Passin, 'The Occupation – Some Reflections' in *Daedalus* Summer 1990, 91–129. Cohen, *Remaking Japan* ch. 7.

mistaken idea that government is something to be executed by some deity, hero or great man', and he lamented that the transference of this worship to MacArthur was 'the worst enemy of democracy'.[9] But many of his compatriots still clamoured even to catch a glimpse of the great man. MacArthur also earned the approval of many Japanese people for intervening personally in 1946 to save the country from mass starvation resulting from the war-ravaged and inflation-wracked economy. He did this by diverting to Japanese civilians surplus army food supplies that became available with a decline in the number of American servicemen in the country from 600,000 to 200,000, a reduction made possible by the peaceful Japanese reception of the occupation. He then used his immense popularity and stature in the US to push Congress into granting Japan much more financial aid than the administration had intended.

However, the increased aid to Japan encouraged a movement within the American Government to halt MacArthur's reform programme. He was accused of damaging Japan's chances for economic recovery and financial self-sufficiency. Important members of the administration, such as Under Secretary of State Dean Acheson, Navy Secretary James Forrestal and the intellectual director of the State Department's Policy Planning Staff, George Kennan, agreed that America's own prosperity and military security required economic recovery in Western Europe and Japan. Their recipe for Japan was to halt the dismantling of the *zaibatsu*, to stop the economic reparations imposed on Japan after the war and to introduce other policies to promote economic growth. Army Under Secretary William H. Draper Jr, who had overall responsibility for the occupation, affirmed after a visit with Kennan to Japan in March 1948 that SCAP had turned the country into an economic 'morgue'. Kennan even claimed that MacArthur's policies had opened Japan to communist influence.[10]

MacArthur strongly resisted this attempt to control and change his policies. He had no quarrel with America's emphasis on strategic containment of international communism, but he saw China, not Japan, as the place to hold the line against it. He also vigorously defended his *zaibatsu* programme as necessary for removing the power of the Japanese old guard. Nor did he desire to see any diminution

9. Quoted in ibid. 53.
10. Schaller, *MacArthur* 145. See also William S. Borden, *The Pacific Alliance: United States Foreign Economic Policy and Japanese Trade Recovery, 1947–1955* (Madison 1984) ch. 2.

in his authority, especially because he had ambitions to become the Republican Party candidate in the 1948 presidential election.

On 6 April 1948, however, MacArthur suffered a decisive political defeat when he won less than a third of the Republican Party convention delegates for his home state of Wisconsin. Opposition in Washington to his economic policies grew. In October 1948 Truman approved a directive to MacArthur to terminate reparations, to eliminate most restrictions on Japanese industry and to promote Japanese exports in the context of wage control and a balanced internal budget. After his surprising election win in November, Truman dispatched banker Joseph Dodge to Tokyo to implement the new approach. The result was that most of SCAP's attack on the *zaibatsu* collapsed. In the end only eleven companies were broken up; the anti-monopoly law was limited merely to regulating the effects of monopoly holdings; and new cartels led by many prewar Japanese business leaders were encouraged in the name of economic growth. New laws were passed in Japan restricting the rights of unionists, such as preventing public servants from striking; and there was a purge of communists and other radicals from union ranks. The whole process has been labelled by Japanese historians, and more lately by American revisionists, as a 'reverse course'.

However, there has been a recent debate about the extent of the 'reverse course'. The revisionist historian Howard Schonberger argues that 'the signals of closer American collaboration with Japanese conservatives and the business class were unmistakable'. SCAP's Labor Division chief, Harry Cohen, agreed that after 1948 a new alliance emerged 'between the conservative and big business elements' of Japan and the US.[11]

There were, indeed, major limitations to the effect of the reforms in Japan. Women's rights in the constitution did not overcome the social prejudice against women's equality. In 1990 women still did not receive equal pay for the same work as men. The universal voting rights have not prevented the conservative Liberal Democratic Party (LDP) from being constantly voted into office. One of the most successful reforms was the renunciation of war, despite the emergence under later American pressure of a 'self defence' force. However, by

---

11. Howard B. Schonberger, *Aftermath of War: Americans and the Remaking of Japan, 1945–1952* (Kent 1989) 282. Cohen, *Remaking Japan* 459. See also 'A Forum: American Democratization of Japan: Correcting the Revisionist Vision', *Pacific Historical Review* LVIII, 1988, 179–218.

1990 many fears were being expressed inside and outside Japan that Japanese militarism would re-emerge in the future.[12]

But how far the so-called 'reverse course' weakened the reforms of the early American occupation of Japan is questionable. Historians, such as Carol Gluck and Robert E. Ward, point to the fact that by the time of the new directives from Washington in 1948 there were clear signs that SCAP was travelling in the same direction, especially the move to stifle emerging communist influence in labour unions after MacArthur banned a general strike planned for 1 February 1947. In this case a brake was being applied to radical Japanese exploitation of SCAP's reforms. Indeed, the latest study of the occupation by Richard Finn, one of the junior members of SCAP and later director of Japanese affairs in the State Department, affirms that MacArthur's suppression of left wing unions was in line with his general policy of encouraging a moderate labour movement.[13] Furthermore, while MacArthur tried to retain his attack on the *zaibatsu*, he had a strong political motive to hold on to his reforming image, and he had admitted to Kennan on 5 March 1948 that he thought the 'reform measures . . . were almost completed'.[14] Japanese international relations scholar, Sakamoto Yoshikazu, agrees that SCAP's reforming agenda was limited and was virtually completed by the end of 1947. Thus the influences of the Cold War and American concern to boost Japan's economic growth were not necessarily pushing SCAP in any new reactionary direction in 1948.[15]

THE COLD WAR COMES TO EAST ASIA

The Cold War was a profound influence on future Pacific Basin affairs and it recently has been argued that it started in Asia by the

12. See Masumi, *Postwar Politics* chs 4–5; Merion and Susie Harries, *Sheathing the Sword: The Demilitarisation of Japan* (New York 1987); and Janet E. Hunter, *The Emergence of Modern Japan: An Introductory History Since 1853* (London 1989).

13. Richard B. Finn, *Winners in Peace: MacArthur, Yoshida, and Postwar Japan* (Berkeley 1992) 142–3.

14. Quoted in Robert E. Ward, 'Conclusion' in Ward and Sakamoto, *Democratizing Japan* 408. See also Gluck, 'Entangling Illusions', 199–207.

15. Sakamoto Yoshikazu, 'The International Context of the Occupation of Japan' in Ward and Sakamoto, *Democratizing Japan* 69.

end of 1945, well before the proclamation of the Truman Doctrine on 12 March 1947 which outlined the policy of containment of the Soviet Union (USSR).[16] The Soviet entry into the Pacific War, six days before the Japanese surrender, raised in Washington the spectre of Soviet domination of Korea, Manchuria and perhaps even northern China. Truman was much less willing to accept such a prospect than was Roosevelt, who had signed the Yalta Agreement of February 1945 between Britain, the US and the USSR. Under its terms the Soviet Union was promised the Japanese Kurile Islands and southern Sakhalin, control of Manchuria's railways and of Port Arthur, and internationalization of the Manchurian port of Dairen. In return Stalin had pledged to support the Chinese Nationalist Kuomintang Party Government and to guarantee to enter the war against Japan within three months of the defeat of Germany.

Though he had been Roosevelt's vice-president, Truman had not been party to his former chief's foreign policy thinking. Nor, as the product of Missouri state Democratic Party machine politics, did he have any foreign affairs background. Therefore he was willing to listen to State Department officials who had been critical of Roosevelt's alleged open-handed policy towards Russia. They advised Truman to take a harder line, especially as they claimed that the USSR was already violating the Yalta Agreement in Eastern Europe. As revealed in new evidence from his private diary, Truman also was given confidence in the potential success of this changed direction by America's possession of the atomic bomb.[17]

The Truman Administration's suspicion of the USSR was heightened when Stalin demanded control of Dairen. He also proposed to confiscate Japanese industry in Manchuria as 'trophies of war', which the US regarded as vital for China's economic recovery. So when Japan signalled on 10 August its desire to surrender, Truman authorized the dispatch of American troops to northern China and to southern Korea. However, the Soviet Union's entry into the war necessitated a division of Korea; and the shortage of available American military manpower, in view of the needs of the occupation of Japan, precluded the US from hindering the USSR's activities in Manchuria.[18]

---

16. See Marc S. Gallicchio, *The Cold War Begins in Asia: American Policy and the Fall of the Japanese Empire* (New York 1988); and Robert L. Messer, 'American Perspectives on the Origins of the Cold War in East Asia, 1945–1949' in Akira Iriye and Warren Cohen (eds), *American, Chinese and Japanese Perspectives on Wartime Asia 1931–1949* (Wilmington 1990) 243–68.

17. Ibid. 251–2.

18. Gallicchio, *The Cold War Begins* chs 4–5.

CHINA AND THE US

The communist victory in China was one of the early major political changes in the Western Pacific Basin and became a major influence on American policy in the region. The alleged purpose of the 53,000 marines Truman sent to China after the end of the Pacific War was to assist in transporting Nationalist troops into the north in order to supervise the Japanese surrender, which was being carried out by the wartime American military adviser to the Kuomintang, Lieutenant-General Albert Wedemeyer. But the rapid troop movement was designed primarily to prevent the Chinese Communist Party (CCP) from extending its control in northern China. Over 400,000 Kuomintang troops were transported to northern China in American planes and ships. Also almost $450 million in American lend lease aid went to Nationalist China in the two months after the Japanese surrender. Additional military equipment was sold to Kuomintang leader Chiang Kai-shek's forces for a fraction of its true value. Moreover, the American marines allowed Nationalist troops to operate against Communist Chinese forces by guarding communication lines, resulting in some clashes between American and CCP troops.

These actions by the Truman Administration continued a bias in favour of the Kuomintang that had been developing in the last year of the Roosevelt Administration under the influence of Wedemeyer and the US Ambassador in China, Patrick Hurley. This preference had occurred despite Roosevelt's policy of working towards a coalition of the Kuomintang and the CCP to rule postwar China. But Hurley and Wedemeyer had underestimated the power of the CCP, which by the end of the war controlled about a fifth of China extending from its base at Yenan in the northwest. They also overestimated the support of the CCP by the USSR, which had no confidence in a CCP victory and was concentrating instead on extracting wealth from Manchuria.[19]

In late 1945 America therefore stood on the brink of heavy military involvement in the Chinese civil war on the side of the Kuomintang. However, in the State Department there was strong opposition to such a prospect. John Carter Vincent, director of the department's

---

19. See James Reardon-Anderson, *Yenan and the Great Powers: The Origins of Chinese Communist Foreign Policy 1944–1946* (New York 1980); and John W. Garver, *Chinese-Soviet Relations 1937–1945: The Diplomacy of Chinese Nationalism* (New York 1988).

Office for Far Eastern Affairs and a former American diplomat in China, advised that 'involvement in civil strife in China would occasion serious difficulties for us without compensating advantages' and would encourage Chiang to resist negotiations with the CCP.[20] General demobilization of the American army was another good reason to withdraw US troops from China. Nor had the Truman Administration abandoned Roosevelt's policy of seeking a Kuomintang-CCP coalition, though helping to load the dice in favour of the Nationalists.

Then on 27 November Hurley suddenly resigned, probably in search of a more peaceful life. But he placed the blame publicly for his resignation on Truman, the State Department and alleged subversive communists in their midst. 'See what a son-of-a-bitch did to me', yelled the outraged Truman.[21] Hurley's accusations generated Republican Party criticism of Truman's China policy, which prompted the President to choose as a special envoy to China, a man far above politics: war hero, General George Marshall, Roosevelt's army chief of staff.

Marshall's appointment muted criticism in the US of the administration's China policy for a time, but it did nothing to solve the dilemma of two parties competing for control of China's government. Instructed to seek a negotiated settlement of the civil war, Marshall arrived in the Nationalist wartime capital of Chungking in December 1945. There he was welcomed by the Kuomintang Government and by CCP negotiators, who were led by Zhou Enlai. The CCP agreed to a truce in the civil war implemented with Marshall's assistance in January and February 1946 which, though not completely effective, greatly reduced the fighting. But the truce was short-lived because the Kuomintang and the CCP did not trust each other, a situation that neither Marshall nor other Americans could fully appreciate. By mid-April the civil war had recommenced. Despite Marshall's threat to cut off financial aid, initial Kuomintang military successes put Chiang in no mood to resume negotiations.[22]

20. Vincent to Byrnes, 12 November 1945, in Ernest R. May, *The Truman Administration and China, 1945–1949* (Philadelphia 1975) 63.

21. Quoted in John M. Blum (ed.), *The Price of Vision: The Diary of Henry A. Wallace, 1942–1946* (Boston 1973) 519.

22. For American policy in China to 1946 see Paul A. Varg, *Closing the Door: Sino-American Relations 1936–1946* (Lansing 1973); Michael Schaller, *The U.S. Crusade in China, 1938–1945* (New York 1979) and John Robinson Beal, *Marshall in China* (New York 1970). See also Bevin Alexander, *The Strange Connection: U.S. Intervention in China, 1944–1972* (New York 1992) chs 60–7.

At first the fighting was centred in Manchuria, where the Kuomintang held the cities and the CCP most of the countryside. But though the American-armed Nationalist troops were better equipped and initially more numerous, they were underpaid, poorly fed and abysmally led. Moreover, their government, whose officials were enriching themselves at the expense of an economy running riot with inflation, was losing its last shreds of public support. Kuomintang troops were soon routed from easily defended positions. By November 1948 communist forces, well armed with captured American weapons and with ranks swollen by defecting Nationalist soldiers, had conquered Manchuria and were driving into central China. After a two-month-long battle, in which the Kuomintang lost over half a million men, the CCP captured Beijing and Tientsin in January 1949. In May 1949 they crossed the Yangtze River and entered Shanghai. The game was up for the crumbling Nationalist regime, whose members were already depositing their riches off-shore in Taiwan. On 1 October 1949 the Chinese People's Republic was proclaimed in Beijing, and in December Chiang Kai-shek and his henchmen fled to Taiwan with the remnants of their shattered army.[23]

The Truman Administration tried to wash its hands of this unfolding disaster. An arms embargo on China had been declared after the re-commencement of the civil war; and a disillusioned Marshall returned to Washington in January 1947, damning both the Kuomintang and the CCP for ruining his efforts to establish a coalition government. There was strong support within the State Department for abandoning the doomed Nationalist regime. Overpopulated and underdeveloped China was not viewed as important in the Cold War. Western Europe, the Middle East and Japan were much more significant regions in American eyes for resistance to Soviet expansionism. Furthermore, defence appraisals viewed the islands from Japan through Okinawa to the Philippines as forming an adequate western Pacific defence perimeter for the US.[24]

But the Republican Opposition did not accept such hard-headed logic about declining Kuomintang fortunes in China. Searching for political weapons to fight the coming 1948 election, Republicans saw

23. See Steven I. Levine, *Anvil of Victory: The Communist Revolution in Manchuria, 1945–1948* (New York 1987) ch. 4; Lloyd Eastman, *Seeds of Destruction: Nationalist China in War and Revolution* (Stanford 1984) ch. 7; E.R. Hooton, *The Greatest Triumph: The Chinese Civil War 1936–49* (London 1981) chs 3–7.

24. Lester J. Foltos, 'The New Pacific Barrier: America's Search for Security in the Pacific, 1945–47', *Diplomatic History* 13, 1989, 317–42.

the abandonment of an anti-communist regime in China to advancing red hordes as very useful heavy artillery with which to batter the administration. There was plentiful ammunition, such as Hurley's denunciation of communist subversion in the State Department and the pro-Chiang Kai-shek propaganda of a very noisy China lobby in America. Many of the congressional critics who jumped on the bandwagon knew very little about China. A leader of this campaign was congressman Richard Nixon, who railed against the 'apologists for the Chinese Communists in the US, both in and out of the State Department'.[25]

Faced with this barrage of criticism and fearful of USSR support for the CCP, Truman and Marshall, now US Secretary of State, were unwilling completely to abandon the Kuomintang. So the arms embargo was lifted in May 1947. In the next month 100,000 rounds of rifle ammunition were sold to the Nationalist Government at 10 per cent of cost price. However, Marshall also sent General Wedemeyer to China to impress on the Kuomintang the need for significant reforms and to assess whether anything was worth salvaging. Wedemeyer found much in Nationalist China to criticize, but his strong anti-communist predisposition induced him to recommend large-scale military and economic aid to the Kuomintang government, including a team of 10,000 officers and troops as military advisers.[26]

This level of support for the Kuomintang was too much for Marshall and Truman. It invited American military participation in a war in distant Asia, with the threat of a military response from the USSR, which was geographically much better placed to intervene. Ironically, a later CCP Ambassador to Moscow, Liu Xiao, has recently claimed that Zhou Enlai told him that Stalin demanded the CCP army stop at the Yangtze because the USSR feared that the Chinese Civil War was overturning the spheres of influence established at Yalta. Stalin feared that the US might be provoked to military intervention in China, thus causing a third world war, which he desperately wished to avoid because of the requirement for economic development in his own war-ravaged nation. But Wedemeyer's report was suppressed. The American Government no longer believed that Chiang would survive as leader of China,

25. Quoted in Gordon H. Chang, *Friends and Enemies: The United States, China, and the Soviet Union, 1948–1972* (Stanford 1990) 26.

26. William Stueck, *The Wedemeyer Mission: American Politics and Foreign Policy During the Cold War* (Athens, Ga. 1984) chs 1–2, 4.

though political pressure in America was maintaining financial aid for him in the form of the China Aid Act of April 1948, which granted $125 million.[27]

A problem was that many Republicans refused to accept that the Kuomintang was a lost cause and during 1949 maintained the political attack on the Administration's China policy. The government responded by releasing in August the 'China White Paper', which contained many of the documents dealing with America's relations with China during the past decade. The aim was to justify its view that no American intervention could have saved the Kuomintang. Acheson, who became Secretary of State in January 1949, privately remarked of Chiang Kai-shek: 'I arrived just in time to have him collapse on me'.[28]

To many members of the State Department the logical step was therefore to recognize the communist government in China. But Truman had decreed that the US should 'be most careful not to indicate any softening toward the Communists but to insist on judging their intentions by their actions'.[29] Nor had the 'China White Paper' abated the intense political criticism in America about the so-called 'loss of China'. So, despite Britain's decision to recognize the CCP Government in January 1950, the US adopted a wait and see policy. Furthermore, new evidence from associates of the CCP's foreign minister, Zhou Enlai, emphasizes that he had been alienated by Hurley's policies in 1945 and that there was no chance of Communist China seeking any rapprochement with the US in 1949. This split between the new potentially powerful communist state in the Western Pacific Basin and the US had the potential to significantly widen the impact of the Cold War in that region.[30]

27. Ibid. ch. 5. John Garver, 'New Light on Sino–Soviet Relations: The Memoir of China's Ambassador to Moscow, 1955–62', *The China Quarterly* no 122, June 1990, 303.

28. Dean Acheson, *Present at the Creation* (New York 1969) 257.

29. Quoted in Chang, *Friends and Enemies* 35.

30. See Nancy Bernkof Tucker, *Patterns in the Dust: Chinese-American Relations and the Recognition Controversy 1949–1950* (New York 1983); June M. Grasso, *Truman's Two-China Policy 1948–1950* (Armonk 1987); David Allan Mayers, *Cracking the Monolith: U.S. Policy Against the Sino-Soviet Alliance, 1949–1955* (Baton Rouge 1986); and Warren I. Cohen, 'Conversations with Chinese Friends: Zhou Enlai's Associates Reflect on Chinese-American Relations in the 1940s and the Korean War', *Diplomatic History* 11, 1987, 283–9.

DIVIDING KOREA

Another early result of the Cold War which had a major influence on subsequent Pacific Basin affairs was the creation of two separate countries in Korea. Initially, at the Yalta Conference, Roosevelt and Stalin had agreed to a Soviet-American-British-Chinese trusteeship over Korea as preparation for ultimate independence of the country. The trusteeship idea was Roosevelt's preferred method for containing the USSR by admitting it to a club of nations which America would lead. This policy expressed the confidence of the leader of the world's greatest economic and military power, but it also appreciated the realities of Soviet military strength in border regions like Korea. However, the news of the successful testing of the atomic bomb, secretly given to Truman while he was attending the Potsdam Conference in July 1945, convinced him to seek American control of the peninsula if Japan could be induced to surrender before Russia entered the war. The declaration of war by the USSR, and its manifest ability to occupy the whole of Korea before any American troops could arrive, upset this aim. So, on the basis of a quick decision by the State-War-Navy Coordinating Committee in the early hours of 11 August, Truman suggested to Stalin a division of the Soviet and American military zones along the 38th north latitude parallel, chosen because it roughly divided the country into half and was north of Korea's capital city, Seoul. Stalin probably agreed to this proposal to secure North Korea as a security zone with the confident expectation that a future friendly government would control the whole peninsula.[31]

However, the Americans had a poor understanding of Korea. While there was a historic division of the peninsula between the populous South and the much more rugged North, the 38th parallel was an arbitrary line that separated the minerals, electric power and heavy industries of the North from the light industries and agricultural production in the South, which had a population – estimated at 15.8 million in May 1945 – about twice the size of the North's.[32] Korea also was in a chaotic state. The Japanese had imposed partial modernization on a traditional peasant society. Conscripted from

31. Bruce Cumings, *The Origins of the Korean War* vol. 1 (Princeton 1981) ch. 4. James Irving Matray, *The Reluctant Crusade: American Foreign Policy in Korea, 1941–1950* (Honolulu 1985) chs 1–2.
32. Cumings, *Origins of the Korean War* vol. 1, 60.

farms to serve in factories, mines and the Japanese army, Korean peasants had been exposed to an outside world unknown to their parents, and many had become dissatisfied with traditional rural society. Korean landlords and bureaucrats were only partially modernized in their attitudes. The Japanese autocracy had stifled all forms of Korean protest, which with the end of the war were released like the contents of a suddenly opened pressure-cooker.[33]

The American commander of the occupying 24th US Corps, Lieutenant General John Hodge, was a former farm boy from Illinois and a tough soldier with little understanding of politics or administration. Selected to head the occupation only because his corps was the most readily available, he had no prior knowledge of Korea. His political advisers had only been briefed on the trusteeship proposal, not about an American military occupation. Korea was an afterthought in American wartime planning which had concentrated on Japan.

The American Military Government (AMG) in South Korea relied for advice, in fact, on the tiny minority of Koreans who spoke English and who belonged mainly to the wealthy classes. So the AMG sided with business leaders and landowners in opposition to the Korean People's Republic, which was proclaimed on 6 September by the Committee for the Preparation of Korean Independence, a coalition of communists and other left wing leaders under the leadership of the centre-left Yŏ Un-hyŏng. This coalition was supported by numerous locally based people's committees, mostly spontaneously formed to oppose all who had collaborated with the Japanese. Hodge had no understanding of the popular basis of this unrest, blaming it on Soviet-backed communists. He also had no belief in the capacity of Koreans to manage their own affairs. In fact the AMG showed gross insensitivity to Korean feelings by temporarily using former Japanese colonial administrators. Washington quickly countermanded this mistake, but the AMG continued to use former Korean members of the colonial bureaucracy and police force who were condemned by most Koreans as collaborators. Also, the criticism of Hodge in Washington was muted by the fact that the Truman Administration shared his aim to stop the spread of Soviet influence in Korea.[34]

The Truman Administration, however, was still committed to the

33. Ibid. chs 2–3.

34. Ibid. chs 3–6, 8. Matray, *The Reluctant Crusade* ch. 3. Melvyn P. Leffler, *A Preponderance of Power: National Security, the Truman Administration and the Cold War* (Stanford 1992) 88–90.

international trusteeship ideal for the whole of Korea as a means of containing Soviet expansion. At a meeting of British, American and Soviet foreign ministers in Moscow in December 1945 there was agreement to create a 'provisional, democratic Korean government', to be determined by an American-Soviet Joint Commission in Korea. Stalin agreed to this proposal because he continued to desire a united Korea with a government friendly to the USSR.[35]

There was strong opposition in South Korea to the Moscow agreement, especially from seventy-year-old Syngman Rhee. He had been imprisoned in 1898 by the Korean monarchy for pro-constitutional agitation. On his release in 1904, he had travelled to the US, gained a PhD degree, and stayed in that country for most of his subsequent life until 1945. A shrewd but obstinate man, he was the self-styled leader of Korean exiles in the US and had long and unsuccessfully badgered State Department officials to support Korean independence under his control. On his return to Korea in October 1945 Hodge gave him a red carpet reception, looking to him to lead the disorganized local right wing groups, which had been weakened by their previous collaboration with the Japanese.[36]

This AMG favouritism towards Rhee and others on the right, who dominated a Representative Democratic Council instituted in February 1946, pushed left wing leaders and communists to stir up popular opposition to the American occupation. They promoted a general strike on 24 September 1946, which was followed by violent incidents known as the October people's resistance. This was suppressed by the police and by right wing youth groups. More than 200 policemen and as many as 1,000 civilians were killed, much of the country's rice crop was destroyed, many left wing leaders were imprisoned and most of the people's committees collapsed. Hodge regarded the left wing protests as Soviet inspired.[37]

The Truman Administration was able to reopen negotiations with the USSR about Korea after another foreign ministers conference in Moscow in April 1947. But discussions in the joint commission in Korea continued to stall over the Soviet insistence that Rhee and Korean conservatives could not join any provisional Korean government on the grounds of their opposition to trusteeship. Indeed, Rhee and his supporters were agitating against trusteeship and in favour of South Korean independence. This included a campaign of

35. For Russian policy see Cumings, *Origins of the Korean War* vol. 1, ch. 7.
36. Ibid. ch. 6.
37. Ibid. ch. 10.

terror against Rhee's political opponents in which Yŏ Un-hyŏng was assassinated.

Washington decided to quit Korea in 1947 in the face of the failure of the Joint Commission negotiations and the refusal of the Republican controlled American Congress to approve financial aid for South Korea on top of large financial assistance to Greece and Turkey. The Joint Chiefs of Staff (JCS) declared Korea of no strategic value. The 45,000 American troops there would be no match for Soviet military power and 'could well be used elsewhere'.[38] The violent actions of Rhee and his henchmen had also ensured that the trusteeship ideal was unworkable. Therefore Washington turned to the United Nations (UN) to conduct elections in Korea that would lead to an independent government, with the expectation that the USSR would object so that the election would only take place in the South. The current historians' consensus is that the Truman Administration hoped that free elections in the South might encourage American Congressional approval for economic aid and that the UN would give the country a legitimate status which the USSR would find difficult to overturn. Then South Korea might have a viable future after the projected post-election withdrawal of American troops.[39]

The government in North Korea opposed elections in its territory. There Stalin had handed over power to a leftist-communist alliance led by Kim Il Sung, who had been born in Pyonyang, the future capital of North Korea, in 1912 and had been a Soviet-backed leader of anti-Japanese guerillas in Manchuria. His government implemented radical land reform on the CCP model and allowed initial popular participation in decision making through people's committees, though power was soon being controlled by Kim's central government.[40]

The UN Temporary Commission on Korea (UNTCOK), with delegates from eight countries, most of which had close defence and economic ties with the US, could only operate in the South. There, escalating violence, with leftist attempts to disrupt the election process and rightist intimidation of political opponents, resulted in nearly 500 deaths in five months and imprisonment of over 10,000 people resulting from an administration crackdown on the

38. Quoted in Richard Whelan, *Drawing the Line: The Korean War, 1950–1953* (Boston 1990) 44.

39. William Whitney Stueck, Jr., *The Road to Confrontation: American Policy toward China and Korea, 1947–1950* (Chapel Hill 1981) ch. 3. Matray, *The Reluctant Crusade* 123–4. Bruce Cumings, *The Origins of the Korean War* vol. 2 (Princeton 1990) 65–8.

40. Ibid. vol. 1, ch. 11; vol. 2, ch. 9.

left wing – not the right. Hodge asked to be relieved of his post because of the hostility towards him expressed by Rhee. But Hodge's successor, General John Coulter, who was second-in-command of the AMG, regarded Rhee as leading the only viable political force. The election, in fact, was controlled by Rhee and his right wing allies, who fielded three-quarters of the candidates and clearly intimidated voters. UNTCOK, which was greatly constrained in its freedom of observation by an election committee dominated by the right wing, declared the election on 9 May 1948 to have demonstrated a 'reasonable degree of free expression'. But the delegates from Australia, Canada and Syria refused to participate in the charade.[41]

Thus, with the connivance of the AMG, the unscrupulous and dictatorial Syngman Rhee became the president of the Republic of South Korea (ROK) with international blessing. The US then withdrew its army, the last troops leaving in June 1949. There had been a Soviet withdrawal from North Korea in the previous December. Confident in Kim Il Sung's position, the Soviets left behind them ninety-three Second World War vintage aircraft, plus tanks and artillery. Also over 80,000 North Koreans were with the CCP army in the Chinese Civil War. Rhee was keen to achieve unity by forceful subjugation of the North. But Washington refused to provide him with arms to wage an aggressive war, giving only enough to equip 65,000 soldiers to defend the country and suppress insurgents, plus a 500 strong American military advisory group. The American Government was suspicious of Rhee's intentions and wanted no open-ended military commitment. It was an ambiguous policy of limited support.[42]

Indeed, in 1949 the ROK was in a parlous state. The economy was in a mess, with the North denying power resources. There was a shortage of technicians, high unemployment and rampant inflation. American occupation had established a climate of press censorship, arbitrary arrest and political violence which Rhee continued to exploit after independence. He also faced leftist guerilla groups, which were being brutally suppressed by his army. While America never had sufficient military power in the country to impose a different political system, the favouritism of the AMG from the start towards Rhee

41. Ibid. vol. 2, 70–8. Matray, *The Reluctant Crusade* 134–49.
42. Ibid. ch. 8. Peter Lowe, *The Origins of the Korean War* (London 1986) ch. 3. Cumings, *Origins of the Korean War* vol. 2, 445–6.

had ensured that he would be victorious and wrecked any hope of a negotiated settlement with the USSR for a united Korea.[43]

CONTEST FOR CONTROL OF VIETNAM

Vietnam was the region in the Western Pacific Basin which was to see the longest actual war of the Cold War era. On 2 September 1945 the independence of Vietnam was proclaimed in Hanoi, the capital of the Indochina province of Tonkin, by Ho Chi Minh. Born in 1890 in central Vietnam, he left in 1912 as a merchant steamer's cabin boy and settled in France, where he joined the French Communist Party. He moved via Russia to Canton in China, where in 1930 he organized the Indochina Communist Party. It participated in nationalist revolts in 1930–31, which were brutally crushed by French military power. Considered a gentle man with a warm personality, Ho was a master organizer. As well as a communist, he was a fervent nationalist whose first aim was the liberation of his homeland. From headquarters in a cave near the Chinese border, he founded in May 1941 the Vietminh (Front for the Independence of Vietnam), which aimed to arouse support among rural Vietnamese by advocating independence and broad 'democratic' reforms, but which played down land reform in order to gain wider support. The Vietminh were assisted greatly by the way French rule was discredited by the easy assumption of control by the Japanese in 1940–41 and the continuation under Japanese control of the Vichy French administration. The suddenness of the Japanese surrender and a spontaneous popular uprising in Hanoi gave the Vietminh force under a gifted general, Vo Nguyen Giap, the chance to seize power in August 1945, with the tacit support of China, which had been designated at the Potsdam Conference to occupy Indochina north of the 16th latitudinal parallel.[44]

43. Okonogi Masao, 'The Domestic Roots of the Korean War' in Yōnosuke Nagai and Akira Iriye (eds), *The Origins of the Cold War* (New York 1977) 299–320. Cumings, *Origins of the Korean War* vol. 2, chs 6–8. Song Kwang Sung, The Impact of U.S. Military Occupation on the Social Development of Decolonized South Korea, 1945–1949, Ph.D. thesis, University of California, Los Angeles 1989, chs 3–6.

44. Anthony Short, *The Origins of the Vietnam War* (London 1989) ch. 1. Jaques Dalloz, *The War in Indo-China 1945–54* (Dublin 1990) chs 1–2. Lloyd C. Gardiner, *Approaching Vietnam: From World War II Through Dienbienphu 1941–1954* (New York 1988) ch. 2. Greg Lockhart, *Nation in Arms: The Origins of the People's Army of Vietnam* (Sydney 1989) chs 2–3.

The Vietminh also had been able to exploit a growing national consciousness among the Vietnamese, who before the war were seventeen million of the twenty-two million population of Indochina. Ninety per cent of the Vietnamese were smallholding peasants, half of whom owned less than a hectare of land, with consequent widespread indebtedness to money-lenders and losses of land to large Vietnamese and Chinese landholders. Vietnamese peasants also had been heavily taxed by the French administration. It did supply them with physical security, improving health services and education and some benefits of economic development. But such benefits were dissipated by the 1930s depression. Few Vietnamese had the right to vote and then only in the colony of Cochin China. This colony and the rest of Indochina, which had a mixture of control ranging from protectorates over indigenous kingdoms to direct French rule, was administered by a governor general. He was supported by 36,000 French subjects, who were mostly soldiers and administrators, and who maintained overall economic control and racial superiority over the 'natives'. The subordination of the Vietnamese people was fertile ground for the work of Vietminh leaders, who mostly came from the small Vietnamese middle class.[45]

American support for the Vietminh was reflected on independence day in Hanoi by Ho's quotation from the American Declaration of Independence, by US army officers standing beside Giap on the Vietminh army reviewing stand, and by a fly-past of American warplanes. Roosevelt had strongly opposed the restoration of French colonialism in Indochina because he viewed France as an exploitative colonial power and because Vichy France had allowed Japanese occupation. His hope was for international control of the region. Truman did not have the same faith in international control and was concerned to support France as a bulwark against communist expansion in Europe. So he did not oppose the resumption of French rule in Indochina. However, his administration offered France no assistance and rejected French requests to provide transportation for troops to enable a quick return to Indochina.[46]

45. Dalloz, *War in Indo-China* ch. 1. David G. Marr, *Vietnamese Tradition on Trial, 1920–1945* (Berkeley 1981) chs 1, 7–10. William J. Duiker, *The Rise of Nationalism in Vietnam, 1900–1941* (Ithaca 1976). Ken Post, *Revolution, Socialism and Nationalism in Viet Nam* (Aldershot 1989–90) vol. 1, 23–45.

46. George C. Herring, 'The Truman Administration and the Restoration of French Sovereignty in Indochina', *Diplomatic History* 1, 1977, 97–117. Peter Dennis, *Troubled Days of Peace: Mountbatten and South East Asia Command, 1945–46* (Manchester 1987) 25–33.

France, however, received British support in Vietnam south of the 16th parallel. Occupation of that area had been assigned at Potsdam to the British South East Asia Command (SEAC), which to some American critics meant 'Save England's Asian Colonies'. Indeed, the British Government had no wish to stop France resuming control in Indochina given its own desire to restore colonial rule in British colonies conquered by Japan. The SEAC commander of the 20th Indian division, Major-General Douglas Gracey, was determined to assist the restoration of French authority and took no notice of Vietminh representatives waiting to greet him when he flew into Cochin China on 13 September. In the region's anarchical climate, with factional struggles, looting and anti-French violence, Gracey established curfews and press control, re-armed French soldiers interned by the Japanese and moved to disarm Vietminh police who were part of significant Vietminh control of the capital city, Saigon. In consultation with the acting French High Commissioner, Colonel Jean Cédile, Gracey supported on the night of 23 September a successful surprise attack, by re-armed and recently landed French troops, on Vietminh-held public buildings and outposts in Saigon. This was denounced as an act of war by the Vietminh-nationalist front in the city.[47]

After this almost bloodless coup, there was an escalation of violence with arbitrary attacks on Vietnamese people by French soldiers, which Cédile condemned as 'unjustified acts of brutality'.[48] The Vietminh responded with attacks on French civilians and fought against the reinforced French troops. With the assistance of Japanese soldiers, France was able to restore significant control in Cochin China and Annam by the end of 1945.[49]

The French Union, planned in March 1945 by the Provisional Government in France, promised 'appropriate liberty' for Indochina but did not spell out what that term meant. A year later, on 6 March 1946, Ho Chi Min signed an agreement with Jean Sainteny, the French Government's political representative in Hanoi, which did provide a definition. Sainteny, concerned to prevent Vietnamese violence against French personnel still awaiting evacuation, and conscious that the Vietminh had substantial control of the Tonkinese countryside, conceded recognition of 'the Republic of Vietnam as a free state

47. Ibid. 33–46. Peter M. Dunn, *The First Vietnam War* (London 1985) ch. 8. Dalloz, *War in Indo-China* 58.
48. Quoted in Dennis, *Troubled Days of Peace* 48.
49. Ibid. ch. 3. Dunn, *First Vietnam War* ch. 8.

with its own government, parliament and finances, forming a part of the Indo-China Federation and the French Union'. He said later that though the government was 'Communist-led' it contained 'as many nationalists as Communists'. Ho Chi Minh agreed to membership of the French Union; to the postponement for future negotiations of Vietnam's diplomatic relations with foreign states and of French cultural and economic interests in Vietnam; and to a future referendum about the status of Cochin China and Annam. Ho also agreed to welcome the arrival of French troops in Tonkin. He signed this accord in recognition of the important role of the French in negotiating the withdrawal of 200,000 Chinese occupying soldiers, who were engaging in significant plunder and whose commanders had pretensions to incorporate northern Vietnam into China. But he faced the absence of recognition of his Democratic Republic of Vietnam (DRV) by any other nation, including the USSR, which was more concerned to support communists in France.[50]

However, this accord was short-lived, especially because France was determined to retain control of the economically richest region – Cochin China. This was the main reason for the failure of negotiations at the Cochin China hill station of Dalat in April 1946 between Vietminh leaders led by Giap and the new French High Commissioner, Admiral Thierry d'Argenlieu, who regarded the Ho-Sainteny agreement as another Munich-style sell out. A visit by Ho and other Vietminh leaders to Paris in June-July produced no solution to the impasse. The decline of the political power of the Socialists meant that the French Government was now led by the Catholic *Mouvement Républicain Populaire* (MRP), which was less concerned about Vietnamese aspirations and keen to restore France's war-shattered national pride, for which a colonial empire was seen as important.

Back in Vietnam there was an inevitable explosion that caused the war to flare up in the North. A French attempt to seize a junk carrying suspected smuggled fuel, and its recapture by Vietminh militiamen on 20 November 1946, was seized upon by the French commander, General Jean Valluy, with approval from Paris, to teach the Vietminh a lesson; even though the incident stemmed from the French administration's breaking of the Ho-Sainteny agreement by taking control of the administration of Vietnam's customs policies.

---

50. Interview with Jean Sainteny in Michael Charlton & Anthony Moncrieff, *Many Reasons Why: The American Involvement in Vietnam* (Harmondsworth 1979) 29. Dalloz, *War in Indo-China* 68–70. Douglas Pike, *Vietnam and the Soviet Union: Anatomy of an Alliance* (Boulder 1987) 29–31.

Three days later, after a two-hour ultimatum to the Vietminh to evacuate the Tonkinese port of Haiphong, the city was mercilessly bombarded by a French cruiser killing at least 1,000 people, most of them civilians. Ho still sought negotiations. On 15 December he sent an appeal to a new Socialist government in France, but d'Argenlieu's administration in Saigon delayed transmission of the cable. With no reply from Paris, Ho ordered Giap with some 60,000 troops to prepare for war. On 19 December 1946, the day after Giap received a French order to disarm his troops in Hanoi, the Vietminh struck. They blew up the Hanoi power station, which blacked out the street lighting, and launched an attack on French military outposts and civilian houses. The war in Tonkin had begun.[51]

Giap's mostly inexperienced army, however, was no match for well-trained French troops, who by September 1947 had a strength of 115,000 supported by heavy artillery and air-power. They expelled the Vietminh from Hanoi and other Tonkin towns, and forced Ho, Giap and his men into the mountainous interior. But because France needed to fight another colonial war, in Madagascar from March 1947, and because Vietminh guerillas were also still at large in Cochin China, the French military command in Vietnam had insufficient power to crush the Vietminh completely. Failing in positional warfare in 1946, the Vietminh had evolved an offensive guerilla strategy using village and regional units and extensive tunnel systems that assisted in keeping French forces dispersed.[52]

The French effort to crush the Vietminh was influenced by political changes in France. In 1947 the French right wing used the Vietnam War and the Cold War in general to force communists from the Socialist Party-led government, though in opposition the Communist Party did not whip up any anti-war movement because at this stage the USSR was indifferent to the Vietnam conflict. The Socialists, who were divided on the Vietnam question, lost popular support over industrial unrest in France during 1947; and in a political reshuffle in November the overseas ministry came under the control of the MRP.[53]

The main MRP policy for Vietnam was an attempt to construct an alternative indigenous regime in Vietnam by turning to Bao Dai. He was the French-educated former king of Annam, who had been used

51. Short, *Origins of the Vietnam War* 49–56.

52. Dalloz, *War in Indo-China* 95–102. Lockhart, *Nation in Arms* 183–93.

53. Edward Rice-Maximin, *Accommodation and Resistance: The French Left, Indochina and the Cold War, 1944–1954* (New York 1986) chs 4–5.

by the Japanese in 1945 as their puppet emperor of Vietnam. He had abdicated under Vietminh pressure after the Japanese surrender and was living in Hong Kong when he was approached by the French Administration to become its tame emperor. He delayed his response by negotiating for an independent state of Vietnam within the French Union. However, when his rule was eventually proclaimed on 2 July 1949, the independence of his state was significantly restricted in military, diplomatic and economic spheres. Nor was Bao Dai's return to Vietnam from a sojourn on the French Riviera greeted with much popular enthusiasm, and his status was clearly revealed when he did not reside in Norodom Palace in Saigon, now the French High Commissioner's residence. Instead Bao Dai and a blonde European concubine retreated to Dalat, where he liked to hunt tigers. Nevertheless, the French Government could now proclaim the creation of a Vietnam nation, which might be the focus of a nationalist alternative to the Vietminh.

However, in 1949 other world governments, including the US, were hesitant to recognize Bao Dai's regime in Vietnam because of its limited independence and doubts about his playboy image. With the emerging Cold War, in which France's role in Western Europe was regarded as crucial, Ho Chi Minh's communism was viewed with increasing disfavour in Washington. By 1948, it was widely believed there, without any evidence, that he was being supported by the USSR. But the US was also critical of France's unwillingness to extend political rights to the Vietnamese and through 1949 was maintaining neutrality in the Indochina War.[54]

Nevertheless, during 1949 a change was occurring in American foreign policy thinking which foreshadowed future support for the French in Vietnam. The Cold War was not progressing well. Despite the extensive Marshall Plan aid for Europe, the British economy was faltering and France faced major domestic turmoil. Ominously, in September Truman announced that the USSR had exploded an atomic weapon, and in October the CCP won control of China. Consequently, the American State Department started developing, for the first time, a comprehensive plan for halting communist advances in Southeast Asia by supporting anti-communist forces. Such a policy would have the added advantage of taking pressure off France and Britain, who were expending money on fighting wars

---

54. Herring, 'The Truman Administration'; George McT. Kahin, *Intervention: How America became Involved in Vietnam* (New York 1986) 3–30; Short, *Origins of the Vietnam War* 62–79.

against communist guerillas. This was a policy development which was to greatly extend intervention by the major power in the Eastern Pacific Basin into its western region.[55]

STRUGGLE FOR INDEPENDENCE IN INDONESIA

Holland, however, did not receive American support for a desperate struggle to crush a nationalist rebellion in the Netherlands East Indies (NEI). On that southwestern edge of the Pacific Basin, Indonesian nationalists had taken the same opportunity as had the Vietminh in Tonkin to exploit the sudden power vacuum created by the Japanese surrender in 1945. On 17 August Achmed Sukarno proclaimed the inauguration of the Republic of Indonesia in Jakarta, as the capital city was later to be renamed.

In contrast to Vietminh leaders, Sukarno and his co-leader, Muhammed Hatta, were not communists. Sukarno, born on Java in 1901, had read Marxist literature, but during his Dutch language schooling at Surabaya he was strongly influenced by a group of Indonesian nationalists who rejected Marxist and Islamic ideology. Their focus was independence from Dutch rule with no prescriptions about what would follow, to which Sukarno added an indomitable belief in his own destiny like the great men of history about whom he avidly read. He became the founding chairman of the Indonesian Nationalist Party (PNI) in 1928, which quickly suffered from Dutch repression. He was jailed in 1930 and, after an early release, was exiled in 1933 along with other nationalist leaders, including Hatta. Under an earlier 'ethical policy', Dutch colonialism had provided European education to a generation of Indonesian leaders, who were then politically suppressed by a more conservative regime in the 1930s. That administration stifled any expressions of Indonesian nationalism and even more moderate requests for Indonesian participation in government. Consequently, by 1942 there was widespread urban hostility towards Dutch rule. Many rural Indonesians had been quiescent under Dutch control, influenced by pervasive Muslim

---

55. Andrew J. Rotter, *The Path to Vietnam: Origins of the American Commitment to Southeast Asia* (Ithaca 1987) ch. 5. Leffler, *Preponderance of Power* 312–40.

fatalism, but they were suffering severely from the effects of the economic depression in the 1930s.[56]

In 1942 the Japanese, who easily overcame Dutch resistance, had freed and returned to Java nationalist leaders to much popular acclaim. The Japanese proclaimed the ideal of Asian brotherhood and by late 1944, under the threat of American attack, firmly promised Indonesian independence. In May 1945 an indigenous constitutional convention, after much disputation, approved an Indonesian constitution, based on five principles of nationalism, humanitarianism, democracy, social justice, and belief in a God who transcended all religions, including Islam. This wartime experience gave a massive confidence-boost to nationalist leaders and greatly increased their potential popular support.[57]

The Dutch Government was even keener to reoccupy NEI than the French in Indochina. The NEI, the centrepiece of the Dutch colonial empire, was before the war the Netherlands' fourth largest market and fifth greatest source of imports, supplying essential raw materials, especially rubber, tin and oil. Even more important was the transfer to Holland of profits from Dutch companies in the colony which, along with interest on and redemption of loans and pensions, and wages of Dutch employees in Indonesia, contributed an estimated 14 per cent of the Dutch national income in 1938. After being occupied by Germany during the Second World War, the Netherlands saw reoccupation of the NEI as a means of salving national pride; and foreign exchange from Indonesian earnings was badly needed to balance Holland's huge postwar balance of payments deficit.[58]

However, though the US Government had a more benign view of Dutch than of French colonialism, allied shipping priorities had frustrated Netherlands plans to establish in Australia an armed force of sufficient strength to reoccupy the NEI. An NEI government in exile had been located in 1942 in Australia and was joined in March 1945 by the re-appointed governor of NEI, Dr Hubertus van Mook. He had very limited military power to re-establish Netherlands control

56. M.C. Ricklefs, *A History of Modern Indonesia* (London 1981) chs 13–16. Anthony Reid, *The Indonesian National Revolution 1945–50* (Melbourne 1974) ch. 1. Colin Wild and Peter Carey, *Born of Fire: The Indonesian Struggle for Independence* (Athens, Ohio 1988) chs 10, 11, 13.

57. Theodore Friend, *The Blue-Eyed Enemy: Japan Against the West in Java and Luzon, 1942–1945* (Princeton 1988) chs 4–5.

58. Pierre van der Eng, 'Marshall Aid as a Catalyst to the Decolonization of Indonesia', *Journal of Southeast Asian Studies* 19, 1988, 336. Ricklefs, *History of Modern Indonesia* 146–7.

in the archipelago. Nor had he sufficient information about wartime conditions to shake a widely-held Dutch delusion that, apart from a few nationalist agitators, Indonesians would welcome the Dutch return.[59]

Consequently, as with the French in Cochin China, Holland had to rely on the British SEAC for initial support in Indonesia. But information from advance personnel there convinced SEAC's commander, Admiral Lord Louis Mountbatten, that his men could face hostility from the Indonesian Republic, which had a potentially large army, well armed with Japanese weapons, though lacking in training. Therefore, Lieutenant-General Sir Philip Christison, the commander of the occupying British force, announced that his task was only to disarm the Japanese, to rescue prisoners of war, and to maintain law and order in main cities. He also announced his intention to convene a conference between Indonesian nationalists and the Dutch, which infuriated van Mook as displaying recognition of the Indonesian Republic.[60]

A difficulty for the Netherlands was that neither Mountbatten nor the British Government believed that there was a military solution to the problem of the Indonesian Republic, certainly not one to be undertaken by British forces. Therefore negotiation with Indonesians was the only recourse. Initially also Mountbatten refused permission for Dutch troops to land in Java so as to avoid violent Indonesian responses. Indeed, British troops faced armed Indonesian resistance, especially in Surabaya, where two brigades of the 5th Indian division, supported by naval firepower and air attacks, took three weeks from 10 November 1945 to establish British control of the city against Indonesians equipped with Japanese machine guns, artillery and tanks. However, the failure of initial negotiations, conducted under British pressure between the Dutch and representatives of the Indonesian republic, further military clashes between British troops and Indonesians, as well as criticism from his local commanders of the 'trigger happy' Dutch approach to the problem, also convinced Mountbatten by April 1946 to withdraw and hand over the control that SEAC had achieved in Java and Sumatra to Holland. Also in Eastern Indonesia Australian occupying forces quickly allowed the Dutch to resume control.[61]

59. Dennis, *Troubled Days of Peace* 66–77.
60. Ibid. ch. 5.
61. William H. Frederick, *Visions and Heat: The Making of the Indonesian Revolution* (Athens, Ohio 1988) 182–296. Dennis, *Troubled Days of Peace* chs 9–10.

Nevertheless, negotiations were revived. The Indonesians, led by Prime Minister Sutan Sjahirir who, as a non-collaborator with the Japanese during the war, was more acceptable internationally than President Sukarno, offered a compromise by insisting only on sovereignty over the islands with substantial Indonesian control: Java, Madura and Sumatra. Under strong British pressure, supported by the US, the Dutch Government accepted this partition proposal in the Linggajati agreement of November 1946. Under its terms the Republic and the Netherlands pledged to cooperate to create by 1 January 1949 a federal United States of Indonesia (USI) in which the Indonesian Republic and the Dutch-held islands would be sovereign states with the Dutch queen as symbolic head.

On both sides, however, there were many political leaders who rejected that compromise. With nationalist sentiment disrupting efforts to consolidate Netherlands control in eastern Indonesia, and a Dutch wish to appropriate more of the wealth of Java and Sumatra to compensate for the cost of NEI reconstruction, the Netherlands Government decided to use the 100,000 troops it had established on Java to assert its authority over the Indonesian Republic in a euphemistically named 'police action'. Launched on 20 July 1947, it consisted of major military thrusts from the Dutch centres on Java. These advances succeeded in capturing all of Java's deep sea ports plus Sumatra plantations and oil and coal installations. Indonesian military forces lacked training, coherence of command, and the sea and air power which supported the Dutch troops.

The 'police action', however, aroused strong opposition in the UN led by newly independent India and by Australia, where the Labor Government had swung from initial support for the restoration of Dutch rule in Indonesia to advocacy of a negotiated solution, which Holland was now seen to be rejecting. Furthermore, the US supported negotiations. The American Government had refused to become involved in Indonesia at the end of the war in recognition of the need to use its troops elsewhere, which had resulted in the assignment of the region to SEAC. The Netherlands had the misfortune of not being a major European power like France. Nor was the Indonesian Communist Party (PKI) influential in the Indonesian Republican Government, which had pledged not to interfere with foreign investment. Holland, dependent on American financial support, was forced to accept a cease-fire on 4 August, without achieving the conquest of Java. Washington also took the lead in UN sponsored Indonesian-Dutch negotiations which led to an agreement signed on the US warship *Renville* in January 1948. The Renville agreement recognized a cease-fire along the so-called van Mook Line, which connected points of the most advanced Dutch incursions into Republican territory, even though it enclosed many Republican-occupied areas.[62]

The Dutch moved to create new states out of the captured territory so that the United States of Indonesia (USI) could outvote the Republic of Indonesia. But in those states there was much sympathy for the republican cause. The Indonesian Republic in turn faced political instability caused by dissension with the Renville agreement. It also suffered from economic distress caused by the Dutch blockade, an influx of as many as six million refugees, and high inflation generated by the government's printing of money to meet costs. In west Java there was a popular revolt led by a Dutch-educated Islamic mystic, Sekarmdji Maridjan Kartosuwirjo. More seriously, the PKI was organizing strikes and peasant takeovers of properties. By mid-September there were violent clashes between communist and government forces leading to a PKI uprising in the town of Madiun, which was crushed by the Indonesian army resulting in the deaths of the PKI's leader, Musso, and at least 8,000 PKI supporters. Meanwhile post-Renville negotiations between the Dutch and the republicans were breaking down, especially over the Dutch strategy to create more USI states. There were also frequent clashes between Dutch and Indonesian troops along the long van Mook line, and there were Indonesian raids within the Dutch zone which had been infiltrated by guerilla bands.[63]

The Netherlands Government's response to these clashes and the stalling of USI negotiations was to launch on 18 December 1948 the second 'police action'. A majority of Dutch Cabinet ministers were hoping to eliminate the Republic. With 99,000 troops in Java and unchallenged air support, the Dutch army considered it could easily defeat the opposing disorganized forces. Indeed, an airborne paratroop landing at the Republic's capital of Yogyakarta resulted in the capture of the republican Cabinet, but the military leaders and most of the Indonesian soldiers there were able to escape. In fact, while capturing key republican positions and major towns, the

---

62. Reid, *Indonesian National Revolution* 111–14. Margaret George, *Australia and the Indonesian Revolution* (Melbourne 1980) chs 3–8. Robert J. McMahon, *Colonialism and Cold War: The United States and the Struggle for Indonesian Independence, 1945–49* (Ithaca 1981) chs 2–6.

63. Robert Cribb, *Gangsters and Revolutionaries: The Jakarta People's Militia and the Indonesian Revolution 1945–1949* (Sydney 1991) ch. 11. Reid, *Indonesian National Revolution* 124–47.

Dutch forces failed to defeat the Indonesian army. It dispersed and engaged in guerilla attacks on military posts, lines of communication, plantations and even towns well into the Dutch rear.[64]

The second 'police action' not only failed in its objectives, it also raised another storm of international protest in which the US took strong action. The suppression of the Madiun uprising had given the Republic of Indonesia good anti-communist credentials. So pressure, including the suspension of Marshall Plan aid, was placed on Holland to halt the military campaign and return to the negotiating table. New research has shown that the suspension of Marshall Aid money was symbolic rather than actual since most of it had already been committed. There was also a realization in Holland that besides strong international opposition and a potential future threat to aid money, the Netherlands could escape from the financial obligation to support Indonesia's economic recovery if it became independent and Dutch economic interests there were protected. Therefore a cease-fire was announced to take effect on 11 August. From 23 August to 2 November there was a round table conference between Dutch and Indonesian representatives in The Hague at which a Republic of the USI was recognized with the Dutch queen as its titular head, and with Sukarno as president and Hatta as prime minister. The new state accepted responsibility for the NEI's debt, which was set, after much haggling, at forty-three billion guilders, much of it being the cost of the 'police actions'. Guarantees were given for the protection of Dutch investments. The status of West New Guinea (Irian Jaya) was postponed for later negotiations. On 27 November 1949 the Netherlands transferred sovereignty of the rest of NEI to the new Indonesian Republic which, with its seventy-eight million people and 1.9 million square kilometres of land, was to become a major Southwestern Pacific Basin power.[65]

OUTBREAK OF INSURRECTION IN MALAYA

In Malaya, there was to be another communist uprising which became linked to the Cold War in the Southwestern Pacific Basin. In contrast

---

64. M.H. Groen, 'Dutch Armed Forces and the Decolonization of Indonesia: The Second Police Action (1948–1949), A Pandora's Box', *War & Society* 4:1, 1986, 79–104.

65. van der Eng, 'Marshall Aid as a Catalyst', 338–52.

to the reception of the Dutch in Indonesia, the British return to Malaya after the Second World War was generally welcomed by its indigenous people, despite Britain's humiliating defeat by the Japanese in 1941–42. The Malays had become a minority: 43.5 per cent of the population of 5,848,910 in the 1947 census, compared with 44.7 per cent Chinese and 10.3 per cent Indians. Before the war the Malays had been largely shielded from western influences by British protection of their mostly subsistence peasant and hierarchical Muslim society. The British administration ruled through the traditional sultans in two sets of Federated and Unfederated States alongside the three Straits Settlements colonies covering the first areas of British commercial penetration – Singapore, Malacca and Penang. Many members of the Malay aristocracy had been transformed into English language-educated public servants. Although a sense of nationalism had been growing in the Malay community, especially among the minority receiving English education, the main nationalist organization, the Malay Association, was conservative and loyal to the British crown. A more radical young Malay union, the Kesatuan Malaya Muda (KMM), was formed in 1938 by Ibrrahim Yaacob. It advocated a pan-Malay union with Indonesians, but it failed to receive significant popular support. The Chinese and Indians had been brought to work in the colony's rubber plantations and tin mines, and the Chinese were prominent in commerce. Among the Chinese, in particular, there was pressure for equal rights. Though by 1931 some 31 per cent of the Chinese were locally born, they had no citizenship rights outside the Straits Settlements, not even possessing the British subject status of foreign born Indians.[66]

From 1942 to 1945 Malays were generally quiescent under Japanese rulers. The Japanese preferred to work with the established public servants rather than with the KMM, which was perceived as having little public support. The Japanese brutally mistreated the Chinese, encouraging many of them to support a resistance movement, the Malayan People's Anti-Japanese Army (MPAJA). This was the armed wing of the predominantly Chinese Malayan Communist Party (MCP), which had been formed in 1930. The MPAJA received British military support during the war and, when the Japanese surrendered, it resisted appeals from the KMM to join in opposing a British return. A frustrated Yaacob left with other KMM leaders to fight for Indonesian independence. However, the MPAJA used the four-

66. See R. Roff, *The Origins of Malay Nationalism* (New Haven 1967); and Victor Purcell, *The Chinese in Malaya* (Kuala Lumpar 1967).

week time gap before the British arrived in the mainland capital of Kuala Lumpur to murder Malay collaborators, provoking retaliatory Malayan attacks on Chinese. Communal violence continued during 1945, and the British Military Administration's (BMA) order for the surrender of all arms was only partially obeyed, leaving many weapons in MCP members' hands. The war had thus generated in Malaya open racial conflict. Furthermore the BMA, which contained only a minority of people with knowledge of the country, had brought disrepute to British authority. It failed to curb the minority of British soldiers who indulged in plunder and rape; it was ineffective in controlling the communal violence; it created mass poverty by declaring Japanese money worthless; and it fostered corruption and black marketeering.[67]

Remaining KMM supporters tried to exploit resultant popular discontent by launching a radical Malay Nationalist Party (MNP). But most Malays refused to support it. They were much more agitated by a British proposal to reorganize the Malay states and two of the Straits Settlements – not strategically important Singapore – into a Malayan Union. The objectionable features of this plan were the stripping of the powers of the traditional rulers, who had religious as well as social and political status; the centralizing of power in Kuala Lumpur; and the granting to non-Malays of equal citizenship rights. These reforms were the result of prewar British discussions about the problem of citizenship rights for non-Malays and a wartime shift in Colonial Office preferences towards the Chinese, who had opposed the Japanese occupation and whose loyalty could be claimed by China. Granting them full citizenship rights also was seen as the only basis for welding together a future independent Malaya in which there was no place for special protection of Malays or their sultans.[68]

Mass Malay protests resulted in the formation in May 1946 of the United Malay National Organization (UMNO), which attracted much popular support. Its opposition to the Malayan Union was

---

67. Richard Stubbs, *Hearts and Minds in Guerilla Warfare: The Malayan Emergency 1948–1960* (Singapore 1989) 11–16; Cheah Boon Kheng, *Red Star Over Malaya: Resistance and Social Conflict During and After the Japanese Occupation, 1941–1946* (Singapore 1983) 294–5. Khong Kim Hoong, *Merdeka!: British Rule and the Struggle for Independence in Malaya, 1945–1957* (Selangor 1984), ch. 2.

68. Albert Lau, 'Malayan Union Citizenship: Constitutional Change and Controversy in Malaya, 1942–48', *Journal of Southeast Asian Studies* XX, 1989, 216–43. A.J. Stockwell, *British Policy and Malay Politics During the Malayan Union Experiment, 1942–1948* (Kuala Lumpar 1979) 35–8, ch. 4. See also Albert Lau, *The Malayan Union Controversy 1942–1948* (Singapore 1991).

peaceful but so widespread that Britain was prepared to back down. This policy change was also influenced by the lukewarm approach to the union by Indians and Chinese and by a concern to stem any anti-British movement among the Malays matching the nationalism of their Indonesian cousins. Independence was still considered well into the future for politically inexperienced Malays; and the colony's tin and rubber exports, which were rapidly recovering from wartime damage, were major earners for Britain of scarce American dollars. So in 1948 the Malayan Union was replaced with the Federation of Malaya Agreement. It restored the power of traditional Malay rulers and retained universal citizenship rights but made them more restrictive by, for example, lengthening the required periods of residence for non-Malays from five to fifteen years. This victory firmly established UMNO's popular support among Malays, many of whom were now dubious about the British connection.[69]

A vociferous opponent of the Federation Agreement was the MCP. It had organized a series of strikes in 1946, exploiting working-class grievances about food shortages and low wages. The BMA responded with military pressure against strikers and arrests of strike leaders, causing the MCP to adopt a lower profile and concentrate on organizing public support. Though gaining little influence in the Indian and Malay communities, it won significant Chinese support, assisted by the nationalistic nature of Chinese language education in Malaya since the 1920s and continuing low wages and high food prices. Nor was there an alternative strong Chinese political association.

However, on 10 May 1948 the MCP central committee decided to authorize armed struggle. This decision was influenced by the lack of wider community support, British Administration pressure on Chinese trade unions, the inspiration of the CCP victories in China and, especially, the unmasking in 1947 of an influential leader, Lai Tek, as a wartime collaborator. He had been the architect of the MCP peace strategy, and he also absconded with most of the party's funds, leaving more radical leaders in charge. The result was a growing escalation of violent incidents culminating in the murder of three British planters on 16 June 1948 by members of the MCP's Malayan Races Liberation Army (MRLA).[70]

The British Administration was soon convinced that this armed

---

69. Ibid. ch. 6. Stubbs, *Hearts and Minds* 27–8. Khong Kim Hoong, *Merdeka* ch. 3.
70. Stubbs, *Hearts and Minds* ch. 2.

uprising was part of a USSR supported anti-colonial strategy since it coincided with the outbreak of a communist-led revolution in Burma and the abortive Madiun uprising in Indonesia. But the British could provide no evidence and the hypothesis is doubtful given the Soviet Union's lack of support for the Vietminh in Indochina before 1950. Furthermore, by 1951 the British Administration in Malaya was discounting external assistance to the MCP, and the only evidence was the arrival that year of some Chinese army officers.[71]

A major source of support for the insurgency – men, food and information – was the large community of Chinese squatters, who had been driven from urban centres into rural districts by economic hardship during the 1930s depression and had been neglected by the government. The area they occupied was vast – forest reserves, Malay reservations and especially European plantations that had fallen into disuse during the war. Their number was unknown to the government; an estimate was 300,000 in 1948.[72]

The first MRLA objective was destruction of the economy and of government authority. Targets were mines, plantations and communications including assassinations of owners, managers and public officials. Operating centres were camps hidden in jungle but close to the squatter areas. The initial insurgent strength was about 2,300 front line men, which grew to a peak of 7,292 in 1951. Their early weapons were those the MPAJA had not surrendered in 1945.[73]

The British Administration declared a state of emergency after the murders of 16 June. Initially its force to combat the insurgents consisted of 9,000 Malay police and ten infantry battalions, seven of them Gurkhas and three British. They were soon supported by army reinforcements, armoured cars, artillery and aircraft. The army was used to pursue and destroy insurgents, at times shooting Chinese suspects indiscriminately. The police had the more difficult job of maintaining security; their numbers increased to 16,220 by the beginning of 1950, but many of the hastily trained recruits treated members of the Chinese community with open brutality. A Malay Special Constabulary, 10,000 strong in August 1948, was used to

71. Pike, *Vietnam and the Soviet Union* 28–32. R.B. Smith, 'China and Southeast Asia: The Revolutionary Perspective, 1951', *Journal of Southeast Asian Studies* XIX, 1988, 97–100.

72. Anthony Short, *The Communist Insurrection in Malaya 1948–1960* (London 1975) ch. 7.

73. Ibid. ch. 4. Robert Jackson, *The Malayan Emergency: The Commonwealth's Wars 1948–1966* (London 1991) ch. 2.

guard plantations, mines and other important installations, and in 1949 a force of Kampong Guards was raised to protect Malay villages. To 1950 the campaign was controlled by the Commissioner of Police with advice from military commanders. Major improvements had been made to the police force after the arrival in 1948 of the British Police Commissioner in Palestine, Colonel W. N. Gray. Regulations were passed giving the administration sweeping powers of arrest and control of transport and food distribution, and in 1949 the Chinese squatter problem was addressed with regulations empowering resettlement. That year 6,343 squatters were detained and 9,062 Chinese were repatriated to China. These were preliminary measures to combat the insurgency, but the process suffered from coordination problems; and the use of force was increasing sympathy in the Chinese community for the rebels. The insurrection in Malaya was to remain a major problem for the anti-communist cause in the Southwestern Pacific Basin.[74]

THE HUK REBELLION IN THE PHILIPPINES

Across the South China Sea, in the Philippines, insurgency also flared up after the end of the Pacific War, which became interpreted as another communist challenge. American colonialism had been much more benevolent than French or Dutch rule in Southeast Asia, and in 1934 the Philippines were promised independence from 1946. Admittedly, a major reason for the move towards independence was pressure within the US Congress to rid the country of an economic burden and to stop immigration of Filipinos and the free importation of Philippines produce, especially sugar. American sugar interests, at the beginning of US rule of the Philippines, had combined with anti-imperialists and anti-trust minded progressives to impose strict limits on American landholdings and a fifty-year limit on American corporations. In 1938 the 8,700 Americans in the Philippines population of sixteen million were mostly military personnel and public servants. In 1916 literate Filipinos were given the right to vote for an almost wholly elected congress, with the

74. Ibid. ch. 3. Stubbs, *Hearts and Minds* ch. 3. Short, *The Communist Insurrection* ch. 5.

US retaining power only over defence and foreign affairs. In 1936 the colony was given Commonwealth status with its own elected president. By then nearly all public servants were Filipinos and educational opportunities were far greater than in any other colony in Asia. Nearly half the population was literate. However, though big church estates were broken up and sold to the people, there were no measures to stop the accumulation of wealth by Filipino landowners and their dominance over the political system.[75]

Indeed, there was growing popular dissent in the 1930s on the large central plain of the most heavily populated island, Luzon. The population of 1,389,000 in 1939 was almost double its level in 1903, creating an acute land shortage problem at a time when landlords were becoming commercially minded and placing more pressure on the predominantly tenant farming population. Under the influence of American education and capitalism, the days of the Spanish-based traditional society of mutual obligations between peasant and landlord were rapidly disappearing. Peasants reacted with acts of violence that were more than matched by landowners and their local authority allies. There were also strikes and the formation of peasant political organizations. The small Philippines Communist Party (PKP) had little to do with this dissent because of government oppression and because its base was urban.[76]

During the Pacific War, however, a PKP leader, Luis Taruc, became the head of the main anti-Japanese resistance on Luzon, the *Hukbalahap* (Huk) movement. He was a central Luzon tenant farmer's son, who had received an English-language education to college level, which gave him a love of American history. Too poor to finish college, he returned to his home district to work as a tailor, and he became a socialist leader until his party merged in 1938 with the PKP. Taruc was not an ideological Marxist. There were some committed communists in the Huk leadership, but they were neither a majority nor a controlling influence. By September 1944 the Huks had over 10,000 guerillas armed mainly with captured Japanese weapons. They were not supported, and at times were actively opposed, by the official American resistance organization. Its members had been commanded to lie low and concentrate on gathering intelligence for

75. Norman G. Owen, *Prosperity Without Progress: Manila Hemp and Material Life in the Philippines* (Berkeley 1984) ch. 7. David Wurfel, *Filipino Politics: Development and Decay* (Ithaca 1988) 8–12.

76. Benedict J. Kerkvliet, *The Huk Rebellion: A Study of Peasant Revolt in the Philippines* (Berkely 1977) chs 1–2. Eduardo Lachica, *The Huks: Philippine Agrarian Society in Revolt* (New York 1971) chs 3–4.

MacArthur's army, which invaded the islands in force in August 1944 and was widely welcomed by Filipinos. The Americans re-established the Philippines Commonwealth government, giving the Huks no chance to launch a social revolution. Indeed, they were only a small minority of the Philippine resistance movement and their activities were confined to central Luzon.[77]

Though the Philippines became an independent republic on 4 July 1946, it gave, under American negotiating pressure, major concessions to the US. Ninety-nine year leases were conceded for twenty-two military and naval base sites. Ironically, economic constraints – free trade for eight years, pegging the Philippine peso to the American dollar and parity for American investors in the republic – paved the way for much more American economic expansion into the new nation than was possible when it was US territory. The investment parity provision aroused much Filipino opposition and was only accepted because of a narrow electoral victory in April 1946 for the conservative pro-American Liberal Party, assisted by smear tactics and money power, and the subsequent unseating from the Congress of representatives elected in Central Luzon, because of alleged fraud and terror there.[78]

This unseating of six elected members of the National Peasants Union (PKM) was one of the grievances that sparked the armed Huk uprising in mid-1946. The Huks, though fighting alongside the invading Americans, had been rejected by the postwar regime, which ordered them to surrender their arms and employed violence against those who refused. Despite this pressure many weapons were successfully hidden. The Huks were victims of the hostility of the official American guerillas and of landowners and other members of the governing elite, which included many pardoned wartime collaborators. The communists in their midst made them unacceptable to Americans. This rejection, the restoration of the power of landowners, and repression of peasants and the PKM, including murders, were sparks igniting rebellion in Central Luzon.[79]

The Huk insurrection grew in strength from 1946 to 1949. Precise numbers of guerillas are unknown, but there were at least 5,000 in Central Luzon by late 1948. So in size they matched the insurgents in Malaya and had a popular base of support among the tenant

77. Ibid. ch. 6. Kerkvliet, ch. 3. Friend, *Blue-Eyed Enemy* chs 8–9.

78. Ibid. ch. 11. Stanley Karnow, *In Our Image: America's Empire in the Philippines* (New York 1989) ch. 12.

79. Kerkvliet, *The Huk Rebellion* ch. 4

farmers of Central Luzon. Their weapons came from wartime caches plus captured arms, and guns and ammunition stolen for them by civilian employees at the American bases. However, the rebellion failed to expand much outside Central Luzon because there was not the same history of peasant radicalism in other regions, nor the same high proportion of tenant farmers. Moreover, there were cultural differences to overcome. Even in Central Luzon problems of manpower and food supplies limited Huk communications, and some of the recruits acted with undue violence against villagers. PKM support for the rebellion also diminished under government repression, which increased the dominance of communist leaders, although Taruc and other Huk leaders remained non-Marxist.[80]

The rebellion was sustained by the Philippine Government's use of violent repression, rather than attempting to redress peasant grievances. The use of troops, aircraft and artillery to support local constabulary resulted in many civilians being killed or arrested for allegedly supporting the rebels. As one witness recalled: 'The mailed fist policy meant open season on all suspected Huk and PKM. And, of course, this also meant trouble for people who were not directly involved'.[81] Evacuation of peasants caused much economic hardship. The American Government, which was quick to believe the Huks were communists, provided by mid-1948 $72.6 million in military aid to equip 22,000 constabulary troops and 33,000 regular army soldiers. But in 1949 the rebellion was continuing to grow in a country recovering from great wartime damage and with a political system dominated by its socio-economic elite. It was to remain a thorn in the side of the anti-communist cause in the Pacific Basin into the 1950s.[82]

CONCLUSIONS

By 1949 the Western Pacific Basin had been dramatically reshaped since 1945. Much stronger postwar forces of Asian nationalism had made a significant gain in Indonesia, had been granted success in

80. Ibid. ch. 5.
81. Quoted in ibid. 194.
82. Ibid. 188–203.

the Philippines but faced French intransigence in Indochina. The outbreak of the Cold War had compromised the nationalist cause by forcing a division in Korea and by increasing the resolve of western world powers to resist independence movements in Vietnam and Malaya. The Communist victory in China now cast a huge shadow over the future prospects for western interests in the region. The US was being deflected from a primary concern about halting the advance of communism in Europe into a decision to start lending its support to the anti-communist cause in the Western Pacific Basin. This reconsideration had already halted the process of socio-economic reform in Japan. It had prompted pressure on Holland to grant anti-communist Republic of Indonesia its independence and to allocate financial support for the campaign against the Huk rebellion. Indeed, the groundwork had been laid for American financial involvement in France's struggle in Vietnam.

The American objectives in the Western Pacific Basin were mixed. 'The reverse course' in Japan has been used as evidence that the US's primary objective was to promote 'Open Door' economic imperialism. This theory can be supported by American approval of the Indonesian Republic, which pledged to protect foreign investment, and by the imposition on the independent Philippines government of policies to assist expansion of American capital there. But it is too simple to say that American foreign policy decision makers such as Truman, Kennan and Acheson were acting at the behest of American capitalists. They all shared the 'corporationist' view that American ideas and values were good for other countries. This was demonstrated by the planning for the occupation of Japan and by opposition to the corruption and elitism of Chiang Kai-shek. But also much of postwar US foreign policy was influenced by 'realist' assessments of American power and security influences. Such realities conceded control of Manchuria to the USSR; they influenced the handing over to SEAC of responsibility for Southeast Asia; and they prompted the withdrawal from Korea in 1949. Reasons for increasing American involvement in the Western Pacific Basin from 1950 will be examined in the next chapter.

CHAPTER TWO

Containing the Advance of Asian Communism, 1950–1960

In the Western Pacific Basin in 1950 the US faced a major communist advance in Korea, an increasingly difficult French struggle to suppress the communist-led insurgency in Vietnam and the growing Huk rebellion in the Philippines. The British Government also was combatting an increasingly militant communist insurgency in Malaya. The attempts to suppress these rebellions, which presaged major communist victories in the Cold War, are major themes in this chapter. Also discussed are the wider influences of the Korean War on the Pacific Basin, US moves to contain Communist China and the impact on Japan of its involvement in the US anti-communist defence network.

THE KOREAN WAR

At 4 a.m. on Sunday 25 June 1950, the army of the Democratic People's Republic of Korea (DPRK) began on the Onjin Peninsula the first of a series of attacks across the 38th parallel. The US State Department did not receive from its ambassador in Seoul confirmation of newspaper reports about the attack until six-and-a-half hours later, 9.26 p.m. local time on Saturday. Telephone consultations with Secretary of State Acheson and President Truman resulted in the issue being referred quickly to the UN. Convened in emergency session on the Sunday afternoon, its Security Council approved a US resolution which declared the North Korean attack 'an act of aggression', ordered a withdrawal of DPRK forces north of the 38th parallel and authorized member states to assist in 'the execution of this resolution'. Only Yugoslavia, which abstained from voting, expressed opposition. Crucially, the USSR, one of the five nations with a power of veto in the Council, was not present because Stalin had been boycotting the UN since mid-January for its refusal to transfer Nationalist China's seat to the People's Republic of China. Washington was attempting to force the DPRK to retreat without American military intervention. However, the rapid advance of the better equipped and much more experienced North Korean People's Army (KPA) into South Korea provoked, under UN authority, a speedy American commitment of air and naval power and then ground forces to prevent a complete DPRK victory.[1]

The US was not acting under any treaty obligation to the ROK. Administration personnel had made public statements minimizing the importance of South Korea, much to the consternation of Rhee. Such speeches, however, were not signals that America would abandon a country to which that year it had granted $120 million in aid; in which there was America's largest overseas embassy; and which was being assisted by a sizeable mission of US military advisers. South Korea was seen to be an important supplier of rice to Japan and a market for the Japanese exports that were being encouraged under the 'reverse course' programme for Japanese economic recovery. Rather, the American public statements were designed to deter the ROK from expecting US support for any aggressive move against the DPRK.[2]

The American decision to seek UN support for military assistance to the ROK was made in the context of increasing Cold War intensity in Europe and Asia. The communist takeover in Czechoslovakia in 1948 and the Russian blockade of Berlin in 1948–49 had signalled to the US a dangerous threat of Soviet expansionism into Western Europe. In Asia, the communist victory in China presented new problems for the region because it was widely believed in America that the CCP and the USSR were closer allies than they really were. This belief had been spelt out in NSC-68, a re-evaluation of US foreign policies and strategic plans by the Departments of State and

1. See Glenn D. Paige, *The Korean Decision* (New York 1968). Matray, *The Reluctant Crusade* ch. 10.
2. Cumings, *Origins of the Korean War* vol. 2, ch. 13. Ronald McGlothlen, 'Acheson, Economics, and the American Commitment in Korea, 1947–1950', *Pacific Historical Review* LVIII, 1989, 23–54.

Defense, which was submitted by the National Security Council (NSC) to Truman on 7 April 1950. There were also the continuing insurgencies in Burma, Malaya, Vietnam and the Philippines that were alleged to be actively supported by the USSR. In this context the attack on non-communist South Korea by the DPRK was seen as another Soviet-inspired aggression that must be resisted in the same manner as was the Russian blockade of Berlin. Not to do so would raise echoes of Munich in 1938, especially given the virulence of the growing Republican Party attack on the 'loss' of China and the alleged softness of the administration towards communism that was being fuelled by the Alger Hiss and other spy scandals.[3]

However, there is no evidence that the USSR masterminded the DPRK attack. Moscow probably received prior notice of the invasion but would hardly have planned it and then have failed to veto the Security Council response. In fact, after receiving a cable from Jacob Malik, the Soviet representative at the UN, about the US request for Security Council action, a senior Foreign Ministry official, Andrei Gromyko, prepared an instruction to 'use the right of veto'. He warned Stalin that, 'in the absence of our representative, the Security Council will do what it likes, including sending troops to South Korea from other countries under the guise of being United Nations forces'. But Stalin instructed Malik to maintain the Soviet boycott of the UN. Nor was the DPRK a puppet Soviet state. Kim Il Sung and his colleagues did not believe they had a benevolent neighbour in the USSR, which had maintained neutrality with Japan for almost the entire Pacific war, which had agreed to a division of Korea, and which had made North Koreans pay for all assistance. The uneasy relationship was demonstrated by the failure of the two countries to sign a mutual defence pact as was concluded between the USSR and Eastern European communist states in 1948. North Koreans publicly lavished great praise on the Soviets, but these nations' real relationship was like that of two actors in a play with rival ambitions.[4]

An alternative charge is that the ROK started the war by attacking first. Certainly Rhee's government had made no secret of its wish to reunite Korea by force. There had been numerous armed clashes along the 38th parallel in 1949 after the American troop withdrawal that were mostly started by the ROK and which the DPRK did

---

3. Lowe, *Origins of the Korean War* chs 5–6.

4. John Merrill, *Korea: The Peninsular Origins of the War* (Newark 1989) 21–9. Andrei Gromyko, *Memories* (London 1989) 102. Cumings, *Origins of the Korean War* vol. 2, ch. 10.

not exploit to commence a war. But even if there was an initial ROK attack across the Onjin Peninsula border, for which there is no conclusive evidence, why did the DPRK convert its response into attacks all along the border? Evidence has been discovered of North Korean preparations of aeroplanes and troops for some big conflict around 25 June, which explains the quick spread of attacks along the border after the initial outbreak. So, even if the DPRK military preparations before that date were for war games rather than for an invasion, the KPA was in readiness either for a massive response to ROK provocation or to launch its own attacks.[5]

So the probability is that the DPRK started the war, though the South was not blameless in its previous military incursions across the border, nor in bellicose statements about subjugating the North. Various reasons have been offered for the Northern attack. One, which has been frequently advanced, is that there was a factional conflict between Kim Il Sung and Pak Hŏn-yŏng, the former leader of the communists in the South who had become the DPRK's foreign minister. He was allegedly now concerned about the loss of his base in the ROK because of the successful suppression of communist guerillas there and consequently argued that a Northern attack would unleash a popular Southern uprising, which would facilitate speedy military victory. But this reasoning could have been advanced by anyone in the DPRK, and the argument was used against Pak in the postwar search for scapegoats for the North's military defeat.

A more acceptable theory is that the DPRK was acting before Korea was irreparably divided. This is supported by a shift in May 1950 in the Northern anti-Rhee rhetoric from accusations of advocating a forceful Southern invasion of the North to a charge that Rhee was seeking a permanent division of Korea. The ROK economy was improving under the impact of good harvests in the previous two years. Rhee's government also had promised land reform, and the elections in May 1950, though demonstrating popular dissatisfaction with Rhee by electing many independents to the National Assembly, had no bearing on his position as president and fulfilled a criterion for continued American support.

However, there was probably another reason impelling urgency to the DPRK attack and a willingness to risk American military support for the ROK. There is plenty of evidence that DPRK

5. Ibid. 588–98. Gye-Dong Kim, 'Who Initiated the Korean War?' in James Cotton and Ian Neary (eds), *The Korean War in History* (Atlantic Heights 1989) 33–50.

leaders were growing alarmed at American efforts to boost the Japanese economy and the establishment of economic and potential military links between Japan and the ROK. Though the military fear was exaggerated, the spectre of an American supported revival of Japanese influence in Korea was terrifying for former victims of Japanese colonialism. Crucially also, the return to the DPRK in early 1950 of most of its veterans in the CCP army greatly assisted in tipping decisively the military balance against the inexperienced South Korean army (ROKA).[6]

The wildfire advance of the KPA into South Korea meant that the first American troops to arrive from Japan only assisted remnants of the ROKA to defend a small area around the port of Pusan. Indeed, many South Koreans, alienated by Rhee's policies, either did not resist or actually welcomed the invaders. By early September, however, America's Far East Commander, MacArthur, directed a UN army (UNA) of 83,000 Americans plus a British Commonwealth brigade composed of British troops from Hong Kong and the Australian battalion engaged in the occupation of Japan. With the addition of surviving ROKA divisions, MacArthur now had 180,000 troops to set against the 98,000 strong KPA. With the reluctant permission of the JCS, MacArthur used this advantage in a brilliantly conceived and successful amphibious landing on 15 September at Inchon on the west coast of South Korea close to Seoul. The capital city was occupied by 28 September, and the main KPA supply line had been severed. This disaster for the DPRK, along with a UNA breakout from the Pusan perimeter, caused a headlong KPA retreat across the 38th parallel.[7]

The subsequent decision to switch the UNA from containment of the DPRK attack to a roll-back attempt to reunite Korea under non-communist rule was uncontroversial in the US. The shock of the initial KPA success, and then the euphoria aroused by MacArthur's dramatic counter-stroke, had aroused widespread public support for an advance across the 38th parallel. Nor did the Administration need any urging to do this, especially because stopping at the border would boost the Republican Party attack on its policy towards communism

---

6. Cumings, *Origins of the Korean War* vol. 2, ch. 14.
7. For good short histories of the war see Burton I. Kaufman, *The Korean War: Challenges in Crisis, Credibility and Command* (Philadelphia 1986); and Callum A. MacDonald, *Korea: The War Before Vietnam* (New York 1986). For an overview of recent literature on the causes and course of the war see Rosemary Foot, 'Making Known the Unknown War: Policy Analysis of the Korean Conflict in the Last Decade', *Diplomatic History* 15, 1991, 411–31.

at a time of imminent mid-term congressional elections. Furthermore, the advance into communist North Korea was in keeping with the hard line the Truman Government had been taking towards communist China, and so it was not the departure from previous policies that historians have claimed.[8]

The US roll-back decision also discounted any threat of Russian or Chinese retaliation. The USSR had responded to the American intervention in the war with proposals in the UN for a joint Soviet-American effort for peaceful reunification of Korea, which the US had brushed aside. China warned that it would not tolerate an American military advance into North Korea, but this was dismissed in Washington as bluff on the grounds that neither China nor the USSR wanted a general war with the US. Also the US, with British support, achieved a big majority in a vote in the UN General Assembly on 7 October, which authorized the UNA to cross the border. This decision avoided the need for endorsement by the Security Council, to which the USSR had returned. America, and the other nations which had been persuaded to support the extension of the war, had deluded themselves that they could safely remove the artificial border in Korea.

But China was not bluffing. On the basis of interviews with Chinese veterans of the Korean War, the British journalist Russell Spurr has reconstructed a conference in Beijing on 6 August 1950 between the field commander of the Chinese People's Liberation Army (PLA), Peng Dehuai, and his generals. Peng told them that China would enter the war 'if the integrity' of the DPRK were 'directly threatened' by 'the American imperialists', though Han Nianlong and Pu Shuan, who served in the Chinese Foreign Ministry at the time, insist that China's concern was for her own security not for the independence of North Korea. Indeed, there is no evidence that China had encouraged Kim Il Sung to start the war, having paid little attention to North Korea and failing to send an ambassador to its capital, Pyongyang, until after the war commenced. At that time there had been only one Chinese army corps stationed along the Yalu River.[9]

In preparation for the intervention option, four seasoned field

8. Chang, *Friends and Enemies* 77–80.

9. Russell Spurr, *Enter the Dragon: China's Undeclared War Against the U.S. in Korea, 1950–51* (New York 1988) 68–9. Cohen, 'Conversations with Chinese Friends', 288. Hao Yufan and Zhai Zhihai, 'China's Decision to Enter the Korean War: History Revisited', *The China Quarterly* no 121, March 1990, 99–100.

armies, of western army corps size, were sent to Manchuria and two more were placed on standby. On 1 October a special enlarged Politburo meeting in Beijing reviewed the pros and cons about entering the war. There was opposition on the grounds that China would be fighting the world's greatest military power, but Mao Zedong insisted that a war with the imperialistic US was inevitable and that to allow an American presence on the Yalu River would pin down a large Chinese force while the US had freedom to attack from Taiwan or through Vietnam. The narrow shape of Korea and its mountainous terrain also would limit the mobility of MacArthur's much more mechanized but numerically inferior armies. Furthermore, Stalin was willing to provide the PLA with major war materiel and air force support, being happy to assist China to fight the war with the US that the USSR strongly desired to avoid. On 14 October, the first PLA 'volunteers' started crossing the Yalu River into Korea. This move occurred six days after UNA troops entered the DPRK and after American planes conducted bombing raids up to the Yalu, which included dropping some bombs on the Chinese side. Ironically, on the next day on Wake Island in mid-Pacific MacArthur assured Truman, at their first ever meeting, that there was no danger of Chinese intervention in the war. [10]

At first the PLA launched probing attacks on UNA and ROKA units as they fanned out into the northern part of the DPRK after capturing Pyonyang on 20 October. But MacArthur in Tokyo and his generals in Korea discounted the danger because the PLA units pulled back after initial sharp engagements. UNA forces continued to advance along a wide front, with one American regiment reaching the Yalu River on 21 November. MacArthur had exceeded his instructions in using American troops so close to the Chinese border. But the JCS was unwilling to challenge his military reputation, which had been heightened by his success at Inchon. Moreover, while Acheson later criticized MacArthur for chasing the 'mirage' of total victory, the American Administration had also succumbed to its allure. On 15 November Peng responded sadly to the failure of his warning attacks: 'All we seem to have accomplished is to convince the Americans that Chinese troops have not entered Korea in any strength'. Therefore there was 'no alternative but to teach the imperialists a lesson', he said as he bent over a relief model to explain

10. Ibid. 103–15. Spurr, *Enter the Dragon* 83–5, 111–19. Kaufman, *Korean* War 90–1.

to his generals how he intended to encircle the American Ninth Army group and destroy it.[11]

Therefore, when MacArthur launched an offensive on 24 November to achieve complete control of North Korea, his widely dispersed 150,000 strong armies were counter-attacked by the PLA, which now had 300,000 troops in North Korea plus 80,000 survivors of the KPA. Furthermore, Peng achieved comprehensive surprise because he moved his troops forward under cover of darkness, and the low level of PLA technology with little radio contact had protected it from American electronic surveillance. Within four days the American, British Commonwealth and ROK forces were in headlong retreat out of North Korea.

In response to this sudden Chinese success, MacArthur wanted to widen the war, using air power – possibly atomic bombs – and a naval blockade of China as well as unleashing the Chinese Nationalist troops on Taiwan to attack the Chinese mainland. But Truman's Administration had tried to contain the war from the beginning, by ordering the 7th fleet to patrol the Formosa Strait between Taiwan and China in order to prevent an attack across it from either side. Because Washington believed the USSR must be supporting China, the weight of government opinion was against any move that might bring the USSR into the war. Such a global contest would place America at a great disadvantage with a rearmament programme only in its early stages and a subsequent inability to stop any Soviet advance in Europe while fighting China.[12]

However, the US Government was equally determined to preserve the ROK. To allow a complete Chinese victory would threaten the whole American policy to contain communist expansion in the Western Pacific Basin and might induce a loss of Japanese confidence in the US. Nor did Truman wish to add the 'loss of Korea' to the lost China theme of Republican propaganda. So he rejected a plea from Prime Minister Attlee of Britain for agreement to a cease-fire in Korea in return for seating China in the UN and reaching a solution about Taiwan.[13]

11. Acheson, *Present at the Creation* 456. MacDonald, *Korea* 57–9. Spurr, *Enter the Dragon* 169.

12. Rosemary Foot, *The Wrong War: American Policy and the Dimensions of the Korean Conflict, 1950–1953* (Ithaca 1985) 101–30. For the US quarantine of Taiwan see Alexander, *The Strange Connection* ch. 10.

13. Rosemary Foot, 'Anglo-American Relations in the Korean Crisis: The British Effort to Avert an Expanded War, December 1950–January 1951', *Diplomatic History* 10, 1986, 43–57.

Fortunately for Washington, the Chinese onslaught, which applied overwhelming numbers against the flanks and rears of UNA forces, ran out of steam after taking Seoul and pushing the UNA south of the Han River. The major problem was the need for Chinese units to stop periodically and regroup to cope with the PLA's primitive communications system, and the difficulties of an ever extending and inefficient supply line. American air power and increasing American artillery strength also hampered the Chinese advance. Then on 25 January 1951 a new American field commander, the hard-driving General Matthew Ridgway, launched a UNA counter-offensive using the principle of maximum use of tanks, artillery fire and air strikes against selected Chinese targets – a 'meat grinder' strategy. Seoul was recaptured on 15 March.

On 11 April Truman stunned the American nation by sacking MacArthur, replacing him with Ridgway. It was the culmination of an emerging fundamental policy difference between the president and his Far East commander, who continued to advocate widening the war to the Chinese mainland. He had communicated that opinion on 20 March to the minority Republican leader of the House of Representatives, who obligingly read the letter to Congress on 5 April, which clinched the case for MacArthur's dismissal. He returned to America to a hero's welcome and made public speeches, using his gifted verbosity, to condemn the government's limited war policy in Korea as 'appeasement', which the Republicans gleefully reiterated.[14]

The war in Korea was heading for a stalemate. Initially the UNA forces faced the most massive Chinese attack of the war launched on 22 April. Though the UNA suffered over 7,000 casualties, huge Chinese losses and army disorganization allowed the UN command to launch a counter-offensive, which pushed the Chinese army north of the 38th parallel. This success influenced a revised American Far Eastern policy, NSC-48/5, which now sought a peace that would preserve the ROK. To force China to the peace conference table, this policy statement endorsed strong military pressure against Chinese forces in Korea – termed 'fighting whilst negotiating' – and encouragement of anti-communist elements in China, but no widening of the military conflict. Pressure from America's European allies contributed to this decision and also to peace negotiations, which the USSR supported.[15]

14. See Richard Lowitt (ed.), *The Truman-MacArthur Controversy* (Chicago 1967).
15. Foot, *The Wrong War* 131–6. Kaufman, *The Korean War* ch. 6.

Negotiations with the Chinese began on 10 July 1951 at Chinese-held Kaesong on the 38th parallel and soon shifted to the nearby village of Panmunjom. But the talks proved long and difficult, particularly over the issue of prisoners of war, who were mistreated by both sides. Nor were there any alternative groups in China for America to encourage to put pressure on the communist regime. On the other hand Peng resisted pressure from Kim Il Sung to launch a second offensive in 1951 to conquer South Korea. There was a continuing air war over North Korea between the American air force and Chinese planes, which were mostly Soviet supplied and piloted. At times there were heavy clashes between troops eyeing each other across intermittently declared cease-fire zones. This stalemate frustrated US military commanders and many members of the American public, who turned to a Second World War hero, General Dwight Eisenhower, who won for the Republican Party the 1952 presidential election. He had promised to end the war on 'honorable terms'. However, despite war weariness in China, which was spending 60 per cent of its revenue on the war, and in North Korea, which had lost over half a million of its people in the conflict, there was more fierce fighting with Chinese and North Korean attempts to seize military vantage points. Rhee also stalled the peace process by an unwillingness to accept the inevitability of a divided peninsula including the release of many of the North Korean prisoners of war to remove a US bargaining chip. However, on 27 July 1953 an armistice was finally signed ending the war. Chinese officials of the time said later that it was approved in recognition of the military stalemate. They denied ever receiving word of Eisenhower's threat to use nuclear weapons to achieve the armistice, despite the many US claims after the war that the nuclear threat was the decisive factor. The weight of the most recent American writing on the subject suggests that, even if a nuclear threat was delivered to China, it had little influence on the outcome of the war. [16]

16. Ibid. chs 7–9. Paik Sun Yup, *From Pusan to Panmunjom* (Washington 1992) 228–34. Cohen, 'Conversations with Chinese Friends', 289. Chang, *Friends and Enemies* 88–9. Edward C. Keefer, 'President Dwight D. Eisenhower and the End of the Korean War', *Diplomatic History* 10, 1986, 267–89. Mark A. Ryan, *Chinese Attitudes Toward Nuclear Weapons: China and the United States During the Korean War* (New York 1989) ch. 7. Foot, 'Making Known the Unknown War', 426–7. See also Rosemary Foot, *A Substitute for Victory: The Politics of Peacemaking at the Korean Armistice Talks* (Ithaca 1990).

REPERCUSSIONS OF THE KOREAN WAR

The influences of the Korean War along the East Asian rim of the Pacific Basin were profound. In Korea it solidified the peninsula into two nations viewing each other with continuing hostility. South Korea continued to be propped up by more than 50,000 American troops to ward off any future attack plus a $700 million aid package. Eisenhower was committed to disengage from Korea. He also introduced a 'new look' defence policy which called for big cuts in the army from its inflated Korean War strength, with a reliance on the armies of US allies backed by a mobile US reserve and massive nuclear superiority to deter Soviet or Chinese aggression. But Eisenhower's Administration was locked into promising continuing assistance to the ROK by Rhee's intransigence over the armistice negotiations and the need to persuade him to attend a conference in Geneva in April 1954 between the USSR, the US, Britain and France to establish peace in Korea. Truman also had turned a blind eye to Rhee's use of thuggery and intimidation in 1952 to force the South Korean Assembly to agree to constitutional amendments that consolidated Rhee's presidential power, which he then used to suppress or frighten away opponents in a presidential election in which he won five million of seven million votes. Truman's Administration knew that any move to replace Rhee would be interpreted by his conservative supporters in the Republican Party as communist-inspired. Furthermore, Washington saw no viable alternative to Rhee as leader of South Korea.[17]

America's relations with China also were influenced greatly by the Korean War. From the outset of the war the US imposed a trade embargo on China. It has been argued that the Eisenhower Administration was trapped into maintaining implacable hostility to Red China because of the public outrage at the sudden Chinese attack on American forces in North Korea and the humiliation of their subsequent retreat. This hostility, along with Senator Joe McCarthy's witch-hunt for alleged communists in the State Department, resulted in the dismissal of China experts from the department. The result

17. Henry W. Brands, Jr, 'The Dwight D. Eisenhower Administration, Syngman Rhee, and the "Other" Geneva Conference of 1954', *Pacific Historical Review* LVI, 1987, 59–85. Edward C. Keefer, 'The Truman Administration and the South Korean Political Crisis of 1952: Democracy's Failure?', ibid. LX, 1991, 145–68. Robert A. Devine, *Eisenhower and the Cold War* (New York 1981) 33–9.

was an alleged failure to spot the signs of Sino-Soviet conflict in the subsequent decade. However, recent studies, using newly declassified US documents, have demonstrated that the administration was aware of Chinese-Soviet divisions. They suggest that a policy of maximum pressure was placed on China to force Beijing to seek assistance from the USSR which might impose strains on the relationship, a policy that was by no means completely unsuccessful.[18]

Sino-Soviet relations had improved during the Korean War. China received valuable air force support and other military assistance from the USSR, though not as much as she wished. During the early 1950s there was significant Soviet technical assistance in the form of machinery, industrial technology and education for Chinese students in the USSR.[19]

CHINA, THE US AND TAIWAN

Continued hostility between China and the US placed strains on the Soviet-Chinese relationship. The conflict stemmed in particular from America's support for Chiang Kai-shek's Nationalist Chinese regime on Taiwan, which had received new strategic status during the Korean War as a potential threat to China and as an offshore defence base. From 1951 to 1957, $683 million in economic assistance and $1.47 billion in military aid flowed from the US to Taiwan.[20]

On that mountainous island of 36,000 square kilometres, which had been a Japanese colony from 1895 to 1945, the Nationalists had established the structure of their former government of China as an outward sign of the resolve to return to the mainland when the 'Chinese bandits', as they called the CCP, were overthrown. Consequently Taiwan's national assembly was controlled by the Kuomintang, which was dominated by mainlanders, with Chiang Kai-shek as a virtual president for life. The 80 per cent of the population who were Taiwanese had no say in this political arrangement,

18. David Allan Mayers, *Cracking the Monolith: U.S. Policy Against the Sino-Soviet Alliance, 1949–1955* (Baton Rouge 1986) chs 4–5. Chang, *Friends and Enemies* chs 3–6.

19. Ibid. 79–80, 203–4. R.K.I. Quested, *Sino-Russian Relations: A Short History* (Sydney 1984) 115–17.

20. Chang, *Friends and Enemies* 160–2.

though they were given democratic control over local government. The Taiwanese were ethnically Chinese, but their long separation from the mainland had given them a distinctive outlook, and relations with the 'mainlanders' had been soured by initial postwar Nationalist rule. Taiwanese who had enjoyed significant economic progress under repressive Japanese rule found themselves after 1945 under equally oppressive but more corrupt masters who plundered the island's resources for their own wealth and for the needs of the Nationalist mainland regime. A consequent Taiwanese riot in February 1947, which developed into an incipient rebellion, was brutally crushed by Nationalist troops, leading to the deaths of as many as 10,000 Taiwanese, especially community leaders. The now leaderless and traumatized Taiwanese retreated into the quiescent and apolitical mode with which they had reacted to the brutal Japanese conquest of their island.[21]

The flashpoint between America and China was the Nationalist retention of three small island groups close to the Chinese mainland: Jinmen (Quemoy) guarding the entrance to the Chinese port of Xiamen (Amoy); Mazu (Matsu) lying on the approach to the port of Fuzhou (Foochow); and the strategically less valuable Dachen Islands to the North. The Nationalists regarded these islands as potential launching pads for their much vaunted determination to return to the mainland. China expressed a firm resolve to capture them, starting on 3 September 1954 with a heavy bombardment of Jinmen, with continuing artillery strikes and air raids on the islands and massing of Chinese troops opposite them. The Nationalists responded in kind, stationing a large proportion of their forces on the islands.

The US Government became involved in the Nationalist defence of China's offshore islands because of a conviction in Washington that their loss would be a devastating blow to the shaky prestige of Chiang Kai-shek's regime. Eisenhower's Administration did place successful pressure on Chiang to withdraw in January 1955 from the Dachens, which were beyond war-plane range from Taiwan. But in the process a secret promise was given to him that America would oppose a Chinese invasion of the Jinmen and Mazu Islands. On 28 January 1955 the American Congress also gave the Administration a free hand to use force to protect Taiwan and 'related positions and territories'. Eisenhower and his Secretary of State, John Foster Dulles, who had

---

21. Thomas B. Gold, *State and Society in the Taiwan Miracle* (New York 1986) 44–64. James C. Hsiung et al. (eds), *Contemporary Republic of China: The Taiwan Experience 1950–1980* (New York 1981) 341–7.

served the Truman Administration as a special diplomatic envoy to Japan, planned in fact to use atomic weapons against China if the islands were attacked. Blunt warnings of this prospect were delivered to Beijing. There was dissent within the NSC about risking such a war with China, but Eisenhower and Dulles presumed correctly that the USSR would not intervene to support Beijing. They were convinced by the new Krushchev regime's efforts to remove sources of dissension between America and the USSR, such as concluding an agreement for a Soviet withdrawal from Austria. Indeed, the most plausible reason why China stepped back from the brink by refraining from launching any invasion of the islands was absence of Soviet support, which is confirmed by China's ambassador to Moscow, Liu. The American position was more than inspired brinkmanship, as biographers of Eisenhower have suggested. It was a firm American game-play that preserved peace in the Western Pacific Basin only because China backed off.[22]

Beijing made another threat against Jinmen in 1958 at a time when the US was preoccupied with Anglo-American intervention in the Middle East. Gromyko, now the Soviet Foreign Secretary who went to Beijing to discuss this and other issues, wrote that he was 'flabbergasted' when Mao Zedong 'showed a willingness to accept the possibility of an American nuclear attack on China'. Gromyko warned him that there 'definitely' would be no 'positive response' from the USSR. However, a longer term minus for the US was China's realization of the need to develop her own nuclear weapons.[23]

COLONIAL REMNANTS IN CHINA: MACAU AND HONG KONG

Despite the complete mainland victory of the communist forces in China in 1949 and the tensions aroused between China and

22. Robert Divine, *Eisenhower and the Cold War* (New York 1981) 61–70; Stephen E. Ambrose, *Eisenhower: The President* (New York 1984) 245. Chang, *Friends and Enemies* ch. 4. Garver, 'New Light on Sino-Soviet Relations', 305–6. See also Alexander, *The Strange Connection* 147–63.
23. Gromyko, *Memories* 251. See also John W. Lewis and Xue Lital, *China Builds the Bomb* (Stanford 1988).

Western countries, no moves were made by Beijing to take over the vestiges of European empires in China: Portuguese Macau and British Hong Kong. There was no military reason for this Chinese restraint. Though Britain reinforced its Hong Kong garrison in 1948, victorious Chinese troops could easily have stormed across the colony's frontier in 1949. Instead the PLA stopped short of the frontier and only communist guerillas occupied the Chinese border posts. The CCP central committee had decided to solve diplomatically remaining colonial problems from the past, announcing that it would honour all China's international treaties. This policy also covered Macau, an even less defensible relic from the long distant days of Portuguese economic imperialism in East Asia.

There had been discussions between Britain and the Chinese Nationalist Government about the future of the British island and the New Territories on the mainland, which had been leased by Britain in 1898 for ninety-nine years. This British enclave in China represented the days of China's diplomatic weakness. However, though the prewar Nationalist Government had voiced the need to overturn 'unequal treaties', it was unwilling to provoke conflict with Britain. China at that stage was seeking international respectability and soon was facing the major problem of Japanese expansionism. After the end of the Japanese occupation of Hong Kong in 1945 there was no significant Chinese opposition to the return of British colonial authorities. Ironically, Hong Kong became an important conduit for arms supplies and a safe haven for the CCP during the Chinese Civil War, a continuation of traditional British laissez-faire policies towards the colony's Chinese residents. Nevertheless, the CCP made it clear that it too regarded both Hong Kong and Macau as remnants of the unequal treaties imposed on China by outside imperialist powers, which would require correction in the future.[24]

After China entered the Korean War, tension developed between Hong Kong and its huge neighbour. A burgeoning commerce between them was stifled by the UN embargo on trade on goods that could assist China's war effort. Hong Kong's exports to China fell from HK$1.6. billion in 1951 to HK$520 million in 1952. This was a major economic burden for Hong Kong's population, which had been swollen by refugees from Communist China, rising from 600,000 in 1945 to nearly 2.2 million by 1952 in a land area of only

24. Kevin P. Lane, *Sovereignty and the Status Quo: The Historical Roots of China's Hong Kong Policy* (Boulder 1990) 41–70.

1,074 square kilometres, which had no raw materials and needed to import most of its food and even water. Resultant poverty was evidenced by people living on rooftops. When a fire in December 1951 destroyed over a thousand squatter shacks, CCP newspapers accused the British Administration of deliberately starting the conflagration in order to allow the extension of Hong Kong's airport. A citizens' group in Guangzhou (Canton) announced that a 'comfort mission' would deliver money raised for homeless victims in Hong Kong. Despite the British Administration's announcement that the mission would be denied entry, some 5,000 Hong Kong people flocked to the colony's railway station and rioted when informed that the mission was not arriving, leading to the death of a rioter. The British Administration reacted by banning a Hong Kong communist newspaper and prosecuting editors for seditious circulation of Chinese lies. Beijing fulminated against 'savage and despotic' British rule in Hong Kong and vowed the territory's liberation 'one day'. However, such propaganda was not converted into action, and after the Korean War there were renewed flows of Chinese goods and people across the Hong Kong border.[25]

There was further tension over a British attempt to impose quotas on Chinese immigrants, which provoked a savage riot in 1956 that left 59 people dead and aroused Chinese condemnation of British collusion with 'cold blooded murderers' from Taiwan. A consequent meeting between Zhou and Hong Kong's Governor in Beijing resulted in a continued Chinese commitment not to challenge British rule and a British agreement not to use the territory as a military base or source of subversion against China and to protect Chinese officials there.[26]

During the 1950s a legacy of the Korean War trade embargo with China was an industrial take-off in Hong Kong led by the textile industry. This was assisted by the influx into the colony after the communist victory in China of many Shanghai mill owners bringing with them machinery and skilled workers. Facilitating the industrial growth was the creation of new markets in Asia for cotton goods created by wealth generated by the Korean War, plus markets in Britain and the US. By 1959, 35 per cent of the colony's domestic exports were products of its textile industry, the beginnings of

25. Ibid. 70–1. Jon Woronoff, *Asia's 'Miracle' Economies* (London 1986) 143. Theodore Geiger and Frances M. Geiger, *The Development of Hong Kong and Singapore* (London 1975) 68.
26. Lane, *Sovereignty and the Status Quo* 71–4.

major economic growth in this small Pacific rim state on the edge of China.[27]

JAPAN AND THE KOREAN WAR

The Korean War proved a salvation for the Japanese economy, which had been struggling under the effects of domestic inflation and an American imposed austerity plan to enhance Japanese exports. MacArthur and the Japanese Prime Minister, Yoshida Shigeru, a prewar diplomat who escaped the postwar purge, were able to reactivate Japanese production of military materiel to supply American forces in Korea, justified on the grounds of providing for an 'emergency'. Japan's propinquity to the war zone and still underutilized industrial capacity not only assisted America's suddenly overstrained armaments production but also provided a decisive boost to the Japanese economy. Between 1950 and 1954 Japan supplied close to $3 billion worth of war-related supplies, which economic historians acknowledge was the decisive ingredient in the postwar re-creation of Japan's industrial might. Japanese technicians also were used in Korea to man harbour facilities, power plants and essential industries. Some forty-six Japanese ships manned by members of the former Japanese Imperial Navy served in Korean waters. About 2,600 Japanese seamen and dockers supported the Inchon landing.[28]

The Korean War also was the catalyst for the signing of peace treaties with Japan which ended the American occupation. The threat to East Asian security presented by the outbreak of the war and the consequent enhanced strategic importance of Japan brought the need for a peace treaty to the fore. The US Administration speedily resolved to send Republican Senator Dulles to negotiate with the nations formally involved in the occupation of Japan for a peace treaty, which he discussed with a wide range of groups in Japan, negotiating in particular with Yoshida. The result was a

---

27. Geiger and Geiger, *Development of Hong Kong* 68–74.
28. William S. Borden, *The Pacific Alliance: United States Foreign Economic Policy and Japanese Trade Recovery, 1947–1955* (Madison 1984) 145–7. Rienhard Drifte, 'Japan's Involvement in the Korean War' in Cotton and Neary, *Korean War in History* 120–34.

conference which began on 5 September 1951 in San Francisco and which was attended by delegates from fifty-two nations, including Japan. Three days later these nations with the exception of three from the communist block – the USSR, Poland and Czechoslovakia – signed the Peace Treaty that formally ended the military occupation of Japan. A second, important part of the process was concluded on that afternoon with the signing of a Japan-US mutual security treaty, which established an alliance of equal partners which was to have a major influence on future Pacific Basin affairs. Japan regarded the treaty as a guarantee of independence under US military protection. The peace treaty process was also a catalyst for America's signing of a mutual defence pact with Australia and New Zealand: the Australia, New Zealand, United States Security Treaty (ANZUS). Those two Pacific nations were particularly fearful of prospects of rearmament in Japan. The Korean War crisis had inspired the US to recruit wider Pacific allies, such as Australia and New Zealand, which had made military contributions to the fighting of that war.[29]

CONTINUING CONFLICT IN VIETNAM

In early 1950, prior to the outbreak of the Korean War, the US became concerned about advancing communism in the Southeast Asia portion of the Pacific Basin. This region was now regarded in Washington as an area for Japanese trade expansion, which would stimulate Japan's economic growth. Britain also had become worried about the growing power of the Vietminh insurgents in Vietnam, as a potential threat to the containment of the communist insurgency in Malaya. So London expressed this concern strongly to Washington, which had been promoting American purchases of Malayan tin and rubber in order to assist dollar-starved Britain. Vietnam was seen as a key to the success of American efforts to promote Japanese trade to Burma, where there was a major communist insurgency,

29. Michael M. Yoshitsu, *Japan and the San Francisco Peace Settlement* (New York 1983) chs 3–5. Finn, *Winners in Peace*, ch. 19. John Welfield, *The Postwar International Order and the Origins of the Japanese-American Security Treaty* (Canberra 1982). David McLean, 'Anzus Origins: A Reassessment', *Australian Historical Studies* 24, 1990, 64–82. For Australia and the Korean War see Robert O'Neill, *Australia in the Korean War 1950–1953* 2 vols (Canberra 1981).

and to Thailand, which was already being viewed as a domino that might fall to communism with communist victories in Indochina. Furthermore, France's efforts to defeat the Vietminh, which cost 167 million francs in 1949, were placing severe burdens on the economy of that key Western European nation. Paying attention to combatting communism in Vietnam also would help deflect the growing Republican attack on alleged communist sympathizers within the State Department. This was especially the case after the DRV had declared publicly in January 1950 its allegiance with the USSR and Communist China, both of which recognized it that month as the only legitimate government in Vietnam.[30]

Therefore, in February 1950, the US recognized the Bao Dai Government in Vietnam. With news of Chinese arms flowing to the Vietminh and the successful Communist Chinese invasion in April 1950 of Nationalist-held Hainandao Island, Truman authorized on 1 May $10 million in aid for the French war effort against the Vietminh. On 5 June Congress approved the granting of $23.5 million to French Vietnam, the largest amount in an economic aid package for Southeast Asian countries. Despite initial scepticism about Bao Dai, Truman's Administration had accepted, without further analysis, assurances that France was working towards the creation of an independent country under that ruler, whose authority depended on French military power.[31]

After the communist victory in China, France was starting to lose the war in Vietnam's northern province of Tonkin. Before 1950 the French had controlled towns and lines of communication, and there was an ebb and flow struggle with elusive Vietminh guerillas in the countryside. But in 1950, with Chinese assistance, the Vietminh were pressing against French outposts in northern Tonkin, causing a strategic need for withdrawal of the French troops there, which in turn opened the northern border over which Vietminh soldiers were moving to and from Chinese camps. There they were being trained and armed with modern weapons to add to those captured from the French. Also the government in Paris was unable to increase the number of French soldiers in Vietnam, who were never much more than 100,000 throughout the war, because of the demands on a volunteer army in other colonial territories and for European

30. Rotter, *The Path to Vietnam* chs 6–8.
31. Ibid. 166–79. Gary R. Hess, *The United States' Emergence as a Southeast Power, 1940–1950* (New York 1957) 355–6. Short, *Origins of the Vietnam War* 78–84.

defence. It was illegal to send French soldiers doing compulsory military service overseas.[32]

American aid for the French military effort in Vietnam increased sharply after the outbreak of the Korean War to $450 million in the fiscal year 1951. The result was a strengthening of French control in southern Vietnam, where Vietminh guerillas were distanced from Chinese aid and were disadvantaged by the way it concentrated Vietminh energies in Tonkin. In January 1951 Giap decided, against Chinese advice, to deliver a coup de grâce in the Red River Delta. He failed because most of his troops were not yet ready for battle against French forces operating on interior lines with well prepared defences.[33]

However, France was unable to suppress the rebellion in the Vietnamese countryside, despite escalating American aid, which by 1953 was paying for over 60 per cent of French military expenditure in Vietnam. Efforts, under American pressure, to increase the Vietnamese proportion of the French army were limited by a French reluctance to rely on Vietnamese officers. The American Administration urged a more aggressive approach to the war, to which Paris reluctantly agreed. But a new French commander, General Henri Navarre, could do little with the need for so many of his troops to protect French-held positions from guerilla attacks. He did look, however, for a showdown with the Vietminh by placing a strong garrison in the Dien Bien Phu valley in Western Tonkin, which was also designed to stop Vietminh incursions across the nearby border into Laos.[34]

The battle of Dien Bien Phu, which began on 13 March 1954, reflected Navarre's gross underestimation of Vietminh capabilities. The 12,000 French troops on the valley floor left control of the surrounding hills to enemy forces, in order to entice them to attack a well-defended position. The sixteen by eight kilometre width of the valley was regarded as adequate protection because of allegedly superior French firepower. However, since the end of the Korean War the Vietminh army had received an increased flow of arms from China. The French artillery in the battle was outnumbered by nearly four times as many Vietminh guns, which were of equal or better

32. Dalloz, *The War in Indo-China* 104–27. Lockhart, *Nation in Arms* 225–9.

33. Ibid. 230–42. Dalloz, *The War in Indo-China*, 132–3. James S. Olson and Randy Roberts, *Where the Domino Fell: America and Vietnam 1945 to 1990* (New York 1991) 31.

34. George McT. Kahin, *Intervention: How America became Involved in Vietnam* (New York 1986) 42. George C. Herring, *America's Longest War: the United States and Vietnam 1950–1975* (Philadelphia 1986) 25–8. Dalloz, *War in Indo-China* 158–62.

capability and were sited in much less exposed firing positions. With this major advantage, the 47,000 Vietminh attackers were able to seize two forward French outposts that commanded the valley's one airport, making inaccurate parachute drops the only source of French supply. Then, with the assistance of trenches creeping towards the remaining French lines and human wave assaults, the defenders were pounded into submission on 7 May 1954.[35]

Dien Bien Phu was not as decisive a battle as has been claimed. It had not dislodged the French from any other major position they held in Vietnam, while the Vietminh had expended much energy in winning the battle. Also, before it began, the French Government was seeking a negotiated end to the war. A victory at Dien Bien Phu would have allowed the government to negotiate from a position of military strength.[36]

One other significance of the battle was pressure applied by Paris on Washington to intervene with air strikes against the attacking Vietminh. Such American intervention, including possible use of nuclear weapons, was supported by Admiral Arthur Radford, the chief of the JCS. It is generally suggested by historians that Dulles was convinced of the need to support this plan, known as 'Operation Vulture', and that he was restrained by his inability to persuade Britain and other allies, a condition imposed by Eisenhower for any American military intervention. Recently, it has been argued that Dulles himself hid behind the attempt to internationalize any intervention knowing that such 'united action' could not be achieved. Whether Dulles or Eisenhower determined the policy, Washington was not willing to embark on unilateral intervention, especially since France was unwilling to concede to the US military control of consequent operations in Vietnam, which could well involve American soldiers. Furthermore, France might withdraw from the war leaving the US to carry the burden of combatting the Vietminh and possibly China as well. However, the NSC was authorized to prepare a contingency plan for American military intervention if China entered the war.[37]

35. For an account of the battle from the Vietminh side see Lockart, *Nation in Arms* 252–63.

36. Dalloz, *War in Indo-China* 168–75.

37. Frederick W. Marks III, 'The Real Hawk at Dienbienphu: Dulles or Eisenhower?', *Diplomatic History* LVIX, 1990, 297–321. Melanie Billings-Yun, *Decision Against War: Eisenhower and Dien Bien Phu, 1964* (New York 1988) chs 4–6. George C. Herring and Richard Immerman, 'Eisenhower, Dulles and Dien Bien Phu: "The Day We Didn't Go to War" Revisited', *Journal of American History* 71, 1984, 343–63. Short, *Origins of the Vietnam War* 128–48.

In fact the war between France and the Vietminh was resolved by a peace conference in Geneva, beginning one day after the fall of Dien Bien Phu, and also attended by Britain, the US, the USSR and China. The two communist powers placed pressure on Ho Chi Minh to agree to a division of Vietnam to the bitter disappointment of many of Ho's colleagues. The USSR and China believed, according to Kruschev's memoirs, that the Vietminh would face great difficulty in retaining their recent military gains. Moscow was keen to portray a peaceful international image and to limit Chinese influence in Vietnam. China was concerned about prospects of American military intervention and had no wish, so soon after the exhausting Korean War, to be embroiled in another war. The DRV also complained later, and one Chinese diplomat of the time has admitted, that Beijing wanted to maintain a divided Vietnam and pressured Hanoi to drop the aim of achieving a communist Indochina confederation by allowing the French-created royal governments of Cambodia and Laos to be represented at the conference. After much negotiation, an agreement was signed on 20 July to divide Vietnam at the 17th parallel north latitude. Assisting this agreement was mediation by Britain's Foreign Secretary Anthony Eden, and the appointment of a new French premier on 17 June, Pierre Mendès-France, who made a public commitment to achieve peace in Indochina within one month. The division of Vietnam was to be only temporary. The Geneva Agreements provided for free elections for a national government to be held in both sections of Vietnam within two years and to be supervised by representatives from a western, a non-aligned and a communist country: Canada, India and Poland. A cease-fire also was established in Cambodia and Laos, which became fully independent.[38]

The US Administration's participation in the Geneva Conference was a negative one that laid the groundwork for the commitment of the US to a future war in Vietnam. Eisenhower and Dulles were distrustful of negotiations with communists. Dulles revealed his uncompromising attitude during his short stay in Geneva by publicly snubbing Zhou Enlai. Washington believed that only a military solution through 'united action' by western powers could stop an eventual communist takeover of the whole of Vietnam and

---

38. Nikita Krushchev, *Krushchev Remembers* (London 1971) 482. Pike, *Vietnam and the Soviet Union* 39–42. Ton That Thien, *The Foreign Politics of the Communist Party of Vietnam: A Study in Communist Tactics* (New York 1989) 123–5. William J. Duiker, *China and Vietnam: The Roots of Conflict* (Berkeley 1986) 30–2.

probably the rest of Indochina. The final agreements were better than expected, but Washington refused to sign them, pledging only not to 'disturb' their provisions and reserving the right to take necessary future action.[39]

Dulles's preferred option was to establish a collective security arrangement for protecting Southeast Asia from further communist advancement. The result was the formation in Manila in September 1954 of the South East Asia Treaty Organization (SEATO). The treaty's signatories – the US, France, Britain, Australia, New Zealand, Thailand, Pakistan, and the Philippines – agreed to consult and cooperate with each other against communist subversion or open attack and to provide a defensive umbrella over the states of Indochina. The Philippines saw the treaty as a means of reinforcing US commitment to its own defence. Thailand, which in the past had followed a 'bending in the wind' policy of conciliating more powerful nations in order to preserve its own independence, was prepared to join in an alliance with the US because of a fear of the growing power of the Vietminh, though initially giving the DRV diplomatic and limited financial support. The Korean War had strengthened this policy change, demonstrated by Thailand's offer of 4,000 troops to assist the beleaguered UN army and a contribution of 40,000 tons of rice for South Korean relief. This commitment expressed Prime Minister Field Marshall Phibunsongkhrum's conservative concern about communist expansion, especially the threat from his neighbour, Communist China. The US had rewarded Thailand with economic and military aid, the latter being worth $56 million by 1953. Therefore Thailand was keen to join SEATO, though there was disappointment in Bangkok that the treaty was not a more cast-iron US guarantee of Thailand's security. The US Senate passed the SEATO treaty by a very big majority, a sign of the American political consensus about the Cold War.[40]

39. Richard H. Immerman, 'The United States and the Geneva Conference of 1954: A New Look', *Diplomatic History* 14 (1990) 43–66. Kahin, *Intervention* ch. 2. Gary Hess, 'Redefining the American Position in Southeast Asia: the United States and the Geneva and Manila Conferences' in Lawrence S. Kaplan, Denise Artaud and Mark R. Rubin, *Dien Bien Phu and the Crisis of Franco-American Relations, 1954–1955* (Wilmington 1990) 123–48.

40. George C. Herring, '"A Good Stout Effort": John Foster Dulles and the Indochina Crisis, 1954–1955' in Richard H. Immerman (ed.), *John Foster Dulles and the Diplomacy of the Cold War* (Princeton 1990) 219–28. Leszek Buszynski, *S.E.A.T.O.: The Failure of an Alliance Strategy* (Singapore 1983) ch. 2. R. Sean Randolph, *The United States and Thailand: Alliance Dynamics, 1950–1985* (Berkeley 1986) 6–32.

The US also decided to support the regime of a new ruler in the southern Republic of Vietnam (RVN), Ngo Dinh Diem. This move was consistent with the post-Korean War policy of supporting anti-communist regimes in other Pacific Basin countries such as South Korea and Taiwan, whatever their political qualities. However, by expressing a willingness to take France's place in South Vietnam, the Eisenhower Administration locked itself into backing a government which became dependent upon its support. Diem was a French-educated Roman Catholic in a predominantly Buddhist country, who had been a civil servant from the age of twenty in 1921 and in 1933 Bao Dai's secretary of the interior. He soon resigned from that post because of French interference. But his nationalist credentials were compromised by his collaboration in 1945 with Japanese authorities, and he spent most of his subsequent time in Europe and the US, though displaying there anti-French nationalist sentiments. Assisted by influential US friends, especially the Roman Catholic Democratic Party senators Mike Mansfield and John F. Kennedy, he became Bao Dai's premier in June 1954. Not consulted in the making of the Geneva Agreements, Diem loudly denounced them as signing away more than half his country, and he turned to the US for support. Convinced that Diem represented a hope of establishing an anti-communist bulwark in South Vietnam, the US willingly supplied financial assistance, particularly to resettle some 900,000, mostly Catholic, refugees from the North, plus military aid for the South Vietnamese army. This financial assistance was worth $322.4 million in the fiscal year 1955–56.[41]

Diem was little better than Bao Dai as a focus for a viable anti-communist regime in Vietnam. His Roman Catholic religion and reliance upon the urban elite were not good qualifications for winning the support of Buddhist peasants. His wartime collaboration and subsequent absence overseas weakened his nationalist image in comparison with Ho Chi Minh, the leader of the long independence struggle against the French. The US recognized that Diem would have little hope of winning the projected 1956 election against Ho.

So Diem was allowed to subvert the Geneva Agreements by demanding free elections and free speech in each zone before reunification elections were held, and then to renege on those terms

41. Gardiner, *Approaching Vietnam* 292–3. Short, *Origins of the Vietnam War* 190–1. Carl A. Thayer, *War by Other Means: National Liberation and Revolution in Viet-Nam 1954–60* (Sydney 1988) 123. Ronald H. Spector, *Advice and Support: The Early Years of the U.S. Army in Vietnam 1941–1960* (New York 1985) chs 12–15.

in the RVN. In 1955, voters were given a referendum choice between himself and Bao Dai as chief of state, which was fraudulently organized to give Diem 98 per cent of the vote. Elections for a RVN national assembly in 1956 were heavily influenced by the government's firm control of the press and suppression of opponents, which ensured that only three of the assembly's 123 members constituted a genuine opposition. Diem's dictatorial pretensions already had provoked a severe internal crisis in 1955 when he alienated three powerful politico-religious sects: the Cao Dai, a syncretic religion based on elements of Catholic Church order; the millenarian Buddhist Hoa Hao; and the mafia-style Binh Xuyen. But with a fund of $12 million secretly supplied by the CIA, Diem bought off key Cao Dai and Hoa Hao leaders, integrating some of their troops into his army, which then crushed a Binh Xuyen revolt. American advisers in Saigon at the time urged Washington to abandon Diem, but the surprise victory of the RVN army (ARVN) in the civil strife, convinced Dulles that he should continue to support the nation, which was kept alive with economic and military aid. From 1955–56 to 1959–60 this assistance was worth $1.584 billion and fostered dependency rather than internal economic development.[42]

Diem paid only lip service to democratic values. There was a widespread campaign of violence and oppression against the regime's political opponents administered by Diem's ruthless brother, Nhu. The French-trained chief of the ARVN's General Staff, Tran Van Don, has commented that Diem and Nhu 'resorted to arbitrary arrests, confinement in concentration camps for undetermined periods of time . . . and assassinations of people suspected of Communist leanings. Their use of Gestapo-like police raids and torture were known and decried everywhere'. Furthermore, their 'repression . . . spread to people who simply opposed their regime such as heads or spokesmen of other political parties and against individuals who were resisting extortion by some government officials'. A later American Defense Department analysis concluded that the Diem Government's 'Communist Denunciation Campaign thoroughly terrified the Vietnamese peasants and detracted significantly from the regime's popularity'.[43]

42. Herring, *America's Longest War* ch. 2. Thayer, *War by Other Means* 123. William S. Turley, *The Second Indochina War: A Short Political and Military History, 1954–1975* (Boulder 1986) 13–15.

43. Tran Van Don, *Our Endless War: Inside Vietnam* (San Rafael 1978) 66. *The Pentagon Papers: The Defense Department History of United States Decisionmaking on Vietnam*, Senator Gravel Edition (Boston 1971) (*PP*) vol. I, 255.

Under American pressure, Diem's government did legislate to redistribute land, much of it abandoned during the first Vietnam War, to landless peasants, who formed 80 per cent of the population of the Mekong Delta. But former landlords now living in urban areas were given the right to impose rents on peasants who occupied the vacated land, which often exceeded the government's 25 per cent maximum rate. There was also corruption and inefficiency in the administration of the land reform, including preference for Catholic refugees from the North. Consequently, only 10 per cent of the landless South Vietnamese became property owners. Diem also took away the traditional right of villagers to elect their own village chiefs, fearing that Vietminh people would win, and appointed instead mostly Northern Catholics.[44]

Diem's regime therefore created fertile ground for a communist-led resistance movement in the RVN. Initially the Vietnamese Communist Party (VCP), which had led the struggle against French rule, accepted the call from Geneva for a cease-fire. The party looked forward confidently to an imminent DRV takeover of the whole country in national elections and therefore stood aloof from the civil strife in the RVN in 1955. However, Diem's survival and the campaign of violent repression, which his government launched against the VCP, drove the party underground. As many as 90 per cent of the party's cells had been destroyed by mid-1956. The party concentrated on rebuilding its rural strength by exploiting the peasant grievances against the inequities of land reform and the imposition of authoritarian and often corrupt village officials. The VCP still faced much ARVN violence which provoked some violent responses by its members. But the party renounced at this stage an armed uprising, influenced by its North Vietnamese members. In the DRV the VCP was concentrating upon rebuilding the war-ravaged countryside, which included coping with a severe threat of famine, for which deliveries of rice from the USSR and China were valuable. The VCP in the North also was facing problems involved in land reform which, it later admitted, involved excessive government repression.[45]

In 1959, however, the VCP decided to launch an armed struggle to overthrow Diem's regime and reunite Vietnam. The party's 15th plenum, meeting in Hanoi in January 1959, resolved to establish a National Front for the Liberation of South Vietnam (NLF) to be controlled by the party's South Vietnamese central committee and

---

44. Ibid. 67–9. Thayer, *War by Other Means* ch. 6. Kahin, *Intervention* ch. 4.
45. Thayer, *War by Other Means* chs 2–7.

to be supported by a 'liberation army'. The main *casus belli* was a riot on 1 December 1958 in a RVN detention centre, which had caused inexperienced prison wardens to open fire, killing more than a dozen protesters, though the number of deaths were inflated to more than 1,000 in DRV propaganda. There were deeper influences on the decision. By 1959 North Vietnam had achieved some economic stability with a record harvest in the previous year, and North Vietnam had established good relations not only with the USSR and China but also with Laos and Cambodia and non-aligned Burma and India. The USSR, China and communist Eastern European countries were providing aid worth over US$570 million from 1955 to 1960, though this was less than half the level of US aid to the RVN. The DRV also had launched a propaganda campaign blaming the Government of South Vietnam (GVN) for reneging on the reunification elections promised in the Geneva Agreements and preserving an arbitrary division of the Vietnamese nation; and the US was vilified for supporting Diem.[46]

North Vietnam had confidence therefore in an uprising in the South. Many party members there had long been calling for a general rebellion, and some, particularly in the highlands of the South and in the Mekong Delta, had been maintaining· armed struggle. So the plenum decision was received enthusiastically by the Southern VCP. To avoid US military retaliation against the DRV, it was decided to rely mainly on South Vietnamese resources, including Southerners returning from the North. The struggle was to be directed by the Southern NLF, which was launched by the VCP in December 1960, though it included non-communist nationalists. Insurgent violence initially targeted GVN officials in rural areas – 1,400 were assassinated or kidnapped by the end of 1960. This violence was designed to destroy GVN influence in rural areas, where armed guerilla units, which in February 1961 were called the People's Liberation Armed Force (PLAF), were being organized. These insurgents, who were contemptuously called Viet Cong by their opponents, already numbered 16,000 by the end of 1960, according to US intelligence.[47]

By August 1960 there was serious concern in Washington about 'the stability and effectiveness of President Diem's government', as expressed in a State Department Special National Intelligence

---

46. Ibid. ch. 8.
47. Ibid. ch. 9. Post, *Revolution, Socialism and Nationalism* vol. 2, chs 5, 9–10. Kahin, *Intervention* 100. Turley, *Second Indochina War* xv, 30.

Estimate. It noted that in South Vietnam there was not only increasing PLAF activity; there was also criticism among intellectuals 'and to a lesser extent in labor and business groups' about the 'pervasive influence' of the GVN's Can Lao party controlled by Ngo Dinh Nhu, which was silencing dissidents with political arrests, beatings, torture and murders, and of 'Diem's virtual one-man rule and the growing evidence of corruption in high places'. The report further acknowledged that the GVN lacked 'positive support among the people in the countryside'. This was principally because of the 'ineptitude and arrogance of many local and provincial officials, . . . the harshness with which many peasants have been forced to contribute their labor to GVN programs, and the unsettling economic and social effects' of a government resettlement programme to enhance GVN authority. However, Diem regarded his critics as 'dupes of the Communists', and was concentrating on a military solution to the problems. Yet the seven ARVN divisions, which were assisted by a 675 strong American Military Assistance and Advisory Group (MAAG), had been trained and deployed mostly to resist 'an overt attack from North Vietnam'. In General Tran's view the Americans 'put us in the same mold as Koreans' and trained the ARVN to fight another Korean War.[48]

However, the State Department report concluded that 'these adverse trends are not irreversible', if Diem could take measures to protect and win the support of peasants and to 'reduce the corruption and excesses of his regime'. There was a strong but blind faith within the Eisenhower Administration that with more time and continued American support Diem's regime could survive as a bulwark against the tide of advancing communism.[49]

SUPPRESSION OF REBELLION IN THE PHILIPPINES

The Truman and Eisenhower Administrations in the 1950s had more success in their support for the suppression of the communist-led

---

48. 'Short-Term Trends in South Vietnam', 23 Aug. 1960, *Foreign Relations of the United States (FRUS), 1958–1960* vol. 1: Vietnam (Washington 1986) 536–41. Tran, *Our Endless War* 149.

49. David L. Anderson, *Trapped by Success: The Eisenhower Administration and Vietnam, 1953–1961* (New York 1992) 196–7.

insurrection in the Philippines. In 1950 the Huk insurgents in Central Luzon had grown in number to at least 12,000 chiefly because of the brutality of the government's attempts to defeat them. The alliance since 1948 between the communist PKP and the peasant-based Huks had improved the insurgency's organizational base. The Huks demonstrated their strength with two waves of daring raids in April and August 1950 on towns and barrios. Their best prize was the seizure of 80,000 pesos from the Lugun provincial treasury in Santa Cruz. This offensive strategy was the idea of the professionally educated and Marxist brothers Joseph and Jesus Lava, who had taken over direction of Huk policy from Taruc. But the Lavas mistakenly believed that a financial crisis in the Philippines would create a genuine revolutionary climate that would soon lead to the downfall of the Liberal Philippines Government, whereas outside Central Luzon Filipino peasants generally remained apathetic to the Huk cause.[50]

Furthermore, the Philippines president, Elpidio Quirino, took an important step, at American behest, when in September 1950 he appointed Ramon Magsaysay as secretary of the Department of National Defense. The son of a school teacher, Magsaysay had been born in 1907 among peasants of Central Luzon. A commerce graduate, he served with US backed guerillas during the Second World War and afterwards became a Liberal member of Congress and chairman of the House Committee on National Defense. In 1950 he travelled to the US to request assistance for the financially harassed government and returned with $10 million as an emergency grant with promises of more money to come.[51]

Magsaysay, as defence secretary, demanded a free hand in order to introduce drastic army reforms aiming to remove the military brutality that had driven peasants to join the Huks. He was successful in giving the army new zeal to pursue Huk groups without stealing from or brutally treating peasants. There were still some military excesses, but the new approach coupled with offers of amnesty for Huk guerillas, which were rigorously honoured, started to thin Huk ranks. Former Huks also contributed to army intelligence. Appreciating the socio-economic reasons for the peasant-based Huk support, Magsaysay convinced the government that it should implement

---

50. Lachica, *The Huks* 123–30. Kerkvliet, *The Huk Rebellion* 203–33.

51. Lawrence M. Greenberg, *The Hukbalahap Insurrection: A Case Study of a Successful Anti-Insurgency Operation in the Philippines, 1946–1955* (Washington 1987) 79–81.

agrarian reforms, which forced landlords to allow peasants to keep more of the harvest. Rural development projects were introduced, and financial assistance was given to former insurgents to settle on land away from Central Luzon, especially on Mindanao. Magsaysay's own adherence to a simple life style and his willingness to travel to talk with peasants made him a very popular leader.[52]

The military and economic reforms implemented or inspired by Magsaysay and his personal popularity were the most important reasons for the decline of the Huk insurgency after 1950. The reforms greatly improved the government's image among Central Luzon peasants. The military reforms also led to much better targeted military pressure against the Huks, even though there were still problems of army indiscipline. Assistance came from the Joint United States Military Advisory Group, which by 1952 consisted of thirty-two officers and twenty-six soldiers to give military advice and administer American military aid. It also was committed to support economic reform on the basis of a correct American Embassy analysis that the Philippine Government had lost the trust of most of the Central Luzon peasant population. The American assistance programme used people who had familiarity with the Philippines, and it drew upon a reservoir of Filipino goodwill towards Americans who had liberated their country from the Japanese and quickly granted them independence. American financial aid, which from 1951 to 1956 amounted to $500 million, was a vital factor in the defeat of the insurrection because it enabled the implementation of the important economic and military reforms. The close relationship between American capital investment and the Filipino ruling classes assured a high degree of compliance with American supported reforms, which greatly eased the way for the implementation of Magsaysay's reform agenda. With declining peasant support and increased government military pressure, the Huks were reduced by 1956 to a few small half-starved bands. Only a few survived by 1960. However, Magsaysay, who was president from November 1953 until killed in an aircraft crash in March 1957, failed to implement fundamental reform of the landlord-dominated society of Central Luzon, which stored serious problems for the future.[53]

---

52. Ibid. 82–95.
53. Kerkvliet, *The Huk Rebellion* 233–48. Larry E. Cable, *Conflict of Myths: The Development of American Counterinsurgency Doctrine and the Vietnam War* (New York 1986) 52–66.

DEFEATING INSURGENCY IN MALAYA

It was a more difficult task to defeat the communist insurgency in Malaya. Although MRLA insurgents never numbered more than 6,000 – about half the largest number of Huks – they operated over a much larger area than Central Luzon and had the protection of a more jungle-covered and mountainous terrain. The MRLA had more definite targets: British personnel, the economic infrastructure and the security forces. Furthermore, they were more tightly disciplined than the Huks, with the assistance in 1951 of some Chinese army officers who infiltrated Malaya. A high point of MRLA success was the ambushing and killing of the British High Commissioner, Sir Henry Gurney, on 6 October 1951. That year the insurgents killed 504 government security men and 533 civilians, many of whom were managers and workers on rubber estates and at tin mines. A new strategy to drive out the British was the killing of wives and children of British planters and miners.[54]

In 1951, however, 1,077 members of the MRLA were killed, the highest number to that point, which was a result of increasing government efficiency and pressure. Improvements on the government side started with the arrival in Malaya in April 1950 of Lieutenant-General Sir Harold Briggs, a retired wartime Indian divisional commander. Appointed the director of all operations against the MRLA, he quickly perceived that a major fault of previous efforts had been the absence of a coordinated plan.

The Briggs plan provided the basis for government operations for the rest of the Emergency. A major aim was to deny supplies and intelligence to the MRLA, which involved relocating Chinese squatters into 'new villages'. Given no choice, 385,000 people had been shifted to 492 of these settlements by the end of 1951. Initially poorly protected and serviced, the new villages were being improved during 1952 with new government revenue generated by a boom in rubber and tin prices. This prosperity was caused by the Korean War, which proved an economic salvation for Malaya as well as for Japan. The Briggs plan also targeted the 60,000 Sakai aboriginal people in the mountains, many of whom had been coerced by the MRLA to provide food and guides. Jungle forts were constructed

---

54. Jackson, *The Malayan Emergency* 38–41. Short, *The Communist Insurrection* ch. 12.

to bring the Sakai under British protection and to provide medicine and trading opportunities. Another important initiative of the Briggs plan was to coordinate all sources of intelligence under one director and an intelligence committee. Information played an increasingly important role in the apprehension of insurgents, as was occurring in the Philippines. Close cooperation between small groups of troops and police further improved operations against MRLA squads with larger military forces blocking insurgent sources of supply. A very tight control of food supplies, to the extent of searching villagers and workers, was a major part of the programme.[55]

Gurney's assassination also provoked more financial support from a new British Conservative Government for the anti-MRLA campaign. General Sir Gerald Templar, the British Director of Military Intelligence, arrived to succeed Briggs, who retired in November 1951. Templar employed mass leaflet drops and broadcasted messages from aircraft in a successful psychological campaign to entice insurgents to surrender. Rewards were increased for the capture of those who kept fighting. Such methods alongside greater military pressure contributed to a downhill run in MRLA fortunes after 1951. However, to combat fewer than 6,000 guerillas 40,500 overseas troops were used in 1952, made up of seven British, seven Gurkha, one African and one Fijian battalions, which were joined in 1955 by one from Australia. There were also 28,500 Malay troops and police supported by 39,000 Special Constables along with the much larger Home Guard. By the end of 1956 the MRLA had shrunk to an estimated 2,063. Fighting still continued, but by 1960 the MRLA, a pale shadow of its former self, had been driven to the Thai border area. Furthermore, the surviving insurgents were being suppressed by the Malayan Government which had achieved independence. It had been delayed by the Emergency but was granted in 1957 when the insurgency had been largely defeated.[56]

Important in the defeat of the MRLA was a new government approach after 1951 to attempt to win more Malay and Chinese support. Important for this process was the commodity prices boom generated by the Korean War, which greatly increased government revenue to spend on the new measures to combat the MRLA and brought widespread prosperity to the people of the colony. Ironically,

55. Ibid. chs 15–17. Stubbs, *Hearts and Minds* ch. 4.
56. Ibid. chs 5–8. Jackson, *The Malayan Emergency* chs 5–8, 13. Cable, *Conflict of Myths* 82.

a MRLA policy decision in 1951 to compete for popularity by stopping attacks on the civilian population also improved government morale and increased Malay support for the government cause. The MRLA had very little support from any Malays and they lacked any direct line of communication with a friendly nation which so benefited the Vietminh in Tonkin. The Huks also had been limited by geographic isolation and minority peasant support. Consequently the MRLA and the Huks suffered from growing arms and ammunition shortages that were the opposite experience of the Vietminh. However, both the Philippines and Malayan Governments needed to change their policies in 1950–51 to seek support from their civilian populations in order to gain supremacy over the insurgents, an approach not really adopted by the French in Vietnam.[57]

OPPOSITION TO THE US-JAPAN SECURITY TREATY

Communists also were blamed in Washington for provoking anti-US demonstrations in Japan in 1960. The demonstrators, however, were mainly members of the Japanese Socialist Party and other non-communists concerned about the signing of a revised security treaty between Japan and the US. The new treaty was long desired by leaders of the Japanese Government to change the terms of the 1952 treaty that gave the US the freedom to move military forces in and around Japan without giving a guarantee to defend that nation. The new treaty, a result of significant negotiation, still gave the US the right to use Japan for military and naval purposes, but it obliged America to defend Japan against foreign aggression, and Japan promised to protect US forces there and to cooperate with America if 'the security in the Far East is threatened'. Japanese critics complained that the treaty would obligate their country to develop armed forces in violation of the Japanese constitution and that the vague 'Far East' provisions would commit Japan to open-ended support for American imperialism. There was also public concern about Japan being linked to the US after the shooting down of an American U2 spy-plane over the USSR when it was known that U2 planes

---

57. Stubbs, *Hearts and Minds* ch. 9.

were based in Japan. The Liberal Democratic Party (LDP) prime minster, Kishi Nobusuke, contributed to the crisis by ramming the treaty through the Japanese Diet without enough time to debate the issues. A result of the violent demonstrations was the cancellation of a projected visit by Eisenhower to Japan in June 1960. Kishi was forced to resign during the protests, which were also directed against him as a previous member of Tojo's wartime Cabinet. But the LDP easily won national elections later in the year and thus preserved the alliance between Japan and the US.[58]

THE US, THE USSR AND INDONESIA

The US was concerned as well about growing communist influence in the important Southwest Pacific Basin state of Indonesia during the 1950s. That nation with its large population and its economic wealth in rubber, tin, oil and other resources was regarded as a vital sector of non-communist Southeast Asia. During the 1950s the communist PKI made a spectacular comeback from its decimation in 1948. Under the youthful and pragmatic leadership of D. N. Aidit, the PKI sought to become the largest political party in the post-revolution democratic state. In the 1955 election it achieved 16 per cent of the vote, only 6 per cent behind the best supported party, the PNI which, along with two Islamic organizations made the PKI one of the four major parties. The PKI was kept out of government by a coalition of the other three parties. However, resultant internal divisions in Prime Minister Ali Sastroamidjojo's Cabinet encouraged President Sukarno to talk of the need for 'guided democracy' rather than party competition, which the PKI supported and thus curried favour with Sukarno. Serious regional troubles, with an army rebellion on Sumatra, supported by American oil companies, and an uprising in Sulawesi in East Indonesia, were threatening to fragment the nation. In this crisis atmosphere, with the support of the army, Sukarno proclaimed martial law and introduced 'guided democracy', under which the PKI moved to improve its

---

58. Tadashi Aruga, 'The Security Treaty Revision of 1960' in Akira Iriye and Warren I. Cohen (eds), *The United States and Japan in the Postwar World* (Lexington, Ky. 1989) ch. 4.

position. It was able to exploit a crisis in November 1957, when a motion calling on the UN to support negotiations about Irian Jaya failed to receive the necessary two-thirds majority in the General Assembly. In the resultant furore in Indonesia about western influence in the UN, all Dutch properties were seized and Dutch personnel were expelled from Indonesia; and PKI and PNI unions started taking over the abandoned Dutch enterprises. In local Java elections the PKI was out-polling the PNI.[59]

The US Administration, now alarmed at growing PKI influence, covertly sent arms to the rebels in Sumatra, and CIA pilots flew planes which bombed Indonesian forces. But early in 1958 Indonesian army and air force action crushed the rebellion and captured one of the American pilots. Consequently, this rebellion seriously damaged US-Indonesian relations, which the PKI exploited. As well, the revolt soured relations between Indonesia and newly independent Singapore and Malaya, which had sympathized with the rebels and provided a conduit for weapons flowing to them. The Philippines and Nationalist China also expressed support for the rebellion. Sukarno's response of imposing a ban on activities of the Kuomintang in Indonesia gave the PKI a chance to increase its support in the local Chinese community. Furthermore, Sukarno had turned to Eastern Europe and the Soviet Union for arms supplies and for economic development projects. For these purposes Kruschev supplied a credit of $US 117.5 million in 1959 and another $US 250 million on a visit to Jakarta in January 1960. Eisenhower left to his successor a serious concern about communist influence in Indonesia.[60]

CONCLUSIONS

By 1960 the Western Pacific Basin had become a major battleground in the Cold War between the communist world, which was still

59. Ricklefs, *History of Modern Indonesia* chs 18–19. Rex Mortimer, *Indonesian Communism under Sukarno: Ideology and Politics 1959–1965* (Ithaca 1974) chs 1–4.

60. Ricklefs, *History of Modern Indonesia* 250–7. McMahon, *Colonialism and Cold War* 323–4. R.A. Longmire, *Soviet Relations with South-East Asia: An Historical Survey* (London 1989) 53–7. John Prados, *Presidents' Wars: CIA and Pentagon Covert Operations since World War II* (New York 1986) 130–44.

expanding in size in the Pacific Basin, and the US led anti-communist coalition. A stalemate had been preserved after the expenditure of much blood and money in the Korean War. That war, however had beneficial consequences for the non-communist cause in providing the impetus for a peace treaty with Japan, by giving a crucial boost to the Japanese economy and by generating extra wealth in Malaya for defeating the Communist insurgency there, which in turn allowed the granting of independence to Malaya and to Singapore. British military power remained in the region to protect its former colonies and its surviving outpost in East Asia, Hong Kong. In Vietnam France, despite strong American financial backing, lost the struggle to hold the free world line in northern Indochina; and France retreated from the Western Pacific Basin, leaving the US to support South Vietnam. However, US pressure on China by supporting the Kuomintang regime on Taiwan had helped to widen cracks in the Soviet-Chinese alliance that had received a boost during the Korean War. Taiwan and South Korea had become front line anti-communist positions in the Cold War, despite their autocratic regimes. Japan had become a major bastion for American power in East Asia, though not all its citizens were happy about this major postwar development in the former dominant power of that region. But the Soviet Union, and to a lesser extent China, supported North Vietnam, where a decision had been made for a major communist-led insurrection in South Vietnam. Furthermore, the Soviet Union was financing an increase in the military muscles of Indonesia, where the Communist Party was growing in influence. The Western Pacific Basin was to remain a major Cold War battleground in the 1960s.

CHAPTER THREE

Confrontations and Cooperation in East and Southeast Asia, 1961–1968

The biggest issue in the Pacific Basin in the 1960s was the war in Vietnam in which a communist-led insurgency struggled against US supported South Vietnam, a conflict that gradually involved and affected many other Pacific Basin countries, some of which cooperated with the US. The war was also generating new economic wealth for Japan and other East and Southeast Asian nations, setting some on a road of increasing economic growth. The nature of that war, the international involvement in it, and its wider influences are the major themes of this chapter. Another subject is one of the last issues involved in the ending of European colonialism in the Southwest Pacific Basin as Indonesia sought to complete its takeover of the whole of the former Dutch empire and launched a military confrontation against a new Malaysian federation. But this conflict ended in the beginnings of a new era of cooperation in Southeast Asia.

THE KENNEDY ADMINISTRATION AND VIETNAM

John F. Kennedy, who in January 1961 at forty-three years of age became the first American president born in the twentieth century, had based much of his campaigning for office as the candidate for the Democratic Party on the theme that the US was losing world power. He complained that Eisenhower's Republican Administration had presided over a decline in the size of US armed forces, had allowed the development of an alleged new Soviet missile supremacy and had failed to prevent an outbreak of communist expansionism in regions such as Cuba, Indochina and the African Congo. Kennedy called for 'New Frontier' policies to get the country moving again.

However, Kennedy sought a new flexibility in US relations with the USSR. He wished to move away from dependence on the Eisenhower Administration's threat of massive nuclear retaliation, though ironically his mistaken belief in Soviet nuclear supremacy started a nuclear arms race between the two powers. Kennedy therefore sought to increase America's conventional military power so that his government could respond in low-key ways to communist expansionism. He also had a strong political reason to beat an anti-communist drum given previous Republican campaigns against alleged Democratic Party softness about communism.[1]

Along with wider world problems of alleged Soviet expansionism in regions such as Cuba and the former Belgian Congo, Kennedy was briefed by Eisenhower about a threat to the independent kingdom of Laos in Indochina. Plane-loads of arms had been arriving in that country from the USSR for North Vietnamese-supported Pathet Lao rebels. Kennedy seized on this Soviet threat to Laos in his inaugural address to Congress and in other public statements in what Roger Hilsman, the State Department's Director of Intelligence and Research, described as 'a very hawkish manner'. Kennedy's public indignation about Soviet aggression masked in fact heavy involvement by the CIA in equipping and training a rival army, which was also aiming to seize power in Laos. There was a clear threat of direct US-USSR military confrontation. This awesome prospect in a distant, landlocked, small Asian kingdom caused Kennedy to pull back from direct US military intervention by reluctantly accepting a Soviet proposal for a cease-fire in Laos in May 1961 in preparation for a peace conference.[2]

However, the Laos scare directed Kennedy's attention to Diem's regime in South Vietnam, which was struggling to suppress another alleged Soviet-backed communist insurgency. Washington also had become alarmed about a well publicized speech by Kruschev in Moscow on 6 January 1961 expressing Soviet support for national

---

1. Thomas G. Paterson, 'John F. Kennedy's Quest for Victory and Global Crisis' in Thomas G. Paterson (ed.), *Kennedy's Quest for Victory: American Foreign Policy, 1961–1963* (New York 1989) 3–23.

2. Interview with Roger Hilsman in Charlton and Moncrieff, *Many Reasons Why* 63. Short, *Origins of the Vietnam War* 227–35.

wars of liberation, though the rhetoric was mostly directed at bolstering USSR communist world leadership credentials in a growing split with China. The Kennedy Administration was also warned from its people in South Vietnam that the PLAF was winning the struggle against the ARVN, which could be reversed with better support for Diem. Also the MAAG in Saigon had submitted a counter-insurgency plan, which advocated American financial aid to increase the size of the ARVN and the Vietnamese Civil Guard. Kennedy endorsed this plan, authorizing an additional $42 million to the existing $70.9 million in military aid, 100 extra personnel for the MAAG and 400 Special Forces troops to train ARVN soldiers in counterinsurgency tactics. Kennedy also appointed a new ambassador, Frederick Nolting, a career diplomat serving with NATO in Paris, who knew little about Vietnam. His instructions were to give more support to Diem and oversee 'a stepped-up' programme of military assistance to the ARVN, which had some focus on economic development.[3]

Kennedy did receive advice from within his administration to resist increasing America's commitment to the RVN. George Ball, the under secretary for foreign affairs, considered that sending more military advisers to the RVN 'would gradually involve us in a military contest', and he privately warned Kennedy that 'if we go down that road we might have within five years, 300,000 men in the rice paddies and jungles of Vietnam, . . . impossible terrain in which to engage our forces'. But Kennedy insisted: 'That will never happen'.[4]

In fact Kennedy was fending off strong advice for a bigger growth in US support for South Vietnam. Vice-President Lyndon Johnson went to Vietnam to show the American flag and brought back in May 1961 a recommendation for a 'major effort' to assist the struggle there against communism rather than 'throw in the towel' and signal to the world that 'we . . . don't stand by our friends'. General Maxwell Taylor, Kennedy's military adviser, and Walt Rostow, an economist and special foreign security affairs adviser, also visited the RVN and produced a joint report advocating increasing US military aid, sending more military advisers and despatching 8,000 US soldiers under the cover of flood relief aid in the Mekong Delta. Kennedy resisted sending any American troops, but he agreed to increase the number

3. Ibid. 236–46. Herring, *America's Longest War* 73–8. Interview with Frederick Nolting in Charlton and Moncrieff, *Many Reasons Why* 70–1.

4. Interview with George Ball in Charlton and Moncrieff, *Many Reasons Why* 78.

of military advisers. Indeed, by the end of 1962 there were 11,000 of them plus 300 US military aircraft and 120 American helicopters in South Vietnam.[5]

Many historians claim that, with this military build-up, Kennedy crossed the Rubicon to the later massive American involvement in the Vietnam War. William Bundy, the assistant secretary for defense and international affairs at the Pentagon, explained the major reason: 'I think it was the sense that you had to stand firm in this area, that otherwise the idea of Communism as the wave of the future would have a very great effect'. This strong support for the RVN reflected the Kennedy Administration's confidence in the ability of American economic and military power to conquer communist expansionism. Furthermore, there was an important political motive. When in September 1963, in the face of grave problems confronting Diem's government, Kennedy was asked if he would reduce aid to South Vietnam, he said 'no' because 'strongly in our mind is what happened in the case of China . . . We don't want that'.[6]

But the task the Kennedy Administration was undertaking in Vietnam was more difficult than many of his advisers had suggested. By 1961 over half of the villages of the RVN had come under NLF influence. Insurgent violence was an important reason. In Long An province near Saigon, during the week of Tet in January 1960, twenty-six village chiefs and other GVN supporters were murdered, which subsequently caused many of Diem's officials in the province to resign or flee; and part of the land in Long An was being redistributed by NLF-established peasant committees. NLF control of the countryside had deprived the GVN of much of its taxation revenue, causing heavy reliance on American aid. Indeed, many formerly fatalistic peasants had been radicalized by their experience of the eight years of the first Vietnam War. Also, as Tran Van Don admits, the NLF in urban areas succeeded in enlisting the help of non-communist 'progressive intellectuals, liberal bourgeois and frustrated nationalists' who 'had been harassed previously, or jailed by President Diem's overzealous

5. Congressional Research Service, Library of Congress, *The U.S. Government and the Vietnam War: Executive and Legislative Roles and Relationships (UGVW)* (Washington 1985) Part II, 45. John Newman, *JFK and Vietnam: Deception, Intrigue and the Struggle for Power* (New York 1992) 130–9. Lawrence Bassett and Stephen E. Pelz, 'The Failed Search for Victory: Vietnam and the Politics of War' in Paterson, *Kennedy's Quest for Victory* 240–1.

6. Short, *Origins of the Vietnam War* 243. Interviews with Maxwell Taylor and William Bundy in Charlton & Moncrieff, *Many Reasons Why* 72–5, 69. *Public Papers of the Presidents of the United States, John F. Kennedy, 1963* (Washington 1964) 659.

secret police'. Furthermore, the first Vietnam War had given many members of the PLAF significant experience of guerilla warfare. Hit-and-run tactics and sophisticated methods of deception, such as long underground communication tunnels, were well developed.[7]

There were also limits to the quality of the American Administration's knowledge about South Vietnam. Taylor admitted that on his visit he 'found very quickly that the information we were getting back in Washington was highly unreliable'. Nolting remained convinced that the increased American assistance 'began to reverse the tide of Communist success' in 1962. But in a letter to the State Department in July 1961 he admitted that it was difficult to discern if the war against the PLAF was 'getting better' but stressed a need to 'create a new and winning psychology'. He therefore wrote: 'I have taken a much more optimistic line in conversations with other diplomats and with the press here . . . and I think we should continue to do so, giving benefit of the doubt wherever possible to optimistic assessment'. He became a victim of his own deception as indicated by his continued faithful support during 1963 of Diem, whose popularity in the RVN was fast diminishing.[8]

Indeed, Nolting's estimate of an improving war situation in 1962 belied the dismal performance of the ARVN. Lieutenant-Colonel John Paul Vann, who arrived in Vietnam in 1962 to act as senior American adviser to an ARVN division, quickly noted how: 'Petty jealousies among battalion and regimental commanders take precedence over, and detract from, the primary mission of closing with and destroying the enemy'. Officers used the artillery and aircraft supplied by the US to bombard villages indiscriminately on the mere suspicion of a PLAF presence. He also was revolted by the torturing and killing of prisoners. He could not think of worse ways to fight the war.[9]

The Kennedy Administration did attempt to introduce into South Vietnam more appropriate policies for fighting a guerilla war. From the outset of his presidency, Kennedy was keen on the idea of developing more effective methods of combatting communist-led

7. Jeffrey Race, *War Comes to Long An: Revolutionary Conflict in a Vietnamese Province* (Berkeley 1973) 113–34. James Walker Trullinger, Jr., *Village at War: An Account of Revolution in Vietnam* (New York 1980) 85–90. Tran, *Our Endless War* 81. Turley, *Second Indochina War* 39–40.

8. Interview with Taylor in Charlton & Moncrieff, *Many Reasons Why* 72–3. Frederick Nolting, *From Trust to Tragedy: the Political Memoirs of Frederick Nolting, Kennedy's Ambassador to Diem's Vietnam* (New York 1988) 43, 147.

9. Neil Sheehan, *A Bright Shining Lie: John Paul Vann and America in Vietnam* (New York 1988) 91, 101–10.

insurgencies. Washington also persuaded Diem to introduce a strategic hamlet system, duplicating the successful scheme adopted during the Malayan emergency, as a non-military option to counter the insurgency.

However, the strategic hamlet programme was not the answer to the NLF insurgency. Vietnamese peasants were far more rooted to their home villages than were Chinese squatters in Malaya. Also, a large number of the strategic hamlets were incapable of being protected from determined guerilla attack, especially because insufficient efforts were made to rid the hamlets of PLAF members living inside them. Nor were the hamlets part of a coordinated anti-insurgent campaign as they were in Malaya. Indeed, many hamlets were deprived of promised resources by the corrupt nature of the GVN management of the programme, which was directed by the thuggish Nhu.[10]

Nor, compared with the Philippines, was there a cooperative and effective personal indigenous leadership to support counter-insurgency programmes. Diem was not the Magsaysay of South Vietnam as so many Americans hoped he would be. Diem and Nhu had no intention of giving up any power by implementing the democratic and social reforms that Nolting urged upon him on behalf of Washington. The Ngo brothers believed that the US needed them more than the reverse, a misconception that Nolting and other Americans fostered.

The day of reckoning came on 1 November 1963 when South Vietnamese army units attacked the presidential palace, from which Diem and his brother fled, to be murdered the next morning by ARVN soldiers. An important background to this coup had been Buddhist riots in May 1963 in Hue, the diocesan seat of another of Diem's brothers, Roman Catholic Archbishop Ngo Dinh Thuc. Buddhist priests had been forbidden by Catholic city officials to celebrate Buddha's birthday in the same public manner that the jubilee of Thuc's ordination had been celebrated in the previous month. Though the Catholic Minister of the Interior overturned the decision, it had already sparked off longstanding Buddhist grievances about the monopolizing of RVN public positions by Catholics. In the two months after the riot, there were five successive self-immolations by Buddhist monks calling for the overthrow of Diem; and anti-

10. Kahin, *Intervention* 140–5. Cable, *Conflict of Myths* ch. 11. Eric M. Bergerud, *The Dynamics of Defeat: the Vietnam War in Hau Nghia Province* (Boulder 1991) 33–8. Louis A. Wiesner, *Victims and Survivors: Displaced Persons and Other War Victims in Viet-Nam, 1954–1975* (Westport 1988) ch. 3.

government elements, including the NLF, used Buddhist protests to further their own anti-Diem cause. This dissent finally convinced the Kennedy Administration that the government in Saigon should change. So Nolting was replaced by a Republican Party leader, Henry Cabot Lodge, in a bipartisan display of American concern for the future of the RVN. There was still nervousness in Washington about backing a coup that might not succeed. On 30 October Lodge was told that if he 'should conclude that there is not clearly a high prospect of success' he should dissuade the plotting generals. But Lodge considered that 'after our efforts not to discourage a coup' any such pressure would be futile, and anyway he was 'not convinced that the coup was going to fail'.[11]

Kennedy himself was assassinated three weeks later. He had left in South Vietnam 16,700 American military personnel who were permitted to engage in battle alongside the ARVN units they advised. He also had approved assistance for covert raids into North Vietnam. He had financially supported an increase in ARVN and Home Guard forces to over 200,000 men. Yet the NLF insurgency was growing stronger, boosted by a DRV decision in 1963 to step up its support. US intelligence acknowledged that more than 90 per cent of the PLAF were Southerners; most of its recruits from the North were Southern returnees. But the Americans were making a strategic mistake of encouraging the ARVN to direct its energies to defending South Vietnam's borders in order to cut off DRV aid to the PLAF, applying a lesson learned in previous postwar insurgencies. Also many ARVN divisions were preserved from the conflict to provide protection for Diem. The US Administration had not appreciated the depth of anti-government feeling in the countryside. The State Department's Paul Kattenburg said, after his return from a fact-finding mission to Vietnam, that he listened to a NSC meeting on 31 August 1963 attended by Johnson, Secretary of State Dean Rusk and other major decision makers. 'There was not a single person there that knew what he was talking about . . . They didn't know Vietnam . . . They simply didn't understand the identification of nationalism and Communism and the more this meeting went on . . . I thought "God, we're walking into a major disaster"'.[12]

11. Kahin, *Intervention* ch. 6. Marylin B. Young, *The Vietnam Wars 1945–1990* (New York 1991) ch. 5. Moya Ann Ball, *Vietnam-on-the Potomac* (Westport 1992) 70–7. *FRUS, 1961–1963* vol. 4: Vietnam August–December 1963 (Washington 1991) 500–1, 484–90.
12. Turley, *Second Indochina War* 40–8. Interview with Paul Kattenburg, 16 Feb. 1979, in *UGVW* II, 161.

THE US, CHINA AND THE USSR

Influencing the increased military commitment by the Kennedy Administration to the RVN was a growing fear of Chinese support for North Vietnam and the insurgents in the South. Bundy explained: 'the idea of China as a menace grew particularly from the time of the Sino-Indian conflict in the fall of 1962 which seemed (and I think exaggeratedly) an example of the Chinese being ready to move hard in peripheral areas'. In fact China had not increased its suppo:t of the DRV in the early 1960s. After joining with the USSR to impose the partition of Vietnam at Geneva in 1954, China's major post-Korean War priority was to avoid another debilitating contest with the US and to develop her own underdeveloped economy. Beijing was contributing some economic and military aid to the DRV, but much less than the USSR. A Chinese motive for such assistance from the late 1950s was to maintain some influence in the region in the face of a growing split between Beijing and Moscow. But China was not interested in a more powerful unified Vietnamese state on her southern border. DRV leaders later complained that China refused to support the VCP uprising in South Vietnam because Beijing's real intention was 'maintaining the political status quo in Vietnam'.[13]

The Kennedy Administration knew of the widening split between China and the Soviet Union. However, that knowledge did not encourage any closer American move towards China. The Democratic Party's memory of the damage inflicted on the Truman Administration by the Republican 'loss of China' propaganda and Kennedy's own longstanding antipathy to Communist China, ensured that the Nationalist Chinese regime in Taiwan remained the only American-recognized Chinese government. Also influencing this policy was a strong suspicion that the Beijing regime was developing an atomic bomb. This was an alarming prospect for Kennedy and other members of his administration who were becoming concerned about Chinese ambitions to dominate Southeast Asia and were prepared to believe that the CCP would be willing to sacrifice millions of its own citizens in a nuclear war. So Kennedy's response was a new urgency in negotiations with the USSR for a nuclear test ban treaty, which had stalled under the Eisenhower Administration. Initially, Kruschev did not respond favourably, being unsure about the emerging rift with

13. Interview with Bundy in Charlton & Moncrieff, *Many Reasons Why* 68–9. Ton That Thien, *Foreign Politics* 125.

China. But in 1963, after the Cuban missile crisis had generated mutual US-Soviet fears of nuclear war, Kruschev came to an agreement with the US to ban open air nuclear tests, which worsened relations between the USSR and China. The Kennedy Administration responded to this minor detente by discussing the possibility of a joint Soviet-US air attack on the Chinese nuclear facilities at Lop Nor on the edge of the Talimupendi desert. But available evidence suggests that this drastic proposition was still-born in Washington.[14]

INDONESIA AND IRIAN JAYA

The USSR-China split even had a significant influence in the Southwestern Pacific Basin. There was a growing Soviet involvement in Indonesia in order to counter Chinese influence. After a dispute in 1959 between China and Indonesia about restrictions placed on Chinese people there, Beijing sought in 1960 an accommodation with Jakarta to counter growing Soviet influence in Indonesia. Moscow in turn provided increased credit to Sukarno's government, resulting in an Indonesian build-up of arms supplied by the Soviet Union and Communist Eastern European countries. By 1961 Indonesia had received its first long-range bombers, submarines and other advanced military hardware. These arms gave Sukarno the confidence to force the Irian Jaya issue with strong support from the PKI and the army. So army 'volunteers' were sent from the beginning of 1962 into Irian Jaya to start guerilla action against Dutch rule.[15]

US concern about Soviet influence in Indonesia affected Washington's policy in the Irian Jaya conflict. A recent study of the Indonesia-Netherlands military balance in 1962 demonstrates that the Dutch forces in the region, especially aircraft, had the capacity to prevent a full-scale Indonesian invasion of Irian Jaya. The Australian Government also supported diplomatically the Netherlands' insistence on retaining control of the territory in order to prepare its Melanesian people for

14. Chang, *Friends and Enemies* ch. 8. Michael R. Beschloss, *The Crisis Years: Kennedy and Kruschev 1960–1963* (New York 1991) chs 17–21. James Fetzer, 'Clinging to Containment: China Policy' in Paterson, *Kennedy's Quest for Victory* ch. 7.

15. David Mozingo, *Chinese Policy Towards Indonesia 1949–1967* (Ithaca 1976) ch. 6. Longmire, *Soviet Relations* 60–8. Franklin B. Weinstein, *Indonesia's Foreign Policy and the Dilemma of Dependence: From Sukarno to Suharto* (Ithaca 1976) 306–14.

self-determination. Australia preferred not to have an expansionist Indonesia camped on the western border of Papua New Guinea. But the US chose to support Indonesia. Hilsman explained that the 'spectacle of the Soviet Union and the other Communist countries supplying Indonesia with a billion dollars of military arms and equipment and the increasing Communist influence that was the logical resultant of this aid' caused the US to abandon its 'policy of passive neutrality'. So the US pressed Holland to agree in September 1962 to transfer control of Irian Jaya to Indonesia on 1 May 1963, with provision for a UN-supervised expression of self-determination by the indigenous people in 1969. Also the Netherlands were not well placed to fight single-handedly a lengthy guerilla war in Irian Jaya. Australia was forced to agree to the capitulation. Its government was unwilling to join the Dutch in a war with Indonesia without US or British support. The British Cabinet had backed away from a previous promise to provide 'logistical support' for a Dutch defence of Irian Jaya.[16]

CONFRONTATION

Indonesia's success in gaining Irian Jaya encouraged further conflict in the South-western Pacific Basin. Sukarno started making threatening gestures towards the Federation of Malaysia, which was inaugurated on 16 September 1963. The concept of Malaysia had been advocated in May 1961 in a speech by Malaya's prime minister, Tunku Abdul Rahman, as a solution to the problem of amalgamating Malaya and Singapore without Malays being subjected to a Chinese majority. By including in the proposed federation the British colonies of

16. Ian MacFarling, *Military Aspects of the West New Guinea Dispute, 1958–1962* Australian National University Strategic and Defence Studies Centre (ASDSC) Working paper, no 212 (Canberra 1990) 21–47. Roger Hilsman, *To Move a Nation* (New York 1967) 374–5. Gregory Pemberton, *All the Way: Australia's Road to Vietnam* (Sydney 1987) ch. 3. Amry Vandenbosch, 'Indonesia, the Netherlands and the New Guinea Issue', *Journal of Southeast Asian Studies* VI, 1975, 109–15. Christopher J. McMullen, *Mediation of the West New Guinea Dispute, 1962: A Case Study* (Washington 1981). The Earl of Home, 'Assistance to the Netherlands Government in the Event of an Indonesian Attack on West New Guinea', 29 Dec. 1961, CAB 129/107/222, Public Record Office (PRO), London.

Sarawak, Brunei and Sabah on the island of Borneo, a non-Chinese majority would be preserved. Singapore's People's Action Party (PAP) Government still envisioned in Malaysia a fruitful wider stage for its political activities, which were facing a serious challenge from the leftist *Barisan Sosialis* (Socialist Front). The island's economic interests also would be advanced in the promised Malaysian common market. However, the Sultan of Brunei was unhappy about sharing the oil riches of his small state with his Malay cousins and did not join the federation.[17]

Emboldened by its victory in Irian Jaya, Indonesia launched a similar military campaign against Malaysia, known as Confrontation. Sukarno condemned the Malaysian federation as a neo-colonialist ploy by a declining empire to ensure continued British influence in the region. Such rhetoric was good propaganda. But probably it also reflected the anti-imperialist ideology that had informed the long struggle by Sukarno and Indonesian nationalists to free themselves from Dutch influence, which had continued after the formation of Indonesia. Now there was a chance for Sukarno to arouse his people to eradicate the last remnants of British influence in Southeast Asia. Britain represented an old established force opposing the new emerging forces that had become a theme of Indonesian foreign policy. Moreover, Anglophobia in Indonesia had been generated previously by the handing back of power to the Netherlands during SEAC's postwar regime; and the antipathy had been aggravated by the support provided by Malaya and British Singapore to the 1958 rebellion in Sumatra. That rebellion and the accompanying Sulawesi revolt indicated the fragility of Indonesian unity, which could be subject to interference by a British-dominated Malaysia. Malaya and Singapore also were economically more prosperous than Indonesia; and the new federation gave them potentially greater economic power in the region, in glaring contrast to Indonesia's economic problems. Furthermore, Confrontation could divert public attention from economic troubles in Indonesia. The expulsion of Dutch enterprise, internal unrest and galloping inflation, fuelled by Sukarno's heavy expenditure on military hardware and on grandiose building projects, had seriously damaged Indonesia's economic health. One suggested motive for Confrontation, for which there is no good

---

17. N.J. Ryan, *A History of Malaysia and Singapore* (Kuala Lumpur 1976) ch. 20. C.M. Turnbull, *A History of Singapore 1819–1980* (Singapore 1989) 264–80.

evidence, is that Indonesia had expansionist ambitions to incorporate some of Malaysia's territory.[18]

The occasion for launching the anti-Malaysia campaign was presented by the use of British troops in December 1962 to crush a left wing rebellion against the Sultan of Brunei. While there is no evidence that Indonesia instigated that uprising, some of the rebels had received training and support from a Kalimantan (Indonesian Borneo) army commander. The military thrust of Confrontation began in April 1963 with army 'volunteer' groups mounting raids across the Kalimantan border into Sarawak and Sabah. Their aim, in particular, was to stimulate popular opposition to Malaysia from groups such as Sarawak communists and the Brunei rebels. At this stage Sukarno seems to have been testing the water with a three-pronged strategy that included diplomatic efforts to prevent the formation of Malaysia and the propaganda campaign against British neo-colonialism.[19]

Sukarno was unable to prevent the inauguration of Malaysia. But having aroused Indonesian public opposition to the new nation, he was unwilling to suspend Confrontation. The campaign also was backed by his two major political support groups, the army and the PKI, for contradictory reasons. The army feared that Singapore's Chinese communists would become more influential in Malaysia, whereas the PKI more correctly viewed Malaysia as strengthening the anti-communist hand of the Alliance Government.[20]

So, after the formation of Malaysia, the Indonesian Government stepped up its raids into Sabah and Sarawak. Commercial relations were severed in an attempt to drive Indonesian trade from Malaysian ports. Diplomatic links between the two countries were broken. The British embassy in Jakarta was burned to the ground by a rampaging mob on 17 September, and two days later all British property in Indonesia was seized. Indonesian regular troops also were sent into action in Borneo and in December 1963 severely mauled a Malay regiment in Sabah.

Malaysia did not have to face Confrontation alone. British troops based there were swung into action, and reinforcements were sent from Britain. Initially they were able to cope with the Indonesian raids. The British commander of Borneo operations, General Sir Walter

18. Ide Anak Agung Gde Agung, *Twenty Years of Indonesian Foreign Policy 1945–1965* (The Hague 1973) ch. 16. J.A.C. Mackie, *Konfrontasi: The Indonesia-Malaysia Dispute 1963–1966* (Kuala Lumpur 1974) 326–33.

19. Mackie, *Konfrontasi* chs 6–7.

20. Ibid. ch. 8. Agung, *Twenty Years* 467–72.

Walker, explained that in 1963: 'the threat was from small, ill-trained and poorly armed gangs', which were met with 'tactics . . . similar to those of the Malayan emergency: platoons operating independently from company bases'. But the increasing frequency and strength of raids late in 1963 caused a request from Britain to Australia for military assistance. The Australian Government did not wish to upset relations with Jakarta which previously had been strained by the Irian Jaya dispute. So Canberra pleaded the unavailability of troops. Further pressure from the Malaysian and British Governments for release of the Australian battalion serving in Malaya succeeded after it was used to capture a small party of Indonesian guerillas landed by sea on the Malacca coast. The Australian troops, along with British, Gurkha and Malay regiments, went into action in Sarawak against Indonesian army units, a development which caused considerable nervousness in Canberra about the possibility of Indonesian retaliation in New Guinea.[21]

However, the undeclared war was not widened. Britain rejected proposals to launch air and sea strikes against Indonesian military bases. Instead, with the availability of 50,000 overseas troops plus three Malay battalions, incursions were authorized into Indonesian territory for up to 10,000 yards (9 km) in order to ambush Indonesian supply parties. In Walker's view the allied troops 'out-guerrilla-ed the guerrilla in every department of the game through sheer good training, based on operational experience'. Consequently, Indonesian insurgents were placed on the defensive to protect supply lines, which limited their offensive capabilities. A 'hearts and minds' programme, as in the Malayan Emergency, also was used to conciliate the local population and to limit support for the insurgency by the small number of communists in Sarawak and Sabah.[22]

Diplomatically, Indonesia received some support. The Philippines condemned the formation of Malaysia, because of a Philippine claim to Sabah, which was based on an eighth-century cession of that region by the Sultan of Brunei to the Filipino Sultan of Sulu. China, which was establishing closer relations with Indonesia, denounced Malaysia as an imperialist plot. The Soviet Union used its veto to block any

21. Sir Walter Walker, 'How Borneo was Won, the Untold Story of an Asian Victory', *The Round Table* 59, 1969, 17. David Horner, 'The Australian Army and Indonesia's Confrontation with Malaysia', *Australian Outlook* 43, 1989, 61–76. Pemberton, *All the Way* ch. 8.

22. Walker, 'How Borneo was Won', 17. Mackie, *Konfrontasi* 258–64.

action by the UN Security Council and continued to ferry arms to Indonesia.[23]

The US did not support Indonesia in Confrontation. The Kennedy Administration welcomed the formation of Malaysia as a nation that would anchor an anti-communist arc across the South China Sea to the Philippines and Taiwan. Kennedy regarded Malaysia as 'the best hope of security for that very vital part of the world'.[24] It was not considered necessary to send any US aid, because the new nation was seen as a British responsibility, and the US was already carrying a major burden in supporting South Vietnam. Washington also tried to cushion the impact on Indonesia of American diplomatic support for Malaysia. A reduced flow of military and economic aid to Indonesia continued, much to the annoyance of Malaysia. This was an American balancing act attempting to stop Indonesia falling into the communist camp. However, increased Indonesian military pressure on Malaysia caused the US in 1964 to suspend all military assistance to Jakarta as well as a $400 million economic aid package. Also Tunku Rahman was invited that year to visit Washington, where he was promised military training for Malaysian troops in the US and was given a credit line for arms purchases.[25]

Sukarno defiantly rejected US attempts to use the threat of withdrawal of economic aid to pressure him to cease Confrontation. The US embassy was burned down in Jakarta and paratroopers were landed in Malaya, though they were quickly rounded up. There were, however, limits to the Indonesian military campaign. There were no attempts to assassinate Malaysian leaders, which could have caused much political instability in Malaysia. No more than 30,000 Indonesian troops were used at the height of Confrontation, which reflected Sukarno's need to station his army in other parts of Indonesia to prevent dissidents using the undeclared war as a cloak to cover local rebellions. Sukarno also refrained from provoking total war against superior British technology. Indeed, he continued throughout the crisis to mount a diplomatic campaign to isolate Malaysia.[26]

Confrontation ended because of violent political change in Indonesia. Growing communist influence there resulted in an attempted coup on 30 September 1965 against the army leadership; five generals were

23. Ibid. 264–89.
24. Hilsman, *To Move a Nation* 385.
25. Pamela Sodhy, 'Malaysian-American Relations during Indonesia's Confrontation against Malaysia, 1963–66', *Journal of Southeast Asian Studies* XIX, 1988, 111–36.
26. Mackie, *Konfrontasi* 221–47.

killed. One of the non-targeted generals, General Suharto, then seized power with the support of loyal troops. The PKI was blamed for the September coup, resulting in an anti-communist popular frenzy, encouraged by the army, which resulted in the slaughtering of as many as half a million known or suspected communists in late 1965 and early 1966. The more likely sponsors of the coup were younger officers acting, with some support by PKI elements, against generals accused of opposing Sukarno's policies and of being influenced by the CIA. Certainly, all of the targeted generals had received military training in the US. Sukarno also was accused of complicity in coup planning, which was a major reason, as well as poor health, why he failed to reclaim power. His actual involvement in the putsch remains uncertain because of the unreliability of the evidence produced after his death in 1970 to implicate him.[27]

Suharto's 'new order' military regime in Indonesia sought an end to Confrontation. With Thailand acting as a mediator, an agreement was signed in Bangkok by the Indonesian and Malaysian foreign ministers to terminate all hostilities. Indonesia gave diplomatic recognition to Malaysia and suspended relations with China, which had already withdrawn its ambassador and cut economic and technical aid to Indonesia. The minimal American military aid to the Indonesian army and probable CIA support for Suharto after the PKI coup paid a rich dividend. Indeed, there is evidence that the CIA assisted in the massive anti-communist purge. Suharto's Indonesia was now secured as a supporter for the US-led anti-communist crusade in the Western Pacific Basin.[28]

27. Nawaz B. Mody, *Indonesia under Suharto* (New York 1987) ch. 1. Oey Hong Lee, 'Sukarno and the Pseudo-Coup of 1965: Ten Years later', *Journal of Southeast Asian Studies* VI, 1975, 119–35. Ulf Sundhaussen, *The Road to Power: Indonesian Military Politics* (Kuala Lumpur 1982) chs 5–6. Harold Crouch, *The Army and Politics in Indonesia* (Ithaca 1978) chs 4–8.

28. Mackie, *Konfrontasi* ch. 12. Brian May, *The Indonesian Tragedy* (London 1978) 125–8. Mozingo, *Chinese Policy Towards Indonesia* ch. 8. William Blum, *The CIA: A Forgotten History* (London 1986) ch. 31. Robert Cribb (ed.), *The Indonesian Killings* (Clayton, Victoria 1990) 7–14.

MALAYSIA EXPELS SINGAPORE

Ironically, the end of Confrontation was accompanied by the separation of Singapore from Malaysia. Singapore's Chinese people, who were three-quarters of the island's population of 1,700,000, were uncomfortable partners for Malays in Malaysia. There was irritation there from the start when Singapore unilaterally declared its independence from Britain fifteen days before the inauguration of the federation and held prompt elections in which Alliance Party-supported candidates were defeated. The PAP also campaigned on the mainland in the March 1964 federal election in an attempt to supplant the conservative Malay Chinese Association in the allegiance of the Chinese population of Malaya. This was a PAP tactical mistake, given the conservatism of communal politics in Malaya. There was in fact little in common between urban Singapore and predominantly rural Malaya, and the Tunku condemned Lee Kuan Yew for breaking a promise to refrain from entering national politics. Racial tensions exploded into communal riots in Singapore in July and September 1964, the latter said to be the work of Indonesian agents. But the PAP blamed Malay extremists for the violence, and Lee Kuan Yew and other PAP leaders started calling for a 'democratic Malaysian Malaysia' in which there was no place for special Malay privileges. In May 1965 the PAP succeeded in organizing a united opposition front, the Malaysian Solidarity Convention (MSC), to compete against the Malaysian National Alliance Party. Many Malays saw the MSC as a Chinese challenge to political leadership in Malaysia, which was achievable if the 42 per cent of the federation's population who were Chinese gained the support of other non-Malays. For many rural, conservative and Muslim Malays, Lee Kuan Yew personified aggressive and materialistic Chinese ambition. A fear of spreading racial violence was uppermost in the minds of the Tunku and his deputy Tun Abdul Razak, when they decided to expel Singapore from the federation, which was ratified by the Federal Parliament on 9 August, to the consternation of Lee Kuan Yew, who tried to stave it off. An alternative move to depose the Singapore Government had been rejected because of likely opposition from Britain and Australia, which played major roles in Malaysia's defence.[29]

---

29. Turnbull, *History of Singapore* 279–85. Chan Heng Chee, *Singapore: The Politics of Survival, 1965–1967* (Singapore 1971) *passim*.

Consequently, Singapore was a small island state forced into independent existence. Lee Kuan Yew publicly wept at the collapse of his dream of the PAP ruling a multi-racial Malaysia. The separation agreement provided for economic, political and foreign policy co-operation between Malaysia and Singapore, and PAP leaders hoped the breach might soon be healed. But competition rather than cooperation was the order of the early days of the relationship as Malaysia erected tariff barriers to protect her own industries and Singapore rejected a defence alliance. Immigration controls also vexed travellers daily crossing the causeway connecting Singapore and Malaya. The island state was forced to find new forms of economic wealth to compensate for the blighted vision of a Malaysian common market. Fortuitously a new source of prosperity was emerging across the Gulf of Thailand in the form of massively increasing US involvement in the conflict in Vietnam.[30]

THE JOHNSON ADMINISTRATION AND VIETNAM

Lyndon Johnson, who stepped into the shoes of the assassinated Kennedy, was a Texas politician and masterful manipulator of Senate votes before he was chosen as Kennedy's presidential running mate in the 1960 election campaign to give the Democratic ticket a Southern sectional balance. From the outset of his presidency, Johnson declared that the US was 'not going to lose Vietnam' and see 'Southeast Asia go the way China did'.[31] The Democratic Party's 'loss of China' memory influenced him as much as Kennedy. Johnson also had Kennedy's confidence in American wealth and know-how to defeat communist insurgencies. Nor did the big majority of the advisers he inherited from Kennedy provide any convincing reasons to go against his political judgement.[32]

An alternative to the Vietnam conflict was being advocated by the ARVN junta which now controlled the GVN, headed by General Duong Van Minh, a French-trained officer who had become an opponent of Diem. Minh and his fellow junta leaders considered

---

30. Turnbull, *History of Singapore* 288–93.
31. *UGVW* II, 209.
32. Ball, *Vietnam-on-the Potomac* ch. 6.

the main problem with Diem's regime was hostility aroused among the large non-Catholic majority in South Vietnam, which prompted many non-communists to support the NLF. Their solution was to conciliate Buddhists and the powerful Cao Dai and Hoa Hao sects, by freeing their leaders from the imprisonment that had been Diem's response to their opposition, and by supporting their religious activities. The junta moved to win rural support by starting to dismantle the mostly ineffective and hated strategic hamlets. The new leaders opposed any increase in the US military presence and advocated pulling Americans back from battalion level in the ARVN in order to reduce their visibility and so improve the GVN's nationalist credentials. The junta preferred to work towards a negotiated peace rather than to prosecute vigorously an unwinnable war, though Minh publicly opposed a neutral South Vietnam. That declaration was in response to a groundswell of support in South Vietnam for an offer by President Charles de Gaulle of France to assist in negotiations for the neutralization of all the states of Indochina.[33]

Such a prospect was particularly disturbing to the French-trained General Nguyen Khanh, supported by dissident ARVN officers who had been demoted by the junta or who had not received expected rewards. The result was another coup which toppled Minh's regime on 29 January 1964. Khanh gave prior warning of the coup to Lodge, who withheld the information from Minh's government. However, there is no evidence in recently declassified documents that either Lodge or his superiors in Washington conspired in the coup. But the stage had been set for a major escalation of the American effort to defeat the NLF insurgency.[34]

Johnson's decisions to escalate American involvement in Vietnam evolved gradually in a climate of indecision. Since late 1963 military chiefs had been urging a bombing campaign against the DRV in order to deter Hanoi's support for the insurgency in South Vietnam. Johnson was not yet prepared to authorize bombing North Vietnam, but he did sanction in January 1964 an increase in support for covert operations against the DRV and across the borders of Laos and Cambodia to interdict supplies from the North. At the same time, drawing on his domestic political experience, he used the

33. Kahin, *Intervention* 182–92.

34. Lodge to Department of State, 29 Jan. 1964, *FRUS, 1964–1968*, vol. 1: Vietnam 1964 (Washington 1992) 37–9. No evidence of any greater US involvement in the coup is provided in the most recent account of it, *viz* Fredrik Logevall, 'De Gaulle, Neutralization and American Involvement in Vietnam, 1963–1964', *Pacific Historical Review* LXI (1992) 83–7.

Canadian representative on the virtually defunct Indochina Control Commission to offer the DRV a deal that would trade peace for a guarantee of the DRV's borders and no permanent US bases in the South. Hanoi's reply was that the US would have to withdraw all its forces from the RVN and allow the establishment of a neutral regime which would include the NLF. To Washington that proposal was a recipe for a communist takeover, so Johnson approved a draft schedule for bombing the North.

Johnson still hesitated to take the bombing plunge, especially as in the latter half of 1964 he was campaigning as peacemaker in an election campaign against the Republican Party's hawkish Barry Goldwater. But reports were arriving about Khanh's irresolute leadership, and the US's Military Assistance Command Vietnam (MACV) was urging the despatch of more American troops. A *casus belli* emerged conveniently when on 3 August three Vietnamese torpedo boats attacked the US destroyer, *Maddox*, which had arrived in the Gulf of Tonkin one day after South Vietnamese raids against two islands in the gulf. There is doubt that a second attack on *Maddox* on the next evening actually occurred. But it triggered a retaliatory response from Johnson's administration in the shape of air strikes against DRV torpedo boat bases and oil storage installations. Congress also dutifully passed, with only two dissenting votes, the Southeast Asia (Gulf of Tonkin) resolution, which gave the President a free hand to take any measures to repel armed attack on American forces and to protect any state covered by SEATO, including all the nations of Indochina. No congressman inquired whether sending more troops or bombing North Vietnam really would force the NLF to capitulate, as Johnson suggested. In reality, at this stage of the war, the MACV could provide little evidence that the PLAF was depending on men and supplies from the DRV. The few arms seized by the ARVN were its own captured weapons or were leftovers from the first Vietnam War.[35]

Johnson did not use the Gulf of Tonkin incident to endorse a continuous bombing campaign in the DRV. His overnight rise in popularity from 42 to 72 per cent in the Harris opinion poll, for his firm but restrained response to the alleged gulf attack, encouraged restraint. Thereby he was able to campaign as a lover of peace

35. Young, *The Vietnam Wars* ch. 6. *FRUS, 1964–1968*, vol. 1, ch. 8. Cable, *Conflict of Myths* 215–39.

compared with the aggressive Goldwater, whom he trounced in the November 1964 election.[36]

But conditions in Vietnam were deteriorating. Khanh, whose popularity had been sliding, used the Tonkin Gulf affair to assume near-dictatorial powers and to clamp down on civil liberties in expectation of military reprisals against the RVN by the DRV, which did not materialize. He received support from Washington except for pressure to soften the most draconian elements of his proposed new constitution, such as no provisions for elections. But he miscalculated. Angry Buddhist mobs rose in mass protests, which had an anti-American flavour and were vigorously encouraged by the NLF. Though Khanh promised constitutional reforms, continuing popular demonstrations against him provoked American intervention to work out a compromise. Minh and a Catholic leader, General Tran Thien, both Khanh's bitter rivals, were added to the leadership – a triumvirate that would serve until promised elections. The Gulf of Tonkin crisis had led to political instability in the RVN rather than generating any sense of national unity.[37]

Furthermore, PLAF aggression was increasing, as exemplified by a mortar attack on the Bien Hoa airfield on 1 November, which destroyed six US B-57 bombers and killed five US servicemen. Johnson responded to that attack by ordering an interdepartmental working group to prepare submissions about increasing pressure on the DRV. He then chose the softest option of continuing covert attacks on the North and implementing controlled reprisals to PLAF attacks rather than fuller bombing 'squeezes' on North Vietnam.[38]

Hanoi was expecting American escalation of the war. The DRV realized that it could be facing air attacks and even a ground assault from the world's most technologically advanced armed forces. Moreover, US entry into the war could bolster the wobbly Saigon Government sufficiently to protect it from popular dissent or from guerilla assaults. A similar DRV response was needed. It was decided to prepare the North to resist such an attack and to strengthen the NLF in the South by sending there, for the first time, regiments of the People's Army of Vietnam (PAVN). A complicating factor was a decline in Soviet aid to the DRV by 1964. Shipments of heavy

36. Larry Berman, *Planning a Tragedy: The Americanization of the War in Vietnam* (New York 1982) 31–4.
37. Kahin, *Intervention* 227–35. Truong Nhu Tang, *A Vietcong Memoir* (San Diego 1985) 91–2.
38. Berman, *Planning a Tragedy* 34–5. Herring, *America's Longest War* 123–8.

machinery and construction equipment had fallen by half since 1962. A major reason was Vietnam's refusal to side openly with the USSR in the Sino-Soviet dispute, because of Hanoi's wish to turn the rivalry to its own advantage without being sucked into the conflict. China also viewed the DRV's fence-sitting with disfavour and continued only its low level aid and its refusal to support the DRV war effort in South Vietnam. The one bright note for the future was the overthrow of Kruschev in October 1964 and his replacement by the quadrumvirate of Leonid Brezhnev, Alexi Kosygin, Mikhail Sislov and Nikolai Podgorny, who promised to increase aid for the DRV, though the promise did not become reality until February 1965.[39]

In the RVN during 1964 the NLF was increasing its stranglehold on much of the country. Decreased GVN control had been caused by political instability, the counter-effect of political rivalry among ARVN officers, desertion of soldiers from its ranks, and continued reluctance of many units actually to fight the enemy. The best ARVN units were preserved to protect the shaky Saigon Government. As well as employing violence against RVN officials, the NLF implemented land distribution, lower taxation, appointment of local people as village officials, and disbandment of the hated fortified villages. By the end of 1964 all the rural areas of Long An province, which was on the southern side of Saigon, were under NLF control, leaving only the provincial capital and six district towns in GVN hands. The same was largely true of the other provinces surrounding Saigon except Bien Hoa on its eastern flank.[40]

The Johnson Administration did not perceive how far the Saigon regime had lost control of its country. William Bundy explained: 'We didn't think that the threat within South Vietnam on the ground was so serious that the South Vietnamese ground forces couldn't continue to handle it'. So, using as justification an attack on 7 February on Pleiku airfield in the Central Highlands, which killed nine Americans, Johnson decided on 13 February to implement the bombing plan, code-named 'Rolling Thunder'. But the use of RVN airfields for this purpose raised the question of their protection, the paucity of which had been demonstrated at Bien Hoa and Pleiku. Hence, a marine regiment, the first ground troops as distinct from reinforcements for the MACV, arrived in Vietnam six days later to protect Danang air

39. Post, *Revolution, Socialism and Nationalism* III, 324–5. Turley, *Second Indochina War* 57–8. Pike, *Vietnam and the Soviet Union* 56–62, 73–4.

40. Race, *War Comes to Long An* 167. Post, *Revolution, Socialism and Nationalism* IV, 235. Bergerud, *Dynamics of Defeat* 68–84.

base on the northern coast of South Vietnam. They were welcomed by a GVN now firmly in the hands of the military after a further coup in February 1965 had installed another triumvirate: a French-trained air force general, Nguyen Cao Ky, the Buddhist First Army Corps commander, Nguyen Chanh Thi, and a US trained ARVN divisional commander, Nguyen Van Thieu. But Bui Diem has pointed out that there had been no attempt to assess South Vietnamese opinion about the US decisions to send troops to the RVN and to bomb the DRV. 'Had the South Vietnamese been consulted early in 1965', he wrote, 'it is likely that they would have preferred either no intervention or a limited effort to stabilize the military situation'.[41]

The decision to widen the war with Rolling Thunder was not taken lightly by Johnson. He had no blind faith that airpower would win the war. He knew that more troops would have to be sent to protect airfields and to counter the expected arrival of additional PAVN troops. He realized that the necessary increased war expenditure could gravely threaten his first priority – his 'Great Society' social reform programme for the US. But he said later that if he abandoned the war and 'let the Communists take over South Vietnam, then I would be seen as a coward and my nation would be seen as an appeaser, and we would both find it impossible to accomplish anything for anybody anywhere on the entire globe'.[42] The problem was that Eisenhower and Kennedy had laid US prestige on the line in South Vietnam. They also had given that small nation a strategic importance which Johnson accepted without question. Furthermore, his decisions to implement Rolling Thunder and despatch US troops were approved by all members of his Cabinet and followed a series of conversations with congressmen and Democratic Party leaders.[43]

The result was a major escalation of US forces in the RVN. In response to Westmoreland's request for troops to counter a threatened PAVN offensive in the highlands, Johnson announced on 28 July that he was sending another 50,000 soldiers to Vietnam. By the end of 1965 there were 155,000 US ground forces in the RVN, a larger number than French troops in the whole of Vietnam at any time during the First Indochina War. A year later the number of US

41. Interview with W. Bundy, Charlton and Moncrieff, *Many Reasons Why* 20. Kahin, *Intervention* 292–344. Bui Diem with David Chanoff, *In the Jaws of History* (Boston 1987) 338.

42. Doris Keans, *Lyndon Johnson and the American Dream* (New York 1976) 252.

43. Henry F. Graff, *The Tuesday Cabinet: Deliberation on Peace and War under Lyndon B. Johnson* (Englewood Cliffs 1970) 39. Berman, *Planning a Tragedy* ch. 3.

troops in South Vietnam had almost doubled. They reached a peak of 441,000 at the end of 1968, when there were also 95,000 US air force and naval personnel serving in the Vietnam War.[44]

However, American soldiers, with their heavy artillery, helicopter gun ships, napalm, and 'agent orange' to defoliate forests, were not the best means for combatting the NLF insurgency. They undoubtedly saved the Saigon Government from being overwhelmed by the PLAF. But the inrush of Americans encouraged the ARVN, with the exception of airborne battalions and the Saigon marines, to engage the PLAF in combat even less energetically than before. Vann, who had resigned from the army but was back in Vietnam as a US provincial pacification representative, wrote in December 1966: 'I consider the performance of the ARVN to be more disgraceful than ever'. He saw no significant progress in winning the war. The Pentagon's own analysis suggested otherwise. It measured an increase in the 'secure' Vietnamese population from 6.8 million in December 1964 to 11 million in June 1967, with a decrease in that period of NLF-controlled population from 3.3 million to 2.4 million, and also a decline from 6 million to 3.8 million in the number of people in 'contested' areas. However, most of the GVN's gains were caused by people moving into the secure areas, rather than from the small increase in the area under GVN control. Furthermore, even in so-called secure areas, especially at night time, the PLAF had some presence. For example, in 1968 PLAF guerillas enjoyed virtual free movement within most of the twenty-seven square kilometres area of My Thuy Phuong village near the central coast city of Hue, despite the presence nearby of an encampment of American marines.[45]

While the massively increased American military presence and the US army's 'search and destroy' strategy did lead to some decrease in NLF controlled areas, it was not winning the war. American firepower that effectively stemmed the Chinese onslaught in the Korean War was far less successful in combatting elusive PLAF guerillas. Only about 5 per cent of ground assaults by PLAF/PAVN units from 1965 to 1967 were conducted at battalion or greater strength. Most PLAF action consisted of long distance fire, harassment and terrorist attacks. The American creation of free fire zones for bombs

44. R.B. Smith, *An International History of the Vietnam War* vol. 3 *The Making of a Limited War, 1956–66* (Houndmills 1991) ch. 9. Thomas C. Thayer, *War Without Fronts: The American Experience in Vietnam* (Boulder 1985) 37.

45. Sheehan, *Bright Shining Lie* 628. Thayer, *War Without Fronts* 137–43. Wiesner, *Victims and Survivors* ch. 4. Post, *Revolution, Socialism and Nationalism* IV, 333–4. Trullinger, *Village at War* 121–2.

and artillery also was, in Vann's view, counterproductive in terms of destruction of civilian life and property. The experienced General Tran explained that 'the Americans were organized to fight a war in which there are well-defined front lines with relatively secure areas against an enemy, and where the overwhelming fire superiority of American weapons could bring decisive results'. After a visit to the RVN in October 1966, Secretary of Defense Robert McNamara doubted whether the war could 'be brought to a satisfactory conclusion within the next two years'.[46]

The political dimension of the struggle in South Vietnam also meant that battlefield defeat would not necessarily lose the war for the NLF. Tran recognized this dilemma when he acknowledged that the military mission of destroying the enemy's bases and preventing infiltration of his supplies had to be accompanied by a rural reform programme capable of 'winning the support of the populace'. This was a fundamental lesson of the Malayan Emergency and the Huk insurrection in the Philippines. But in Vann's opinion the GVN was incapable of carrying out the necessary social reform because it was 'oriented toward the exploitation of the rural and lower-class population'.[47]

Johnson's Administration did pay some attention to the need for pacification programmes in South Vietnam. Initially it relied on the ARVN to carry them out. But, as McNamara acknowledged, the ARVN 'do not understand the importance (or respectability) of pacification nor the importance . . . of proper, disciplined conduct'. He also admitted that 'bad management on the American' side was 'part of the problem'. However, he thereby committed the error of thinking that improved management was the solution. It arrived in South Vietnam in May 1967 in the shape of the Civil Operations and Rural Development Support programme. This organization circulated propaganda, which at times was composed without reference to Vietnamese customs or circumstances. The food and medicines distributed for villagers often found their way into the hands of corrupt officials. New rural schools and hospitals lacked trained staff to run them. Paramilitary Vietnamese were trained to carry out PLAF-style tactics against NLF villages, but irregular troops

46. Tran, *Our Endless War* 149. Bergerud, *Dynamics of Defeat* 109. Turley, *Second Indochina War* ch. 4. Douglas Pike, *PAVN: People's Army of Vietnam* (Novata 1986) ch. 9. *PP* IV, 253.

47. Tran, *Our Endless War* 117. Thayer, *War Without Fronts*, 25–6. Cable, *Conflict of Myths* 211. Vann quoted in Bergerud, *Dynamics of Defeat* 108.

were peasants who were often left without military support from upper-class ARVN officers and so suffered high casualties.[48]

An improvement to counter-insurgency operations later in 1967 was the Phoenix programme implemented by American-led Vietnamese paramilitary personnel and supported by the CIA. Despite official US denials, Phoenix carried out a large amount of kidnapping, torturing and assassination, though a CIA agent in Hau Nghia province, Orrin DeForest, avers that Phoenix took the credit for the work of the provincial regional force. But people also were killed and kidnapped on the basis of lists compiled by informers, who had other agendas to fulfil when naming alleged supporters of the NLF. One such group was an extreme right wing Vietnamese organization, which arranged in this way to murder Buddhist political opponents. Furthermore, Phoenix was responsible for providing the misinformation that resulted in the massacre by US troops of 400 to 500 men, women and children in the village of My Lai on the northeast coast of South Vietnam on 16 March 1968. Many of the women were raped before they were shot.[49]

Nor did Rolling Thunder serve its purposes of seriously damaging the DRV's war effort and persuading its government to sue for peace. The political restraints imposed on the bombing were a reason. Fear of provoking China kept the bombs thirty miles from the Chinese border. Airfields were off-limits to avoid killing Russian technicians. Haiphong and Hanoi were initially out of bounds to avoid any international outcry about murdering civilians. The earliest targets were military installations and lines of communications mainly south of the 20th latitudinal parallel. There was a month's pause from 27 December 1965 to allow for a Soviet peace initiative, which gave the DRV breathing space. When Hanoi denounced the pause as a sham, the bombing was widened to include oil storage areas, industrial plant and electric power stations; but installations in civilian areas were exempt. The controls on the air campaign also were influenced by Johnson's concern to limit the impact of the war on his Great Society programme.[50]

48. *PP* II, 596. James William Gibson, *The Perfect War: Technowar in Vietnam* (Boston 1986) ch. 8.

49. Douglas Valentine, *The Phoenix Program* (New York 1990) ch. 24, 192 and *passim.* Orrin DeForest and David Chanoff, *Slow Burn: The Rise and Bitter Fall of American Intelligence in Vietnam* (New York 1990) 54–5. Michael Bilton and Kevin Sim, *Four Hours in My Lai* (New York 1992) *passim.*

50. Mark Clodfelter, *The Limits of Air Power: The American Bombing of North Vietnam* (New York 1989) 73–134.

However, a major factor in the limitation of Rolling Thunder was the Second World War basis of the air-force's strategic bombing doctrine, which emphasized attacks on economic infrastructure in order to destroy the DRV's war-making capacity. The manifestly smaller industrial capacity of the DRV made such attacks allegedly more important. But this approach ignored North Vietnam's ability to mobilize manpower to repair damaged communications quickly, to build by-pass roads and to disperse oil reserves. The thick vegetation over much of the country and the frequency of cloudy weather during the monsoon season were aids to hidden transportation and reconstruction. In the DRV by 1968, 35 per cent of oil storage capacity, 41 per cent of power plants and 45 per cent of major bridges had survived the 643,000 tons of bombs dropped by US and RVN planes. The bombing further generated increased imports from China and the USSR to compensate for the American damage. Beijing maintained that 320,000 Chinese were sent to the DRV to support air defence, engineering assistance and repair of damage, though there are doubts about the magnitude of that claim. The Vietnamese war effort, depending on low technology, was only marginally damaged. Even railway engines were powered by coal rather than by the targeted oil. For the North Vietnamese people, many of whom were evacuated from Hanoi and Haiphong, the bombing was of little more than nuisance value, and it encouraged the same spirit of resistance as was exhibited by the people of Britain during the Second World War.[51]

The limits to the effectiveness of Rolling Thunder were most dramatically demonstrated with the NLF Tet offensive, which began on 30 January 1968. Taking advantage of a truce called during the traditional Tet holiday time, 84,000 PLAF troops and popular militia, who had smuggled themselves into most of South Vietnam's provincial and major cities, staged a well coordinated series of attacks. They blew a hole in the wall of the American embassy in Saigon and engaged in a night-long battle with troops landed on the embassy roof by helicopter. The insurgents attacked Saigon's Presidential Palace and the ARVN general staff headquarters. They seized a large sector of Hue, where it has been claimed that 2,800 officials and other supporters of the GVN were massacred while the NLF flag flew above the citadel. However, some of the bodies found in the

---

51. Ibid. 134–46. William J. Duiker, *China and Vietnam: The Roots of Conflict* (Berkeley 1986) 50.

mass graves were victims of South Vietnamese teams which carried out revenge attacks.[52]

The PAVN's Major-General Tran Do admitted: 'We didn't achieve our main objective, which was to spur uprisings throughout the south'.[53] The PAVN had supported the offensive with attacks and threats in border areas, especially besieging a 6,000 strong garrison at Khe Sehn near the DRV border, which provoked Johnson in early mornings to pace White House floors fretting about a second Dien Bien Phu. But the US defenders were easily reinforced. Also, while much of the US army in Vietnam had been drawn out to the frontiers, US and ARVN troops were still able to gain the upper hand over the urban insurgents. However, the efforts to blast the PLAF from the Cholon District in Saigon and from Hue caused many civilian deaths, and throughout the whole country more than half a million South Vietnamese lost their homes. Eleven hundred Americans were killed.[54]

The Tet offensive was a strategic failure for the NLF and the DRV. While the US estimate of the death of 40,000 PLAF and PAVN troops probably was inflated, many died in second and third offensive waves against RVN cities in May and in August-September. The urban South Vietnamese people had not risen to support the insurgents. The Hue massacre, which NLF leader Huyen Tan Phat admitted had been a case of 'seriously inadequate' PLAF discipline, also diminished public support for the NLF. Furthermore, the absence of so many warriors fighting in the towns and cities in the three offensives of 1968 left many NLF hamlets, including My Lai, unprotected against attack by GVN and US forces. In Hau Nghia province, where the presence of an American division in the previous year had only freed main roads during daytime between GVN-held provincial cities, the GVN was able to extend control over most of the province by 1969.[55]

However, the Tet offensive was a watershed in US public attitudes to the Vietnam War. Dramatic television and newspaper pictures – such as MACV commander General William Westmoreland claiming

52. Turley, *Second Indochina War* 106–7. Valentine, *Phoenix Program* 179–80. Young, *The Vietnam Wars* 217–9.

53. Quoted in Olson and Roberts, *Where the Domino Fell* 186.

54. Larry Berman, *Lyndon Johnson's War: The Road to Stalemate in Vietnam* (New York 1989) ch. 9. Keith William Nolan, *The Battle of Hue: Tet, 1968* (Novata 1983). Herring, *America's Longest War* 191. Turley, *Second Indochina War* 97–108.

55. Tang, *Vietcong Memoir* 154. Valentine, *Phoenix Program* 179–92. Bergerud, *Dynamics of Defeat* 205, 215–22.

victory in the compound of the allegedly secure embassy, and of the GVN police commissioner shooting a PLAF prisoner in the head in a Saigon street – were shattering illusions about a winnable war for the glorious cause of freedom. The grisly statistics of American deaths in the offensive reinforced rising resentment at the price paid by the 30,347 Americans who had died in combat in Vietnam by the end of 1968. Already in 1967 there had been a huge demonstration in New York of over 200,000 people protesting against the war and big protest marches in other cities. Resistance by young people to being drafted for the war was spreading. There was a growing disquiet caused by reports and photos of massacres of innocent people by indiscriminate bombing and napalm attacks on Vietnamese villages. The 10 per cent surtax in 1967 for an increasingly expensive war diminished public support for it. After the Tet offensive, a Gallup Poll result published on 10 March revealed that 49 per cent of Americans believed that the US was wrong to have entered the Vietnam War, and only 33 per cent believed that America was making any progress in it. A majority of Johnson's closest advisers now opposed any expansion of the war and advocated more reliance on the ARVN, which had demonstrated surprising resilience and tenacity during the Tet offensive. Johnson then announced publicly his refusal to agree to Westmoreland's call for 206,000 more troops for an offensive strategy across the DRV border. But on 31 March the physically and emotionally exhausted president told the nation that he would not stand for re-election. He also announced a halt to bombing north of the 20th parallel in a search for a negotiated peace, though his government insisted on the preservation of an independent and non-communist RVN.[56]

The months of 1968 after the Tet offensive saw mounting opposition to the Vietnam War with large street demonstrations in American cities. In August the Democratic Party held its national convention in Chicago, while outside the convention hall street battles raged between police and anti-war demonstrators. The administration's search for peace talks did evoke a favourable response from Hanoi if the bombing ceased and if the NLF was included in negotiations for a peaceful settlement of the conflict. Johnson responded by halting all bombing of the DRV on 31 October. This announcement also was aimed at boosting the popularity of the Democratic Party

56. Berman, *Lyndon Johnson's War* ch. 10. Gabriel Kolko, *Vietnam: Anatomy of War 1940–1975* (New York 1985) ch. 25. Herring, *America's Longest War* 171–210. Charles DeBenedetti and Charles Chatfield, *An American Ordeal: The Antiwar Movement of the Vietnam Era* (New York 1990) ch. 203–15.

candidate, Hubert Humphrey, who had been loyally supporting the president's Vietnam policy. But the Republican candidate, Nixon, who had publicly declared the Vietnam War above politics, used private Republican Party connections to support RVN President Thieu's refusal to attend any peace talks in Paris in order to stymie Johnson's peace initiative. The announcement of Thieu's intransigence did deflate a surge of public euphoria about peace prospects before the 5 November election, which Nixon won narrowly, with a mere 0.7 per cent advantage in the popular vote. However, Thieu would have opposed the peace plan without the Republican Party pressure, since the whole rationale of his regime depended on war-based US support. There was also no diminution of US military efforts in South Vietnam; and bombing of suspected DRV transportation routes in Laos continued.[57]

OTHER NATIONS AND THE VIETNAM WAR

Many other countries in the Pacific Basin became actively involved in or were strongly influenced by the Vietnam War. Though this time the US had entered a war without UN sanction, pressure was placed on allies of America to make it a 'free world' crusade against communism. By 1968 there were 65,802 allied military personnel in Vietnam, nearly all from five other Pacific Basin nations: South Korea, Thailand, the Philippines, Australia and New Zealand.[58]

The Australian Government in 1964 was eager to join the contest because of its belief in Chinese complicity in the war and the threat to Australia that would flow from expanding Chinese influence in Vietnam and the rest of Southeast Asia. Sending Australian troops to South Vietnam also was considered an insurance policy for future support from the US, especially if Confrontation developed into a war between Indonesia and Australia. By 1968 Australia had a task force in Phuoc Tuy province, plus an air squadron and a naval destroyer, totalling 7,661 men. Their previous counter-insurgency

57. Ibid. 215–37. Young, *The Vietnam Wars* chs 10–11. Stephen E. Ambrose, *Nixon: The Triumph of a Politician 1962–1972* (New York 1989) 206–22.

58. Stanley Robert Larsen and James Lawton Collins, Jr., *Allied Participation in Vietnam* (Washington 1975) 23.

experience in Malaya and Borneo encouraged the three Australian battalions to operate more effectively at foot patrol level than did the Americans with their abundance of helicopters. Australia also provided economic and technical aid worth over $10.5 million from 1966 through 1968.[59]

New Zealand's contribution of two infantry companies, an artillery battery plus army and air force support personnel, numbered 516 men by 1968. They supported the Australian task force but were little more than a token gesture in response to US pressure for more foreign flags in the RVN. The National Party New Zealand Government had preferred united action by SEATO, which had not been able to come to any agreement about military intervention in South Vietnam. The strong opposition to the military commitment by the New Zealand Labour Party reflected the comparative isolation of the country from Southeast Asia.[60]

Among America's Asian allies, Thailand sent 6,005 men to the RVN by 1968 and was providing pilot training for its air force plus two naval ships to patrol its waters, the cost being paid for by the US. More valuable were the US airfields in Thailand which made major contributions to Rolling Thunder and to American air strikes in Laos and South Vietnam. American bases in the Philippines were important repair stations and staging posts for American ships and planes serving in the war zone. A new president, Ferdinand Marcos, sent in February 1966, at American expense, a 2,061 strong engineering battalion to the RVN. By far the biggest manpower contribution, 50,000 troops, came from South Korea, as repayment for American support during the Korean War and for continued US military protection. Washington, however, rejected Chiang Kai-shek's enthusiastic offer of troops for South Vietnam because of fear of provoking Chinese intervention in the war. Nationalist China provided only some technical and medical assistance. Japan, which remained loyal to its US ally, supplied medical teams and over $50 million worth of economic assistance to South Vietnam. US bases in Japan and Okinawa were also valuable for prosecuting the war.[61]

59. Ian McNeill, 'The Australian Army and the Vietnam War' in Peter Pierce, Jeff Doyle and Jeffrey Grey (eds), *Vietnam Days: Australia and the Impact of Vietnam* (Melbourne 1991) 11–61. Pemberton, *All the Way* ch. 9. Larsen and Collins, *Allied Participation* 88–101.

60. Ibid. 23, 104–10, 116–35. Mark Pearson, *Paper Tiger: New Zealand's Part in SEATO 1954–1977* (Wellington 1989) 95–100.

61. Larsen and Collins, *Allied Participation* 26–42, 52–76, 161–2. Randolph, *United States and Thailand* ch. 3. Thomas R.H. Havens, *Fire Across the Sea: The Vietnam War and Japan 1965–1975* (Princeton 1987) 223.

However, protests against American involvement in Vietnam emerged in Japan after the start of Rolling Thunder. Liberals, socialists, neo-nationalists and politically uncommitted intellectuals joined in public statements and street rallies which tapped widespread anti-war sentiment. The Japanese anti-Vietnam War campaign became violent in October 1967 when helmeted and stave-carrying students, who were protesting against a planned visit by Prime Minister Satō Eisaku to South Vietnam, battled with riot police. This confrontation caused the first death of a Japanese anti-Vietnam War demonstrator. Other riots followed, provoked by incidents such as the first visit of a nuclear-powered American warship to Japan in January 1968; and the tension exploded into widespread violence on a day of national protest on 21 October 1968. Opinion polls showed that a clear majority of Japanese people wanted the Americans to stop using Japanese facilities for the war and to withdraw from Vietnam. But Satō did not budge from supporting the US in recognition of the US defence treaty that allowed Japan to ignore heavy expenditure for self-defence.[62]

Even Canada, while maintaining official neutrality in the Vietnam War, provided significant support for South Vietnam and for the American war effort. Canadian economic assistance to the RVN increased by 250 per cent in 1965–66 to Can.$1,254,700, and rose again to Can.$2,694,000 in 1967–68. The Liberal Party Canadian Government insisted that it was not shipping arms to South Vietnam. In literal terms this statement was true. Canadian arms merely found their way to Vietnam via the US with the full knowledge of government authorities in Ottawa, who actively encouraged their production and sale and even suggested ways around Canada's own arms-export control legislation. A possible reason for this government duplicity was the estimated 125,000 jobs in Canada that had some relationship to the arms sales. Also about 10,000 Canadian volunteers joined the US army in South Vietnam.[63]

On the other side of the Vietnam War, the Soviet Union, after Kruschev's fall, became a major supporter of the DRV. A visit by Kosygin to Hanoi in February 1965 sealed the new relationship with the signing of a defence pact between the USSR and the DRV. The USSR condemned the American bombing of North Vietnam as a violation of the rules of the Cold War and declared its duty to give full support to North Vietnam's defence capability. Washington breathed

62. Ibid. chs 2–6.
63. Victor Levant, *Quiet Complicity: Canadian Involvement in the Vietnam War* (Toronto 1986) 68–78, 210–11, chs 6, 11–12.

a sigh of relief that the criticism was so relatively mild. Indeed, Moscow's main motive in supporting the DRV was to gain a march on China. The USSR launched a worldwide propaganda campaign against American war-mongering, but Washington interpreted correctly that there was no prospect of any Soviet military intervention in Vietnam. As demonstrated in the 1962 Cuba missile crisis, the Soviet Government was anxious to avoid the possibility of a nuclear war with the US. The USSR also appears not to have expected a DRV victory. Hence there were Soviet offers to mediate for peace, starting with the one that prompted the US bombing pause of December 1965. However, an alternative view advanced by János Radványi, the Hungarian Chargé d'Affaires in Washington at the time and a later defector to the US, was that Moscow was merely buying time for the DRV and was happy to see the US waste men and money in Vietnam. Indeed, Soviet materiel support for the DRV was significant. Soviet military aircraft and air defence systems accompanied by Russian military and technical advisers gave North Vietnam the capacity to shoot down US aircraft. Soviet artillery, machine guns and modern rifles gave the PAVN more fighting power. Soviet trucks, railway stock and telegraphic equipment assisted DRV communications. Such aid allowed a diversion of DRV resources for prosecuting the war, as did a wide range of other supplies, including food and fuel. USSR goods shipped through Haiphong rose from 500,000 metric tonnes in 1965 to two million metric tonnes in 1967. There was also extensive training of Vietnamese military and civilian personnel in the USSR.[64]

China was a less enthusiastic supporter of the DRV. Hanoi later complained that Beijing welcomed the American military expansion in South Vietnam to prevent a DRV victory there and charged China with opposing peace negotiations, so that North Vietnam would be weakened by protracted warfare. Chinese military advisers also were said to have opposed large-scale PAVN attacks and supplied only light weapons and ammunition. Such accusations were made at the time of the Sino-Vietnamese war in 1979 and may have been largely propaganda. The Chinese insistence on the DRV fighting a protracted war could also have been aimed at tying down the US in a long struggle that would preclude any potential Sino-American confrontation. However, other evidence supports the case that China

64. Pike, *Vietnam and the Soviet Union* 72–122. János Radványi, *Delusion and Reality: Gambits, Hoaxes, & Diplomatic One-Upmanship in Vietnam* (South Bend 1978) *passim*.

was a lukewarm supporter of the DRV. Chinese troops were sent to North Vietnam, but only to protect the railway line from China to Hanoi over which China sent food and other aid, which in total was only about a quarter as much as the aid flowing to the DRV from the Soviet Union and Eastern Europe. Beijing loudly denounced the USSR's refusal to send military forces to assist the DRV, while making sure that no Chinese troops became involved in the fighting. The long shadow of the Korean War influenced Mao Zedong's caution. His political opponents called for joint China–USSR action to fight American imperialists in Vietnam, but they were suppressed in the Great Proletarian Cultural Revolution, which broke out in May 1966.[65]

Whether the Beijing leadership wanted the DRV to win the war or not, it is clear that the Kennedy and Johnson Administrations were overreacting to any threat of Chinese expansionism in Southeast Asia. Indeed, this fact was gradually being appreciated in Washington, so that by 1966 Johnson stopped talking about Chinese involvement in the war and started informal talks with Chinese officials in Warsaw. Ironically, the Vietnam War was encouraging the small beginnings of a later rapprochement between the US and China.[66]

A by-product of the war, which has been claimed to have influenced improvements in US relations with China and Russia, was the capture on the high seas by North Korea on 23 January 1968 of the USS *Pueblo*. The humiliating capture of a ship of the world's largest navy by one of the world's smallest prompted talk by members of Johnson's Administration of declaring war on North Korea. It had used the distraction of the Vietnam War for provocations against the ROK, the latest being an attempt on 21 January by a DPRK commando squad to assassinate President Pak Chung-hee. But the National Security Agency had not informed the US Cabinet that the *Pueblo* had originally been designed to yield to North Korean captors a code machine which, when used by them, would allow the US to break the USSR codes used by the PAVN. When the *Pueblo* unwittingly intercepted a Soviet message about plans to attack China and returned to Japan, the NSA sent the ship back with misinformation circulated to Moscow and Peking that it still carried the intercepted message. Consequently, the *Pueblo* was seized by a boat-load of Chinese soldiers, and then was fired upon by a

65. Pike, *Vietnam and the Soviet Union* 72, 77–82, 86–9. Thien, *Foreign Politics* 125–8. Eugene K. Lawson, *The Sino-Vietnamese Conflict* (New York 1984) ch. 2. Duiker, *China and Vietnam* 48–51.
66. Chang, *Friends and Enemies* 253–75.

Soviet warship in a vain attempt to stop it falling into Chinese hands. When no message was found, the *Pueblo* was handed over to the DPRK, which used the rigged code machine and allowed the US to break the PAVN's code. Consequently, MACV in Saigon received a prior inkling of the Tet offensive, but not of its surprising extent, while the *Pueblo's* crew languished for eleven months in North Korean prisons. However, the wider claims that the Kremlin called off a pending attack on China, that the incident encouraged Beijing to seek a détente with the US, and that the USSR, weakened by the perceived need to revamp its intelligence services, also sought better relations with the US, need verification from as yet unrevealed Chinese and Soviet sources.[67]

Japan was a major beneficiary from the Vietnam War. It provided a base for an estimated 40,000 American troops during the war and served a greater number of Americans on rest and recreation leave, all of whom contributed to the Japanese economy. Japan's exports to South Vietnam boomed from about $35 million per year before 1965 to $199 million in 1968. Some of the exports were American procurements, but South Vietnam's American-injected wealth attracted a host of Japanese consumer goods. Japan further benefited from the increased buying power of other Southeast Asian states, which also were experiencing a Vietnam War-driven economic boom. The year 1965 was a turning point for the entry of Japanese capital into Southeast Asia, which by 1969 was worth $355 million. The Vietnam War assisted Japan's gross national product (GNP) to climb back to the levels of the 1950s from a low of 4 per cent per annum in 1965 to 14 per cent per annum in 1968. That year's GNP of $141.9 billion moved Japan past West Germany into second place behind the US, though the Japanese per capita GNP was only about half that of West Germany and one-third of the American level.[68]

The other East Asian non-communist economies started to experience accelerated growth rates under the influence of the trade boom generated by the Vietnam War. South Korea was well placed to take advantage of increased trading opportunities as a result of a military coup in 1961, which overthrew Rhee, who displayed little interest in economics and presided over a country still suffering from

67. Robert A. Liston, *The Pueblo Surrender: A Covert Action by the National Security Agency* (New York 1988) 1–25, 61, 234–43.

68. Havens, *Fire Across the Sea* 103–5. *The Far East and Australasia: A Survey and Directory of Asia and the Pacific* (London 1969–) (*FEA*) 1969, 709; 1970, 779.

the ravages of war and dependency on US aid. The new president, Pak, placed a priority on economic development, inaugurating fiscal reform and emphasizing expansion of exports by freeing them from restrictive regulations. With the assistance of the Vietnam War trade boom, the ROK's exports of goods and services, at prices adjusted for inflation, rose from 57.06 billion won in 1964 to 235.03 billion in 1968. This era marked the beginnings of the South Korean 'economic miracle'. Taiwan also enjoyed an export-led economic boom that started earlier in the 1960s as a result of economic reforms centring on export incentives, but which received a fillip from the Vietnam War. Taiwan's exports rose from NT$17.998 billion in 1965 to NT$31.567 billion in 1968.[69]

The general growth of trade generated by the Vietnam War also was benefiting Hong Kong. The colony experienced a five-fold growth in the value of its manufacturing, which was diversifying from its textiles base into electronic and other goods and which contributed to 80 per cent of the colony's exports by 1969. Whereas in 1951 there were 2,000 factories in Hong Kong supporting 95,000 workers, by 1966 there were 10,413 factories employing 635,000. But there had not been commensurate increases in personal wealth for many of Hong Kong's people, who had swollen in number to 3.7 million in 1966. That year protests over increased ferry fares boiled over into two nights of ugly rioting. There was a four-month-long period of rioting in 1967 emerging from an industrial dispute that became a left wing challenge, influenced by the cultural revolution in China, to the paternalistic British Hong Kong administration.[70]

In Southeast Asia a new cooperative arrangement was developing in the wake of the international turmoil in that region. On 8 August 1967 the foreign ministers of Indonesia, the Philippines, Singapore and Thailand and the deputy prime minister of Malaysia signed in Bangkok an agreement to establish an Association of Southeast Asian Nations (ASEAN). The main objectives of ASEAN were to promote economic growth, to foster social and cultural relations and to preserve peace among its members. Provision was made for an annual meeting of foreign ministers and for a standing committee,

---

69. Paul W. Kuznetz, *Economic Growth and Structure in the Republic of Korea* (New Haven 1977) 90–2, 220. Rong-I Wu, 'The Distinctive Features of Taiwan's Development' in Peter L. Berger and Hsin-Huang Michael Hsiao, *In Search of an East Asian Developmental Model* (New Brunswick 1990) 179–96. Samuel S. Ho, *Economic Development of Taiwan, 1860–1970* (New Haven 1978) 198, 392.

70. Geiger and Geiger, *Development Progress of Hong Kong* 78–9. Felix Patrikeeff, *Mouldering Pearl: Hong Kong at the Crossroads* (London 1989) 43–51.

but there was no permanent secretariat. Though accused by China of being an anti-communist league, ASEAN had no pretensions to be a defensive alliance or to project military power. However, Indonesia's foreign minister, Adam Malik, commented 'it was the fact that there was a convergence in the political outlook of the five prospective member-nations . . . which provided the main stimulus to join together in ASEAN'. Indeed, the idea grew out of Thailand's facilitating of the agreement between Malaysia and Indonesia to end Confrontation. A forerunner to ASEAN was the concept of Maphilindo promoted by the Philippines, prior to Confrontation, in an unsuccessful attempt attempt to resolve diplomatic disputes involving the formation of Malaysia. In 1968 there was a suspension of ASEAN meetings when the Philippines reactivated claims to Sabah, with a consequent disruption of diplomatic relations between Kuala Lumpur and Manila. This dispute demonstrated the early fragility of ASEAN, but it was to be resolved in 1969.[71]

CONCLUSIONS

The Western Pacific Basin in 1968 was therefore a mixture of international conflict and cooperation. The US and its Asian and Australasian allies were locked in a bitter conflict with the NLF in South Vietnam and North Vietnam, supported by the USSR and less enthusiastically by China. The Johnson and Kennedy Administrations had continued Eisenhower's policy of supporting South Vietnam, which was propped up from the beginning by US aid. The US takeover of the war effort in 1965 was partially a repetition of the Korea experience with the development of a similar military stalemate. However, a fundamental difference was that in Vietnam there was a mainly guerilla conflict rather than a conventional war, and there was a failure in Washington to understand the strength of home-grown support for the NLF, resulting in inadequate pacification programmes.

The Vietnam War had other major Pacific Basin consequences. The massively increased US war effort in Vietnam was generating major

---

71. Roger Irvine, 'The Formative Years of ASEAN: 1967–1975' in Alison Broinowski (ed.), *Understanding ASEAN* (London 1983) 8–20 (quotation 14).

economic growth in Japan and in the emerging East Asian economies of South Korea, Taiwan, Hong Kong and Singapore. The war was also boosting Japanese economic expansion in East and Southeast Asia. ASEAN was a new venture in Southeast Asian cooperation after the failure of Sukarno's military confrontation of Malaysia. Bases had been established for major future economic growth in the Western Pacific Basin. Furthermore, there were signs of future rapprochements between the US and China and the US and the Soviet Union that were to have a tremendous future effect on international relations in the whole of the Pacific Basin.

CHAPTER FOUR

Détente, Disengagement and Invasion in East and Southeast Asia, 1969–1979

The main theme of this chapter is the way the new US Administration sought to disengage from the Vietnam War and how the process included the beginnings of a new détente between the US and China plus improvements in US-Soviet relations that were to have a profound influence on weakening the impact of the Cold War in the Pacific Basin. Another theme is how new conflicts in the Indochina part of the Western Pacific rim were to emerge after the US disengagement. Another subject is how the withdrawal of one of the last small vestiges of European colonialism in the Southwestern Pacific Basin caused an Indonesian invasion and subsequent war in East Timor. Economic growth in the Western Pacific Basin is further discussed, including the beginnings of future economic conflict between Japan and the US.

SEARCHING FOR AN END TO THE VIETNAM WAR

The Vietnam War was one of the most pressing concerns facing Nixon when he became the US president in January 1969. He and his special adviser in national security affairs, Henry Kissinger, a German-born political science professor and government international affairs consultant, realized that no military victory was feasible, given the strength of the anti-war movement in the US. Determined to make their mark in history, they refused to contemplate a 'dishonorable' withdrawal, which could leave them open to the accusation of 'losing

117

Vietnam' to communism. Nixon had been prominent in such attacks on the Truman Administration's China policy. Furthermore, as new administrators of the awesome power of the US, Nixon and Kissinger believed they could pressure Hanoi into agreeing to a peace that would preserve the integrity of the RVN. However, they also saw the iridescent anti-Vietnam War writing on US political walls and were determined to commence a process of withdrawal of American troops from Vietnam. Hence the Nixon Administration supported increasing the size and power of the ARVN, so that it could eventually defend a non-communist South Vietnam; a policy known as Vietnamization, which had commenced under the Johnson Administration in 1968. But initially Nixon did not publicly announce any plan to withdraw troops from Vietnam.[1]

On the diplomatic front, Nixon and Kissinger secretly proposed to Hanoi, through French intermediaries, a mutual US-DRV troop withdrawal from South Vietnam. But they also wished to project an image of American toughness by demonstrating their willingness to remove constraints imposed on the US war effort by Johnson. So, they secretly implemented Operation Menu, which extended the bombing campaign to Cambodia. The main military targets were PLAF sanctuaries and a reported NLF command structure, the Central Committee Directorate for South Vietnam (COSVN).[2]

Since achieving independence in 1954, Cambodia had been walking on a neutral tightrope under its leader, Prince Norodom Sihanouk. Born in 1922 and ruler of his country since 1941, he was a flashy potentate, who boasted of his sexual prowess. But he was also an intelligent and shrewd politician, whose overriding aim was to preserve his country's independence. His refusal to join SEATO and his rejection of American pressure to suppress communists, engendered hostile relations with the US. Consequently, American money for military and economic aid was used to win support for the US among army officers and the social elite. This undermined their loyalty to Sihanouk. The prince, who considered that Hanoi would win the war in South Vietnam, in 1964 rejected US aid and expelled American citizens. In the next year he broke diplomatic relations with the US after *Newsweek* accused his family of running brothels in the capital city, Phnom Penh. More fundamentally, he was protesting at the arrival of the first American ground troops in South Vietnam. The

1. Ambrose, *Nixon* 2, 256–8.
2. William Shawcross, *Sideshow: Kissinger, Nixon and the Destruction of Cambodia* (New York 1981) ch. 1.

US army's 'search and destroy' strategy forced PLAF units to seek shelter in Cambodia, which Sihanouk tolerated. He also submitted to Chinese pressure in 1966 to use the port of Sihanoukville as a source of supply for the PLAF. His 6,557,000 subjects in 1968 lacked power to resist such pressures. The US, in turn, had been launching covert sabotage operations inside Cambodia, and there were haphazard US artillery and air attacks across the border.[3]

Starved of military supplies and accusing China of supporting communist Khmer Rouge rebels in his country, Sihanouk turned back to the US in 1967. One result was a visit to Phnom Penh in January 1968 by the US ambassador in India, Chester Bowles. The Nixon Administration later claimed that Sihanouk gave Bowles the green light for Operation Menu. This is very doubtful, given that the purpose of Bowles's Mission was to smooth relations between the two countries, including the easing of Cambodian fears about American 'hot pursuit' of NLF insurgents across the Cambodian border.[4]

The inappropriately named Operation Menu, which in the next fifteen months dropped over 100,000 tons of bombs on Cambodia, did not achieve its aim of frightening the DRV into offering negotiating concessions. COSVN had reacted to the debilitating failure of its Tet offensive by reducing large-scale military actions in South Vietnam. Though there was another offensive during Tet in 1969, it was carried out mainly by small units. Battalion or greater size attacks on US/ARVN forces declined from 126 in 1968 to 34 in 1969, the lowest rate since 1964. However, small-scale attacks and other terrorist activities did not diminish in number, which represented COSVN's switching of strategy back to the 'swarm of gnats' technique of destabilizing the enemy. This strategic change demonstrated the versatility of the PAVN/PLAF war machine, which could suffer a major military defeat in the 1968 Tet offensive and still actively survive, despite serious losses of manpower. Hanoi therefore had no military reason to seek a compromise peace, especially because the Tet offensive had delivered a major political victory by boosting the anti-war movement in the US. North Vietnam could confidently expect that the US would be the first side to capitulate in an ongoing war. Nixon and Kissinger therefore learned from Hanoi that the only

3. Ibid. ch. 3. *FEA* 1971, 422–7.
4. Shawcross, *Sideshow* ch. 4.

condition for peace would be a total US withdrawal from South Vietnam and abandonment of the Thieu Government.[5]

Hanoi was buttressed in its rejection of US peace initiatives by increased Soviet military materiel. A major reason was Moscow's fear of a US-China rapprochement. Nixon had early signalled that he would be seeking better relations with China, whereas the Sino-USSR dispute had intensified to the level of armed conflict along the Ussuri River on Manchuria's eastern border. Moscow responded to the threat of a US-China détente by sending more troops and equipment to Chinese border regions and by bolstering the DRV, with the aim of making it dangerous for the US to withdraw from Vietnam. The Kremlin hoped that maintenance of a large US army in Vietnam would deter improvements in Sino-American relations, an ironical contrast to the claims of anti-peace movement conservatives in the US.[6]

However, Nixon and Kissinger realized the need to convince the American public that they genuinely sought peace. So on 29 April 1969 Nixon announced that during the next twelve months 150,000 men would be withdrawn from Vietnam in concert with improving the ARVN. In May he publicly revealed his peace initiatives to the DRV. In June, after a conference with Thieu on Midway Island in mid-Pacific, Nixon announced the evacuation of the first 25,000 US troops from South Vietnam.[7]

Nevertheless, anti-war protesters were soon disillusioned by the absence of any announced progress in US-DRV negotiations. The planned troop withdrawal was soon condemned as much too slow. On 15 October tens of thousands marched and attended teach-ins in American cities in a 'Moratorium' day of protest. Nixon, already showing intolerance of dissent by authorizing FBI surveillance and legal harassment of left wing organizations, went on a counter-offensive with an organized pro-Administration campaign. Especially effective was a nationally televised address on 3 November, in which he plucked his audience's patriotic heart strings, dismissed the anti-war movement as a noisy minority and appealed for the support of the 'great silent majority' of Americans. This speech regained for him the

5. Thayer, *War Without Fronts* 44–5. Pike, *PAVN* 226–8. Lawson, *Sino-Vietnamese Conflict* 122. Turley, *Second Indochina War* 124–7.

6. F. Charles Parker IV, *Vietnam: Strategy for a Stalemate* (New York 1989) 231–2. Chang, *Friends and Enemies* 276–7.

7. Herring, *America's Longest War* 225–6.

political initiative. A Gallup Poll soon declared that 77 per cent of American people were supporting the President's Vietnam policy.[8]

The Vietnamization policy had resulted by 1970 in a growth of the ARVN, including marine corps, from 311,000 in 1967 to 429,000. Including air, naval and irregular forces, the RVN had nearly a million men under arms. A huge stock of US arms also had been handed over, and many US troops were pulled out of large-scale offensive operations to join the ARVN in an accelerated pacification programme.[9]

However, relations between US troops and Vietnamese people were bedevilled by racism and cultural arrogance. A feature of the closer contact was the often contemptuous American attitude towards the ARVN, which many US soldiers regarded as reluctant to fight and a threat to the safety of Americans. The US troops brought with them a 'civic action' programme to South Vietnamese villages aimed at improving agricultural production, education and other facilities. But too many Americans regarded Vietnamese, especially peasants, as subhuman, calling them 'gooks', 'dinks' and other derogatory names. The consequent arrogant and at times brutal behaviour of the soldiers, who also were becoming disillusioned with withdrawal from active fighting and disaffected by the peace movement at home, was counter-productive. In My Thuy Phuong village, which in 1968 experienced the establishment of the US 101st Air-borne Division 'Camp Eagle' on its boundary, villagers had few good words for the aid programmes.[10]

Furthermore, there were still grave inadequacies in the quality of the ARVN and popular forces. ARVN officers continued to be drawn mainly from the urban elite. Corruption was rife in promotions and even in the supply of basic services to poorly paid troops. The popular forces, on which village security mostly depended, were even less effective. A study of their operations in Hau Nghia province during 1970 concluded that a very large percentage of contacts with insurgents were made by a very small percentage of the province's 33 regional and 77 popular force units. In My Thuy Phuong village few popular force soldiers could shoot straight; most preferred to stay in base and could not be trusted to stay awake on guard duty. A fundamental morale weakness was summed up by a villager's

8. DeBenedetti and Chatfield, *An American Ordeal* 238–61.

9. Turley, *Second Indochina War* 128–30.

10. Bergerud, *Dynamics of Defeat* 223–34. Wiesner, *Victims and Survivors* 356. Trullinger, *Village at War* 138–9.

comment: 'How could the Regional Forces be good? None of the soldiers wanted to fight and die for Mr. Thieu'.[11]

There were members of Thieu's administration who advocated reforms in order to create wider popular support, and also to counter a growing view in the US that the GVN was a corrupt autocracy unworthy of the blood and treasure that the US had poured out to save it. The RVN ambassador to the US, Bui Diem, sent a stream of such advice in his regular correspondence with Saigon, reinforcing it on a home visit in July 1970. His complaint was that he did not receive enough US support because: 'The real problem was that South Vietnamese corruption and political reforms were simply not high on the American list of priorities'. Thieu was prompted to redress some of the worst errors of the Diem regime with a return to local election of village officials, and in 1970 he launched a 'land for the tillers' programme. But such efforts had little impact on peasant opinion. Capable villagers were unwilling to stand for office. Nor did the new village councils have sufficient authority to break the power of the often corrupt provincial chiefs. Also in Hau Nghia province the PLAF did not attempt to disrupt village elections, an indication of their low threat to the influence of the People's Revolutionary Government (PRG), as the NLF called itself from 1969. The land reform in that province had limited impact. Much of the government land distributed to landless peasants was soon abandoned because of continuing guerilla warfare, and the GVN land reform paled into insignificance compared with previous NLF land redistribution.[12]

Thieu also in 1971 destroyed much of his credibility by using CIA money, Phoenix Program assassinations and voting instructions to provincial chiefs to convince political opponents that there was no point in standing against him in that year's presidential election. Bui Diem regarded the consequent one-man election as 'a point of no return, at which the search for a vivifying national purpose was finally discarded in favor of the chimerical strength of an autocrat'.[13]

The GVN had benefited from a short breathing space in its struggle with the PRG. The failed offensive strategy in 1968, and a continued bleeding of PRG resources during the lower-level attacks of 1969, placed the insurgent cause on a back foot. In both Long An and Hau Nghia provinces, which were considered of high strategic importance for the RVN because they surrounded the southern and western sides

11. Ibid. 169–70. Bergerud, *Dynamics of Defeat* 294–5.
12. Ibid. 268–72, 298–300. Bui Diem, *In the Jaws of History* 277.
13. Ibid. 293. Young, *The Vietnam Wars* 264–6.

of Saigon, GVN influence extended dramatically under the impact of US army action at village level. In Long An surrenders of PLAF members rose dramatically in March-April 1969 and remained high into 1970, when US intelligence calculated 427 surviving insurgents in the province. In Hau Nghia PLAF units had retreated into jungle hideouts or into Cambodian sanctuaries. Local recruiting for the PLAF also had fallen off, forcing reinforcement by PAVN troops.[14]

However, communist influence in the RVN had not been eliminated. A major reason was the flexible small cell basis of PRG organization and the way many of its members blended into the community, including serving in GVN popular militia and police. In Hau Nghia intensive Phoenix hunting of PRG personnel was bedevilled by inadequacy of information, by GVN police corruption and by PLAF retaliatory assassinations. Thus during 1970 in South Vietnam, while battalion-sized attacks on US/ARVN forces dramatically declined to thirteen, smaller unit attacks fell only to 3,526 from 3,578 the year before.[15]

An American-GVN response to continuing insurgent aggression was a joint US-ARVN invasion of the NLF's Cambodian sanctuaries in April 1970. A green light for this campaign was shone by a new regime in Cambodia which overthrew Sihanouk on 18 March. The coup was led by Lieutenant-General Lon Nol, a French-educated former minister for national defence, who had been appointed as Sihanouk's prime minister in January 1970. Sihanouk, who was visiting Europe at the time of the coup, blamed the CIA for organizing it. Nixon and Kissinger claimed they were surprised to hear of the coup, but if so, their administration had been ignoring intelligence reports. Furthermore, Nixon on the next day was issuing instructions 'for maximum assistance to pro-US elements in Cambodia'. There were good reasons for Washington to support a coup. Operation Menu had failed in its objectives. Sanctuaries for NLF forces were still being used, and COSVN had not been destroyed. Nor had Sihanouk, in Washington's opinion, done enough to expel the PLAF. A CIA agent in Saigon at the time, Frank Snepp, says that his agency and the MACV believed that Lon Nol 'would welcome the United States with open arms and we would accomplish everything'.[16]

14. Race, *War Comes to Long An* 269. Bergerud, *Dynamics of Defeat* 251–4.

15. Ibid. 255–61, 313–5. Thayer, *War Without Fronts* 44.

16. Henry Kissinger, *The White House Years* 465. Snepp quoted in Shawcross, *Sideshow* 115.

The Cambodian invasion was a poisoned chalice for Cambodians and for Nixon. The much sought after COSVN prize was never found. The invasion's main result was to drive PLAF forces deeper into Cambodia. When the US troops pulled out, the ARVN engaged in an orgy of indiscriminate violence and looting of the civilian population. In Beijing Sihanouk formed a government in exile containing members of the Khmer Rouge, who now were receiving support from Hanoi and China. The invasion of Cambodia thereby gave a major push to Cambodia's roller-coaster ride to the abyss of mass destruction. In the US, the Cambodian invasion served to reignite the anti-war movement, especially on university campuses, resulting in the killing on 4 May of four students at Kent State University in Ohio by national guardsmen. Even Cabinet members protested, resulting in the sacking of Secretary for the Interior Warren Hickel. The new wave of anti-war anger was feeding the growth of a siege mentality in the White House that was to lead to the destruction of Nixon's presidency.[17]

The Nixon Administration, however, was continuing its phased evacuation of troops from South Vietnam. By the end of 1969 a withdrawal of 90,000 army, air force and naval personnel had been authorized; further major reductions occurred in the next two years. By the end of 1971 the US army and marine corps had shrunk to 120,600 plus 37,000 air and naval personnel. US combat deaths also had dropped dramatically from 14,592 in 1968 to 1,380 in 1971.[18]

The major reduction in US forces and casualties in Vietnam helped to quieten the American peace movement. There was a small bout of protests after the ARVN was sent on a disastrous incursion into Laos in February 1971. There was a major anti-war public campaign in late April-early May with an encampment in Washington of Vietnam Veterans Against the War and the arrival in that city of thousands of others to declare their opposition to the war. Military-style police action against these protesters after 1 May, including mass arrests, deterred future potential demonstrators. The violence of the college protests in 1971, which had included the torching of buildings, had created an anti-demonstration backlash among many students. The winding down of the hated draft, which finally ended in January 1972, also decreased much personal anger with the war. Nixon was

17. Shawcross, *Sideshow* ch. 10. Turley, *Second Indochina War* 134-5. Young, *The Vietnam Wars* 245-50.

18. Thayer, *War Without Fronts* 37-8, 107.

spared from living out his apocalyptic vision of 'a thousand incoherent hippies urinating on the Oval Office rug'.[19]

Nixon, however, had further reasons to be aggrieved with opponents of the Vietnam War. In July 1971 the *New York Times* started publishing excerpts from 7,000 pages of a secret Defense Department dossier and supporting documents about the war, the *Pentagon Papers*. These extracts revealed the duplicity of many of the statements of the Kennedy and Johnson Administrations about the escalation of US military involvement in Vietnam, and exposed the US role in supporting the RVN's breaking of the 1954 Geneva Agreements. An enraged Nixon sought a Supreme Court order against their publication, but he was overruled. Obsessed with a perception that leaks from his government might become a deluge that would politically drown him, Nixon authorized the formation of a group of 'plumbers' to take preventive action, employing illegal phone taps, surveillance, infiltration of 'enemy' groups and even burglary. Nixon thereby primed a political time bomb that was later to blast him from office.[20]

Furthermore, despite diminishing street protests, a majority of Americans had become demoralized about the war. An opinion poll in November recorded that 65 per cent of respondents considered the war was 'morally wrong'. Encouraging this view was a national controversy over the sentencing on 31 March 1971 of Lieutenant Calley to life imprisonment for murdering at least twenty-two of the many more Vietnamese victims at My Lai in 1968. Many Americans justifiably considered he was a scapegoat for a much wider disorder in the American army in Vietnam. A hundred disillusioned young Vietnam veterans publicly testified for three days at a Detroit motel about many rapes, tortures and murders of Vietnamese civilians by American soldiers that they had participated in or had witnessed.[21]

The Nixon Administration, however, was still hoping to preserve a non-Communist RVN. It was relying on the Vietnamization programme with continued US air support. Nixon and Kissinger also were working towards an international agreement to impose a Korea-style solution upon Vietnam.

19. Melvin Small, *Johnson, Nixon and the Doves* (New Brunswick 1988) ch. 7. Nixon quoted in Benjamin F. Schemmer, *The Raid* (London 1977) 164.

20. *The Pentagon Papers as Published by The New York Times* (New York 1971) ix–xi. DeBenedetti, *An American Ordeal* 314–5.

21. Ibid. 318. Young, *The Vietnam Wars* 255–6.

US MOVES TOWARDS CHINA AND THE USSR

A key to this diplomatic game was improving US relations with Beijing. Prior to Nixon's election, some Republican Party leaders showed a willingness to sink the party's previous implacable hostility to Communist China. Their eight year period out of office, and their freedom from the 'loss of China' spectre that haunted the Democrats, gave them an ability to face new strategic realities. Nixon was one of them. He confessed later that he had not appreciated the Sino-Soviet split until 1966, but then he publicly argued that the US should reassess its China policy, though maintaining 'a policy of firm restraint'. In his first news conference as president in 1969 he struck a new foreign policy note by expressing an interest in any changes in Chinese government attitudes. Beijing responded positively. There were good diplomatic reasons for China to seek an accommodation with the US. Beijing had condemned, more vehemently than Western nations, the Soviet invasion of Czechoslovakia. Brezhnev's proclamation of the right of the USSR to intervene in the affairs of socialist countries was ominous for China. In March 1969 the first of a series of armed clashes between USSR and Chinese forces on the Sino-Soviet border reflected the freezing of relations between the two nations. However, Beijing's initial approach to Washington was pursued very cautiously because of disputes about such a radical step within the Chinese Government. The US made the running in a gradual process that led to a secret visit by Kissinger to Beijing in July 1971. Two months later, dissension inside China came to a head with a failed plot to assassinate Mao Zedong and a subsequent massive purge of dissidents. The dramatic breakthrough occurred in February 1972 with Nixon's triumphant visit to China, the first by an American president.[22]

Nixon and Kissinger were also able to exploit Sino-Soviet tensions in their relations with the leaders of the USSR. According to a high-ranking Soviet defector, Arkady Shevchenko, Washington firmly turned down a discreet Soviet enquiry about US support for a Soviet attack on China's nuclear facilities, which had been producing

---

22. Chang, *Friends and Enemies* 281–90. Alexander, *The Strange Connection* ch. 19. Richard M. Nixon, 'Asia After Viet Nam', *Foreign Affairs* 46, 1967, 123. Seymour M. Hersh, *Kissinger: The Price of Power. Henry Kissinger in the Nixon White House* (London 1983) chs 26–7. Richard Nixon, *In the Arena: A Memoir of Victory, Defeat, and Renewal* (New York 1990) 11–15.

atomic bombs since 1964. But the USSR's concern about a US–China détente, and a need for grain imports from America, prompted the Kremlin to invite Nixon to Moscow in May 1972. Nixon was delighted to be the first American president to visit the Soviet capital city and returned with agreements to foster trade and scientific cooperation, a pledge of peaceful co-existence and a commitment to further talks on arms reduction. In Gromyko's view this détente was a case of 'a more realistic posture' by Washington in recognition that 'Soviet military strength [had] achieved parity with that of the USA'.[23]

ENDING THE VIETNAM WAR

While the Nixon Administration was breaking the ice of US relations with the two communist superpowers, Hanoi launched another major military attack on South Vietnam. During 1970–71 the DRV had been playing a waiting game for the withdrawal of US troops. There were only two PLAF/PAVN attacks of battalion size or greater during 1971. The guerilla insurgency was kept up in order to counter pacification efforts by the GVN; but small-scale attacks also declined by more than a third during 1971. In May of that year the decision was made in Hanoi to launch another major offensive in the South in 1972. The US talks with China and the USSR were creating a sense of urgency about a potential diplomatic isolation of the DRV. Already there had been a slackening of Chinese aid since 1968. With the American troop withdrawal nearly complete and an election year looming in the US, it was reasoned that the Nixon Administration would not be able to send an army back to aid the GVN. So by showing up the ARVN as incapable of defending South Vietnam, the US might be willing to accept Hanoi's peace terms.[24]

However, Nixon and Kissinger were still prepared to use air power to frustrate the DRV objective. Upon receiving reports of military stockpiling on the northern side of the demilitarized zone, Nixon used

23. Chang, *Friends and Enemies* 285–6. Ambrose, *Nixon* 525–6, 544–8. Gromyko, *Memories* 277. Harry Harding, *A Fragile Relationship: The United States and China since 1972* (Washington 1992) 33–47.

24. Thayer, *War Without Fronts* 44. Turley, *Second Indochina War* 138–9.

the excuse of an insurgent artillery attack on Saigon, which broke the terms of the 1968 bombing halt, to resume on 26 December bombing of North Vietnam south of the 20th parallel. US air units in the RVN also were strengthened. Washington was hoping to dissuade Hanoi from the invasion that his military advisers predicted for February 1972. This strategy, however, failed. The DRV attack on the RVN commenced on 30 March, the day before Easter.[25]

The DRV's 1972 Easter offensive was more powerful than Washington expected. Three PAVN divisions, backed by 200 Soviet-supplied tanks and heavy artillery, smashed across the RVN's northern border demilitarized zone to quickly overrun Quang Tri province. Another division attacked in the western highlands. On 2 April a third front was opened by three more PAVN divisions from across the Cambodian border to the north of Saigon. Within five days they were besieging the provincial city of An Loc. When the ARVN 21st division was rushed north from the Mekong Delta to defend that city, a fourth front was opened in that rice bowl region by three PAVN regiments supported by PLAF guerillas.[26]

Nixon was furious at the news of the Easter offensive. The US response was massive air strikes against PAVN forces in South Vietnam and their supply routes plus the most comprehensive ever bombing campaign against North Vietnam. On 8 May Nixon ordered the mining of Haiphong harbour, correctly calculating that the USSR would not intervene. Moscow launched verbal protests but did not allow the détente process to be upset by the American 'aggression' against the DRV. Despite the damaging of Soviet ships in Haiphong harbour, Nixon's Moscow visit went ahead. With this Soviet acquiescence, Nixon and Kissinger increased their pressure on North Vietnam by launching Operation Linebacker I against targets in Hanoi and Haiphong, using new laser-guided 'smart' bombs. 'The bastards have never been bombed like they're going to be bombed this time', remarked Nixon to his White House aides.[27]

Initially the intense bombing of PAVN troops did not stop their continued advance into the RVN. Much of the central highlands region was overrun. Quang Tri city in the north fell on 1 May with some 8,000 berserk ARVN troops fleeing to Hue, which was swelling with thousands of civilian refugees. Unprotected hamlets

25. Clodfelter, *Limits of Air Power* 151–2.
26. Turley, *Second Indochina War* 140–1.
27. Clodfelter, *Limits of Air Power* 147–63. Nixon quoted in DeBenedetti and Chatfield, *An American Ordeal* 333.

in the Delta also were rapidly falling to the PAVN/PLAF offensive there. But the PAVN offensive, suffering the most intense bombing of the whole war, ran out of steam by mid-June. An Loc was saved and, under a new more efficient commander, the ARVN inched forward to recapture Quang Tri city on 16 September, a major victory. Nevertheless, the PAVN retained control of northern Quang Tri province, much of the central highlands and over a million additional people in the Delta. It was only a partial ARVN victory, helped greatly by US air power.[28]

The battlefield stalemate in Vietnam encouraged both the US and the DRV to search for peace. Nixon faced a renewal of the anti-war movement. It was more muted than previously, with less massively attended public rallies. But it had a new institutionalized focus, with important Congressmen, such as Democratic Party Senators Edward Kennedy and John Tunney, taking a public stand with peace demonstrators alongside a host of media and other national celebrities. Most ominously, there were threats in Congress to cut off funds for military action in Vietnam. Nixon had been able to keep ahead of his anti-war opponents by publicly announcing before the Easter offensive his peace terms, in which he offered to trade a complete American withdrawal for guarantees for the preservation of a non-Communist South Vietnam and the return of US prisoners of war from the DRV. He was able to represent the PAVN attacks on the RVN as a breach of faith by Hanoi, and he justified the bombing as a means to achieve peace on honourable terms. He demonstrated his peace credentials with continued withdrawal of US military personnel from Vietnam to a level of only 39,000 by September 1972. His foreign policy prestige also was boosted by his trips to Beijing and Moscow.

Furthermore, the anti-war movement succeeded in derailing the Democratic Party. Helped by democratizing reforms in party nominating proceedings after the 1968 Chicago Convention, peace activists succeeded in nominating Senator George McGovern as presidential candidate on a platform of unilateral withdrawal from Vietnam. But he was weakened by dissension within his party, by an early image of indecisiveness and by vulnerability to charges of lack of patriotism. His campaign was damaged further by much more lavish Republican spending and by covert destabilizing activities. Nevertheless, though Nixon enjoyed high opinion poll advantages

28. Turley, *Second Indochina War* 142–4. G.H. Turley, *The Easter Offensive: Vietnam 1972* (Novato 1985).

over McGovern, Kissinger was enamoured with the prospect of adding peace in Vietnam to the Administration's China and USSR foreign policy triumphs before the presidential election.[29]

Hanoi also was interested in achieving a peaceful settlement. Its offensive in the South had stalled. The mining of Haiphong harbour had blocked a major conduit of supplies. The USSR had ordered its ships back to Russia rather than confront the US, a sign of the success of Washington's détente initiatives with Moscow as well as with China, which was sending no extra aid. North Vietnam was in danger of political isolation. Nor with McGovern's faltering campaign could it look confidently at any favourable political change in the US. At resumed talks between Kissinger and the French-educated DRV negotiator, Le Duc Tho, in Paris, Hanoi retreated from its demands for Thieu's removal and for a coalition government in South Vietnam. Hanoi was now prepared to accept a standstill cease-fire in the whole of Indochina, arrangements for political movements in the RVN to consult together about future elections and a promise to free US prisoners. The major condition was a US withdrawal of all forces from Vietnam within sixty days. Though such an agreement provided a much less secure guarantee for a non-communist state, especially the retention of the PAVN's substantial gains from the Easter offensive, Kissinger was prepared to make a deal based on Tho's revised terms on 8 October 1972.[30]

However, a peace settlement in Vietnam was stymied by strong opposition from Thieu. The demand that he consult with the PRG would sanction the communist cause after the many years of trying to eradicate it, and the continued presence of PAVN troops within the RVN was too threatening for his political survival. He knew the shaky basis of his own public support and the implacable determination of the VCP to control the whole of Vietnam. Nixon also backed away from the agreement, in order to prevent any questioning of his motives prior to his landslide electoral victory over McGovern on 7 November. After the election Kissinger, now the Secretary of State, presented to Tho some of Thieu's many demands for changes to the draft agreement. Nixon confirmed to Thieu that 'in the event the enemy renews its aggression' the US would 'take swift and severe retaliatory action'. But Thieu persisted in his objections.[31]

29. DeBenedetti and Chatfield, *An American Ordeal* 323–40.
30. Turley, *Second Indochina War* 144–5.
31. Nixon to Thieu, 14 Nov. 1972 in Nguyen Tien Hung and Jerrold L. Schecter, *The Palace File* (New York 1986) 124.

Nixon made one more military attempt to extract further concessions from Hanoi. In eleven days from 18 December, with the exception of Christmas Day, over 20,000 tons of bombs were dropped on communications and storage facilities in Hanoi and Haiphong with many of the 'smart' bombs missing their targets; landing, for example, on Hanoi's largest hospital. The DRV had braced itself for the onslaught. Over half of the city's population had been evacuated, and the destruction was minor compared with Second World War bombing of European and Japanese cities. But 2,196 North Vietnamese civilians died in the raids. The US also lost fifteen B-52 bombers and ninety-two crew members.[32]

It was a high cost for the one major concession wrung from Hanoi, which was the deletion of the requirement for political negotiations in South Vietnam. US air chiefs claimed an extra week of bombing would have won much more. But re-elected Democratic majorities in both Houses of Congress were threatening to choke the money supply for all US forces in Vietnam. So Nixon knew he could achieve little extra. Thieu remained opposed to the retention of PAVN troops in the RVN. But Nixon used the stick of threatening the cancellation of all economic and military aid and the carrot of a renewed absolute commitment to come swiftly to the RVN's aid if the agreement was violated in future by the DRV. On 23 January Tho and Kissinger signed the agreement which concluded US involvement in the second Indochinese War, for a cost of 45,662 US and 5,221 allied combat deaths.[33]

But the war had not ended for the GVN nor for the DRV. While the VCP decided to respect the Paris agreement, it did not do so with the same naivety as after the 1954 Geneva Agreements, which had allowed Diem to attack its members. This time the VCP was determined to offer military resistance to any GVN encroachments on its areas of control, and prior to the signing of the agreement it maximized military efforts to win more territory. Even then, by the party's own admission, fewer than four million of South Vietnam's 19.5 million people were under its control, a smaller number than on the eve of the 1968 Tet offensive. After the signing of the peace agreement, violent land-grabbing by both sides continued, with the ARVN initially gaining the upper hand. The GVN was acting with the assurance that the US would bail it out if North Vietnam launched

32. Turley, *Second Indochina War* 147–9. Clodfelter, *Limits of Air Power* 179–95.
33. Ibid. 196–202. Nguyen and Schecter, *The Palace File* ch. 9. Thayer, *War Without Fronts* 105.

another invasion. Furthermore, South Vietnam had the world's fifth largest army, replete with hardware and supplies left behind by the departing US troops, and still assisted by US military advisers, re-classified as civilians. The ARVN had a clear advantage in numbers and firepower over its opponent in the South.

But strategically, Thieu overstretched his forces in a futile attempt to control the whole of South Vietnam, a feat previously unattainable with the assistance of half a million Americans. He also ran an increasingly authoritarian state, with a rapidly deteriorating economy suffering from the withdrawal of the previous $400 million annual US expenditure in the RVN, combined with sharp rises in world commodity prices, especially oil, and decreasing US aid. Inflation in South Vietnam in 1974 was 100 per cent, while ARVN wages rose by only 25 per cent. Thieu never had a wide basis of popular support. He now faced a rising tumult of public criticism and the emergence of non-communist anti-government movements.[34]

Furthermore, the guarantee of US support for the RVN was fast dissipating. The 1972 Christmas bombing campaign increased the resolve of many members of the majority Democratic Party not only to stop any further funds for military action in Vietnam but also to curb the president's war-making power. This movement was boosted by the revelation in March 1973 of continued US bombing in Cambodia, where the Paris agreement had not halted a Khmer Rouge offensive against Lon Nol's pro-American government. Bolstered by American opinion polls reporting a two-to-one public opposition to the bombing in Cambodia, the Senate voted to restrict money for that campaign. Nixon found this challenge to his foreign policy much harder to shrug off than before, even though he vowed to find money for the Cambodia air campaign elsewhere. His authority was being crippled by growing allegations of an Administration cover-up of the pre-election burglarizing by the 'plumbers' of the Democratic Party national office in the Watergate building in Washington. In June Congress voted to stop all money for the bombing which, after Nixon exercised his veto power, became a compromise promise to curtail it by 15 August. But the revelations in Senate hearings in July of the secret US bombing of neutral Cambodia ever since March 1969, and the falsifying of relevant records, provoked Congress in November 1973 to pass, over Nixon's veto, the War Powers Act.

34. Turley, *Second Indochina War* 157–69. Timothy J. Lomperis, *The War Everyone Lost – And Won: America's Intervention in Viet Nam's Twin Struggles* (Baton Rouge 1984) 96–7.

It required the President to inform Congress within forty-eight hours of the deployment of any US forces abroad and obligated their withdrawal if, within sixty days, there were no Congressional endorsement. While that act still gave the US President short-term freedom to use military force, the spirit behind it ensured no more American military action in Indochina. Congress also in 1974, misconceiving that nothing serious was wrong in the RVN, slashed the Administration's request for $1.5 billion in military aid to South Vietnam to $700 million, which was a crippling blow on top of the rampant inflation that year to the fighting capacity and morale of the ARVN. Moreover, Nixon resigned on 9 August 1974 to escape becoming the second president in US history to face impeachment by Congress.[35]

Hanoi in January 1975 considered the time was ripe for an invasion of South Vietnam. CPV leaders safely predicted that the US Congress would not allow the new Republican Administration, headed by the former party leader in the House of Representatives and vice president, Gerald Ford, to honour Nixon's promises to speedily come to the GVN's aid. Military clashes in late 1974 clearly revealed the sagging morale of the ARVN, which was becoming disaffected by the mounting opposition to Thieu's regime. Indeed, the ARVN collapsed like a house of cards when on 9 March 1975 the PAVN launched the first concentrated offensives against its overstretched defensive positions. On the last day of the next month PAVN tanks rolled unopposed into Saigon after frantic helicopter evacuations of Americans. Many of their former Vietnamese supporters were left behind to face the bloody revenge of the victors of twenty-one years of warfare.[36]

The long war had a brutal impact on many people in South Vietnam. It has been estimated that 171,331 ARVN soldiers died in the war and that the death toll of their communist opponents, including PAVN units fighting in the RVN, could have been as high as 850,000. While numbers of civilians who died or were wounded because of the war are unknown, an estimate of South Vietnamese civilian casualties, based on hospital admissions and other statistical data, from 1965 through 1972, is 1,025,000, including some 250,000 deaths. From 1954 to 1975 over half the South Vietnamese people fled from their homes, some more than once. The majority

35. Ibid. 97–9. Arnold R. Isaacs, *Without Honor: The Defeat in Vietnam and Cambodia* (Baltimore 1983) 303–21.
36. Ibid. 321–487.

of them moved because of the effects of the war rather than because of political commitment, though the stories of what happened when the PLAF conquered Hue in 1968 made fear a major reason for the flight of South Vietnamese from advancing PAVN forces in 1972 and 1975. While US aid prevented starvation or epidemics among the refugees, many became permanent camp dwellers dependent on handouts, though there were job opportunities near US, Korean and ARVN bases, including prostitution. There was also some movement back to villages during the pacification programmes of 1969–71. But the refugee problem contributed to the collapse in support for the GVN. The people who felt compelled to flee from ancestral lands and homes blamed mostly the GVN and the US for the shells and bombs that were the most powerful reasons why they became refugees.[37]

There has been a major American debate about whether the US could have won the Vietnam War. American officers who fought in the war, such as Westmoreland and Colonel Harry G. Summers, have argued that they were crippled by Johnson's restraints. If they had been given more troops to attack across the DRV border and into Cambodia and Laos after the 1968 Tet offensive, along with more intensified bombing of the DRV, its government would have capitulated.[38]

But how US forces would have maintained control of regions in Cambodia, Laos and in the DRV against concerted guerilla opposition is a question unanswered by the military theorists. A PAVN colonel explained in 1984: 'Look what happened in 1970. Americans and ARVN forces did cross the border into Cambodia, but it was easier for us to fight in Cambodia than in South Vietnam'. He pointed out how any American invasion of the DRV would have encountered a population 'well-prepared to wage people's war'.[39]

Furthermore, Americans who were involved in counter-insurgency programmes in the RVN, such as the later director of the CIA, William Colby, have maintained that insufficient American attention was given to meeting the NLF challenge at village level. Thomas

37. Thayer, *War Without Fronts* chs 10, 12, 18. Wiesner, *Victims and Survivors* ch. 16.

38. Westmoreland, *A Soldier Reports* 410. Harry G. Summers, *On Strategy: A Critical Analysis of the Vietnam War* (Novato 1982). See also, especially, Shelby L. Stanton, *The Rise and Fall of an American Army: U.S. Ground Forces in Vietnam, 1965–1973* (Novata 1985); and Philip Davidson, *Vietnam at War: The History* (Novata 1988) and *Secrets of the Vietnam War* (Novata 1990).

39. Quoted in Turley, *Second Indochina War* 190–1. See also Lawrence E. Grinter and Peter M. Dunn, *The American War in Vietnam: Lessons, Legacies, and Implications for Future Conflicts* (Westport 1987) 95–109.

Thayer, a Pentagon systems analyst during the war, provided statistics showing that 95 per cent of attacks on US and ARVN forces were carried out by groups of less than battalion strength during the whole of the American involvement in the war, including the years of the Tet and Easter offensives. Other academic historians support this view; Larry Cable, for example, pointed out that, based on previous experience with guerillas in Greece in the late 1940s and in South Korea, the US high command mistakenly viewed the insurgents in the RVN as partisans belonging to an outside army, whereas they were basically a South Vietnamese revolutionary force with outside support.[40]

Other scholars of the Vietnam War have emphasized that it was unwinnable for Americans because of Vietnamese realities. A micro-study of Hau Nghia Province by Eric Bergerud demonstrates that the war there against the NLF was lost by the Diem regime and that no amount of US firepower or counter-insurgency pressure, both applied to a great extent in that province, could eradicate the NLF. A permanent US occupation might have preserved a degree of GVN control, but such a commitment was never an American aim. When the occupying US division left the province, the PRG quickly reasserted its dominance. This conclusion is supported by the studies by Jeffrey Race of Long Tan province and by James Trullinger of My Thuy Phuong village. These local analyses clearly demonstrate that the NLF/PRG won the 'hearts and minds' battle against corrupt RVN governments that were incapable of introducing meaningful land and other social reforms because they were beholden to the country's ruling classes.[41]

INDONESIA'S INVASION OF EAST TIMOR

A new war commenced on the edge of the Southwestern Pacific Basin when in December 1975 Indonesian forces invaded the former

40. William Colby, *Lost Victory: A Firsthand Account of America's Sixteen-Year Involvement in Vietnam* (Chicago 1989) part 8. Thayer, *War Without Fronts* ch. 5. Cable, *Conflict of Myths* chs 2, 3, 14.

41. Bergerud, *Dynamics of Defeat* 1–7, 323–35. Race, *War Comes to Long An* ch. 5. Trullinger, *Village at War* chs 11–12. For a good survey of the debate see Grinter and Dunn, *The American War in Vietnam*. See also Ben Kiernan, 'The Vietnam War: Alternative Endings', *American Historical Review* 97 (1992) 1118–37.

Portuguese colony of East Timor. In 1974 that territory was a colonial backwater with most of its 653,211 people, who were of a Malay-Melanesian stock, engaged in subsistence agriculture; 93 per cent of them were illiterate. A small educated Timorese elite was working for the Portuguese colonial administration, which maintained authoritarian control.[42]

A military coup which overthrew the fascist government in Portugal in April 1974, provided the catalyst for dramatic change in East Timor. A sudden lifting of restrictions on free speech, and comments by radical members of the Portuguese junta in favour of independence for Portugal's African and Asian colonies, inspired the founding on 12 September 1974 of an independence movement in East Timor named Fretlin (*Frente Revolucionara do Timor Leste Independente*), which was led by young members of the educated Timor elite in the colony's capital city, Dili. Fretlin aimed to work for independence and for economic development, concentrating on land reforms, on the establishment of agricultural cooperatives and on promotion of literacy. Revolutionary brigades were formed to carry out these programmes at village level, influenced by a Marxist minority within the Fretlin leadership. A more conservative party seeking autonomy within the Portuguese empire, the Timorese Democratic Union (UDT), also had been formed in 1974 by more established members of the educated Timorese elite. A third political movement, called *Apodeti* (the Timorese Popular Democratic Association), had been organized by members of the colony's small Muslim community in favour of joining Indonesia and was being supported by *Bakin* (the Indonesian Army's Intelligence Coordinating Agency).[43]

Bakin was committed to work for the integration of East Timor into the Indonesian republic with the support of its military masters in Jakarta. The inherent political instability of the Indonesian archipelago, with previous major separatist revolts, induced great concern within the Indonesian Government about a small independent nation on the southeastern flank, which could be subject to communist influence. The initial strategy was to achieve annexation of East Timor by political means. However, it soon became apparent that *Apodeti* commanded little public support in the colony, compared with UDT and Fretlin, which joined together in January 1975 in a coalition

42. James Dunn, *Timor: A People Betrayed* (Milton, Queensland 1983) chs 1–2. John G, Taylor, *Indonesia's Forgotten War: The Hidden History of East Timor* (London 1991) ch. 1.
43. Ibid. chs 2–3. Dunn, *Timor* ch. 4..

to support independence. Indonesian agents therefore worked to convince UDT leaders that communists were in charge of Fretlin and were seeking to import arms from China to launch a coup. In August 1975 UDT launched a counter-coup, with the support of most Timorese members of the colonial police force, after their Portuguese police chief was kidnapped. But more than 2,000 Timorese soldiers of the colonial defence force joined Fretlin along with additional arms from the Dili arsenal, which clearly tipped the military balance. The speedy success of Fretlin forces, which pushed its UDT opponents towards the border of Indonesian West Timor, forced a rethink by *Bakin*. It had been hoping that the civil war would be protracted enough to warrant Indonesian intervention to stop the bloodshed. So a Confrontation-style low-level military campaign was launched with incursions by Indonesian troops across the West Timor border to rescue UDT leaders and to destabilize the Fretlin Government. One major Indonesian attack on the border town of Balibo resulted in the murdering by Indonesian soldiers of one New Zealand, two Australian and two British journalists working for two Australian television networks.[44]

The Indonesian border crossings met with stiff resistance from Fretlin forces. Fretlin also rapidly formed a government, which had the clear majority support of the Timorese people. The Portuguese governor, deprived of his police and army, had left the island. The reform government in Portugal, embroiled in pulling out of Africa, had washed its hands of East Timor. With increasing Indonesian military border action, Fretlin on 28 November 1975 declared East Timor's independence.

However, East Timor had no international support. Its nearest non-Indonesian neighbour, Australia, already had given the green light to Indonesia to annex the territory. In September 1974, on a visit to Indonesia, the Australian Labor Party leader, Prime Minister Gough Whitlam, told Suharto that: 'An independent East Timor would be an unviable state, and a potential threat to the area'. Within the Australian Government there was a pro-Indonesian group, which included Whitlam and the Australian ambassador in Jakarta, Richard Woolcott. Their concern was not to allow the aspirations of East Timorese people to upset the good relations with Indonesia which had emerged since Confrontation. Woolcott's attitude was demonstrated in a cable in August 1975: 'We should show as much understanding as we can of Indonesia's position and . . . there is no inherent reason

44. Ibid. chs 8–9. Taylor, *Indonesia's Forgotten War*, 30–2, 38–62.

why integration with Indonesia would in the long run be any less in the interests of the Timorese inhabitants than a highly unstable independence'. Washington supported Australia's appeasement, not wishing to upset the cosy relationship established with the anti-communist Suharto regime in Indonesia, which Nixon had labelled 'by far the greatest prize in the Southeast Asian area'. Fretlin also had been successfully damned by Indonesian propaganda as 'communist', though only a minority of its members were Marxists.[45]

With such international support, on 7 December 1975 Indonesia launched a full-scale invasion of East Timor, code-named *Operasi Seroya* (Operation Lotus). The delay after Fretlin's declaration of independence was influenced by an official visit by US President Ford and Secretary of State Kissinger which ended on 6 December. The air and sea attack on Dili was ruthless. Some 2,000 people, including most men of the city, were slaughtered, according to eyewitness reports. At one of the main killing areas, the harbour, one resident of Dili later reported to Amnesty International: 'We were told to tie the bodies to iron poles, attach bricks and throw the bodies into the sea'. On the first day of the attack, women and children were herded out of the town while troops ransacked their homes. Cars, radios, items of furniture, cutlery, and even windows were taken to ships in the harbour. Then Indonesian troops 'demanded women and girls to help them celebrate their victory'.[46]

One reason for the Indonesian ferocity was the strength of the Fretlin resistance, bolstered by some 2,500 regular soldiers, 7,000 part-time militia plus more reservists, all armed with Portuguese weapons. In preparation for the invasion, bases had been established in the interior to which many people retreated. The Indonesian forces, which increased to 25,000 by the end of December, found themselves involved in a bitter guerilla war in a mountainous environment which favoured the insurgents. The use of paratroops in the interior failed because they were rounded up by Fretlin before coastal-based Indonesian forces could reinforce them; and captured Indonesian arms added to Fretlin's firepower. The burning of villages and massacring of their inhabitants by Indonesian troops further fuelled the anger of Fretlin defenders of their homeland. However, by March 1979

45. Ibid. 32. Dunn, *Timor* ch. 7. Woolcott to Department of Foreign Affairs, 24 Aug. 1975, in G.J. Munster and J.R. Walsh, *Documents on Australian Defence and Foreign Policy 1968–1975* (Sydney 1980) 217. Nixon, 'Asia after Vietnam', 111.

46. Amnesty International, *East Timor: Violations of Human Rights: Extrajudicial Executions, 'Disappearances', Torture and Political Imprisonment, 1975–1984* (London 1985) 26. Dunn, *Timor* 285.

Jakarta was confident enough to proclaim the end to *Operasi Seroya*. A strategy of encirclement of areas of Fretlin resistance, saturation bombing, chemical spraying to poison crops, widespread use of torture, and herding of the population into strategic camps, where many died of starvation, had assisted the Indonesians to gain an upper hand. In the process the population of East Timor had been reduced by 130,778 since 1974, when under normal conditions it would have increased. Furthermore, despite this awful human cost, Fretlin had not been eradicated and would continue to trouble the Indonesian Government during the 1980s.[47]

The Indonesian invasion of Timor did receive some, but ineffective, international condemnation. On 22 December 1975 the UN Security Council called for Indonesia to withdraw its forces from East Timor and for a genuine act of self-determination by the indigenous people. But no enforcement provision was part of the motion as in the case of Korea in 1950. The US reaction to the invasion was indicated when Ford was interviewed in Hawaii about it on the day after he left Indonesia. He said: 'We'll talk about that later'. Australia protested against the invasion, but Whitlam correctly admitted three days before it occurred 'we would do absolutely nothing'. His successor, Malcolm Fraser, kept up a moral protest, and in June 1976 his foreign minister 'regretted' that the UN had not played 'a more decisive role'. But the Ford Administration in the US was trying to persuade other members of the UN to come to an accommodation with Indonesia and firmly told Australia not to upset the 'good will' of Suharto's government. Canberra was reminded of the strategic importance of Indonesian waters for the access of US ships and nuclear submarines from the Pacific to the Indian Ocean. Oil interests in Australia also were lobbying for appeasing Indonesia in order to allow exploitation of suspected oil reserves in the Timor Sea. Consequently, Fraser visited Indonesia in October 1976 and tacitly recognized the Indonesian occupation of East Timor; formal *de jure* recognition was given in January 1978. The UN General Assembly in December 1975 rejected the Indonesian annexation of East Timor by 67 votes to 12, with 53 abstentions. Significantly all the ASEAN states supported Indonesia, except Singapore which abstained. The US was among the abstentions. General Assembly motions in the remaining years of the 1970s continued to condemn Indonesia, but support for them was dwindling, with countries such as Australia shifting to abstention.[48]

---

47. Taylor, *Indonesia's Forgotten War* chs 6–8.
48. Ibid., 64, 74. Dunn, *Timor* chs 11–12.

ASEAN, CAMBODIA, VIETNAM AND CHINA

ASEAN's general support for the Indonesian invasion of Timor reflected the growth of cooperation between its member states by the mid-1970s. The fifth ministerial meeting in 1972 declared that 'the important changes that had taken place in the relations among the major powers' necessitated ASEAN members 'cooperating even more closely' in the future. However, there was no move towards a European Economic Community (EEC) model. A UN report tabled at that meeting pointed out that only 6 per cent of the annual trade of ASEAN nations was between them, excluding Singapore's entrepôt trade. But the report praised the growth rate of the member countries, which had reached 6 per cent per annum in the second half of the 1960s. The 1972 meeting expanded the number of permanent committees to cover economic issues, and more economic cooperation flowed from a summit meeting of heads of state in Bali in 1976. Subsequent meetings of economic ministers resulted in the first set of preferential trading arrangements in 1977 and an agreement in 1978 on cooperative industrial projects. Also in 1978 a Japan–ASEAN Economic Council was established to coordinate Japanese investment in ASEAN countries. These developments were small beginnings of ASEAN economic cooperation reflected in an increase in the proportion of intra-ASEAN trade to 9 per cent in 1979.[49]

There was a greater sense of insecurity within ASEAN in the 1970s leading to the beginnings of diplomatic cooperation. In July 1969, as part of his decision to commence withdrawing US troops from Vietnam, Nixon had declared on the North Pacific island of Guam that in future, except for a threat from a nuclear power, the US was 'going to encourage and has a right to expect' Asian nations to 'increasingly' take responsibility for their own defence. This statement became known as the 'Guam' or 'Nixon' Doctrine. It was taken seriously by ASEAN nations in the context of the decreasing US involvement in the Vietnam War. Malaysia and Singapore also were perturbed when Britain withdrew its commitment to their defence in 1971. ASEAN foreign ministers responded to such developments by calling in November 1971 for a 'Zone of Peace, Freedom and

49. Ronald D. Palmer and Thomas J. Reckford, *Building ASEAN: 20 Years of Southeast Asian Cooperation* (New York 1987) 40, ch. 5. Broinowski, *Understanding ASEAN* 37–65, 70–88. United Nations, *Yearbook of International Trade Statistics (YITS) 1980* (New York 1981) vol. 1, 477, 617, 770, 856, 928.

Neutrality' in Southeast Asia, which was being promoted by Malaysia. But Singapore, conscious of its vulnerable small island status, had more faith in the Five Power Commonwealth Defence Agreement, which it had signed with Malaysia, Britain, Australia and New Zealand to cover its defence needs. Thailand and the Philippines were unwilling to give up their hosting of US military bases, though they agreed in 1973 to abandon the military component of SEATO, in response to US acceptance of pressure for this downgrading of that virtually moribund alliance from Labour governments in Australia and New Zealand. Indonesia was sceptical about foreign powers guaranteeing neutrality in Southeast Asia and opposed Singapore's idea of allowing the naval forces of all the major naval powers to patrol the region's waters. A dispute also arose when Indonesia and Malaysia tried to declare the Straits of Malacca as a non-international waterway, which Singapore strongly and successfully resisted with the assistance of the major maritime powers, including the US and the USSR. Such disagreements were major barriers to early diplomatic cooperation in ASEAN.[50]

However, more concern was aroused in ASEAN with radical political changes in Indochina in 1975. In Cambodia, the Chinese-supported Khmer Rouge won a rapid victory over Lon Nol's government when the DRV overran South Vietnam. After achieving victory in an internal party struggle, from October 1976 to 1978 the Khmer Rouge chief, Pol Pot, and party cadres killed well over a million – possibly as many as two million Cambodians. The Khmer Rouge, who had won their recruits among illiterate peasants rather than in urban areas, slaughtered in particular the educated elite, other urban dwellers and perceived enemies of the revolution. One reason was that in response to overcrowded Phom Penh the Khmer Rouge leadership, which had difficulty in feeding all of its army, drove the city's inhabitants into the countryside. There many died of malnutrition and the brutality of Khmer Rouge supervisors forcing them to work with little more than their bare hands to plant crops, dig canals and other rural work. The slaughter, however, was also part of an overzealous and frantic effort to 'socialize' the nation in the style of the Chinese cultural revolution. The death of

50. *Public Papers of the Presidents of the United States, Richard M. Nixon, 1969* (Washington 1971) 549. K.K. Nair, *Words and Bayonets: ASEAN and Indochina* (Selangor 1986) ch. 1. Michael Leifer, *ASEAN and the Security of South-East Asia* (London 1989) 52–62. Turnbull, *History of Singapore*, 298, 316. Buszynski, *SEATO* ch. 6.

Mao Zedong in September 1976 and uncertainty whether Chinese support for the Khmer Rouge would continue probably influenced the sense of urgency. A military coup in Thailand in October 1976 also introduced a more anti-communist regime there, removing a previous parliamentary government which had been prepared to cooperate with Democratic Kampuchea, as the Khmer Rouge now called their country. Furthermore, there were frequent border clashes with the DRV over their French-drawn boundary. Many Khmers who were killed by Pol Pot's regime were condemned as friends of Vietnam. In Kampuchea there was a sense of embattled isolation, like revolutionary France in 1793, as expressed in a December 1976 party manifesto: 'Enemies without continue to approach; enemies within our frontiers have not been eliminated'.[51]

Increasing border fighting culminated in a full-scale Vietnamese invasion of Cambodia, beginning on 25 December 1978. There is a debate about Vietnam's motives. Most of its neighbours and other contemporary commentators claimed that Vietnam seized an opportunity created by the the chaos of the Pol Pot regime to dominate the whole of Indochina, a linguistically and culturally diverse region brought together only by French colonialism. An alternative hypothesis is that the border between Vietnam and Cambodia is the great divide between Indian and Chinese cultural influences. On the Indian side Khmers and Thais regarded borders as fluid and, even though Cambodia had shrunk in size under Thai conquests, the nature of Thai rule was more acceptable to Khmers than the Chinese-influenced Vietnamese who sought to impose their social and political order on those they conquered. But such an explanation does not explain the ferocity of Thai-Khmer conflicts in the past nor the causes for antipathy between Kampuchea and Vietnam after 1975. From that year there were border clashes, the start of which have been blamed on alleged Vietnamese slowness in leaving their Cambodian sanctuaries. However, Pol Pot's regime

---

51. 'Report of Activities of the Party Center According to the General Political Tasks of 1976', 20 Dec. 1976, in David P. Chandler, Ben Kiernan and Cahnthou Boua (eds), *Pol Pot Plans the Future: Confidential Documents from Democratic Kampuchea, 1976–1977* (New Haven 1988) 190. Grant Evans and Kelvin Rowley, *Red Brotherhood at War: Vietnam, Cambodia and Laos since 1975* (revised edit. London 1990) 81–92. Elizabeth Becker, *When the War was Over: Cambodia's Revolution and the Voices of its People* (New York 1986) chs 5–8. Craig Etcheson, *The Rise and Demise of Democratic Kampuchea* (Boulder 1984) ch. 7. For eyewitness accounts of the Khmer Rouge era see Martin Stuart-Fox, *The Murderous Revolution: Life & Death in Pol Pot's Kampuchea* (Chippendale, New South Wales 1985); and James Fenton (ed.), *Cambodian Witness: The Autobiography of Someth May* (New York 1986).

boasted about driving the Vietnamese out of the region before the agreed departure date. Phnom Penh resisted Hanoi's requests to deal with border disputes by diplomatic means, a mark of the hysterical Kampuchean reaction to enemies of their revolution. Vietnamese attempts to encourage popular resistance to Pol Pot failed in the face of the murderous Khmer Rouge repression, which was spilling over the Vietnam border. The response from Hanoi was the invasion of Kampuchea by 120,000 troops.[52]

Khmers greeted the invading Vietnamese as 'liberators', reported the American journalist William Shawcross, who visited Cambodia in 1980. Ill-equipped to fight one of Asia's most powerful armies, the Khmer Rouge retreated to the jungles and mountains of southwestern Cambodia near the Thai border, where they were able to regroup to fight again.[53]

The country the Khmer Rouge left behind them had been desolated. Shawcross was taken to mass graves of the thousands killed in the last days of the Khmer Rouge regime, full of blindfolded skulls. The terror of starvation stalked the land during 1979 because of economic dislocation and non-planting of rice. That year an estimated 188,000 Cambodians fled across the Thai border, joining over 100,000 others, who were refugees from Pol Pot's regime. A demographic estimate is that the population had declined to 6,100,000 in 1980 whereas, without the oppression of Pol Pot's regime, famine and emigration, it should have been over nine million.[54]

China was alarmed about the Vietnamese invasion of Kampuchea. Since the DRV conquest of South Vietnam, Beijing had been publicly condemning Hanoi's alleged imperialistic ambitions in Indochina. This propaganda was in line with China's longstanding policy since 1954 to prevent the creation of a greater Vietnam. There were also border disputes involving ambiguities in the French demarcated land boundary between China and Vietnam. Differences in definition of the border line across the Gulf of Tonkin were another source of discord. Most contentiously, there were counter-claims between

52. Becker, *When the War* 337–43. Evans and Rowley, *Red Brotherhood* 102–11. Stephen P. Armstrong, The Causes and Implications of the Vietnamese Invasion and Occupation of Kampuchea, MA Thesis, California State University, Long Beach, 150–92.

53. Shawcross, *Sideshow* 404.

54. Ibid. Nair, *Words and Bayonets* 95. William Shawcross, *The Quality of Mercy: Cambodia, Holocaust and Modern Conscience* (New York 1984) passim. Meng-Try Ea, 'Recent Population Trends in Kampuchea' in David A. Ablin and Marlowe Hood (eds), *The Cambodian Agony* (Armonck 1987) 3–15.

China and Vietnam to the Paracel and Spratly Islands in the South China Sea. Those islands were mostly barren islets, reefs and sandbanks, but they possessed strategic command of the South China Sea, and from the late 1960s their region was known to have rich undersea oil deposits. In 1974 China took military control of the Paracels, which was promptly followed by Vietnamese occupation of six of the Spratly Islands, and another five islands were taken over by the Philippines. Worsening relations between China and the DRV were further poisoned in 1978 by a mass exodus of many of Vietnam's more than one million, largely urbanized, Chinese residents. Most fled overland to China, but many took to the high seas in assorted boats which were prey to pirates, storms and the hostility of inhabitants of the ASEAN states where they landed. The anti-Chinese campaign in Vietnam grew with China's denunciation of it. Increasing armed border clashes marked the rapid deterioration in China-DRV relations. Chinese support for the Khmer Rouge and USSR support for the DRV exacerbated these tensions. The breaking point for Beijing came with the prospect of Vietnam overrunning Cambodia. Having stood aside from any military involvement in Indochina during the era of US military action there, Beijing, on 17 February 1979 launched an invasion of North Vietnam.[55]

According to China's new leader, Deng Xiaoping, a former CCP general secretary, the invasion was a response to Vietnamese border provocations. Like the Sino-Indian border war of 1962, the attack involved only ground troops, not air or sea forces, though they were on standby. The official aim was to teach Hanoi a sharp lesson. Hence it was called the Punitive War. But more important objectives were almost certainly to weaken Vietnamese pressure on Kampuchea by causing a withdrawal of Vietnamese troops to protect the border zone with China and to demonstrate that China was a major power to which Vietnam should defer.[56]

The Chinese force which had been collected for the invasion consisted of 330,000 soldiers, of whom about 200,000 were used in the fighting plus 1,200 tanks. The 600,000 strong PAVN had a third of its force occupying Cambodia and another third stationed in South Vietnam and in Laos. But the numerically superior Chinese army was hampered by the absence of any significant modernization since the Korean War. Attacking on three fronts, the troops were greatly

55. Pao-Min Chang, *The Sino-Vietnamese Territorial Dispute* (New York 1986) 11–53. King C. Chen, *China's war with Vietnam*, 1979 (Stanford 1987) chs 2–4.
56. Ibid. 94–5. Evans and Rowley, *Red Brotherhood* 117–19.

hampered by their lack of modern logistical equipment, forcing them to rely on old trucks, donkeys and human labour in the mountainous terrain, which also compelled them to break down divisions to companies and even platoons. The Vietnamese defenders, who were mainly local militia and border guards, were able to exploit a defensive system of tunnels, trenches, land mines and other booby traps. A concerted series of Chinese attacks enabled the capture of the city of Lang Son 16 kms inside the border, situated on the edge of an open plain and only 136 kms from Hanoi. But on 5 March, the day Hanoi ordered mass mobilization for war, Beijing ordered a withdrawal. The attack had destroyed six Vietnamese missile sites and many bridges, roads, railways and buildings, systematically levelled by the retreating Chinese. But the invasion did not succeed in destroying any PAVN division; indeed, only one extra division was actually deployed to reinforce the border guards and militia at Lang Son. The war did not affect the Vietnamese conquest of Cambodia; nor did it diminish the campaign against Chinese residents in Vietnam. The PLA had faced unexpected Vietnamese resistance bolstered by the more modern PAVN artillery. Such was the ferocity of the fighting in the sixteen-day war, that China admitted 20,000 casualties, and its losses were probably considerably higher. Beijing realized, and admitted in the more open post-Mao environment, that the PLA needed much modernization before it ventured on any similar military expedition.[57]

There was a significant international reaction to the Sino-Vietnamese War. The USSR, which had a naval squadron in the South China Sea based at the former US naval base of Cam Ranh Bay in South Vietnam, sent an additional cruiser and destroyer to the region. Soviet arms were airlifted to Hanoi. Moscow warned Beijing about playing with fire, though Soviet officials admitted there was no thought of any Soviet military intervention. The US called for a Chinese withdrawal and supported an ASEAN resolution at the UN for the evacuation of all foreign troops in Indochina, including Vietnamese troops in Cambodia. But the Soviet Union used its veto to prevent any Security Council action.[58]

For the ASEAN states, Vietnam's invasion of Cambodia was a challenge to the principle of respect for the rights of nation states and raised a fear of an expansionist Vietnam. The latter concern was greatest in Thailand, since Vietnam had also assumed de facto control

57. Ibid. 115–19. Chen, *China's War with Vietnam* ch. 5.
58. Ibid. 109–12.

of Laos. A new threatening superpower had loomed on Thailand's eastern border, with a further threat of Vietnamese support for communist subversion in Thailand. The Thai disquiet extended to the opening of secret negotiations with China for mutual support for a Khmer Rouge insurgency against Vietnam's occupation. The Thai premier also visited Washington in February 1979 and received a public reiteration of the US guarantee of Thailand's security.[59]

Fellow ASEAN members gave support to Thailand on the Cambodia issue. However, there were underlying differences of opinion. Indonesia was more interested in coming to an accommodation with Vietnam, because China was viewed as the main threat to Indonesia's security. Malaysia also was mostly concerned about China, being influenced like Indonesia by Chinese involvement in internal communist threats in the past. Singapore, however, was alarmed at Soviet support for Vietnam. Its leaders, especially Lee Kuan Yew, who perceived that superpower competition was the best guarantee for world peace, viewed the US withdrawal from Vietnam as creating a power vacuum in Southeast Asia, which the USSR was now moving to fill. The Philippines was in dispute with Vietnam and China over the Spratly Islands and opposed the invasion of Cambodia on legalistic grounds and its concern for ASEAN consensus. However, at an emergency meeting in Bangkok in January 1979 the ASEAN foreign ministers deplored the armed intervention in Cambodia and called for an immediate withdrawal of foreign troops from its soil. A follow-up statement urged Vietnam to stop the increasing flow of the mostly ethnically Chinese 'boat people' from Vietnam who were landing on ASEAN shores. Despite the doubts of some of its members, ASEAN was throwing its diplomatic weight on the China-Kampuchea side of the Indochina conflict.[60]

Consequently, the Vietnamese-supported People's Republic of Kampuchea (PRK), headed by Heng Samrin, the commander of a Cambodian anti-Pol Pot force, faced strong diplomatic opposition. China, the US and ASEAN supported a call by Pol Pot's deposed Democratic Kampuchea government, which had retreated to the Thai border region, for condemnation of Vietnam. This coalition in September 1979 gained 71 votes to 35 in the UN General Assembly with no Western nation in opposition, although some European

59. Nair, *Words and Bayonets* chs 2–5.
60. Ibid. Leifer, *ASEAN and Security* ch. 4. Chen, *China's War with Vietnam* 135–8. Lau Teik Soon, 'Singapore in South-East Asia' in C.T. Chew and Edwin Lee (eds), *A History of Singapore* (Singapore 1991) 378–9.

nations abstained; but a vote in the Security Council calling for a withdrawal of Vietnamese troops ran into a Soviet veto. Washington initially tried to stop any aid to the victims of the massive famine in Cambodia but in July 1979 relented with the television pictures and news reports of the devastation stirring public humanitarian concern. However, then the Carter Administration insisted that aid must also be given to the 1 to 2 per cent of people under Khmer Rouge control, a precondition that the PRK government resisted until the overwhelming nature of the disaster forced it to agree. Even then about half of over US$600 million of relief went to the Thai border region resulting, according to Shawcross, in an average of $1,124 per head for refugees in Thailand compared with $439 to those living under PRK control. This was another reason for the stream of Cambodians crossing into Thailand during 1979.[61]

THE US AND EAST ASIA

ASEAN's diplomatic assertiveness in the late 1970s was also a reaction to a general lack of interest in the Western Pacific Basin region by the Administration of Jimmy Carter, the Southern Democratic Party president of the US since 1977. Carter was much more interested in détente with the Soviet Union centring on arms reduction negotiations, which produced the Second Strategic Arms Limitation Treaty (SALT-2) in 1979. However that treaty was withdrawn by Carter's Administration from ratification proceedings in the US Senate after the Soviet invasion of Afghanistan in December 1979.[62]

However, Carter did not abandon East Asian defences against communism. The US Seventh Fleet still patrolled the Taiwan Straits to protect the regime of Chiang Kai Shek, who died in 1973, and his Kuomintang Party successors, who still ruled the Taiwanese people. However with the passing of the old guard Nationalists who had arrived in 1940, the distinction between Taiwanese and mainlanders was blurring, and both groups had a common interest in remaining

61. William Shawcross, *The Quality of Mercy: Cambodia, Holocaust and Modern Conscience* (London 1984) 391–3. Evans and Rowley, *Red Brotherhood* 155–60.

62. Larry H. Addington, 'The Nuclear Arms Race and Arms control: An American Dilemma in a Historical Perspective', *War & Society* 1:1, 1983, 106–8.

free from the rule of Communist China. The Nationalist China regime still clung to Jimmen and Mazu, in the now forlorn hope of returning to the mainland. In the new spirit of détente with the US, China's shore-based guns were silent in acknowledgement that the US fleet would act to prevent any Nationalist invasion attempt. Nationalist China also had suffered the ignominy in 1971 of being replaced by Communist China, with US blessing, in the UN. When the new US-China relationship was marked with a visit by Deng Xiaoping to Washington in 1978, the US withdrew its recognition of Taiwan as the Republic of China. However, under continuing American military protection and close economic relationships with the US, Taiwan's economy was booming. After a hiccup caused by the sharp oil price rise in 1973 and the post-Vietnam War recession, during the 1970s the average annual growth rate of GNP was 9.75 per cent, just above the high level of the 1960s. The island's 17.1 million people in 1978 were enjoying a GNP per capita six times higher than the GNP per citizen of China.[63]

South Korea also enjoyed good economic growth under continued US defence protection. However, in 1979 the export-driven economy was suffering from a lack of new markets, another big rise in oil prices, and an over-investment in heavy and defence industries. This economic distortion was influenced by the Park Government's concern to improve the country's war-making strength in the light of the Nixon Doctrine. It was reinforced by the withdrawal of one of the two US divisions from the ROK in 1970. Carter in 1977 decided to implement a phased withdrawal of the other division over five years. However, pressure from the ROK via the US Congress and evidence of North Korean military growth stopped that process after only 3,600 troops were evacuated. South Koreans felt aggrieved at this US military retreat after the major South Korean contribution in the Vietnam War. Carter repaired some of the damage in 1979 with a strong statement committing the US to defend the ROK.[64]

North Korea's military expansion in the 1970s was a sign that Kim Il Sung's regime had not given up hope of conquering the South. But it faced a much more powerful ROK than in 1950. The presence of US troops, including tactical nuclear weapons, was also a deterrent,

63. Stephen P. Gibert and William M. Carpenter (eds) *America and Island China: A Documentary History* (Latham 1988) 54.

64. *FEA* 1981–2, 646. Ralph N. Clough, *Embattled Korea: The Rivalry for International Support* (Boulder 1987) chs 3, 7. Youngnok Koo and Dae-Sook Suh (eds), *Korea and the United States: A Century of Cooperation* (Honolulu 1984) ch. 6.

as was the ready availability of US air power from bases in Japan. The USSR in fact declined to provide North Korea with modern arms to counter those being acquired by the ROK. Moscow was not interested in encouraging the union of a highly industrialized nation of 60 million people on its doorstep. The prevailing rapprochement between the US and China suggested that a united Korea might well be drawn into an anti-USSR camp. So North Korea made no move to attack the ROK even with the political uncertainty in the South after the assassination of the increasingly authoritarian Park in October 1979 by the Director of the ROK's Central Intelligence Agency for harsh repression of labour unrest. There were also student protests caused by the 1979 economic crisis.[65]

Japan remained a firm anchor in the American alliance, but there were growing frictions. A new security treaty between the US and Japan was signed in 1970 amidst greater public protests than in 1960. The US invasion of Cambodia provided political ammunition for communists, socialists and other peace activists. A police-estimate of 774,000 Japanese protested against the treaty on 23 June 1970; the organizers claimed two million. There were further, often violent, protests until the treaty was passed by the Diet by a big majority on 19 October.[66]

Trade frictions between the US and Japan also were emerging from Japan's huge economic expansion. The average annual Japanese GNP growth rate of 10 per cent since 1965 fell sharply in 1973 with the big oil price rise and the effects of the wind-down in the Vietnam War. The average annual GNP growth rate for the rest of the decade was 4.7 per cent. But the gap between Japan's exports to and imports from the US was widening because of the good quality of the cars, electrical goods, textiles and other Japanese goods, and because the raw materials and foodstuffs that the US had traditionally supplied to Japan were coming from cheaper sources, such as Australia and Canada. The influx of Japanese textiles especially was alarming to US textile manufacturers, and Washington responded to these and complaints about other imports from Japan with tariff rises and pressure for voluntary restrictions. Nevertheless, the trade imbalance grew from US$1.7 billion in 1974 to US$10.4 billion in 1979. There was an increasing perception in the US of Japan as a dangerous economic competitor and even a potential military

---

65. Clough, *Embattled Korea* 108–9, 243.
66. John Welfield, *An Empire in Eclipse: Japan in the Postwar American Alliance System* (London 1988) 280–2.

threat. The Japanese Government, however, observing a growth in the size of the USSR's Pacific fleet, wanted no reduction in the US defence commitment, which allowed Japan to concentrate on economic growth with only a minor diversion of funds to its Self Defence Force (SDF). The US also remained Japan's most important market throughout the 1970s.[67]

One new opening for Japanese trade and investment was occurring in China. Progress, however, was slow during the 1970s because of political turbulence in China and the Japanese Government's own problems after Prime Minister Tanaka was condemned for corruption. But by 1979 China had become Japan's sixth most valuable market after the US, South Korea, Taiwan, West Germany and Saudi Arabia; and Japan contributed 17 per cent of China's imports. That year Japan joined the US in extending diplomatic recognition to China and disavowing the Republic of China in Taiwan.[68]

A by-product of China's increased openness to the wider trading world was a boom in the late 1970s in its major gateway to the outside world, Hong Kong. Following a post Vietnam War recession there, domestic exports from Hong Kong leapt by 43 per cent in 1976 and continued to grow strongly for the rest of the decade. There was a significant growth of manufacturing in Hong Kong centring on textiles, plastics and electronics. This British colony also was emerging as a major financial sector, with the number of licensed banks increasing from 74 in 1977 to 105 in 1979. In this new prosperous environment there was no repetition of the riots of the previous two decades.[69]

The oil shock of 1973 with concomitant price rises for other raw materials also encouraged Japan to control sources of raw materials in Asia, being dependent on overseas sources for over 90 per cent of energy needs and other supplies. Already there had been capital investment in Asian countries to exploit cheaper labour costs because of the rising price of Japanese labour engendered by growing prosperity. By 1974 Japanese accumulated direct foreign investment in manufacturing in Asia was worth US$1.2 billion and was 38 per cent of all Japanese overseas manufacturing investment, a third of which was in Latin America. Textiles and electrical machinery

67. Ibid. 325–34. Akira Iriye and Warren I. Cohen (eds), *The United States and Japan in the Postwar World* (Lexington, Ky 1989) ch. 8.
68. *FEA* 1981–2, 364, 585.
69. Patrikeeff, *Mouldering Pearl* 76–8.

were the principal Asian products, and the main countries for such investment were Japan's former colonies: Taiwan and South Korea. While this development continued after 1974, particularly in Southeast Asia, there was a deliberate emphasis on moving offshore into Asia primary processing stages of basic materials industries, such as steel, petrochemicals and paper. Furthermore, large Japanese corporations were moving into Asian and wider world investments, such as Mitsui Company, which by 1979 had fifty-nine subsidiaries in twenty-nine nations covering a large range of basic materials industries like iron ore in Australia, petrochemicals in South Korea and rubber, timber and cement in Indonesia. The largest proportion of the investment was in mining to secure the raw materials needed by Japanese industry, such as oil and natural gas in Indonesia, Brunei and Malaysia, copper in Malaysia and the Philippines and iron ore in Australia. Japan's increasing economic interest in Southeast Asia was marked by a visit there by Prime Minister Fukuda Hideko in 1976, where he promised to cooperate as an 'equal partner' with the member countries of ASEAN in building 'peace and prosperity'. Unspoken was his underlying concern to promote further Japanese economic penetration in the region.[70]

Japanese investment was assisting the creation of an economic dynamism in the Western Pacific Basin. In particular the economies of Singapore, Hong Kong, Taiwan and South Korea were among the fastest growing in the world and had earned for them the title of newly industrializing countries (NIC) or 'little dragons'. Their rapidly growing economies, along with the continued remarkable economic growth in Japan, were in the process of making the Pacific Basin more economically important than the Atlantic Basin, which had been dominant in the world for the previous half millennium. During the 1970s most economies of the East Asian region had been achieving annual growth rates of 6 to 8 per cent, compared with between 3 and 4 per cent in Western Europe. By 1979 US trade with non-Soviet Asia was worth $121.3 billion and was $23.9 billion greater than US trade with non-Soviet Europe.[71]

---

70. Rob Steven, *Japan's New Imperialism* (London 1990) 64–85. Bernard Eccleston, *State and Society in Post-War Japan* (Cambridge 1989) 242–51. William W. Haddad, 'Japan, the Fukuda Doctrine and ASEAN', *Contemporary Southeast Asia* 2, 1980, 10–29.

71. Bernard K. Gordon, 'Pacific Futures for the USA' in Lau Teik Soon and Leo Suryadinata (eds), *Moving into the Pacific Century: The Changing Regional Order in the Asia-Pacific* (Singapore 1988) 11. *YITS*, 1981, 1028.

CONCLUSIONS

Major changes had taken place in the Western Pacific Basin between 1969 and 1979. Prominent was the US withdrawal from Vietnam and the subsequent ending of the long war there. The impact of that war on the US itself resulted in no American effort to save South Vietnam. But the DRV faced new enemies in the region with China's failed attempt to teach it a military lesson and the decision by the ASEAN nations to oppose the Vietnamese occupation of Cambodia, even though Khmer Rouge aggression was the most important reason for the Vietnamese action.

The US retreat from Vietnam included a signal in the Nixon Doctrine of a wider American withdrawal from Asia. However, despite emerging détente with China, in 1979 the US still maintained army and naval forces to protect Taiwan and South Korea, and the US was still responsible for the defence of Japan, though a noisy minority of Japanese wished otherwise. Also tensions were emerging over Japan's continued economic expansion and the growing US deficit in bilateral trade. Japan's economic expansion was further influencing economic growth in the 'little dragon' nations of South Korea, Taiwan, Hong Kong and Singapore, which were increasing the economic importance of the Western Pacific Basin.

Though the Cold War was diminishing in significance in the Western Pacific Basin, in 1979 conflicts were still simmering in Southeast Asia. In Cambodia, North Vietnam was facing a foreign power-backed insurgency. In the Philippines the dictatorial and corrupt government of Ferdinand Marcos was combatting a rebellion by the Marxist New People's Army. Fretlin's insurgency in East Timor had not been completely suppressed. Indonesia was fighting another guerilla conflict in Irian Jaya against a Melanesian independence movement, which will be discussed in the next chapter.

CHAPTER FIVE

Independence for some Pacific Islands, 1945–1980

The Pacific Islands are defined as the island groups whose indigenous people are not of Asian stock and who belong to the Melanesian, Polynesian and Micronesian ethnic groups. Micronesia incorporates the relatively small islands of the North Pacific, many of which are coral atolls. Melanesians, who generally have darker skins and more negroid features, inhabit the island chain extending from New Guinea southeastwards to Vanuatu and New Caledonia, which includes the biggest of the Pacific Islands. Melanesia is also the region of greatest linguistic and cultural diversity, with a general absence of hereditary authority. Polynesians are natives of the South Pacific Islands to the east of that island chain, with the exception of Fiji, where the indigenous people are mostly Melanesian but have a Polynesian culture, such as a strong chiefly system. Many of the Polynesian islands are also coral atolls, where coconut palms and the surrounding sea provide the only economic resources for rapidly growing populations. Only Fiji and Melanesia contain significant mineral wealth or have a sufficient area for major production of introduced crops, such as sugar and coffee.

Many of the islands of the Pacific experienced during the Second World War the traumas of Japanese invasion and US counter attacks, leaving much physical devastation. After the war there were isolated islander protests against the return of colonial administrations. But there were not the same concerted movements for independence as in Southeast Asia. By the 1960s, some colonial administrations were pushing for independence more than were islanders. However, in the 1970s French and US administrations were resisting emerging islander independence movements, and one set of islanders were struggling against Indonesian rule. This chapter deals with the processes and struggles for independence by Pacific Islanders to 1980 plus inter-relationships of the independent island states and relations with and between the two former South Pacific colonial powers, Australia and New Zealand.

POSTWAR RECONSTRUCTION AND ISLANDER ASPIRATIONS TO 1949

The one postwar political change in the Pacific Islands occurred in the North Pacific, where Japan's League of Nations mandated islands became an American mandate under UN trusteeship. The JCS wanted outright annexation, the Pacific war having made the Pentagon conscious of the region's strategic importance to the US. But the State Department continued Roosevelt's ideal of international control, though changing it to a UN mandate with special provisions enabling the US Government to draft its own terms for administering the islands. This allowed the US to keep out foreign powers, which accorded with the JCS strategic argument. Truman endorsed this approach because he opposed outright annexation and wished to support the UN. In these American considerations no thought was given to asking the opinion of the islanders. However, their experience of oppressive Japanese rule, the trauma of wartime destruction, the exhibition of US military power in expelling the Japanese and the generosity of many of the occupying American troops made most Micronesians happy about US rule.[1]

Elsewhere in the Pacific war zone, returning colonial powers easily re-established control. However, there were some challenges from islanders, the most serious being the Maasina Rule movement in the mountainous British Solomon Islands, centred on the island of Malaita. Many Malaitans had experienced for generations the wider Pacific world as contract labourers, and Maasina (brotherhood) Rule reflected the contrast islanders had drawn between the fleeing British Administration in 1942 and the Americans, who treated them more

---

1. Foltos, 'The New Pacific Barrier' 316–36. Harold F. Nufer, *Micronesia Under American Rule: An Evaluation of the Strategic Trusteeship (1947–77)* (Hicksville 1978) 26–30. Geoffrey M. White and Lamont Linstrom (eds), *The Pacific Theater: Island Representations of World War II* (Honolulu 1989) chs 3–6, 12.

like equals. Maasina Rule opposed the British return by setting up its own administration, by levying taxes and by demanding higher wages. The British Administration responded by banning Maasina Rule, and after it spread to other islands, 2,000 of its supporters were arrested in 1949, which helped deflate the movement. It was further discredited in 1950 when a predicted arrival of American planes to drive out the British, for which many Malaitians dug bomb shelters, failed to materialize.[2]

In other Melanesian islands there were some millenarian movements making prophecies about the arrival of planes, tanks and machine guns to liberate the coloured people from their white masters. Major examples were Skin Guria on the Huon Peninsula in the Australian mandated territory of New Guinea and John Frum on the island of Tanna in the Anglo-French administered New Hebrides Islands (Vanuatu). But a feature of such movements, called 'cargo cults' by Europeans, was their localized influence in the Melanesian region with its many languages and great cultural diversity. Consequently, none of the returning colonial administrations – British, Australian or French – had any major difficulty with protest movements.[3]

The main task of those administrations was reconstruction after massive war damage. For this purpose, the Australian Government increased its financial subsidy to its territories of Papua and New Guinea, which was only AUS£45,000 per annum in the 1930s, to AUS£2.6 million per annum. This massive increase reflected the new Australian appreciation of the territories' defence value and a sense of responsibility in Australia to the many Papua New Guineans who had assisted the Australian war effort. The previously separated territories of Papua and New Guinea were combined under the one administration under UN mandate, even though Papua had been a colony.[4]

In the French colony of New Caledonia the postwar French Socialist Government gave Kanaks citizenship rights and freedom from the prewar restrictions that had confined them to small reserva-

2. Judith Bennett, *Wealth of the Solomons: A History of a Pacific Archipelago* (Honolulu 1987) ch. 13.

3. Peter Hempenstall and Noel Rutherford, *Protest and Dissent in the Colonial Pacific* (Suva 1984) ch. 5. Michael Allen (ed.), *Vanuatu: Politics, Economics and Ritual in Island Melanesia* (Sydney 1981) ch. 14.

4. Ian Downs, *The Australian Trusteeship, Papua New Guinea 1945–75* (Canberra 1980) chs 2–3.

tions. A few educated Kanaks received voting rights. However, the colony also became an integral part of France, which did not bode well for its future independence. Another barrier to Kanak aspirations was the existence of a community of Europeans, known as Caldoche, with nineteenth-century roots and numbering 18,500 in 1946 compared with 31,000 Kanaks. Furthermore, Europeans controlled the best land and the colony's wealthy nickel production.[5]

Only in one Pacific Islands group was there a strong indigenous independence movement: New Zealand's mandated territory of Western Samoa. Samoans, who were largely self sufficient in their mostly subsistence economy, had expressed violent dissent from New Zealand rule in the Mau movement of the 1920s and early 1930s. Heavy New Zealand military action and the granting to Samoans of village level autonomy had worked to suppress this movement. However, during the Second World War, the presence of 2,000 American troops in Western Samoa, who treated Samoans better than did New Zealanders, prompted some islanders by 1944 to call for an end to New Zealand rule. But they were mollified by the visit to Samoa of the New Zealand prime minister, Peter Fraser, followed by the appointment of more sympathetic administrators and a firm promise to work towards independence. However, there was more dissent when the neglectful New Zealand Parliament approved the conversion of the League of Nations mandate to a UN trust territory without consulting the elected representatives of the Samoans. Many expressed a preference to join their East Samoan cousins under American rule. But they were persuaded by one of their high chiefs, Tamasese, to cooperate with New Zealand efforts to prepare them for independence.[6]

In Fiji, the 117,488 Fijians in 1946 were outnumbered by 120,063 Indians; Indians were brought into the colony in the nineteenth and early twentieth centuries to work in the predominant export crop, sugar, and now dominated, as well, the middle sections of an economy which was controlled by Australian companies and by the 4,594 European and part-European residents. Like Malayans, Fijians had been shielded by the British Administration from European

5. John Connell, *New Caledonia or Kanaky? The Political History of a French Colony* (Canberra 1987) 97, 241–3.
6. Malama Meleisea, *The Making of Modern Samoa: Traditional Authority and Colonial Administration in the Modern History of Western Samoa* (Suva 1987) ch. 6. J.W. Davidson, *Samoa Mo Samoa: The Emergence of the Independent State of Western Samoa* (Melbourne 1967) chs 5–6.

economic influences, though not from Christianity, which they had widely embraced. In the face of prewar Indian demands for equal rights, Fijian chiefs, who commanded strong Fijian loyalty, supported the continuation of a European-dominated legislative council. Further alienation between Fijians and Indians occurred during the Second World War when many of the former volunteered for military service and most of the latter stayed at home. More tension arose when in 1944 Indian sugar farmers went on strike against the Australian Colonial Sugar Refining Company (CSR), which had monopoly control over the milling of cane. Rising prices for sugar after the war reduced Indian cane farmer militancy, but Indian political grievances had not been requited.[7]

SLOW POLYNESIAN ROADS TO INDEPENDENCE

Independence was a slow process in the postwar Pacific even in Polynesia which had more culturally united societies than Melanesia. Independence for Western Samoans was delayed by their strong attachment to traditional culture. Modern anthropological research suggests that Samoan social conservatism was related to the widespread 'matai' system of chiefs, who were heads of extended families, elected by their kindred, giving Samoans great faith in their own social and political organizations.[8] Their attachment to traditional culture created a prejudice in the minds of New Zealand officials about the readiness of Samoans for independence. Furthermore, the insistence of most islanders, except a few western-educated Samoans, on enfranchising only the matai for elections to a self-governing assembly offended New Zealand notions of democracy. Nevertheless, the New Zealand Government was committed to bring the islands to independence, and new more culturally sensitive New Zealand officials in Samoa facilitated an agreement to graft the matai electorate

7. Timothy J. Macnaught, *The Fijian Colonial Experience* (Canberra 1982) chs 8–10. K.L. Gillion, *The Fiji Indians: Challenge to European Dominance 1920–1946* (Canberra 1977) chs 7–9. Michael Moynagh, *Brown or White? A History of the Fiji Sugar Industry, 1873–1973* (Canberra 1981) ch. 7.

8. Lowell D. Holmes, 'Factors Contributing to the Cultural Stability of Samoa', *Anthropological Quarterly*, 53, 1980, 188–96.

onto a Westminster system of government. On the voting register for the first Samoan legislature in 1957 there were only 5,030 matai voters in a Samoan population of 94,665, to elect 41 members. Two other seats were reserved for 5,790 'Europeans', who were mostly part-Samoans. On this electoral basis, Western Samoa became in 1962 the first Pacific Islands group, apart from New Zealand, to be granted independence.[9]

The next territory to become independent was the small equatorial island of Nauru. It was a 'treasure island' for Australian and New Zealand farmers, who benefited from Nauru's phosphate production supplied to them at half world prices, a saving in 1939 of 32 shillings per ton. By contrast Nauruans then received only eight pence per ton in royalties, and their island was being transformed by the mining into a moonscape-like desert. After the Second World War, during which Japanese armed forces deported many Nauruans to other islands, some Nauruans were looking forward to more self-rule rather than a continuation of heavily paternalistic Australian rule. Nauruans were also demanding big increases in their phosphate royalties. They achieved an increase to three shillings and two pence per ton by 1960. But neither Australia nor the UN, which had assumed the League of Nations trusteeship for the island, were contemplating independence.[10]

However, the Nauruan Head Chief from 1956, Hammer DeRoburt, who had received secondary school education in Australia and had led a strike in 1952 for wage increases for Nauruans, was pushing by the late 1950s for still higher phosphate prices and for self-government. In the early 1960s Nauru's leaders envisaged that they would achieve self-rule on another island, perhaps one offshore from Australia, to compensate for the destruction of much of their island. A precedent had been created by the shifting of the Banaban people from Ocean Island (ruined by phosphate mining) to Rabi Island in Fiji. However,

9. Davidson, *Samoa Mo Samoa* chs 10–12. *Pacific Islands Year Book (PIYB)* (8th edit., Sydney 1959) 79. *Report by the New Zealand Government to the General Assembly of the United Nations on the Administration of Western Samoa* 1959 (Wellington 1960) 31.

10. *Nauru Annual Report* 1939, 10. Maslyn Williams and Barrie Macdonald, *The Phosphateers: A History of the British Phosphate Commissioners and the Christmas Island Phosphate Commission* (Melbourne 1985) 273. Roger C. Thompson, 'Australasian, British and German Paternalism in Polynesia, 1900–39', in Kerry Howe, Brij Lal and Robert Kiste (eds), *Waves of History: The Pacific Islands in the Twentieth Century* (forthcoming). Barrie Macdonald, *In Pursuit of Sacred Trust: Trusteeship and Independence in Nauru* (Wellington 1988) 37–40.

negotiations for an Australian island foundered on the Nauruan demands for sovereign independence, though willing to concede to Australia control of defence and foreign affairs. DeRoburt's response in 1964 to this impasse was to demand the independence of Nauru by January 1967. The Australian Government was prepared to concede only a self-government that would not impede continued supply of cheap phosphate for Australian farms at least until the mid-1970s, when much of the supply would be exhausted. But DeRoburt took the issue to the UN, and New Zealand, one of the other two partners, with Great Britain, in the Phosphate Agreement, supported independence for Nauru. New Zealand took less phosphate from Nauru than did Australia and had already granted independence to Western Samoa. The UN and New Zealand pressure caused Australia to capitulate, leading to the birth of the world's smallest independent state in 1968. Its twenty-one square kilometres supported about 3,000 people.[11]

Fijians were much less keen than Samoans or Nauruans about independence. In the 1950s Fijian chiefs were happy to rely upon their alliance with the local European community and the maintenance of colonial rule in order to preserve their Christianized Polynesian social order from any challenge by the more numerous Indians. Nor in that decade, with high sugar prices and rising returns to Indian cane farmers, were there pressures from the Indian community for political change.

However, in 1959 a strike in the capital city, Suva, was a portent of a more unsettled future for the colony. The wages of unskilled workers had not increased since 1955, despite significant price inflation, and this was uniting Fijian and Indian workers against a common European enemy. Leading the workers was James Anthony, a young Indian-Irish-Polynesian secretary of the mixed race Wholesale and Retail Workers General Union, who was blessed with a charismatic personality and whom the governor described as 'probably the only true Communist resident in Fiji'. The industrial action started with an oil strike, though enough oil was exempted to maintain essential services. Two days of crowd action, aiming to prevent wider distribution of petrol, culminated in riot police moving with batons and tear gas into an unauthorized meeting of about 5,000 people listening to Anthony. The crowd of Indians and Fijians that streamed away left a trail of destruction through the Suva shopping centre, targeting especially European-owned stores. Rioting in Suva continued through the

11. Ibid. 40–54.

night. But on the next morning Fijian chiefs patrolled Suva's streets in motor cars calling on Fijian workers to abandon the strike and lecturing them about the shame that the violence had brought upon their community. The subsequent return of Fijians to work demonstrated the continued social power of Fiji's chiefs. They had been aghast at the implications of Indians and Fijians joining to attack the Europeans who were close allies in maintaining chiefly domination and keeping Indians at bay. After the strike, prompt action was taken by the chiefs to organize separate Fijian trade unions. Anthony was removed from the scene by the British Administration, which arranged a scholarship for him at the University of Hawaii. There he did a Master of Arts thesis on guerilla warfare, but he is not known to have put such theory into practice.[12]

In the 1960s Indian cane farmers in Fiji became more restive. A cane growers' strike in 1961 reflected dissatisfaction caused by an expansion of the sugar industry into marginal lands and its inability to keep up with a growing Indian population. A more immediate cause was that, with falling world sugar prices, the monopolistic CSR had cut the price paid to growers and imposed on them extra costs. An underlying problem was that CSR repatriated its profits to Australia rather than investing them in improvements to the industry, and the company was maintaining its successful prewar opposition to diversification of the Fijian economy. In 1960 sugar earned 60 per cent of the colony's export revenue. The cane grower's strike, however, failed because of previous CSR stockpiling of sugar.[13]

But the strike stimulated Indian leaders in the early 1960s to agitate for equal political rights for Indians. Such a move would give dominance in Fiji to the Indian population, which by 1970 comprised 51 per cent of the total population, compared with 43 per cent Fijians, 3 per cent Europeans and part-Europeans and 1 per cent Chinese. The remainder were other Pacific Islanders. In the postwar years until the 1960s there was no change to the legislative council arrangement of 1936, which had sixteen official members and five each from the European, Fijian and Indian communities. Significantly, the Fijian members were nominated by the Council of Chiefs. The chiefs did not agree to universal suffrage for Fijians until 1960, and only to prevent erosion of their authority by having such a

12. Hempenstall and Rutherford, *Protest and Dissent* ch. 3. Governor K.P. Maddox to the Earl of Ripon, 8 July 1959, CO 1036/380, PRO. Personal knowledge (the author shared a room with James Anthony at the Australian National University in 1968).

13. Moynagh, *Brown or White?* ch. 8.

change enforced upon them. The 1963 council elections saw another new phenomenon, the beginnings of an Indian political party, the Federation Party, led by the leader of the cane farmers' strike, A. D. Patel. This party demanded security for Indian cane farmers, the release of more Fijian-owned land for their use and equal voting rights for Indians. It also attacked European socio-economic domination and was supported by Patel's fellow merchants. However, the party urged its supporters not to offend Fijians and tried to woo them, with some success in Western Viti Levu where there was opposition to the power of the dominant chiefs of the Eastern region of Fiji. An alliance with a small Fijian party in that region created the National Federation Party (NFP).[14]

Britain responded to the Indian pressure. The new Labour government was keen to hand over the responsibility of governing Fiji to the local people. Fijian chiefs, who had formed their own political party to meet the Indian challenge, tried to resist the process, and they were able to achieve parity with Indians in a new legislative council which emerged from a constitutional conference in London in 1965 attended by leaders of Fiji's communities. In this arrangement 'general electors', who were members of the European community and of other races, would hold the balance of legislative power. It was a communal system designed to preserve Fijian-European political dominance against the majority Indians. The NFP accepted this imbalance as a first step towards achieving more political power for Indians, in the hope of future electoral change. After more political discussions, Fijian chiefs agreed to independence in 1970 on the understanding that with their European allies they would still maintain political control. The fifty-two seat House of Representatives had twelve seats for each of the Fijian and Indian communities and three for the general electors, with ten Fijians, ten Indians and five general electors to be elected in national seats. There was also an upper house, with eight members to be nominated by the Council of Chiefs, seven by the prime minister, six by the leader of the Opposition and one by the council of the island of Rotuma.[15]

In 1970 the British protectorate of Tonga also became an independent nation. Tonga was the one Pacific Islands group which had retained significant self-government under British colonial control, and where Europeans were denied land ownership in a nation of

14. *Fiji Annual Report* 1970, 12. Robert Norton, *Race and Politics in Fiji* (2nd edit. St Lucia 1990) 77–9, 89–104.
    15. Ibid. 104–5, 190.

mostly small farmers. This freedom had been won by the Wesleyan mission-supported King George Tupou I, who in the 1860s established a British-style parliamentary government dominated by the king and the Tongan nobility. After the declaration of the British protectorate in 1901 a partnership developed between the royal Tongan Government and British authority represented by the consul and European heads of government departments. The process was assisted significantly by Tonga's Queen Sālote III, a politically gifted and gracious ruler, whose long reign extended from 1918 until her death in 1965. By then, British involvement in the kingdom had diminished as overseas-educated Tongans assumed senior public service positions. With the British keenness to leave the Pacific, there was an easy transition to independence in 1970, the only real change being the independence celebrations.[16]

The British Government had more difficulty in shedding its governing responsibilities in its other Polynesian colony, the Gilbert and Ellice Islands. The colony was a widespread collection of small low-lying atolls, except for phosphate-rich but largely worked-out Ocean Island. In the Gilbert and Ellice Islands there were no demands for independence from the islanders. The colony was a quiet backwater of minimal government spending, and its subjects were relatively undisturbed by the challenges of secondary or tertiary education. As late as 1970 there were only 622 islanders enrolled in two secondary schools compared with 12,164 in primary schools. Furthermore, stretching across 1,600 kilometres of the Pacific Ocean, their small islands had few connections with each other, so that there was no sense of national unity. The relative poverty of the islanders made inter-island travel too expensive. Nevertheless, with orders from London, the colony's administration in 1967 transformed a nominated advisory council, established in the early 1960s, into an elected but still advisory House of Representatives. Seven years later, this legislature gained full self-governing power. This rapid transformation from autocratic colonial rule to self-government gave few islanders any real interest or understanding of the changes. The only political party, the Gilbertese National Party, was started in 1965 by civil servants from the Gilbert Islands, who were determined to protect their culture and interests from better educated Ellice Islanders. The concern of the Gilbertese diminished in the 1970s with the realization,

---

16. Noel Rutherford (ed.), *Friendly Islands: A History of Tonga* (Melbourne 1977) chs 9–11. Penelope A. Lavaka, The Limits of Advice: Britain and the Kingdom of Tonga, 1900–1970, PhD thesis, Australian National University, 1981, chs 2–6.

after the first parliamentary elections, that they would easily control the colony after independence. In a house of twenty-three members, there were nineteen Gilbertese, reflecting the fact that in 1968 they numbered 44,897 to 7,465 Ellice Islanders.[17]

This demographic reality encouraged Ellice Islanders to seek secession, although they spoke of it as separation. In one sense this demand was a reflection of history and geography. The two island archipelagos had been arbitrarily joined together in 1916, when two protectorates were made one colony for economic and administrative convenience. For census purposes the colony's people were always classed as ethnically different. The Ellice Islanders are Polynesians and the Gilbertese Micronesians, a difference that is observable by physical appearance and which was related to different linguistic and cultural patterns, such as a stronger chiefly social system in the Ellice Islands. The biggest separating factor was education. With much more keenness for Western education, Ellice Islanders considered themselves superior to Gilbertese and, indeed, Ellice Islanders gained a majority of overseas educational scholarships and senior civil service positions during the 1960s despite being only one-seventh of the population, a dominance which provoked the creation of the Gilbertese National Party. That party in turn encouraged Ellice Islanders to fear they would be discriminated against by the Gilbertese in a united independent country.[18]

The British Government was caught unawares by this Ellice Islander outcry for separation. Having done nothing to foster any sense of national unity in the islands in the past, London was prepared to accept partition of the colony, remembering the violence that had occurred on the Caribbean island of Anguilla in 1969 when it was arbitrarily included in a federation of the West Indies. In a referendum observed by the UN in 1974, 92 per cent of Ellice Islanders voted for separation. By 1976 arrangements for partition of the colony were complete, and in October 1978 the Ellice Islands became the independent state of Tuvalu, which with 7,357 people living on twenty-six square kilometres of land was the world's second smallest state. In July 1979, after further negotiations about remaining phosphate revenue, the Gilbert Islands plus Ocean Island, became the independent state of Kiribati. Though much more populous than

17. *Gilbert and Ellice islands Annual Report* 1970, 38–9, 6. Barrie Macdonald, *Cinderellas of the Empire: Towards a History of Kiribati and Tuvalu* (Canberra 1982) ch. 13.
18. Ibid. 244–53.

Tuvalu, its 726 square kilometres of low lying atoll land also rendered its economic future dependent on outside aid. [19]

PUSHING INDEPENDENCE FOR PAPUA NEW GUINEA

In the much bigger islands of Melanesia, greater cultural diversity and less educational and economic development than in Polynesia were major impediments to independence. So too were the prevailing views of colonial authorities that 'primitive' Melanesians would be incapable of governing themselves for many more decades. In 1951 the Australian minister for territories, Paul Hasluck, said: 'It is to be hoped that New Guinea will develop first towards greater participation in the local management of purely local affairs, and eventually beyond that to some form of self-government . . . That is a long way ahead. It may be . . . more than half a century ahead'. [20]

Using this model of development, in his twelve years of administration from 1951, Hasluck concentrated on extending primary school education with an aim of universal literacy as a basis for future development towards self-management. However, a rapidly expanding population and the discovery of more people in previously unopened areas of the vast highlands region of the country defeated what was too idealistic an aim. In 1960 only 10 per cent of the known 1,815,391 Papua New Guineans were attending schools, compared with 31 per cent of Gilbert and Ellice Islanders. [21]

Attempts to promote indigenous economic development were also limited. In 1960 Papua New Guineans produced only 38 per cent of the territory's coffee production, the largest proportion for any crop except rice. Agricultural production was dominated by Europeans who, with the opening of the climatically attractive highlands to settlement in the 1950s, had increased in numbers during that decade from 10,854 to 18,978. The one success story in indigenous develop-

---

19. Ibid. 253–75. *PIYB* (14th edit., Sydney 1981) 468.

20. Quoted in Hank Nelson, *Taim Bilong Masta: The Australian Involvement with Papua New Guinea* (Sydney 1982) 212.

21. *Papua Annual Report* 1960–61, 255–6. *Territory of New Guinea Annual Report* 1960–61, 163.

ment had been Hasluck's policy of establishing local government councils, which by 1960 covered over a third of the population.[22]

A major step forward in Papua New Guinea's progress towards independence came at the time of a visit in 1962 by a mission from the UN Trusteeship Council led by Sir Hugh Foot, a former British governor who had presided over the introduction of self-government into Nigeria and Jamaica. He was astounded to hear from Australian officials that they would still be ruling the territory in the next century. His report firmly recommended a nationally elected parliament by 1964, concerted efforts to promote national unity, and an end to discriminatory practices, especially the repeal of laws banning the sale of alcoholic drinks to Papua New Guineans. This report challenged the Australian Government at a time when it was realizing that the slow pace of preparation of the territory for independence should be quickened. So Foot's report assisted the implementation of reforms already in the pipeline, such as lifting the alcohol ban. Consequently, an elected House of Assembly was introduced in 1964 after a mammoth administrative programme to inform people about how to vote and to deliver waterproof ballot boxes, mainly by aircraft, to 2,919 polling places.[23]

However, there was no demand for independence among Papua New Guineans in the early 1960s. There were some signs of dissatisfaction with the paternalistic colonial order. The most marked was on the island of Buka, where postwar opposition to returning Australians had been expressed in cargo cult movements. That spirit resurfaced in 1960 with the appearance of the Hahalis Welfare Society, which refused to cooperate with the establishment of a local government council and was soon urging people not to pay new taxes levied to support the council. The movement also upset local Catholic missionaries by encouraging teenage girls to offer sexual services to any takers; the consequent children were communally raised in a baby farm. The Australian Administration in the distant capital of Port Moresby responded to the tax strike in 1962 by sending police to hunt for tax evaders, leading to confrontations with angry mobs. Judicious handling of the police by their Australian officers prevented any bloodshed; and widespread arrests and delivery of more government expenditure for economic development in Buka deflated the protest. But the Hahalis movement was a sign of future dissent in a region which was culturally distinct from the rest of Papua

22. Downs, *The Australian Trusteeship* ch. 7.
23. Ibid. 239–51, 305–9.

New Guinea. The people of Buka and neighbouring Bougainville are mostly black rather than the shades of brown of other Papua New Guineans. Buka-Bougainvillians are culturally allied to the Western Solomon islands, from which they had been arbitrarily separated by colonial boundaries drawn principally because German and Australian administrations in New Guinea had valued the work of Bougainvillians as plantation labourers.[24]

A more concerted protest movement developed in the late 1960s in one of Papua New Guinea's most economically developed regions, the Gazelle Peninsula on the island of New Britain. The Tolai people of that region had experienced the longest contact of any Papua New Guineans with Europeans, going back to the 1870s. Since then, 40 per cent of Tolai land had been alienated to European planters. With postwar population growth, land shortage was becoming a Tolai grievance by the 1960s. The catalyst for protest was the transformation in 1968 of the Tolai local government council into a multiracial one that included the European and Chinese residents of the region and its principal town, Rabaul. This move was part of an Australian Government plan to make local government councils more efficient on a multiracial basis. But the change was seized upon by Oscar Tammur, a Roman Catholic-educated Tolai who had received army training in Australia and was campaigning in 1968 for a House of Assembly seat in the second national election. Tammur charged that the new council was a denial of Tolai rights and skilfully linked the issue with land rights grievances.

After winning a House of Assembly seat in 1968, Tammur became convenor of the Mataungan Association, which campaigned for a dissolution of the new council, for Tolai land rights and for Tolai control of their own affairs. 'They have taken our land, now they want our Council', was a prominent catch-cry. The movement also called for Tolais to stop paying taxes. The Administration refused to back down from its 'progressive' local government policy, failing to understand Tolai grievances. Riot police were flown to Rabaul in September 1969 after Mataungan supporters seized the legislative council building. Two Mataungan leaders were arrested. The association responded in November with a large protest march in Rabaul and a Sunday morning of violence as truck-loads of club-wielding men descended on the houses of pro-administration

24. Ibid. 202–6. Hugh Laracy, *Marists and Melanesians: A History of Catholic Missions in the Solomon Islands* (Canberra 1976) 135–42.

Tolais, who received beatings, some very severe. Subsequent mass arrests of Mataungan leaders quietened the movement, but it did not die out. On a visit to Rabaul in January 1970, when he was greeted by a 10,000–strong crowd, the Australian Labor Party leader, Gough Whitlam, expressed support for Tolai land rights and for local self-government. Six months later a similarly huge crowd in Rabaul confronted the Australian prime minister, John Gorton, raising fists and brandishing banners, with slogans such as 'Gorton go to hell'. More violence between Mataungan supporters and police followed. But the movement lost ground after the Australian district commissioner in the Gazelle peninsula, Jack Emmanuel, was murdered in August 1971, which shocked the largely church-attending Tolai people. The Papua New Guinea Government also was able to reach an acceptable compromise in 1973 with Mataungan leaders on local government and land issues.[25]

Though the Mataungan Association was agitating for local rights, its militancy gave a significant push to the independence process for Papua New Guinea. After 1963, preparations for independence had slowed down under Charles Barnes, a more conservative Australian minister for territories than Hasluck. Barnes stressed economic development to give Papua New Guinea a secure financial base for independence before any move to self-government. This policy included welcoming European capital and settlers, who raised the non-indigenous population of the territory to 48,960 in 1970. However, this was not a troublesome expatriate community as in Kenya or in New Caledonia since, unlike those colonies, most of the settlers arrived after the Second World War, when ultimate independence for Papua New Guinea was settled government policy. Nor did Barnes make any promises about permanent settler rights after independence. But the Mataungan demonstrations in Rabaul convinced a new minister for territories in 1971, Andrew Peacock, to push rapidly for independence, a process which Whitlam, when he became the Australian prime minister in December 1972, firmly continued. Full self-government was implemented in 1973 with a commitment to independence in two years' time.[26]

By this stage there was a Papua New Guinean political party advocating independence, the Pangu Parti. It had been organized in 1967 by young graduates from the territory's administration

25. Downs, *The Australian Trusteeship* 330–40, 424–37, 465–7, 475–7, 510–25.
26. Ibid. chs 10–13. *Papua New Guinea Annual Report* 1970–71, 238.

college led by Michael Somare, a journalist and radio announcer from the Sepik River district. They were assisted by some liberal minded Australians who became party members. However, Pangu gained only twenty-four seats in the expanded House of Assembly's 108 seats in the 1972 election. Local loyalties dominated the election except in the case of a United Party, organized by highlanders, which won forty-two seats. However, it was a conservative party unenthusiastic about the rush to independence because highlanders feared domination by more sophisticated coastal and island Papua New Guineans. Nevertheless, Somare was able to become the prime minister of the self-governing country with the support of independents and small parties in the assembly.[27]

The independence preparations were a crash programme. Though education of Papua New Guineans had improved, including the founding of a university in 1966, there were in 1970 only 19,947 secondary school students in an indigenous population of 2,466,986. There was, consequently, a great shortage of skilled people to run an administration created on Australian lines. The time to train ministers and public servants for independence was less than two years. Furthermore, the nation had been given a Westminster system of government without much consideration of the wide linguistic and cultural diversity in the country, a recipe for political instability. However, the self-governing parliament was given freedom to shape constitutional provisions, such as incorporating customary law.[28]

The cultural and geographic diversity of Papua New Guinea produced separatist movements. In Papua, outnumbered nearly three-to-one by New Guineans, some politicians were calling for separation. Few Papuans spoke pidgin, the lingua franca in most of New Guinea. Papuans also had been more sheltered than New Guineans from economic development. However, cultural diversity within Papua and the cosmopolitan nature of its capital city, Port Moresby, limited the separatist appeal. More ominous was a movement in Bougainville for separation based on the distinct cultural and racial differences there – black Bougainvillians called other Papua New

27. Ibid. 385–92, 486–94. David Stephen, *A History of Political Parties in Papua New Guinea* (Melbourne 1972) ch. 5.

28. J.A. Ballard (ed.), *Policy Making in a New State: Papua New Guinea 1972–77* (St Lucia 1981) 19–74. Tony Delkin, 'In Search of a Home-Grown Constitution: The Constitutional Development in Papua New Guinea between 1962 and 1975' in Sione Lātūkefu (ed.), *Papua New Guinea: A Century of Colonial Impact 1884–1984* (Port Moresby 1989) ch. 21.

Guineans 'redskins'. The giant Australian-owned Panguna copper mine on the island, which since 1967 had been pumping money into the national treasury, was a particular grievance. However, at this stage a nationalist-minded Bougainvillian parliamentarian, Paul Lapun, had satisfied the owners of the land occupied by the mine by sponsoring legislation granting them five per cent of the central government's copper royalties. Somare's government also skilfully manoeuvred Bougainville and the other regions into the new nation by establishing provincial governments which controlled significant powers. However, national unity was to continue to be a major problem facing the new nation, which celebrated its independence in September 1975.[29]

INDEPENDENCE FOR THE SOLOMON ISLANDS AND VANUATU

There were contrasting styles of progress to independence in two other Melanesian island groups, the Solomon Islands and Vanuatu. The Solomons were one of the backwaters of the British Empire. In 1960 there was one boys' secondary school in the protectorate, and primary education was in the hands of the Christian missions, with varying standards of quality. There were few all-weather roads, transport being mostly confined to sea and air. Revenue was based heavily on a single product, copra, which in the two years 1959–60 earned 98 per cent of domestic export revenue. Government attempts to diversify the economy had failed, none more so than an ambitious cocoa-planting scheme. Little attention had been paid to climate and soil suitability; the imported seeds grew into plants that were blighted by insects and disease. During the 1960s the British Government injected more funds to provide a wider economic base for an independent state. Education was improved, and an advisory council in 1960 was transformed into a nationally elected legislature by 1970. Nevertheless, that year there was a smaller proportion of the 156,066 Solomon Islanders attending secondary schools (0.6 per cent) than of the much more numerous Papua New Guineas

29. Downs, *The Australian Trusteeship* 340–62, 440–1, 449–50, 525–9, 540–6. *Papua New Guinea Annual Report* 1970–71, 200, 238.

(0.8 per cent). The reliance on copra had declined to 54 per cent of domestic export revenue in 1969–70 because of a big increase in much less renewable and far greater land-destructive timber exports (42 per cent). There had been a major fall in copra prices because of wider world competition from synthetic substitutes; in 1970 copra earned 25 per cent less than in 1960, despite significant price inflation during the decade. The copra and timber industries were also vulnerable to unpredictable cyclone damage.[30]

In the 1970s, with Britain's keenness to abandon remaining colonies growing under the impact of balance of payment problems at home, independence was strongly pushed in the Solomon Islands. However, a crash programme to equip Solomon Islanders to run their own government ran into problems. There was no islander demand for independence, apart from a few graduates from overseas universities. A committee system of government after 1970 based on British experience in other small colonies, and said to be suited to the major role of consensus in Melanesian culture, displeased aspiring islander politicians because they were deprived of publicity platforms. The slowness of decision-making also discredited the system. Therefore, the government was reorganized in 1974 on Westminster lines, under which limited self-government was introduced in 1976.[31]

A more serious problem was a threat of secession by the Western Islands of New Georgia, Choisel and nearby smaller islands. That sector, which contains the blackest of the Solomon Islanders, was better educated than the rest because of longstanding Methodist mission schooling. The Western Islands' lighter population density gave their people larger average landholdings than in other islands, supplemented by good fishing resources. Western Islanders were proud of their status as independent producers who were not reliant on migratory labour. Their better economic resources, superior education and racial, cultural and religious distinctiveness encouraged Westerners to look down upon other islanders, especially those from much more densely populated Malaita, which supplied the bulk of the protectorate's labour force. Fearing being swamped by uncouth Malaitans, one of whom, Peter Kenilora, became chief minister in 1977, some Western leaders were calling for secession from the coming independent nation. However, the sentiment was more fear for the future than a concerted independence movement

30. *British Solomon Islands Annual Report*, 1959–60, 21, 35, 54–5; 1970, 10, 15, 142. Bennett, *Wealth of the Solomons* 312–13.
    31. Ibid. 318–22.

and attracted only a minority of the people in the region. The central government headed off the separatist movement by giving the Western Islanders more autonomy and increased financial resources. Independence arrived in the Solomons on 7 July 1978 with no significant dissension.[32]

In contrast to the Solomons, there was an active independence movement in Vanuatu. Its main cause was the Anglo–French division of the administration of those islands. The bizarre New Hebrides Condominium, locally known as 'Pandemonium', had created separate health, education, police and other administrative systems for French and British nationals, leaving the islanders as stateless people. French citizens were more numerous because of the geographic propinquity of New Caledonia with its large European population. In 1967 there were 2,835 French nationals in Vanuatu, compared with 621 British in a population of 77,982. But the Australian-based Presbyterian mission had a predominant influence over the islanders, with the Anglican Melanesian Mission covering most of the rest. By contrast, French Roman Catholic missionaries had gained only a small foothold in the islands. The French Administration woke up to this mission legacy too late. Though by 1960 a new French school building programme had commenced, the emerging islander leaders were almost entirely educated by the Anglo-Protestant missions.[33]

In 1971 the New Hebrides National Party (NHNP) was formed in Vila, the capital of the Condominium. The party's leader was Walter Lini, an Anglican priest. Its main policies were the promotion of islander culture (*kastom*) and land rights, which tapped emerging islander grievances about the 36 per cent of the territory's land alienated to Europeans – 32 per cent to French citizens. The French Administration tried to head off the dissent by releasing much of the French-owned properties for islander use, but the choicest 6 per cent of the archipelago's land remained in European hands. In response, the NHNP agitated for independence. But this campaign ran into a brick wall of French opposition, whereas the British Government was eager to facilitate a quick preparation for independence.[34]

32. Ibid. 327–9. Information from Ian Blaikie, an Australian school teacher in the Solomon Islands from 1978 to 1986.

33. Norma McArthur and J.F. Yaxley, *Condominium of the New Hebrides: A Report of the First Census of the Population, 1967* (Sydney 1978). Howard Van Trease, *The Politics of Land in Vanuatu: From Colony to Independence* (Suva 1987) chs 3–4. R. Hodgson to A. Tange, 22 Sep. 1960, A1838/T53, 338/1 Pt. 1, Australian Archives, Canberra.

34. Van Trease, *Politics of Land* 206–24.

However, having granted all its colonists elsewhere universal suffrage, France could not object to the British proposal for an elected national assembly. In the elections in 1976 the NHNP won 59 per cent of the vote, gaining seventeen of twenty-nine elected seats. But other seats were reserved for community groups, including the French-dominated Chamber of Commerce, producing a deadlock in the assembly. The NHNP responded by boycotting the assembly, depriving it of a quorum. Consequent public demonstrations organized by the party and by its opponents during 1977 included the wielding of sharpened sticks and stones and police teargas responses. By the end of the year the NHNP, now renamed the Vanua'aku (Our Land) Party, declared the independence of the islands and the establishment of a People's Provisional Government. It proceeded to control large sections of the territory.[35]

Paris could not respond, as desired, by sending troops to crush the provisional government without the agreement of the British Government, which was embarrassed by public criticism of the use of teargas against pro-independence demonstrators. The French minister for overseas territories, Paul Dijoud, travelled to Vanuatu and negotiated a compromise agreement for a constitution for an independent state that would respect French language and culture and allow some regional autonomy. Land would be returned to customary owners and future expatriate land ownership would be banned. Under the terms of this Dijoud Plan elections were held on 14 November 1979 for a new representative assembly under UN supervision. Despite intensive campaigning by the French local administration in favour of two francophone parties, the Vanua'aku Party won with 62 per cent of the vote and a two-thirds majority of the thirty-nine assembly seats. Self-government had been achieved with Lini as prime minister, with the required majority to make constitutional changes.[36]

This degree of supremacy for an anglophone party was too much for some French settlers and for francophone ni-Vanuatu, as the islanders were calling themselves. A prominent dissident was Jimmy Stephens, a part-European, who had been leading since the late 1960s a political organization, *Nagriamel*, based on land rights issues, which became a francophone opponent of the Vanua'aku Party. On 28 May

35. Ibid. 224–31. Christopher Plant, 'New Hebrides 1977: Year of Crisis', *Journal of Pacific History* 13, 1978, 194–204.

36. Van Trease, *Politics of Land* 231–46. Stephen Henningham, *France and the South Pacific: A Contemporary History* (Sydney 1992) 38–9.

1980, with the backing of French colons, Stephens launched a rebellion on the island of Santo against Lini's government. There were attacks on British and Vanua'aku Party property with smashing of buildings and looting of possessions, forcing Vanua'aku Party supporters to flee into the bush or retreat from the island along with the British police. There was no attack on any French property nor any attempt by the French police to stop the violence. Lini declared a blockade of Santo, but his government had no military force. France intervened with the despatch of troops from Noumea to the Condominium, ostensibly to stop further violence. Britain responded by sending a force of marines, with the result that armed forces of two NATO allies were confronting each other in a remote Pacific Islands group while doing nothing to stop the rebellion. Clear evidence emerged afterwards that the French Administration in Vanuatu supported the insurrection. Whether such complicity was sanctioned by Paris is unknown, but the highly centralized French state normally kept a tight control of its colonial administrations.[37]

Lini's government responded with a declaration of independence on 30 June 1980 under the terms of the Dijoud Plan. The rebels on Santo greeted the news with more violence against non-French property. But Lini played a totally unexpected trump card. On 6 August 1980 a contingent of Papua New Guinea troops, accompanied by police from Vila, were landed on Santo by Australian military aircraft. This Australian logistic support for English speaking Melanesian troops was decisive. The insurrection quickly collapsed with the arrest of Stephens and many of his supporters. All of Vanuatu was now fully independent.[38]

OPPOSITION TO INDEPENDENCE IN THE FRENCH PACIFIC

The attempt to retain a French presence in Vanuatu was part of the maintenance of France's status as a *puissance mondiale moyenne* (middle-sized world power). A Pacific centrepiece to this 'grand

---

37. Ibid. 28–31, 38–43. Van Trease, *Politics of Land* 246–56. John Beasant, *The Santo Rebellion: An Imperial Reckoning* (Honolulu 1984) chs 5–6.
38. Ibid. ch. 7. Van Trease, *Politics of Land* 257–8.

design' was the *Centre d'Expérimentation du Pacifique* (CEP), the euphemistically named nuclear testing facilities on Moruroa Atoll, which lies on the southern edge of the Tuamotu Archipelago in French Polynesia, about 110 kilometres southeast of that territory's main island of Tahiti. This remote sector of the Pacific Basin assumed a new importance in France's efforts to maintain world power status after being expelled in 1962 from Algeria, the previous centre for atomic testing. Open-air nuclear testing began at Moruroa in 1966 and quickly attracted world criticism and opposition within French Polynesia.[39]

An early postwar independence movement had emerged in the widely scattered island groups of French Polynesia where, in 1956, 87 per cent of the 73,202 people were Polynesians (Maohi), 9 per cent were Chinese and 3 per cent were French. More than half of the Maohi were Protestant in religion, a legacy of the London Missionary Society which reached the islands before French occupation and reinforced anti-French popular attitudes.[40]

A Maohi advocate for independence was a First World War veteran, Pouvanaa a Oopa, an eloquent Tahitian orator who was apt to use biblical comparisons of his people under French rule with the captive Hebrews in ancient Egypt. He won notoriety in 1947 when he led a large crowd of Tahitians to block, for two days, the landing of three new French officials, arguing that administrative positions should be reserved for islanders. After a naval vessel whisked the officials ashore in early morning hours, Pouvanaa was arrested, held in custody for five months and charged with rebellion. However, the jury acquitted him and his associates after their defence council pointed to their wartime medals and argued that they were not anti-French. The affair conferred martyr status on Pouvanaa. From 1949 he was the territory's elected member in the French Parliament, and his political party, the *Rassemblement Démocratique des Populations Tahitiennes* (RDPT), achieved majorities in the territory's legislative assembly in 1953 and 1957. But the assembly had limited powers, and internal rivalry weakened the party. Nevertheless, French settlers felt threatened by the RDPT, especially after it used its seventeen-to-thirteen seat majority in the legislature in April 1958 to pass resolutions in favour of independence

39. Jean Chesneaux, 'The Function of the Pacific in the French Fifth Republic's "Grand Design": Theory and Practice of the "Puissance Mondiale Moyenne"', *Journal of Pacific History* 26, 1991, 256–72.

40. *PIYB* 8th edit., 139.

and to impose an income tax which hit the richer French members of the population. A shopkeepers' strike in Papeete, the capital of Tahiti, against the tax and a large protest march forced a climb-down by the RDPT on the tax and independence issues. Pouvanaa campaigned strongly for a 'no' vote in the referendum on the continuation of French rule in September 1958, which President de Gaulle arranged for all France's colonies. But a split in the RDPT reduced Pouvanaa's ability to deliver a majority vote for independence; 76 per cent of the voters in the territory favoured continuing French rule. Pouvanaa's opponents achieved their revenge when in October 1959 he was tried and convicted to eight years' imprisonment and sixteen years' exile for conspiring to burn down the legislature building in alleged bitterness at the defeat of the referendum, though in defence Pouvanaa said his threats were no more than a metaphorical use of biblical analogies.[41]

The independence issue was subsequently played down by Maohi parties after the RDPT was banned in 1964 for circulating petitions opposing the stationing of French troops in the territory. The fragmented Maohi parties now argued for autonomy as a first step to independence. The conservative majority in the legislature after Pouvanaa's imprisonment rescinded the independence motion and handed back some powers to the governor.[42]

Furthermore, a major economic transformation was taking place in French Polynesia. The CEP brought new prosperity. The proportion of French financial transfers to the territory's GNP expanded from 16 per cent in 1960–63 to 59 per cent in 1964–69. The attraction of Tahiti as the economic and administrative centre increased, with its share of the territory's population growing from 49 per cent in 1951 to 70 per cent in 1977. By that year new French settlers to French Polynesia had trebled the proportion of the European population since 1956 to 9 per cent. Also 7 per cent of the population were part-Europeans, though labelled 'Polynesians'.[43]

The CEP was opposed by a coalition of pro-autonomy parties, called the *Front Uni*, which achieved a majority of seats in the two legislative assembly elections of 1967 and 1972. The French Government strongly resisted the autonomy aim because it was seen as a step towards independence, which could threaten the

41. Henningham, *France and the South Pacific* 117–26. Robert Langdon, *Tahiti: Island of Love* (5th edit. Sydney 1979) ch. 22.

42. Henningham, *France and the South Pacific* 132–3.

43. Ibid. 127–9. Barry Shineberg, 'The Image of France: Recent developments in French Polynesia', *Journal of Pacific History* 21, 1986, 153–7. *PIYB* 14th edit., 131.

future of the CEP. However, after the election to the presidency of France of Valéry Giscard d'Estaing in 1974, the nuclear testing went underground, partially in response to the *Front Uni*, but more as a concession to wider world opposition to the open-air testing. The elected legislature was given more responsibility, and the governor became high commissioner, with the legislature appointing a council of government with local administrative responsibility, but still under overall French control. Nevertheless, in return for the concessions, the *Front Uni*'s leaders, Francis Sanford and John Teariki, stopped campaigning against the nuclear tests or for more autonomy. Teariki recognized a new economic dependency that the CEP had created in his comment: 'the people want independence, but how would they live?'.[44] This dependency was indicated by a growth in food imports, which by 1980 had more than doubled from their 37 per cent of food consumption in 1960. Indeed, the French Government increased its expenditure in the territory in the late 1970s in order to strengthen the economic chains binding its people to France. Only two small parties, *Ia Mana Te Nunua* and the Polynesian Liberation Front, were keeping the pro-independence light burning.[45]

STRUGGLE FOR INDEPENDENCE IN NEW CALEDONIA

A reverse independence process was occurring among the Kanaks of New Caledonia. In 1951, their franchise was increased close to adult suffrage, a spin-off from reforms in France's wider colonial empire. With 8,700 voters, their political power nearly matched that of the 10,888 European voters. Also an educated Kanak elite had been formed through educational programmes run by the Roman Catholic and Protestant Churches in New Caledonia. At first Kanak leaders mostly gave their support to a new multiracial political party, the *Union Calédonienne* (UC), led by Maurice Lenormand, a French-born pharmacist, who had a Kanak wife and who was willing to support Kanak social and economic advancement. Though such policies placed him at odds with many Europeans, the UC's liberal

44. Quoted in Langdon, *Tahiti: Island of Love* 257.
45. Henningham, *France in the South Pacific* 127–40. Shineberg, 'Image of France' 162–3.

policies, such as redistributing land and more territorial control over the dominant nickel mining company, *Société le Nickel* (SLN), attracted votes from the economically depressed white small farmer community and from the urban working class in a society dominated by a landholding and mining investment elite. In 1953 UC won fifteen of the twenty-three seats in New Caledonia's legislature. Two years earlier Lenormand had been elected as New Caledonia's sole representative in the French Parliament because of divisions among conservative opponents. Outraged European conservatives could not agree on any united opposition to the UC.[46]

Entrenched in power for the rest of the 1950s, the UC introduced a minimum wage for all people in the territory, family allowances and holiday pay and increased opportunities for Kanak education. Lenormand's emphasis was on integrating Kanaks into the community, and he strongly affirmed the link with France. The UC's campaign for a 'yes' vote in the 1958 referendum on retention of French rule produced a 95 per cent affirmative majority in New Caledonia. However, the UC found the land reform problem too hard to solve, because of competing demands from its Caldoche and Kanak supporters and because of the entrenched nature of the existing pattern of land holdings in white society. Nevertheless, the party was bolstered by the election in 1956 of a socialist government in France, which introduced universal suffrage in all France's overseas territories, and ensured that the New Caledonian territorial assembly would have much local power, though France retained control over defence, finance, international communications and the civil service.[47]

However, from 1957 the UC's power started to wane. Conservative political propaganda about defending European society against upstart Kanaks was draining Caldoche support from the party. The advent of the conservative de Gaulle to power in France in 1958 inspired conservatives to demonstrate in Noumea for the resignation of Lenormand and his government. A threat of Kanak counter-demonstrations caused Europeans in Noumea to dig trenches and raise barricades. But the governor defused the situation by banning the carrying of arms, and the agitation temporarily collapsed. De Gaulle's government also started stripping the powers of the legislature in a calculated bid to oust Lenormand. De Gaulle had visited New

46. Myriam Dornoy, *Politics in New Caledonia* (Sydney 1984) 154–64. Connell, *New Caledonia or Kanaky* 241–5.

47. Ibid., 194–7, 245–8. Dornoy, *Politics* 60, 164–8. Henningham, *France in the South Pacific* 54–6.

Caledonia in 1957 and had made contacts with conservatives there. A downturn in the price of nickel, the mainstay of the colony's economy, was exacerbating tension. In 1962, two days after the UC government rejected a request from the SLN for export tax exemption, a bomb exploded in the legislative assembly. The governor, who had supported the SLN request, closed the assembly, but in a new election the UC still won eighteen of the thirty seats. More violence followed including a bomb blast at UC headquarters. Of three suspects, two were members of the UC but recent immigrants with suspected French secret service connections. They confessed that Lenormand had consented to the planting of the bomb in order to discredit conservatives, but later retracted that accusation. Despite obvious weaknesses in the prosecution evidence, Lenormand was convicted for allowing a crime to occur and was awarded a year's suspended jail sentence. Crucially, for his political power, his civil liberties were suspended for five years. Conservatives had achieved their revenge for his desertion of racial ranks.[48]

The UC remained in existence under Lenormand's Kanak deputy Roch Pidjot. However, the assembly lost much of its autonomous power in this decade. The importance of the territory in French Government eyes was growing, in contrast to diminishing British interest in Pacific colonies. One reason for the difference was the CEP and the feeling in French government circles that independence for New Caledonia could inspire the independence movement in French Polynesia. The CEP also enhanced the importance of all French Pacific territories in supporting France's world power aspirations. Under de Gaulle's Fifth Republic, the traditional French colonial attitude of regarding French dependencies as extensions of metropolitan France was reinforced. The people of New Caledonia were all encouraged to think of themselves as French, even though Kanaks suffered from socio-economic discrimination at the hands of local Europeans. Furthermore, New Caledonia's nickel exports were increasing, making the colony the world's second largest nickel producer, with 20 per cent of the world's production by 1970. New laws increased French Government control of the economy including all aspects of the mining industry. Electoral changes, such as increasing seats in Noumea, weakened the UC, though it still won enough European working-class votes to remain in power throughout the 1960s. Continued divisions also inhibited the UC's political opponents.[49]

---

48. Ibid., 56–60. Connell, *New Caledonia or Kanaky* 248–51.
49. Ibid. 251–6. Henningham, *France in the South Pacific* 47–8.

However, demographic changes were eroding the position of Kanaks in their own country. European immigration was growing, boosted by a Vietnam War-driven boom in nickel prices and by deliberate French Government policy. The French prime minister, Pierre Messmer, told his secretary of state for overseas departments and territories in 1972: 'It is necessary to seize this last chance to create another Francophone country so that the French presence . . . [is not] threatened . . . by nationalist claims from the indigenous people . . . The success of this task, essential to support French interests east of Suez, depends on our ability to succeed . . . with an operation to populate this overseas country'.[50] Many of the new settlers were former French colons expelled from independent Algeria, who were strongly racist in their views. These immigrants contributed to the formation in 1968 of the *Comité d'Action Civique*, with a commitment to struggle against opponents of French rule. The influx of Europeans, and also workers from the French Wallis and Futuna Islands, decreased the Kanak proportion of the colony's population from 51 per cent in 1956 to 46 per cent in 1969. During those years the proportion of Europeans rose from 37 per cent to 41 per cent; and 9 per cent of the 100,579 people in New Caledonia in 1969 were from other Pacific islands, especially the Wallis and Futuna Islands. The conservative and strongly Roman Catholic Polynesian inhabitants of those islands had voted overwhelmingly in 1958 to convert their French protectorate into an integrated French overseas territory. Many of these islanders were using their French citizenship to escape from the subsistence economy and high population growth of their islands.[51]

Kanaks in New Caledonia also were suffering from the greatest land inequity in the Pacific Islands. While there was some transfer of land to Kanak reservations, which grew from 126,000 hectares in 1945 to 161,932 hectares in 1969, Europeans still owned 370,000 hectares, much of it of better quality than Kanak land. The economy was dominated by the nickel industry, shared by the SLN in which the French Government had direct vested interests, and by ten Caldoche families, inappropriately named 'small miners'. The European dominance was increasing with the nickel boom and was widening the gap between wealthy urban Europeans and Kanaks. Many Kanaks were still living on marginal rural land, and few Kanaks in urban areas had better than unskilled employment.[52]

50. Quoted in Connell, *New Caledonia or Kanaky* 218.
51. Ibid. 211. Henningham, *France in the South Pacific* 179–80, 183–4.
52. Ibid. 63–6. Alan W. Ward, *Land and Politics in New Caledonia* (Canberra 1982)
10. Connell, *New Caledonia or Kanaky* 125–7.

This contrast helped spawn a new Kanak radicalism in the late 1960s. This development also was influenced by the return to New Caledonia of a small number of the first Kanak university students from France, where they had been influenced by radical French students and were encouraged to reflect on colonial oppression in their home islands. Another important cause of radicalism was dissatisfaction among politically aware Kanaks with the failure of the UC to introduce major reforms, especially land reform. Riotous protest meetings and arrests and imprisonment of Kanak leaders began in 1969. The arrests stoked the fires of Kanak anger. Slogans like 'Calédonie libre' were being daubed on Noumea walls, and Kanak rebellions during the colonial past were being commemorated in song and story.[53]

Kanak protests grew in the early 1970s and inevitably provoked a right wing back lash. In December 1975 communal violence produced its first death when a young Kanak, Richard Kamouda, acting out a mock boxing match with a friend in a Noumea street, was shot at point blank range while resisting arrest by a French policeman, who escaped with a suspended sentence. Kamouda's death was to most Kanaks an assassination; to most Europeans it was justified homicide. The two communities were moving further apart.[54]

Kanak frustration with French intransigence about self-government also had a radical political fallout. In 1970 some of them launched the *Union Multiraciale de Nouvelle Calédonie* (UMNC), led by Yann Celene Uregei. Despite its name, it was the first wholly Kanak political party, the beginning of the break-up of the political alliance of the previous two decades between left wing Europeans and Kanaks. In 1975 Uregei shocked Europeans with a speech in the Assembly calling for independence for New Caledonia. Disagreements, however, about the extent of radical social policies and rivalries among Kanak leaders caused further divisions. A major example came in 1974 when the more radical *Union Progressiste Multiraciale*, broke away from the UMNC. It soon dropped its fictitious multiracial title to become the *Union Progressiste Mélanesienne* (UPM) in 1977.[55]

A Kanak cultural festival in 1975, called Melanesia 2000, reflected growing Kanak cultural and political consciousness. It was a massive festival attended by Kanaks from all over the territory to celebrate their Melanesian culture. A central organizer was Jean-Marie Tjibaou,

---

53. Ibid. 248–50.
54. Dornoy, *Politics in New Caledonia* 207–8.
55. Ibid. 178–82, 185–7. Connell, *New Caledonia or Kanaky* 262–3.

a former Kanak Catholic priest and UC leader on the East Coast of New Caledonia. The festival had obvious political overtones and boosted Kanak nationalist fervour. Symptomatic was the formation of a new radical and socialist Kanak party, the *Parti de Libération Kanak* (PALIKA).[56]

The UC also was losing most of its remaining European supporters. In 1967 some radical working–class leaders left to start a socialist party. More seriously a group of moderate European supporters broke away in 1971 and formed the *Mouvement Libéral Calédonien*. However, with continued political fragmentation among conservatives, the UC, with Lenormand back as its leader from 1971, remained the majority party in the territorial legislature until 1977, with support from the more radical Kanak parties. But this coalition had much less freedom to introduce reform policies with French economic control of the territory. Indeed, in response to the tightened French control, the UC was moving towards the more radical Kanak viewpoint in favour of independence from France, further eroding its European support.[57]

Consequently, in the 1977 election the UC and other Kanak parties lost the majority they had held in all elections since the founding of the UC. The election produced the first clear political polarization in the territory between the European dominated Noumea plus the West Coast and the Kanak controlled East Coast and Loyalty Islands. Supporting the anti-independence centre and right were Polynesian immigrants, who feared for their future under a Kanak dominated independent state. The moderate and conservative parties also picked up a minority of Kanak voters, who saw their economic future as dependent on the French presence or who otherwise feared the radicalism of the majority Kanak opinion. After this election, for the first time the centre and right parties gained a majority in the legislature and the governing council.[58]

By the late 1970s all the Kanak political parties had declared their support for independence. The UC advocated a gradualist approach. The UMNC was arguing for an independent state which would disenfranchise recent immigrants to New Caledonia. PALIKA called for immediate independence on socialist principles. In 1979 these parties and the UPM formed a coalition, the *Front Indépendantist* (FI),

---

56. Ibid. 265–6. Dornoy, *Politics in New Caledonia* 209–12. Henningham, *France in the South Pacific* 67–8.

57. Dornoy, *Politics in New Caledonia* 170–8, 187–90.

58. Ibid. ch. 7.

in order to outmanoeuvre an electoral law that sought to diminish their representation by imposing a 7.5 per cent minimum of votes cast for a party to gain a seat. The FI won fourteen seats. A new conservative coalition, the *Rassemblement pour la Calédonie dans la République* (RPCR), formed in 1978, won fifteen of the thirty-six seats, which formed a majority with the seven elected members of the centrist *Fédération pour une Nouvelle Société Calédonienne* (FNSC). A big minority of Kanaks had deserted the FI, and it attracted very few non-Kanak voters. Ominously for the future, by 1979 violence was breaking out again as radical Kanaks took their protest against French hegemony to the streets with militant conservatives spearheading counter-demonstrations.[59]

The French Government, however, was starting to realize the dangers of racial confrontation in New Caledonia. In 1979 Dijoud advanced a plan for social and economic reforms to correct the previous discrimination against Kanaks if they abandoned their calls for independence. However, all parties of the FI refused angrily to be seduced from their independence struggle. Violence escalated in 1980 when two Kanaks were shot by two Europeans, who escaped with limited prison sentences rather than being charged with murder. The territory was facing a stormy future.[60]

PACIFIC OUTPOSTS OF THE AMERICAN EMPIRE

In the three decades after 1950 strategic and economic bonds were tying Pacific islands to the American empire nearly as tightly as in the French empire. The economic benefits of American rule in East Samoa, established in 1900 to utilize the magnificent harbour of Pago Pago as a naval base, were sufficient to prevent most islanders there from wishing to join their cousins in independent Western Samoa. In 1980 East Samoa's population of about 31,000 Samoans in a total of 32,395 were all American citizens, with their own song 'Amerika Samoa' and a territorial flag, which included the American eagle. More than twice as many of their kindred were living overseas, mostly in Hawaii and on the American west

59. Connell, *New Caledonia or Kanaky* 266–80.
60. Ibid. 276–7, 281–2.

coast. With significant government employment, a prosperous fishing industry and emerging tourism, there was a median household annual income in 1980 of US$9,241, which was much higher than in Western Samoa.[61]

Some North Pacific Islanders became less content with US rule because of nuclear testing in their area. The worst case occurred on 1 March 1954, when at Bikini Atoll in the northwestern corner of the Marshall Islands the US exploded the world's first hydrogen bomb in an operation code-named *Bravo*. An unexpectedly huge explosion, that seemed for many Marshall Islanders as if the sun was rising in the west as well as in the east, deposited a cloud of radioactive dust for a distance of over 360 kilometres to the east, not into the vacant ocean to the north as weather forecasters had predicted. The US blamed this horrendous accident on an unexpected wind shift. However, the eighty-two islanders on the closest inhabited atoll, Rongalep, who started to experience itching, nausea, burns to exposed limbs and hair falling out, became convinced they were guinea pigs for American experimentation. In support of this condemnation, meteorologists involved in *Bravo* knew that the wind had started blowing in an easterly direction before the detonation, but were ignored by their superiors. There was also a delay of two days to evacuate the Rongalep people, whereas a US destroyer spent the day of the test at the entrance of the island's lagoon, with its men sheltered from radiation and measuring its extent, and then sailed away. There was a further day's delay to evacuate the 157 islanders on more distant Utirik Atoll, who were also adversely affected by the fallout from *Bravo*. A counter-argument is that American ships were in the fallout area and that twenty-eight American servicemen involved in meteorological and radiological testing on Rongalep were forced to shelter in an aluminium building when they saw the level of radiation suddenly soar. But these men and the other US servicemen in the area had radiation-proof protection to resort to. There was no protection for islanders, nor any warning given to them. There is still no proof that the indigenous people were deliberately exposed; at best it was a case of Americans looking after their own people before they considered the needs of islanders after an unexpectedly huge nuclear explosion.[62]

61. *PIYB* (16th edit., Sydney 1989) 1–24. Gordon R. Lewthwaite, Christiane Mainzer and Patrick J. Holland, 'From Polynesia to California: Samoan Migration and its Sequel', *Journal of Pacific History* 8, 1973, 133–57.
62. Stewart Firth, *Nuclear Playground* (Sydney 1987) 14–20.

There was some diplomatic fallout for the US from *Bravo*. A Japanese fishing vessel was near Bikini at the time and sailed home with its crew obviously suffering from effects of nuclear radiation that many Japanese knew only too well from their 1945 experiences at Hiroshima and Nagasaki. One of those fishermen later died from the exposure. The Eisenhower Administration felt compelled to pay compensation to the dead man's family after a Japanese Government protest. Marshall Islanders also petitioned the UN about the harmful effects of the radiation and called for an immediate end to nuclear testing in their islands. However, the US was able to contain the damage by keeping secret much of the evidence and assuring the world there would be no lasting ill-effects to the Marshallese people. The US still used the Marshall Islands for nuclear testing until the long negotiated open-air test ban was concluded with the USSR in 1963, though by 1961 concern about adverse UN opinion was prompting a US request to use British atomic testing facilities on Christmas Island, far to the east of the Marshall Islands.[63]

In the North Pacific Trust Territory the US honoured the UN commitment to develop the people towards self-government. In the island group of Palau (or Belau) in 1955 an elected congress was given limited self-government, with a commitment to eventual self-rule. On other islands in the 1950s there were developments of islander controlled local government. There was little self-assertion among Micronesians who had been cowed by increasingly oppressive Japanese rule in the prewar and Second World War years and who had not previously been provided with opportunities to express their views. The Marshallese nuclear test protest in 1955 was couched in very polite terms and was regarded in Washington as an aberration. However, in 1959 a Micronesia Club was formed by young islanders attending university in Hawaii. When its members returned to the islands, they started pressing for faster progress towards a US withdrawal from their homelands. This small agitation contributed to the establishment of a territory-wide Congress of Micronesia in 1965, which was also influenced by the more critical attitude towards trust territories in the UN in the 1960s and by some pressure from within the US Administration. The congress had an upper house with two members from each island group and a lower house elected on a population basis; but the US high commissioner still controlled administration. For many educated

63. Ibid. 21–6. Cabinet Minutes, 14 Nov. 1961, CAB 128/35, PRO.

Micronesians the progress towards self-government was too slow. However, in 1963 a secret report of an investigating commission, headed by Harvard University Professor Anthony Solomon, had recommended a permanent association of the islands with the US because of their strategic importance.[64]

Nor did the hasty development of the Congress of Micronesia engender a strong sense of national unity among the scattered island groups. The Chamorro and Carolinian people of the Northern Mariana Islands were aware of their distinctive Spanish colonial heritage and their status as the Micronesian area of greatest US strategic interest, being the islands closest to Asia. They also looked forward to joining their ethnic cousins on the island of Guam, a separate American possession, gained as a naval-base prize in the War of 1898 against Spain. Also the Northern Marianas were the wealthiest of the island groups at that stage, assisted by US military expenditure, by the presence on Saipan of the Trust Territory Administration, and by developing tourism. So there were objections by islanders in this region to sharing financial resources with poorer Micronesians. Therefore in 1972 the Northern Marianas sought separate talks with the US, and in a plebiscite in June 1975, 79 per cent of voters opted to withdraw from the Trust Territory and to negotiate Commonwealth status with the US. Washington was happy to oblige, since the Commonwealth agreement, which was implemented in January 1978, gave to the US control of defence and foreign affairs and the right to station armed forces in the now self-governing North Mariana Islands.[65]

The granting of separate political status to the Northern Marianas became a precedent for a rash of separatist movements in the Trust Territory. Palauans were concerned about their limited voice in the lower house of the Micronesian Congress because of their smaller population (14,800 in 1980) compared with the bigger island groups of Phonpei (23,140), Truk (38,650) and the Marshall Islands (29,670). Palauans also were determined to preserve their own culture, though many valued American education. Furthermore, there was a divisive community debate in the mid-1970s in Palau about the introduction of a super-port for a Japanese-American oil storage and petrochemical scheme, which would utilize the archipelago's good harbours and its

64. Nufer, *Micronesia Under American Rule* 49–68. Deryck Scarr, *The History of the Pacific Islands: Kingdoms of the Reefs* (Canberra 1990) 299–302.

65. Agnes McPhetres, 'Northern Mariana Islands: US Commonwealth' in Ron Crocombe and Ahmed Ali (eds), *Politics in Micronesia* (Suva 1983) 148–60.

strategic position to the east flank of Japan's main oil supertanker route from the Middle East. The argument between supporters of development and opponents concerned about threats to the environment and Palauan culture, who were supported by American environmentalists, came to physical blows. Supporters of economic development favoured separation from the rest of the Trust Territory in order to give Palau freedom to make its own arrangements with outside developers, even though the super-port proposal was blocked in the US Congress by Democrats concerned about its environmental impact on Palau. Consequently, in a plebiscite in 1978 to establish a Micronesian Federation, 55 per cent of Palauan voters approved separation from it. There was a further public argument over a constitution for the Palauan state in a compact of free association with the US. American pressure to remove a clause preventing the usage, testing, storage or disposal of any nuclear weapons in Palau, which included three separate plebiscites, did not stop 78 per cent of Palauan voters finally approving the constitution with its anti-nuclear clause intact.[66]

There was one other secession from the projected Federation of Micronesia. In the 1978 plebiscite, 62 per cent of Marshall Islanders voted 'no'. This vote was influenced by disagreements over the Congress of Micronesia's taxation policy, fear of domination by the more numerous Truk Islanders, opposition to provisions in the draft constitution for a continued US base on Kwajaleen and personality-based factionalism. In 1980 Marshall Islanders were still negotiating about a compact of free association with the US, which was dangling the bait of economic aid to capture the use of Kwajaleen Lagoon as a missile landing zone, after already spending $20 million to clean up Enewetak Atoll from nuclear contamination and more money on a still unsuccessful effort to make Bikini inhabitable. Therefore the Federated States of Micronesia (FSM) consisted only of Truk, Phonpei and the lesser populated islands of Yap and Kosrae, which in 1980 had respectively 9,320 and 2,940 people. In 1980 the FSM was still negotiating a compact agreement with the US.[67]

Full-scale independence for Micronesians had been compromised by their economic dependence on the US and by the strategic value

66. Gwenda L. Iyechad and Frank Quimby, 'Belau: Super Port, Fortress or Identity' in ibid. 102–23. David Robie, *Blood on their Banner: Nationalist Struggles in the South Pacific* (Sydney 1989) 168–9.

67. Daniel Smith, 'Marshall Islands: Tradition and Dependence' in Crocombe and Ali, *Politics in Micronesia* 55–78. David Hanlon and William Eperiam, 'Federated Micronesia: Unifying the Remnants' in ibid. 79–99.

of their islands. The long memory of the Second World War made US administrations as reluctant to relinquish the right to establish military forces in Micronesia as was the Soviet Union in the states of eastern Europe. The value of the North Pacific for nuclear testing and missile landing enhanced their military worth. The greatest defence impact was on the island of Guam, where in 1978 only about 62 per cent of the 109,000 people had indigenous Chamorro ancestry and where the economic value of a major naval base and widespread American educational services had seduced most islanders to believe their destiny was with the US. Their struggle was to become an American state, as Hawaii did in 1959, where the predominant population was Asian, not Polynesian. Guam's importance as a military base and its otherwise economic non-viability were major stumbling blocks for the islanders in their quest for statehood.[68]

MELANESIANS UNDER INDONESIAN RULE

In 1969 Indonesia organized the takeover of the Melanesian territory of Irian Jaya, which is called West Papua by indigenous nationalists. When Indonesia took control of the territory on 1 May 1963 to prepare it for a UN supervised self-determination plebiscite in 1969, as set out in the agreement with the Netherlands, every effort was made to obliterate Papuan nationalism and culture. The process started on 2 May with a huge bonfire of symbols of Papuan life, school textbooks and West Papuan flags in the central square of the principal city of Jayapura, which was located on the north coast close to the Papua New Guinea border. The next day a Papuan council elected under Dutch rule was replaced by an appointed Regional People's Assembly to operate on Guided Democracy principles. The first governor was a Papuan, Eliezer Bornay, who later said, after he was removed from office in 1964, that he first thought there would be a genuine free choice for his people in 1969 but that such hopes were snuffed out by 'numerous brutalities, thefts, torture, maltreatment,

---

68. Carlos Taitano, 'Guam: the Struggle for Civil and Political Rights' in ibid. 131–45. For Hawaii see Roger Bell, *Last Among Equals: Hawaiian Statehood and American Politics* (Honolulu 1984).

many things that had not happened before'.[69] The result was the emergence in 1965 of Papuan armed resistance led by Arfak tribesmen, some of whom had been trained by the Dutch Papuan Volunteer corps. They used weapons surviving from the Second World War as well as traditional bows and arrows and called themselves *Organisasi Papua Merdeka* (OPM) (Free Papua Movement). Indonesian responses to the rebellion included air force strafing and army burning of Papuan villages and mass executions. The act of 'free choice' was carried out in 1969 by 1,025 Papuan 'representatives' who were carefully trained to vote unanimously on behalf of 800,000 Papuans to 'remain with Indonesia', in front of UN representatives and foreign diplomats who duly declared that the farce was a legitimate expression of the will of the Papuan people.[70]

The OPM did not give up its struggle, even though it suffered from disunity, a paucity of firearms and mass reprisals by the Indonesian army assisted by US-supplied helicopter gun ships. The OPM had neither the cohesiveness, the degree of military training nor the many modern weapons possessed by Fretlin in East Timor. However, the OPM was assisted by a much vaster mountainous and jungle-clad terrain. The Indonesian Government soon realized that large-force action was counterproductive, since villagers were driven further into the mountains, where they were much harder to control and where the guerillas had plenty of hiding places. So from 1973 a strategy was introduced to use security agencies in the style of dictatorial Latin American governments to detain or kill educated Papuans suspected of OPM leanings and thus deprive the organization of its leadership. Such tactics did not drive villagers away but increased their hostility to the brutal administration. Concerted attempts to impose Indonesian culture on Papuans were also bedevilled by cultural insensitivity. For example, traditional tribesmen who wore nothing but penis sheaths were ordered to wear trousers that caused itching and sores. The sentiments of many Papuans became obvious in 1977 when Suharto chanced his popularity with a national election which included Papuans, who were all considered Indonesian citizens. There were OPM-influenced mass uprisings all over the country trying to catch wider world attention and to urge fellow Papuans to boycott the election, much of which was suspended by the authorities.

69. *West Papua: The Obliteration of a People* (revised edit. London 1984) 25.

70. Ibid. ch. 2. Nonie Sharp, *The Rule of Sword: The Story of West Irian* (Malmsbury 1977) 15–23. Robin Osborne, *Indonesia's Secret War: The Guerilla Struggle in Irian Jaya* (Sydney 1985) ch. 1.

The uprisings did attract wider publicity. Also insurrection in the region bordering Papua New Guinea, where OPM activity was strongest, caused many people to flee across the border after the inevitable Indonesian reprisals. But the OPM lived on to continue the struggle during the 1980s.[71]

There was no international support for the OPM. The Papua New Guinea Government did not have the means to stop 'border crossers'; so its army was not ordered to hunt down OPM personnel. At the same time, fearful of Indonesian hot pursuit across the border, Michael Somare's government gave the OPM no support; and Somare made a state visit to Indonesia in 1977 to express his desire for mutual friendship between the two countries. The Australian Government, which showed its willingness to appease Indonesia over the invasion of Timor in 1975, also gave no support to the OPM. Nor did the US abandon its staunch anti-communist ally, Suharto.[72]

INDEPENDENT PACIFIC ISLAND STATES

Political instability was a problem for some of the newly independent island states. In Papua New Guinea, Somare's Pangu Parti improved its performance in the 1977 election but still won only 40 of the 106 seats. To govern, it needed to form a coalition with the 22 members of the People's Progress Party led by Julius Chan, based primarily on the islands and sections of Papua. Pangu had the advantage of being the most truly national party but had the disadvantage of no strong support bases in many provinces, where more local parties or candidates polled better. The coalition soon split in 1978 when Somare pushed for a strong anti-corruption leadership code, which would have forced Chan to divest himself of his many business interests. Somare continued to govern with the support of his old political foes, the twenty-four member-strong United Party. But Somare's government was weakened by the resignation of half of the

---

71. Ibid. 50–76.
72. Ibid. 59–63, 153–60. R.J. May, 'East of the Border: Irian Jaya and the Border in Papua New Guinea's Domestic and Foreign Policies' in R.J. May (ed.), *Between Two Nations: the Indonesia-Papua New Guinea Border and West Papua Nationalism* (Bathurst 1986) 85–100.

supreme court judges when he released from jail his justice minister who had been committed for contempt of court. In March 1980 a no-confidence motion, which set a pattern for future Papua New Guinea politics, overthrew the government and installed Chan as the prime minister. But he headed a more diverse coalition, which did not augur well for future political stability.[73]

There was a portent of much more serious future trouble in Fiji in the first general election in 1977. After achieving independence, the Alliance Party, led by a prominent chief, Ratu Mara, had held power with the support of general electors and some Indians, especially from the Moslem minority in the Hindu dominated Indian community. But in 1977 the Alliance won only twenty-four seats to twenty-six for the NFP. There was one independent and one member from the new Fiji National Party. That party was the principal reason for the Alliance defeat. It captured 25 per cent of the Fijian vote by campaigning on the racist themes that Fijians had been denied adequate control of their country because they were guaranteed only a minority of seats in the parliament, that Fijians should always control the appointment of the prime minister and other ministries affecting the Fijian people, and that Indians should be repatriated to India. However, since the death of Patel in 1969, the NFP was affected by divisions which, after the election, resulted in a leadership struggle. There was a consequent delay in forming a cabinet, which allowed the Fijian governor general to call instead on Ratu Mara to form a minority Alliance government. The NFP denounced this 'insult' to Indians, but some of its members doubted whether an Indian government would have been able to command the loyalty of Fijians. Mara's minority government did not survive long. However, in new elections in 1977 the NFP factionalism boiled over into an open split, which reduced the party's parliamentary representation to only fifteen seats. The racially charged atmosphere of the election campaigning also deprived the NFP of most of its small Fijian support and reduced the Indian vote for the Alliance. But the Alliance was able to appeal sufficiently to Fijians to reduce the National Party's support to 17 per cent of the Fijian vote, resulting in thirty-six seats to the Alliance. Fijians felt safe again.[74]

73. Ralph R. Premdas, 'Papua New Guinea: The First General Elections After Independence', *Journal of Pacific History* 13, 1978, 77–89. Sean Dorney, *Papua New Guinea: People, Politics and History since 1975* (Sydney 1990) 62–6.

74. Ahmed Ali, 'The Fiji General Election of 1977', *Journal of Pacific History* 12, 1977, 189–201. Norton, *Race and Politics in Fiji* 111–20. Victor Lal, *Fiji Coups in Paradise* (London 1990) ch. 4.

The other independent states were blessed with more political stability. However, Tonga's royal and noble dominated government invited future challenges from Tongan commoners. The Samoan matai system was also potentially a weak base for government which, along with divisions among the matai, was soon to produce a constitutional crisis. Nauru's political stability depended on the dominance of DeRoburt, who briefly lost political power for eighteen months in 1977–78.

Few of the newly independent island groups in the 1970s had economic self-sufficiency. Nauru stood out because of continued phosphate mining, now managed by a national corporation. Its people also were benefiting from accumulating overseas investments. In 1979–80 the Phosphate Royalties Trust reported a 22 per cent profit rate on its AUS$292 million investments. They included the 52–storey Nauru House which, from its completion in 1977, dominated the top end of the most fashionable street in the heart of Melbourne, Australia's leading financial centre. The per capita income of the 4,600 Nauruans was among the highest in the world. Much of it was locked up in investments, but available income was sufficient to provide one or two modern motor cars for most Nauruan families, compared with the predominance of bicycles in the prewar era.[75]

All the other independent Pacific Islands states depended to some extent on overseas aid or assistance. The most self-reliant state, Tonga, relied on remittances from its many people who had migrated to Australasia and the US. Papua New Guinea was depending in 1980 on Australia to finance 30 per cent of its budget. There was also a growing reliance in Papua New Guinea on revenue from the Panguna copper mine on Bougainville, which by 1980 was providing 45 per cent of export earnings. More dependent on a single commodity was Fiji. In the three years 1977–79 sugar was worth 54 per cent of Fiji's exports. However, Fiji's total exports were sufficient to pay for only 56 per cent of the nation's imports in the same period, with a consequent need for assistance to Fiji from the International Monetary Fund. The most vulnerable state was Tuvalu, which in 1980 depended on aid from Britain for nearly a third of its small budget and upon Britain, Australia, New Zealand and international agencies for development aid.[76]

75. Ron Crocombe and Christian Giese, 'Nauru the Politics of Phosphate' in Crocombe and Ali (eds) *Politics in Melanesia* 39–2. Macdonald, *In Pursuit of Sacred Trust* 61–2. *PIYB* 14th edit., 275.

76. *FEA* 1981–82, 941–989.

Australian aid to the Pacific Islands was influenced by fear of growing Soviet Union interest in the South Pacific during the 1970s. A particular shock wave was news in 1976 of a USSR offer of economic assistance to the king of Tonga; and there was increasing activity in the South Pacific by Soviet fishing trawlers, which were suspected of intelligence gathering. There were also signs of an emerging Chinese interest in the South Pacific with Beijing's opening of embassies in Fiji and Western Samoa, though the Sino-Soviet split and Australian and New Zealand establishment of diplomatic relations with China made that country less of a potential threat than the USSR. Concern about these new outside great power influences in the South Pacific contributed to an increase in Australian development assistance aid to South Pacific states other than Papua New Guinea, from AUS$15 million over the three financial years 1973–76 to AUS$60 million for 1977–79; as well as increasing contributions to international agencies and non-government organizations working in the South Pacific. Australia also had economic reasons for assisting the newly independent nations of the South Pacific, which, including Papua New Guinea, were the location of 27 per cent of Australia's overseas capital investments in 1975–76, though the source of only 3 per cent of Australia's overseas trade.[77]

New Zealand played a significant aid role in the South Pacific. In 1980 NZ$58 million was spent on economic assistance to South Pacific islands, but a third went to New Zealand's continued dependencies: the Cook Islands, Niue and Tokelau in Polynesia. The 18,128 people in the Cook Islands (1976 census) and the 3,578 in Niue (1979 census) enjoyed self-government but had opted for free association with New Zealand, which looked after their defence and foreign affairs and provided economic aid. This arrangement allowed free access for the islanders to New Zealand, where more lived in 1980 than in their home islands. The economic aid in 1977–78 contributed to 55 per cent of the budget of Niue and 27 per cent of Cook Islands government revenue. The 1,615 people on Tokelau were still ruled directly by New Zealand. With weakening ties between New Zealand and her traditional trading partner and patron, Britain, as a result of the latter's entry into the EEC, New Zealand was pursuing a

---

77. Greg Fry, '"Constructive Commitment" with the South Pacific: Monroe Doctrine or New "Partnership"?' in Greg Fry (ed.), *Australia's Regional Security* (Sydney 1991) 126–8. Parliament of the Commonwealth of Australia, *Australia and the South Pacific: Report from the Senate Standing Committee on Foreign Affairs and Defence* (Canberra 1978) 19, 30–2, 39, 47.

more independent foreign policy as a small island state. 'Now we all accept that New Zealand is a Pacific country on the periphery of Asia' declared H. C. Templeton, a Nationalist Government minister in 1979. Consequently, economic aid to South Pacific Islands was linked to a concern, announced in the 1978 New Zealand Defence White Paper, that New Zealand should assist to 'preserve peace and security in our own part of the world'.[78]

New Zealand's greatest foreign policy concern was to maintain close relations with her big neighbour, Australia. No two independent countries in the world are more alike in culture, social composition and political institutions. Apart from geographic and economic differences between a continent and Pacific islands, the only other major difference was the much larger indigenous and immigrant Pacific Islander population in New Zealand; but the majority of its people, like Australians, were white Anglo-Saxons. Though experiencing past trade frictions and rivalry in the South Pacific, the two nations enjoyed past and present close defence cooperation extending to the training of New Zealand's senior army officers in Australia's premier military college. In the 1970s a process of freeing trade relations between the two nations commenced. In policies towards Pacific Islands there was a growing cooperation between Australia and New Zealand in the 1970s. There were joint protests against French nuclear testing, Australian naval support for New Zealand naval monitoring of the tests, and cooperative support for Fiji's initiative for the establishment in 1971 of a Pacific Forum of heads of governments of independent Pacific nations. That move was a response to France's banning of the discussion of political issues in the South Pacific Commission (a club of colonial powers in the Pacific, established in 1947 to foster development in the islands), into which independent island states were admitted.[79]

Wider cooperation between Australia, New Zealand and the Pacific Islands states was emerging with the establishment of the Pacific Forum. The most dramatic example of this was the agreement at

78. *FEA* 1981–82, 857, 892, 918. *PIYB* 14th edit., 68, 404. K. Janaki. 'International Regimes, New Zealand and the Pacific' in Roderic Alley (ed.), *New Zealand and the Pacific* (Boulder 1984) 303 (quotations).

79. Mary Boyd, 'Australian New Zealand Relations' in William S. Livingston and Wm. Roger Louis (eds), *Australia, New Zealand and the Pacific Islands since the First World War* (Canberra 1979) 47–61. J.D.B. Miller, 'Australasia and the World Outside: Foreign Policies Since World War II' in Keith Sinclair (ed.), *Tasman Relations: New Zealand and Australia, 1788–1988* (Auckland 1987) 183–201. Graeme Thompson, 'New Zealand and the Wider Pacific' in Alley (ed.), *New Zealand and the Pacific* 232–5.

the July 1980 Forum meeting in Tuvalu by Papua New Guinea's Prime Minister Julius Chan and Malcolm Fraser of Australia. They cooperated in the despatch of Papua New Guinea troops to Vanuatu, after they heard a direct appeal from Walter Lini. Such cooperation revealed a new style of military intervention different from the 'gunboat diplomacy' in the inter-World War years employed by Australia and New Zealand to suppress striking Indians in Fiji, militant tribesmen in the Solomons and protesting Samoans.[80]

Relations between Forum members were not always amicable. Nauru's development of an independent airline was at odds with a push for a regional air consortium. There were differences of opinion about the extent of opposition to French colonialism, with Papua New Guinea and the Solomons calling for strong diplomatic protest on behalf of their Melanesian brothers in New Caledonia and Vanuatu, and Australia and New Zealand fearing a French backlash against their important trade links with the EEC. The upshot was a typical Forum compromise at the 1979 meeting in Honiara with an expression of concern about islanders still under colonial rule, but without explicitly naming France. There was also a cleavage developing between Melanesian and Polynesian members of the Forum because of the greater size of the Melanesian states and Polynesian fears of Melanesian assertiveness.[81]

CONCLUSIONS

The Pacific Islands were by 1980 a potentially more unstable region in the Pacific Basin than before. Restive islanders were contesting French control, especially in New Caledonia. The continued strategic demands of the US in Micronesia were creating dissent despite the economic dependency of the islanders. Papuans were proving difficult for Indonesia to control. The newly independent states were also potential sources for instability. The cultural diversity of Papua New Guinea was a recipe for political instability, and secessionist feelings among Bougainvillians were soon to re-emerge. The racial divide

80. Van Trease, *Politics of Land* 257.
81. R.A. Herr, 'South Pacific Regionalism' in ibid. 165–76.

between Fijians and Indians was a threat to stability, particularly if Indians threatened the political and social control of Fiji's chiefs. Undemocratic political systems in Tonga and Western Samoa were open to future challenge. Most of the island states were dependent on outside economic aid. Furthermore, there were threats of disunity between the former colonial powers of Australia and New Zealand and the island states, and between the Melanesian and Polynesian regions. However, the Pacific Forum was a medium for potential cooperation between the disparate island states. The 1980s were destined to be a stormier decade for the Pacific Islands than had been preceding postwar years.

CHAPTER SIX

Arresting Communism in Latin America, 1945–1979

Along the long eastern rim of the Pacific Basin after the Second World War the Latin American republics were relatively peaceful under their mixture of democratic, single party and military governments. But American economic interests, exploitation by ruling elites and widening gaps between rich and poor were storing troubles for the future. The determination of the US to prevent radical movements, which were readily condemned as communist-led, is a major theme of this chapter, which was a mirror along the Eastern Pacific Rim to the Cold War struggle in the Western Pacific Basin. The effects of the US support for right wing regimes and political movements in the Pacific Basin's Latin American countries are examined, because it contributed to a continuation of revolutionary wars and US intervention into the 1980s, compared with the relative peace in the Western Pacific Basin by then. Relations between the Pacific Basin's Latin American countries, especially attempts for free trade agreements and the disputes that hindered them also are discussed. The chapter concludes with an analysis of increasing Japanese economic links with Latin America that were breaking down the previous isolation of Latin America from the Western Pacific Basin.

THE CIA AND GUATEMALA

In 1954 the Eisenhower Administration demonstrated its commitment to fight the Cold War in Latin America, especially in the Central American region that was strategically close to the US, by supporting the overthrow of the government of Guatemala. In 1951 Jacobo Arbenz Guzmán had been elected as the Guatemalan president, promising a radical reform programme. The reforms included a move in 1953 for widespread expropriation of large-scale landholdings, including 225,000 acres of mostly unused land owned by the American United Fruit Company (UFC), which dominated the Guatemalan economy. The company was offered a compensation payment of $627,000, which was its valuation for taxation purposes, but which the UFC now claimed was worth $16 million. This radical agrarian reform programme of the Arbenz Government suggested communist influence, though Eisenhower's Administration privately conceded that it would be difficult to prove any Soviet involvement. In fact Arbenz was not a communist; nor were there any communists in his Cabinet; and the UFC land was to be handed over to small farmer private ownership. There was a local Communist Party, which strongly supported Arbenz, but its influence was exaggerated by Arbenz's opponents. They included, as well as the UFC, other members of the 2 per cent of landowners who controlled 72 per cent of the nation's agricultural land, the conservative Catholic Church, members of the armed forces and other Guatemalans upset by radical policies. The right wing dictators of Honduras, El Salvador, Nicaragua and Venezuela also opposed the Arbenz regime. There is a debate among historians about the extent of popular opposition in Guatemala to Arbenz's government, which depends on the use of primary sources that are heavily influenced by propaganda. However, there is agreement that the US supplied arms and organized assistance to a rebel invasion of Guatemala from neighbouring Honduras on 18 June 1954 led by American-educated Colonel Castillo Armas.[1]

One allegation is that the Eisenhower Administration's willingness to back a revolution against the Arbenz Government was influenced by the UFC. There is circumstantial evidence for this viewpoint in the involvement of some members of the administration in that company. For example, Dulles had been a legal counsel for the UFC and had drafted the contract in 1936 that gave it exceptional privileges in Guatemala.[2]

1. Frederick W. Marks III, 'The CIA and Castillo Armas in Guatemala, 1954: New Clues to an Old Puzzle' and Stephen G. Rabe, 'The Clues Didn't Check Out: Commentary on "The CIA and Castillo Armas"', *Diplomatic History* 14, 1990, 67–95.
2. Stephen Schlesinger and Stephen Kinzer, *Bitter Fruit: The Untold Story of the American Coup in Guatemala* (London 1982) chs 6–7. Richard H. Immerman, *The CIA in Guatemala: The Foreign Policy of Intervention* (Austin 1982) 125–32.

However, the propaganda from the UFC and other Guatemalan and Latin American sources about communist influence would have been a sufficient cause for Eisenhower's administration actively to oppose the Arbenz Government, given its determination to prevent communist expansion in the Pacific Basin, especially in a neighbouring region. Thus Armas's rebel force of some 200 troops had received training from the CIA and were bristling with American arms to distribute to supporters in Guatemala. They also were supported by American-supplied aircraft. Crucial assistance came from dissidents in Guatemala City, possibly bribed by the CIA, who grounded Arbenz's air force and overstated the size of the rebels. Arbenz acceded to a demand from his own army officers for his resignation only nine days after the start of the invasion. The important American involvement in the rebellion was covered up. It clearly breached the principles of the Good Neighbor policy established by Roosevelt in the 1930s and the Eisenhower Administration's own public renouncement of the use of force in the internal affairs of Latin American nations. The Guatemala coup added one more right wing dictatorship – Castillo soon disfranchised most Guatemalans – to the many other dictatorial governments in Latin America at that time.[3]

The intervention in Guatemala was part of a consistent policy pursued by Eisenhower's Administration in Latin America. It was seeking to ensure continued Latin American support for the US in the Cold War and to preserve free trade and investment, which benefited American economic interests and supported the capitalist alternative to communism. It also was argued that US economic influence would increase standards of living, which would help preserve the region from communist influence. But there were no significant improvements in overall living standards of Latin American people, given the elitist nature of economic power in most of the republics and falling prices for the region's agricultural exports. Vice-President Nixon discovered consequent popular resentment against 'Yanqui' influence in hostile demonstrations against him on his Latin American tour in May 1958.[4]

---

3. Ibid. ch. 7. Marks, 'The CIA and Armas Castillo', 69, 73–4. Bryce Wood, *The Dismantling of the Good Neighbor Policy* (Austin 1985) 152–90.
4. See Stephen G. Rabe, *Eisenhower and Latin America: The Foreign Policy of Anticommunism* (Chapel Hill 1988) chs 2–6.

THE ALLIANCE FOR PROGRESS ERA

Kennedy sought to implement a new set of American policies towards Latin America under the title of Alliance for Progress. The aim of the programme was to eliminate illiteracy, hunger and disease in Latin America by the end of the decade. This would be achieved by the application of American money and know-how with the same confidence in the capabilities of the US that inspired Kennedy's policy towards Vietnam. His kick-start of $500 million plus $100 million for reconstruction after a severe earthquake in Chile, expanded to a total of $18 billion in public and private American aid during the 1960s, including over $10 billion from US government agencies. But results fell far short of aims. Literacy programmes barely kept pace with big population increases, and the number of unemployed people grew from eighteen million in 1960 to twenty-five million by 1969. The average annual economic growth rate for Latin American countries in the decade was 1.5 per cent. At the end of the 1960s more than half of the Latin American population lived in poverty.[5]

Furthermore, the main aim of the Alliance for Progress was to remove conditions for the breeding of communist subversion which could be fed by the communist regime established in 1959 by Fidel Castro in Cuba. That communist penetration of Latin America was interpreted as a major Soviet Cold War victory, to the extent that at the beginning of his presidency Kennedy launched against Cuba a Guatemala-style of intervention which was a miserable failure. Kennedy was determined that there should be no more communist successes in Latin America. So, while Kennedy extolled the virtues of democracy, his administration supported military regimes with good anti-communist credentials, and assistance was provided to political opponents of left wing groups. Among the Eastern Pacific Basin countries a prominent example was Chile. There, Colby admitted, the CIA 'had been clandestinely funneling a wide variety of support to the center democratic parties and political forces in Chile since 1963, in an effort to ward off a Castro-supported Communist takeover'. This included providing $3 million to support the Christian Democratic Party's (CDP) Eduardo Frei Montalva in the presidential election campaign to stop his main opponent, the Marxist leader of the

5. Stephen G. Rabe, 'Controlling Revolution: Latin America, the Alliance for Progress, and Cold War Anti-Communism' in Paterson, *Kennedy's Quest for Victory* 105–10.

Socialist Party, Salvador Allende Gossens. With this assistance, which concentrated on a scare campaign linking Allende with atheistic communism to frighten especially women voters, the CIA gave itself the credit for Frei's victory in 1964 with 56 per cent of the vote, the first absolute majority in a Chilean presidential election since 1938. However, that was an inflated claim, since Frei was a moderate reformer supported by conservatives and liberals.[6]

The Kennedy Administration also acted to protect other Pacific Basin Latin American countries from the threat of radicalism. In 1963 the government of Carlos Julio Arosemena in Ecuador was overthrown by a military coup because it was 'soft on Communism'. Philip Agee, a CIA officer serving at that time in the capital city, Quito, later explained the CIA's aims in Latin America: 'we were fighting to arrest the influence of the Cuban Revolution which had an enormous impact throughout Latin America' and to 'buy time' for 'friends' of the US against its 'enemies', who ranged 'from left social democrats . . . to armed revolutionaries'. In Guatemala after a military coup in 1963 to stop the election of a radical government, Johnson's Administration lived comfortably with the subsequent anti-communist military regime. When the progressive government of President Ramón Villeda Morelles in Honduras, who had been strongly anti-communist, was overturned by a coup in 1963, Kennedy suspended aid to and recognition of the military administration, but both were restored in the next year. Kennedy also viewed with distaste the Somoza family, who treated Nicaragua as their personal fiefdom. But Anastasio Somoza Debayle supplied the base for the CIA's abortive attempt to invade Cuba in 1961 and continued to be a staunch ally of the US in quarantining communist Cuba. So Washington continued to support him.[7]

Nor were Alliance for Progress programmes under Kennedy and Johnson allowed to upset the huge American economic interests in

6. Ibid. 109–22. William Colby and Peter Forbath, *Honourable Men: My Life in the CIA* (London 1978) 302. Blum, *The CIA* 232–5. James R. Whelan, *Out of the Ashes: Life, Death and Transfiguration of Democracy in Chile, 1833–1988* (Washington 1989) 130–42.

7. Philip Agee, *Inside the Company: CIA Diary* (Harmondsworth 1975) 295. Philip Agee, *On the Run* (Secaucus 1987) 15, 89. Edwin Lieuwen, *Generals vs. Presidents: Neomilitarism in Latin America* (London 1964) chs 1–2. George Philip, *The Military in South American Politics* (London 1985) 338. Lester D. Langley, *The United States and the Caribbean in the Twentieth Century* (revised edit., Athens Ga. 1985) 237–9. Bernard Diedrich, *Somoza and the Legacy of U.S. Involvement in Central America* (New York 1981) ch. 5.

Latin America, which in 1960 absorbed 25 per cent of US overseas investments and 20 per cent of American exports. For example, in Honduras, Villeda was successfully pressed by Washington in 1962 to rescind a law which confiscated unused land belonging to the UFC and another US company. Moreover, a significant amount of financial aid was devoted to equipping Latin American military and police personnel to strengthen their ability to resist Communist subversion. But such assistance gave them greater abilities to establish and maintain authoritarian rule. Military and economic aid also was fraudulently directed to line the pockets of military leaders, as in the case of El Salvador.[8]

In Central America the Kennedy Administration financially supported moves towards a common market. Road building, including the completion of the Inter-American Highway to Panama in 1964, and other economic aid facilitated industrial growth. But the new industries tended to be capital rather than labour intensive. Also the common market was not fully developed, especially because of the fears of the most developed republic, Costa Rica, of competition from cheaper labour elsewhere in Central America. Costa Rica was also distrustful of Nicaragua. There had been an armed confrontation between the two nations in 1954 over alleged Costa Rican support for a plot to assassinate Anastasio Somoza García and retaliatory Nicaraguan support for Costa Rican rebels.[9]

In Panama in the 1960s there was a growing nationalist opposition to US ownership of the Panama Canal Zone which divided the country into two halves. The seizure of the Suez Canal by Egypt in 1956 prompted Panamanian pressure on the US to concede Panama's sovereignty over the sixteen kilometre-wide Canal Zone, that had been ceded 'in perpetuity' to the US by newly independent Panama in 1903. Eisenhower's Administration had insisted that the Panama Canal had been constructed solely by the US under the terms of a bilateral treaty. Panamanian students responded with a march into the Canal Zone to plant Panamanian flags there. After sending his brother to investigate, Eisenhower was inclined to allow a symbolic flying of the Panamanian flag in the Canal Zone, but he ran into strong Congressional opposition, where there was dark talk of communist agitators inciting the Panamanians. This opposition only served to provoke anger in Panama with another flag-planting attempt in the

8. Rabe, 'Controlling Revolution', 108, 121.
9. Ralph Lee Woodward, Jr., *Central America: A Nation Divided* (2nd edit., New York 1985) 270–5.

Canal Zone in 1959, which caused an outbreak of rioting and an inrush of US troops to restore law and order. Eisenhower responded with an agreement for a symbolic flag in one area of the Canal Zone, while maintaining that it in no way impugned US sovereignty. Kennedy encouraged negotiations with Panama's president, Roberto Chiari, about economic aid to Panama and wider flying of Panamanian flags, but Chiari pressed for renegotiating the Canal treaty. Johnson soon faced in January 1964 another foray by Panamanian students to plant flags that degenerated into four days of armed conflict, which left four US soldiers and twenty-four Panamanians dead and led to Panama's severing of diplomatic relations with the US. Johnson defused the crisis with a promise to negotiate a new treaty, which proposed revoking the US perpetual right to the Canal Zone in favour of American occupation expiring in 1999. But the US claim for continued unfettered military presence plus nationalist sentiment for an immediate end to American occupation aroused enough popular opposition to the treaty to cause the Panamanian Government to refuse to ratify it. Furthermore, continued strong opposition in the US Senate to relinquishing permanent ownership of the zone threatened the treaty's ratification there.[10]

Panama and the Central American republics, except democratic Costa Rica, were characterized by oligarchic or dictatorial rule, with small percentages of the population holding enormous economic power. Five per cent of Panamanians earned more than a third of the national income. In El Salvador 2 per cent of the populace owned 60 per cent of the land, and the thirty-six largest landlords controlled two-thirds of the capital of the 1,429 largest companies. US policies did little to lessen the yawning gaps between rich and poor in Central American republics, and even less to prevent dictatorial political control. The results were growing rebellions that were to prove major headaches to later American administrations. A prominent sign was the Cuban-supported Marxist-led guerilla movement in Nicaragua, the *Frente Sandinista de Liberación Nacional*, which drew its name from a Nicaraguan rebel hero, Augusto Sandino, who was assassinated in 1934 by Somoza's US-supported National Guard. This movement, whose members were called Sandinistas, was founded in Honduras in

---

10. Langley, *United States and the Caribbean* 241–51. Michael Hogan, *The Panama Canal in American Politics: Domestic Advocacy and the Evolution of Policy* (Carbondale 1986) 71–80. Michael L. Conniff, *Panama and the United States: The Forced Alliance* (Athens 1992) 111–26.

July 1961. In the 1960s the Nicaraguan National Guard, well equipped by the US, had little difficulty in containing the Sandinistas.[11]

During the 1960s, there were guerilla movements feeding on political and economic oppression in other Pacific Basin Latin American republics, which were significant consumers of American military aid. In Peru two insurgencies, with Marxist and anti-American biases and drawing their inspiration from Cuba, required 5,000 American-equipped soldiers and police to suppress them in 1965. In August 1968 guerillas in Guatemala shot the American ambassador, who in the previous year had presented the Guatemalan military forces with a great range of US weapons with which to combat another insurgency against the entrenched landed aristocracy and authoritarian military government. In 1968 the US was confronting Marxist insurgencies on both sides of the Pacific Basin, which were major foreign policy problems for the next American administration.[12]

CRUSHING MARXISM IN CHILE

Though in the Western Pacific Basin the Republican administrations of Nixon and Ford abandoned South Vietnam to communist rule and worked for a détente with China, they were as much concerned about the threat of communist expansion in the Eastern Pacific Basin as were the preceding postwar administrations. Therefore, the CIA tried to stop the Marxist Allende winning the 1970 presidential election in Chile. As in 1964, the agency channelled money to opposing

11. Walter La Feber, *The Panama Canal: The Crisis in Historical Perspective* (Oxford 1979) 150. Thomas P. Anderson, *The War of the Dispossessed: Honduras and El Salvador, 1969* (Lincoln 1981) 33. James Dunkerley, *Power in the Isthmus: A Political History of Modern Central America* (London 1988) 342–50. Langley, *United States and the Caribbean* 121–5. James D. Rudolph (ed.), *Nicaragua: A Country Study* (Washington 1987) 189.

12. George D.E. Philip, *The Rise and Fall of the Peruvian Military Radicals 1968–1976* (London 1978) ch. 1. Richard F. Nyrop (ed.), *Peru: A Country Study* (Washington 1981) 36–70. Hector Béjar, *Peru Notes on a Guerilla Experience* (New York 1969) *passim*. Thomas and Marjorie Melville, *Guatemala Another Vietnam?* (Harmondsworth 1971) 6–11. Richard F. Nyrop (ed.) *Guatemala: A Country Study* (Washington 1984) 30–4. Dunkerley, *Power in the Isthmus* 425–58. Michael McClintock, *The American Connection* vol. 2 *State Terror and Popular Resistance in Guatemala* (London 1985) ch. 4.

parties and funded propaganda with themes such as: 'An Allende victory means violence and Stalinist repression'.[13] However, Allende headed the poll, even though his 36.2 per cent of the national vote was 2.4 per cent less than he received in 1964. This time the CDP was internally divided, and Chile's constitution prevented Frei from running for a second term. The party's candidate Rodomero Tomic Romero received only 18.7 per cent of the vote compared with 34.1 per cent for former conservative president, Jorge Alessandri Rodriguez. Colby acknowledged a CIA mistake in concentrating on a 'spoiling campaign' and not in directing funds to one of Allende's two opponents with pressure on the other one to withdraw.[14]

'Nixon was furious', said Colby. 'He was convinced that the Allende victory meant the spread of Castro's anti-American revolution to Chile, and from there throughout Latin America'. Nixon insisted, wrote Kissinger, 'on doing something, *anything*, that would reverse the previous neglect', which threw 'all agencies . . . into a frenzied reassessment'. Richard Helms, the CIA director, was called to an Oval Office meeting with Nixon, Kissinger and the Attorney General. Helms was ordered to implement a programme of covert action. He was to exploit the Chilean constitutional requirement for congress to elect the president when there was no absolute majority in the popular vote. The CIA was to arrange for bribing CDP congressmen to vote for Alessandri or, if that failed, to turn 'to the Chilean military for help'.[15]

The CDP was determined to respect the political convention that the candidate with the most votes should become president. So the military coup option was pursued. However, the army's commander, General René Schneider Chreau, declared that the military should not interfere with the constitutional process. 'In desperation', wrote Colby, 'an attempt was made to kidnap him'. When the kidnappers in four cars pushed Schneider's car off the road, he drew his revolver in self-defence but was shot and died in hospital three days later. This first major political assassination in Chile since 1837 was carried out by a group which the CIA 'had given up as ineffective'; the agency had provided weapons to another group for the kidnapping job. The assassination back-fired, because the leaders of the army, navy and air force reacted by reinforcing their constitutional loyalty. Also an attempt to create economic chaos so as to invite a military coup

13. Blunt, *The CIA* 235.
14. Colby, *Honourable Men* 303.
15. Ibid. 303–4. Henry Kissinger, *The White House Years* (London 1979) 670.

failed. The CIA and the International Telephone and Telegraph Company, one of the largest US private investors in Chile, which contributed $350,000 to Alessandri's election campaign, initiated this move. However, other US companies and banks refused to cooperate. So Nixon failed to prevent Allende's election as president.[16]

A major problem with the schemes to stop Allende was their last-minute nature. In the years prior to the election, the CIA had concentrated on funding non-Marxist political parties. This policy recognized a fundamental feature of the Chilean polity. Chileans had great pride in their constitutional system of government, which had survived since the mid-nineteenth century, despite a period of military rule from 1924 to 1932. The military forces, after the chaos created by military factionalism in 1931–32, accepted the principle that they should stay out of politics and acquiesce in a democratic constitution. There were officers who distrusted constitutional government, some of whom supported the CIA's coup option. But their marginality in 1970 was indicated by the closing of military ranks behind the constitution after Schneider's assassination. Furthermore, most members of the CDP, which held the congressional balance of power, did not have the fears of Allende that haunted Nixon's administration. Communists in the 1930s and 1940s had participated in popular front governments in Chile, and Allende's commitment to democracy was respected.[17]

Allende's 'Popular Unity' government, a coalition of the Marxist Socialist and Communist parties, the Radical Party and a leftist breakaway group from the CDP, still faced strong US hostility during its three years of existence. In a speech to the UN General Assembly on 4 December 1972, Allende complained that Chile was the victim of a US 'financial-economic blockade'; 'not an open aggression . . . but an attack at once oblique, subterranean, but no less lethal to Chile', which aimed to 'strangle our economy'.[18]

Certainly, the Inter-American Development Bank and the World Bank granted no new loans to Chile, in line with a NSC memorandum of November 1970, which stated that: 'The U.S. would use its predominant position in international financial institutions to dry

---

16. Frederick M. Nunn, *The Military in Chilean History: Essays on Civil-Military Relations, 1810–1973* (Albuquerque 1976) 266–8. Mark Falcoff, *Modern Chile 1970–1989: A Critical History* (New Brunswick 1989) 207–17. Whelan, *Out of Ashes* 1027–43.

17. Ibid. ch. 4. Nunn, *Military in Chilean History* chs 5–11.

18. Quoted in Falcoff, *Modern Chile* 218.

up the flow of new multilateral credit and other financial assistance' to Chile. That memorandum also called for the withdrawal of US government 'financial assistance or guarantees' to American companies investing in Chile and to ensure that 'U.S. businesses would be made aware of the government's concern and its restrictive policies'.[19] Accordingly, private US bank lending to Chile declined sharply during Allende's regime. However, it can be argued that his government's expropriation of the American copper mining companies in July 1971 and other nationalization of business enterprises would have influenced investor reluctance, especially as Chile decided that the excess profits of the copper companies did not justify any financial compensation. US public aid programmes to Chile were drastically reduced, though this reflected a high level of aid to Frei's government and the Nixon Administration's abandonment of much of the Alliance for Progress. Military aid to Chile actually increased during Allende's regime, encouraged by his policy of conciliating the Chilean armed forces, and by a US policy of maintaining its influence with that powerful sector of Chilean society. Though the US also attempted to stop the supply of industrial spare parts to Chile, there was no implementation of such a programme. The shortages which occurred were caused by a decline in the country's short-term financing capacity after 1971. Furthermore, the drying-up of US capital was compensated for by credit supplied by Western European and communist countries, though on less generous terms.[20]

Indeed, the major economic problems plaguing the Allende Government in its second and third years were caused much more by wider world conditions, by the weaknesses of the Chilean economy and by the government's own policies than by US economic pressure. Chile's economy depended heavily on mining exports, which produced 85 per cent of export earnings in 1969 and caused a neglect of agriculture, resulting in the need to import food. Copper mining revenue was the principal source for industrial development and even for the food imports for a population in 1970 of 9,340,200 that was the most literate (90 per cent) in Latin America and one of the most highly urbanized (75 per cent). But the dominance of mining in Chile's economic history had created high dependency on

19. United States Congress, *Hearings before the Select Committee to Study Governmental Operations with Respect to Intelligence Activities of the United States Senate, Ninety-Fourth Congress, First Session* vol. 7, *Covert Action in Chile 1963–1973* (Washington 1973) Appendix A, 180.
20. Falcoff, *Modern Chile* 217–30.

world prices. A fall in the world copper price from 64 cents per pound in 1970 to 49 cents in 1971, caused by the wind-down of American involvement in the Vietnam War, burst the bubble of the previously war-inflated copper boom. There were also increases in world food prices by 8 per cent in 1971 and by 41 per cent in 1972.[21]

The Allende Government's policies compounded the resultant economic squeeze on Chile. There was a boom in consumer spending in 1971 influenced by redistribution of income policies, higher wages for workers, expansion of production assisted by government take-overs of industries, a more than doubling of the money supply and strict price controls. But in the next year the expansion was overtaken by an inflation rate of 163 per cent, inducing much black marketing and hoarding to escape the government's retention of price controls. The euphoria of 1971 became black despair for many Chileans in 1972–73.[22]

The Chilean democracy's other major problem was sharp political diversity. The mining-dominated economy had created a wide gap between the rich and the poor in Chile's community. The latter were a minority of the population living mainly in depressed agricultural regions and in the three big cities, Santiago, Valparaíso and Concepción, which contained 45 per cent of the population. The urban and rural poor provided a breeding ground for the communists and the uniquely Marxian Chilean socialists. But this was not a big enough base for those parties to enjoy a political majority, since the larger middle classes of the big cities mainly supported the CDP or more conservative parties. The result was that the Allende Government pursued radical socio-economic reforms, which did not have majority popular support. When the bottom fell out of the economy in 1972 many members of the non-Marxist majority started to protest vehemently against the government, including strike action and violence. Especially effective were protests by middle-class women banging pots and pans, and who had always voted more conservatively than their menfolk. The CDP also veered to the right. Extremist Popular Unity supporters responded with heightened militancy, fuelling increasing social conflict. By August 1973 the country was polarized between bitter protagonists for and against the government, a struggle bordering on civil war.[23]

21. Ibid. ch. 6.
22. Ibid. ch. 3.
23. Edy Kaufman, *Crisis in Allende's Chile: New Perspectives* (New York 1988) chs 10, 11.

This social conflict was a major cause of the violent military coup in Chile on 11 September 1973 carried out by middle-class military officers. The officers perceived a clear anti-government majority, reinforced by the 'popular' women's protests and by the congressional elections of March 1973, in which Popular Unity made only a small gain and remained a minority with 44 per cent of the vote. Allende also had compromised the separation of military and civil power by bringing officers into his government as a means of countering anti-government activities. But by April 1973, having supervised the congressional election, all officers had stepped down from the Cabinet, opening the way for a coup. Allende's chief military supporter, the army commander General Carlos Prats Gonzales, remained loyal. However, he was pressured by most of his generals to resign on 23 August, freeing his successor General Augusto Pinochet Ugarte to organize the coup which ousted the elected government and resulted in the death of its president. Moreover, despite Allende's policy of conciliating the military, many officers were alienated by pressure from militant government supporters to form an armed popular militia. This was a response to a violent right wing group, the Partria y Libertad.[24]

Nixon's Administration has been blamed for complicity in the Chilean coup. Certainly, the CIA had remained active during the Allende regime by providing funds to opposing political parties and newspapers and by maintaining links with the military. In the American Senate hearings on the subject, which were controlled by the majority Democratic Party, Helms insisted that the CIA deliberately distanced itself in 1973 from the military in order to avoid any hint of involvement in a coup. Democrats on the investigating committee had difficulty in believing this claim, given the information they uncovered about the attempted CIA-supported putsch of 1970. But they discovered no firm evidence of US involvement in the 1973 coup. However, Prats, who went into exile in Argentina after the coup, remarked that Allende's government had not appreciated 'how profound the North American influence is in our armed forces, and especially on the mentality of the Chilean military man'. He accused his former military colleagues of not liberating their country from 'the enemy within' but of rendering it dependent on 'the enemy without', namely the US. For such views he was assassinated in Argentina

24. Ibid. chs 4, 12. Nunn, *Military in Chilean History* 276–308. Israel Z. Ricardo, *Politics and Ideology in Allende's Chile* (Tempe 1989) ch. 7.

in 1974 by agents of Chile's military strongman, Pinochet, while many other Chilean supporters of Popular Unity were subjected to imprisonment, torture and execution.[25]

THE NIXON/FORD ADMINISTRATIONS, PERU AND CENTRAL AMERICA

North of Chile, Peru also was 'heading in directions that have been difficult to deal with', wrote Kissinger in 1970. The left wing Peruvian military junta, headed by General Juan Velasco Alvarado, had expropriated the oilfields controlled by the American International Petroleum Company. In the junta's view, the company had been illegally granted in 1922 ownership of all the oil reserves under its fields, which offended Peruvian nationalist sensibilities. No financial compensation was offered to the company on the grounds that it owed Peru US$690 million in foregone revenue because of the 1922 agreement. This refusal caused a crisis in US-Peruvian relations, given the existence of the Hickenlooper Amendment to the Foreign Assistance and Sugar Acts passed by the US Congress in 1961, which required the president to suspend all aid and also sugar import quotas for any country expropriating an American company's assets without adequate compensation. Not wanting to push the Velasco regime further down a pro-Cuban path, Kissinger wrote that the US sought to 'reach an equitable settlement', which was achieved with a compromise compensation agreement. However, the Peruvian junta remained a nuisance to Washington by enforcing a 200–mile sea zone and seizing US fishing boats. This provocation caused the cessation of US military aid to Peru, with a consequent shift by its military regime to the USSR for arms. The junta pursued a conspicuously neutralist foreign policy. It was also an enthusiast for the Andean Common Market (ANCOM), which included Venezuela, Colombia, Ecuador, Bolivia and Chile, though Chile withdrew in 1976 because of ANCOM's code restricting foreign investment. Also,

---

25. Falcoff, *Modern Chile* 230–40. Salvatore Bizzarro, *Historical Dictionary of Chile* (Metuchen 1987) 411.

bristling with Soviet-supplied arms, Peru indulged in sabre rattling with Ecuador and Chile over border issues.[26]

In Central America the Nixon-Ford Administrations maintained a hard line against left wing insurgencies. From 1970 the Sandinistas became more active in Nicaragua. Assisting their rising popularity was a weakening of Somoza's authority, particularly after he pocketed aid money sent to Nicaragua after a devastating earthquake in 1972 that destroyed part of the capital city, Managua, and killed nearly 10,000 people. Somoza received US military aid to launch in 1975 a major campaign against Sandinista insurgents.[27]

Central American unity was shattered in 1969 by the 'Fútbol' War between El Salvador and Honduras. Their mutual border, which had never been properly defined, was a simmering dispute. It was exacerbated by population pressures in small El Salvador and by its landowning elite, which concentrated on coffee exports at the expense of food production. There was a consequent increase of migration of Salvadorians to Honduras in the 1960s, which caused an increasing Honduran clamour to expel them from land they occupied. This was carried out in 1968. Subsequently, there was a wave of violence against Salvadorians in Honduras after attacks on Hondurans attending the 1969 World Cup soccer match in San Salvador. The arrival in El Salvador of Salvadorian refugees from the violence triggered the invasion that started the war. The superior Salvadorian army was soon well on its way towards the Honduran capital, Tegucigalpa. But four days after the commencement of the war a cease-fire was arranged by the Organization of American States (OAS). As many as 2,000 people had been killed, and over 100,000 Salvadorian refugees fled back into El Salvador. Dissension between El Salvador and Honduras continued through the 1970s and wrecked the Central American Common Market ideal of the previous decade. El Salvador was the long-term loser of the contest. Its previous valuable trade with Honduras was lost, refugees contributed to rampant unemployment and there was further concentration of land into the hands of the landowning oligarchy. In 1979 the 116 families

26. Kissinger, *White House Years* 673, 657. Philip, *Rise and Fall* ch. 2. Daniel M. Masterson, *Militarism and Politics in Latin America: Peru from Sánchez Cerro to Sendero Luminoso* (Westport 1991) chs 9–10. Virginia Gamba-Stonehouse, *Strategy in the Southern Oceans: A South American View* (New York 1989) 35.

27. Langley, *United States and the Caribbean* 282–3. Dunkerley, *Power in the Isthmus* ch. 6. Dennis Gilbert, *Sandinistas: The Party and the Revolution* (New York 1988) 3–8. Robert A. Pastor, *Condemned to Repetition: The United States and Nicaragua* (Princeton 1987) chs 4–10.

of this oligarchy received 60 per cent of the country's commercial income.[28]

THE US AND MEXICO

Mexico was causing a different kind of concern to the US in the mid-1970s. After the Second World War relations between the two countries had improved since the prewar tension over Mexican nationalization of American oil companies. In the postwar era Mexico was still ruled by the Partido Revolucionario Institucional. However, the party had lost much of its revolutionary zeal and was concerned to build up industrial development in order to improve the country's agricultural-mining economic base. This economic policy involved protectionism to foster import replacement industries, which incurred displeasure from the US Government, which was emphasizing free markets for US exports, especially in Latin America. Mexico also maintained a non-interventionist foreign policy, which resulted in disapproval of the US intervention in Guatemala in 1954 and, more seriously, a refusal to agree to isolate Castro's Cuba. From 1964 to 1970 Mexico was the only Latin American country to maintain diplomatic relations with Cuba. Mexico also pursued a policy of reducing its economic dependence on the US, resulting in a decline in the US proportion of Mexico's overseas trade from 78 per cent in 1955 to 69 per cent in 1963. However, Mexico generally supported the US in the UN and was careful not to ruffle the feathers of the dominant American eagle excessively, such as by courting the USSR. Consequently, the American administrations of the 1960s were prepared to allow Mexico a measure of diplomatic independence, and US investment in the country continued.[29]

However, in 1976 there was a sharp deterioration in US-Mexico relations. One background factor was an economic crisis, caused principally by deteriorating prices for mineral exports in the post-Vietnam War recession and the populist policies of President Luis

28. Woodward, *Central America* 274–6. Anderson, *War of the Dispossessed passim.* Dunkerley, *Power in the Isthmus* 345.

29. Josefina Zoauda Vázquea and Lorenzo Meyer, *The United States and Mexico* (Chicago 1985) ch. 9.

Echeverría Alvarez. A consequent 50 per cent devaluation of the Mexican peso alarmed American investors, who controlled 62 per cent of the country's burgeoning foreign debt. Of more serious concern in US right wing circles was Echeverría's widespread efforts to reduce Mexican economic and diplomatic dependency on the US, including a growing warmth in Mexico's relations with Cuba and support for Allende's Chile. After the coup there, Mexico severed diplomatic relations with Chile and harboured many Chilean refugees. A concern that Mexico was drifting into the communist camp caused some US congressmen to warn President Ford of leftist trends in Echeverría's government. However, the Mexican Government accepted a dose of financial austerity imposed by the International Monetary Fund, to the consternation of left wing groups in Mexico who accused the government of selling out to the US. Mexico's relations with the US were restored temporarily to an even keel, though Echeverría's successor, José López Portillo, continued an independent stance by breaking diplomatic relations with Somoza's Nicaragua in 1978 and by welcoming that year a visit to Mexico by Cuba's Castro. But in the next year US-Mexican relations slumped again with Mexico's active support for the Sandinistas in Nicaragua and, in particular, because López broke a pledge to give sanctuary to the fleeing Shah of Iran, which drove President Carter into a fury.[30]

THE CARTER ADMINISTRATION AND LATIN AMERICA

One of Carter's major foreign policy concerns, stemming from his evangelical Christian beliefs, was to promote human rights. It was an erratic policy which in Nicaragua did not extend to US support for the Sandinista rebellion, which was regarded as communist inspired. The Carter Administration did not even support the demand of moderates in Nicaragua for American pressure on Somoza to resign. Instead Washington sought an accommodation between Somoza and his critics, which was too late. Moderates were now switching

30. Ibid. 183–90. Lester D. Langley, *Mexico and the United States: The Fragile Relationship* (Boston 1991) 75–87.

support to the Sandinistas who, despite continued US military aid to Somoza's regime, won a bloody war and swept to power in 1979, with Somoza and his cronies fleeing to Miami in the US. The Carter Administration, however, did show a new face to the advent of a radical regime in Central America by offering recognition to the new government and economic aid.[31]

Carter's Administration also became concerned about human rights abuses in El Salvador. There a Marxist guerilla movement was exploiting the growing economic power of the oligarchy, employing in particular bomb attacks in urban areas. The government responded with campaigns against any forms of radicalism, such as closing down the National University in July 1972 for a year and murdering suspected leftist activists. US congressional criticism was aroused in 1977 by violence directed at church workers who were influenced by Latin American liberation theology and who were supporting and organizing peasant movements. Carter threatened to cut off economic aid to El Salvador. A new government under General Humberto Romero, who gained office in a fraudulent national election, promised to respect human rights. However, after the threat of US aid suspension was removed, his government renewed state terrorism to stifle political opposition and to maintain the power of the oligarchy. So the US did not oppose, indeed some US officials supported, a coup in October 1979 against Romero by army officers concerned to introduce a reform government which would address the social conditions that were assisting active Marxist guerillas.[32]

Another Central American republic, Guatemala, earned the ire of the Carter Administration. Rural unrest, exacerbated by commercialized agriculture which was swallowing up peasant land, resulted in repressive government policies. The most notorious case was the mass slaughter in May 1978 of over 100 protesting Indian peasants who had been called by the army to a meeting in the town of Panzós to discuss their grievances. Troops were waiting for them around the town square to machine-gun them down and then bury them in a previously prepared mass grave. But already in 1977 Carter had banned military aid and sales of arms to Guatemala, a decision which the Panzós massacre reinforced.[33]

31. Langley, *United States and the Caribbean* 284–5. Gilbert, *Sandinistas* 8–13.

32. Michael McClintock, *The American Connection* vol. 1 *State Terror and Popular Resistance in El Salvador* (London 1985) 171–195, 243–50. Enrique A. Baloyra, *El Salvador in Transition* (Chapel Hill 1982) 47–74.

33. Dunkerley, *Power in the Isthmus* 434, 437–84. McClintock, *American Connection* vol. 2, 140–1.

Carter's administration solved the problem of simmering dissent in Panama by negotiating a new treaty guaranteeing a US withdrawal from the Panama Canal in 1999. The treaty allowed four Panamanians to join five Americans in a commission to administer the canal, with the formal disbandment of the Canal Zone. There was a long tussle to achieve the necessary two-thirds majority in the Senate for the treaty's ratification. Die-hard nationalists were defending American perpetual ownership of the canal, their zeal reinforced by desires to efface the shameful memories of US abandonment of South Vietnam. But the JCS supported the treaty on the grounds that a 'friendly Panama' was important for the defence of a canal that was less significant in the nuclear age. This opinion assisted the final passage of the treaty through the Senate by one vote.[34]

A Pacific Basin South American country especially targeted by Carter for human rights condemnation was Pinochet's Chile. It had become a pariah of the international scene for killing hundreds of its citizens and causing many others to flee into exile. Carter even put pressure on the Philippines to suspend an invitation for Pinochet to visit that country in March 1980. The US Congress also imposed an arms embargo on Chile after Allende's overthrow, and US economic aid to Pinochet's government was confined to surplus food and other humanitarian assistance. The arms embargo was a worry to Chile in 1974 when the possibility of war loomed with Soviet-armed Peru. Appreciating its military disadvantage, Chile sought a diplomatic solution, which was assisted by a coup in Peru which replaced the physically ailing Velasco with the more moderate General Francisco Morales Bermúdez Cerrutti. Washington probably supported this coup, which removed from South America the only remaining radical Soviet-supported regime.[35]

LATIN AMERICA AND THE WIDER PACIFIC BASIN

After the end of the age of Spanish trade across the Pacific, Latin American states became isolated from the Western Pacific Basin.

34. Conniff, *Panama and the United States* 127–139. Hogan, *The Panama Canal* chs 4–8.
35. Whelan, *Out of the Ashes* 672–711, 780–8. Falcoff, *Modern Chile* ch. 9. Philip, *Rise and Fall* 150–6.

This isolation was influenced by competing agricultural and mineral exports with many other Pacific Basin countries, by tariff-protected economies, by poor communications with the Western Pacific, and by the traditional dependence on the US and Europe for trade and investment. However, in the 1960s the isolation was weakening. The major influence was the spreading of Japan's growing economic empire across the Pacific. During the 1960s Japanese trade with Latin America was increasing at an average annual rate of 15 per cent per annum and rose to an average of 20 per cent per annum in the 1970s. Feeding this growth was Japan's increasing need 'or raw materials, which along with rising commodity prices raised the value of Latin America's exports to Japan from $1.3 billion in 1970 to $4.3 billion in 1979. In turn there were increasing Latin American demands for Japanese manufactured goods, including machine tools for industrial development. Japan's favourable trade balance with Latin America was demonstrated by her $6.3 billion exports to the region in 1979. Though this was only 6 per cent of Japan's total export trade, Japan had become the second most important source of Latin American imports behind the US. Latin America also was attracting Japanese capital, which had risen to $1.2 billion directly invested in 1979. Brazil was the main location for this capital; the second most important country was the Pacific Basin's Peru. Mexico, with its emphasis on import substitution development was not yet a major Japanese investment target. Japanese direct investment in Mexico was increasing, but only from 0.5 per cent of all foreign direct investment in Mexico in 1960 to 5.3 per cent in 1979. Throughout the whole of Latin America, Japan was still well behind the United States and Western Europe as a source of capital, and the main emphasis of Japanese investment in Pacific Basin Latin America was on mining operations.[36]

However, Japan's emerging interest in Latin America was stimulating a greater interest in Pacific Basin affairs in Latin American countries. Mexican presidents visited Japan in 1962, 1972 and 1978 and there were return trips to Mexico by Japanese prime ministers plus exchange visits by foreign ministers and other high-level officials.

36. Claudio Veliz, 'Latin America's Opening to the Pacific' in Joseph Grinwald (ed.), *Latin America and the World Economy: A Changing International Order* (London 1978) 212–32. Susan Kaufman Purcell and Robert M. Immerman (eds), *Japan and Latin America in the New Global Order* (Boulder 1992) 9–10, 18–21, 72–4. Yale H. Ferguson and Sang-June Shim, 'Mexico's North American and Pacific Relations' in Gavin Boyd (ed.), *Region Building in the Pacific* (New York 1982) 216–9. *YITS*, 1981, 537.

A Joint Mexico-Japan Economic Commission was established in 1967, and in 1969 the two countries granted each other most-favoured trading nation status. In the late 1970s Pinochet's Chile looked to Japan as a means to break the country's diplomatic isolation, arranging a visit there by the Chilean Chancellor in 1979. Pinochet also was eyeing Southeast Asia in a new diplomatic strategy, called the 'Pacific drive'. But the campaign had a shaky start when a trip to the Philippines by Pinochet in 1980 was prevented by Marcos's submission to Carter's pressure against it. Pinochet only travelled as far as Fiji, which he saw as having access to Australasia, but where he encountered hostile public demonstrations.[37]

CONCLUSIONS

By the end of the 1970s the Cold War, which was declining in intensity in the Western Pacific, was very much alive in the Eastern Pacific Basin. This was due to the US determination to oppose allegedly pro-communist political movements spawned by the same kind of concentration of wealth in the hands of oligarchic rulers and repression of peasant masses as had occurred in China and Vietnam. The coup in Guatemala in the early 1950s was matched by US support for coups in Latin America into the 1970s against perceived communist threats to US dominance in the region. Even the Alliance for Progress of the 1960s can be viewed as mostly an attempt to prevent communist subversion, which was not allowed to upset American economic hegemony. The link between US political and economic control was demonstrated by the close relationship between the government and US companies in pressure on Chile, though US businesses were not united in this action; and there were fundamental Chilean reasons for Allende's overthrow. In the case of Peru there was a US attempt at compromise in the interests of keeping the radical military junta away from an embrace with Cuba. But US patience wore out when American fishing boats were seized. The unwillingness of even the Carter Administration to pressure the unpopular Somoza in Nicaragua to resign demonstrated

37. Ibid. 206. Gamba-Stonehouse, *Strategy in Southern Oceans* 38–9.

the continuity of American fear of Latin American radicalism during the whole of the 1945–1979 era. Carter made a small advance in accepting the Sandinista regime and keeping bans on aid to Chile, but even this degree of respect for the wishes of Latin Americans was to disappear after his electoral defeat in 1980. The US also supported many military governments in Latin America in 1979. Attempts at economic cooperation between Latin American republics were further limited by conflicts between countries, which produced threats of war, and the short one between El Salvador and Honduras.

Japan's emerging trade and investment in Latin America was a small challenge to the US economic empire there. It reflected the bigger growth elsewhere in the Pacific Basin of Japan's new economic order, which was causing the Americans trading headaches. In turn Japan's growing economic contact was stimulating Latin American interest in the Western Pacific Basin.

CHAPTER SEVEN

Asian Economic Expansion and Strategic Change since 1980

The first major theme of this chapter is the growth and nature of Japanese economic dominance in the Pacific Basin and its implications for Japan's relations with the US and other Pacific Basin countries. The effect of Japanese investment on the economic development of East and Southeast Asian countries is also examined. The second major theme is an analysis of changes in the strategic balance in the Western Pacific Basin resulting from growing rapprochement between the US, China and the USSR and its implications for the US-Japanese defence relationships. Relations between the two Koreas and the Cambodian conflict are subthemes including developments among the ASEAN states.

JAPAN'S NEW ECONOMIC ORDER IN THE PACIFIC BASIN

In 1980 Japan was achieving, by trade and capital investment, the economic order in Asia and the wider Pacific that she had failed to establish by military means before 1945. Japanese accumulated direct investment in Asia increased from US$2.359 billion in 1974 to US$8.643 billion in 1980, which was 27 per cent of Japanese worldwide direct investments, compared with 26 per cent in North America and 18 per cent in Latin America. A total of 404,682 Asians were working for Japanese affiliated companies, 57 per cent of such overseas workers. This was influenced by Asian wages, which in

1980 averaged only 20 per cent of Japan's. Most of Japan's Asian investment continued to be in manufacturing, with textiles still the major sector though their proportion had fallen from 40 per cent in 1974 to 23 per cent in 1980. There were big rises in metals and chemicals, reflecting new Japanese investment trends in the late 1970s. Also the mining component of the Asian investments had soared from US$605 million in 1974 to US$2.815 billion in 1980. Asian countries generally were willing to accept such new capital despite the environmental degradation that mining can produce. Other overseas Japanese industries had damaging effects, such as illness and death caused by iron dust among Filipino workers at Kawasaki Steel's sintering plant in Nabacaan village on the Philippines island of Mindanao. Anti-pollution agitation in Japan was influencing such offshore industrial relocation.[1]

Japanese overseas relocation of industries was linked to trade expansion. In 1980 Japan was the most important trading partner of ASEAN countries, accounting for 27 per cent of their exports and 22 per cent of their imports. Exceptions were Japan's smaller role in the exports of Singapore, with its lack of raw materials; and the US was ahead of Japan in the commerce of the former American colony, the Philippines. Indonesia was the ASEAN nation most closely tied to Japan, the source of 32 per cent of Indonesia's imports and 49 per cent of her exports.[2]

Japan's competitiveness in world markets grew during the 1980s. After the oil price shock of 1973 there had been an emphasis on the introduction of new technologies and rationalism into Japanese home industry, which improved industrial competitiveness. The second oil price shock in 1979 convinced Japanese captains of industry that they were on the right track in re-establishing resource-hungry industries overseas. The Japanese business emphasis was now to concentrate on high technology products for export. The result was a turnaround of a Japanese current account trade deficit in 1979–80, influenced by the oil price rises, to surpluses, which grew from US$8.74 billion in 1981 to US$82.743 billion in 1986. There was an accompanying rise in the value of the Japanese currency from 296 yen per US dollar in 1976 to 168 ten years later, which made Japanese investment in the US increasingly profitable. A growing American trade imbalance

---

1. Steven, *Japan's New Imperialism* ch. 3. William R. Nestor, *Japan's Growing Power over East Asia and the World Economy* (London 1990) ch. 4.

2. Narongchai Akrasanee (ed.), *ASEAN-Japan Relations: Trade and Development* (Singapore 1983) 1–35. *YITS* 1981, 483, 623, 787, 879, 952.

also influenced the comparative fall in the value of the dollar. The US trade deficit with Japan increased from \$18.1 billion in 1981 to \$59.825 billion in 1986, though its proportion of the total US trade loss fell from 46 per cent to 35 per cent.[3]

The declining terms of America's trade with Japan caused growing tension in US-Japanese relations by the second half of the 1980s. Initially, the ballooning trade deficit was cushioned by the large surplus in the American international capital account and by explanations that the problem was a temporary one caused by the second oil shock. Furthermore, the government, headed since 1981 by President Ronald Reagan, a conservative Republican and a former governor of California, was wedded to free trade ideology. So, rather than any US protectionist measures, Reagan concentrated on negotiations with Japan and other countries for freer access to US exports with only minor successes. But by 1986 there was mounting American business and Congressional anger centred on Japanese import restrictions and unfair trade practices, especially the dumping of goods at low prices, though higher US labour costs were a major reason for the trade imbalance. In 1987 a punitive 100 per cent tariff on Japanese semiconductors was one response to dumping accusations. Then, after a hysterical reaction in the US to the Japanese Toshiba company's sale of computer software and silent motor technology to the USSR, Congress passed by huge majorities the 1988 Omnibus and Competitiveness Trade Act, which improved procedures under the 1974 Trade Act that authorized the imposition of penalties against countries committing unfair trade practices. Japan was named as one of those nations in 1989.[4]

By the late 1980s Japan's imports of manufactured goods were increasing under the impact of the rising value of the yen, which improved to an average rate of 128 per US\$ in 1988, falling only slightly to an average of 135 in 1991. The Japanese Government was also starting to emphasize the value of imports, and tariff rates

3. Steven, *Japan's New Imperialism* 18–30. Bela Balassa and Marcus Noland, *Japan in the World Economy* (Washington 1988) 23–7.
4. Chris C. Carvounis, *The United States Trade Deficit in the 1980s: Origins, Meanings and Policy Responses* (Westport 1987) chs 1–2. Edward J. Lincoln, *Japan's Unequal Trade* (Washington 1990) 1–11, 142–55. Thomas A. Pugel, 'Limits of Trade Policy toward High Technology Industries: The Case of Semiconductors' in Ryuzo Sato and Paul Wactel (eds), *Trade Friction and Economic Policy: Problems and Prospects for Japan and the United States* (Cambridge 1987) 184–223. Clyde V. Prestowitz, Jr., *Trading Places: How We Allowed Japan to Take the Lead* (New York 1988) chs 1–3, 9–10.

on manufactured products were lowered to an average rate of 2.6 per cent in 1986, the lowest among major industrial countries. A changing trend was evident in a rise of imported manufactured goods into Japan from US$28.8 billion in 1984 to US$84.4 billion in 1988. The benefit to the US was smaller. But America's unfavourable trade balance with Japan did fall to US$44.9 billion in 1989, a 25 per cent decline from the peak deficit in 1986, and more if inflation is taken into account. This Japanese trend was notable, given the entrenched anti-import prejudice in Japan, which was hard to change because of the strength of group behaviour in Japanese society, reinforced by barriers to outside economic interests presented by the cooperation between Japanese firms against foreign takeover bids and by the linkages between Japanese manufacturers and retailers. There were other anti-importation factors. There was a large home market created by Japan's 122 million people, so that the proportion of manufactured goods in Japan's exports was less than the average level of industrial countries. There were also the subsidies to Japanese farmers in the form of much higher than world prices paid for their production. In 1990 Japan escaped from the claws of the US 1988 Trade Act, and the successor to Reagan, his Vice-President George Bush, praised the cooperativeness of Japan's Prime Minister Toshiki Kaifu in discussions on the Structural Impediments Initiative started by the US in September 1989 for negotiations for freer trade between the two countries. However, US business and Congressional antipathy towards Japan remained, and there was no guarantee that serious trade conflict between Japan and the US might not re-emerge in the 1990s.[5]

The nature of Japanese overseas investment also was changing during the 1980s. The rising value of the yen inspired Japanese capitalists to seek foreign partners or outright purchase of businesses in the advanced industrial countries. In the US real estate was a major area. However, there was also a search for involvement in productive industries, such as the Sony Company's buying of CBS Records for $2 billion in 1987 and of Columbia Pictures in late 1989 for $5 billion. At the end of 1989 the number of Japanese factories in

5. Ibid. ch. 5. *FEA* 1991, 502–3. *Japan: Country Report* 1992:1, 4. Organization for Economic Co-operation and Development (OECD), *OECD Economic Surveys 1988/89: Japan* (Paris 1989) 83–102. *OECD Economic Surveys 1989/90: Japan* (Paris 1990) 133. Kent E. Calder, 'Japan in 1990: Limits to Change', *Asian Survey* XXXI, 1991, 21–35. Research Institute for Peace and Security, *Asian Security 1990–91* (London 1990) 23–32, 114–16.

the US topped 1,000, and by 1991 total Japanese direct investment in the US since 1951 was worth $130.5 billion, 42 per cent of all Japan's worldwide direct investments. Such investment contributed to American bitterness about Japan's economic dominance, with accusations after the Columbia Pictures sale that Japan was even trying to take over American culture as well as the US economy.[6]

On the other hand mergers with US companies have created an alliance between Japanese and American capitalists. Indeed, Japanese money was being used to prop up failing American enterprises, such as providing an emergency loan to the Bank of America. In 1990 seven US states applied to the Japanese Export-Import Bank for low-interest loans that were normally extended to Third World nations, and the US Government asked Japan for $2.6 billion to assist in the construction of a giant superconducting supercollider. A special area of Japanese involvement in American production was the selling of motor car parts for assembly in the US by joint Japanese-US firms, such as production by Toyota and General Motors in California of the Nova and Corolla makes, and wholly-owned Japanese firms, such as the Honda plant in Ohio. Electronics was the other major joint US-Japan venture area, whereby Japan supplied cheap components for assembly in factories in the US. To avoid tariff restrictions over the imports of electronic equipment which were creating the most trade friction, there was a new drive in the late 1980s for Japanese companies involved in electrical goods production in the US to increase the use of locally produced parts, not only for American sales but also, with the high value of the yen, for re-export to Japan. A similar process was occurring in other countries, which was another reason for the increase of foreign manufactured imports into Japan in the late 1980s. Imports into Japan of electrical equipment rose from US$4.5 billion in 1986 to US$9.3 billion in 1988.[7]

In the changed patterns of Japanese investment in the 1980s Asian nations took on a new role. The little dragon Asian NICs – South Korea, Taiwan, Singapore, and Hong Kong – became the major Asian centre for Japanese investment in new forms of manufacturing, particularly electronics and automobile components. Japan was taking

6. Ibid. 11, 43. Calder, 'Japan in 1990', 21–2. Steven, *Japan's New Imperialism* ch. 4.

7. Jeffrey E. Garten, *A Cold Peace: America, Japan, Germany and the Struggle for Supremacy* (New York 1992) 202. *FEA* 1991, 502. Masataka Kosaka (ed.), *Japan's Choices: New Globalism and Cultural Orientations in an Industrial State* (London 1989) ch. 2.

advantage of cheaper wages, which in South Korea, Taiwan and Singapore in 1987 ranged from one-fifth to a quarter of the Japanese wage level.[8]

South Korea also was being used by Japan as an offshore production site for the export of manufactured goods to other countries. By 1988 cumulative Japanese direct investments in the ROK were worth US$3.3 billion, a tenth of the total Japanese direct investment in Asia. Consequently, South Korea's imports of electrical and other equipment for industrial production, principally from Japan, nearly doubled from the 1986 level to a value of US$6 billion in 1988; while in the same years the ROK's exports of electrical machinery and transportation products nearly doubled to US$12.9 billion. A notable item in this export rise was motor cars. In 1983 only 8 per cent of automobiles made in South Korea were exported; by 1988 70 per cent of Korean cars were being sold overseas. The major automobile exporter, Hyundai Motor Company, received 50 per cent of its capital equipment from Japan, and 15 per cent of its capital was owned by the Japanese Mitsubishi corporation. In another major export growth area, electronics, which increased from 7 per cent to 25 per cent of the ROK's exports between 1983 and 1988, the technology employed by the Korean companies came from Japan. There were resultant licensing fees of as much as 10 per cent of export revenue being paid to Japanese corporations. However, a growing balance-of-payments surplus, and a rise in the value of the Korean won, were encouraging South Korean direct investments abroad, which grew from US$633 million in 1986 to US$1.2 billion in 1988, principally in North America, Southeast Asia and the Middle East.[9]

There was a similar story of Japanese involvement in Taiwan's industrialization, though in 1988 the island had absorbed only 6 per cent of Japan's Asian direct investment. The emphasis of the Japanese investment there in the 1980s was in electrical goods production and in other manufacturing. Consequently, Taiwan's exports of calculating

8. Steven, *Japan's New Imperialism*. 150.

9. Ibid. 146–68. Alice H. Amsden, *Asia's Next Giant: South Korea and Late Industrialization* (New York 1989) 175–6. *FEA* 1991, 570. Bon-Ho Koo, 'The Korean Economy: Structural Adjustment for Future Growth' in Chong-Sik Lee (ed.) *Korea Briefing, 1990* (Boulder 1991) 55–73. Walden Bello and Stephanie Rosenfeld, *Dragons in Distress: Asia's Miracle Economies in Crisis* (San Francisco 1990) 113–15. James Riedel, 'Intra-Asian Trade and Foreign Direct Investment', *Asian Development Review*, 9, 1991, 140.

machines and television and radio receivers increased during the period 1980–89 from 5.5 to 9.1 per cent of total exports. The contribution of manufacturing to Taiwan's GNP grew from 26 to 36 per cent in those years, compared with 31 per cent in 1989 in South Korea. Assisted by the high value of the yen and the movement of Japanese industry into high technology areas, Japan was becoming a market for mid-technology electronics exports from Taiwan and from the other little dragons. For example, their exports of colour television sets to Japan boomed from 25,000 in 1986 to 370,000 a year later. [10]

Such exports, however, did not weaken the dependency of Taiwan and South Korea upon Japan for imports to fuel their industrialization. In 1989, 31 per cent of Taiwan's and 28 per cent of the ROK's imports came from Japan, proportions that were slightly higher than in 1980, with the value of the imports inflated by the rising value of the yen. Both countries still had unfavourable trade balances with Japan, with deficits of US$6 billion for Taiwan and US$4 billion for the ROK. However, for both little dragons the US remained their leading export market. They contributed to the US trade deficit in 1989, to the extent of a US$12 billion profit to Taiwan and US$4.7 billion to South Korea, though its trade surplus had almost halved since 1987. Pressure was placed by the US on Taiwan and South Korea to raise the value of their currency. The ROK, especially, in 1985–86 drew US protests for unfair trading practices and maintenance of high protectionism, leading to a major trade confrontation between those two closely allied nations. The falling imbalance of trade for the US in the late 1980s reflected a significant relaxation of restrictions in South Korea on American exports, which almost doubled in value from 1987 to 1989 to only US$1.5 billion less than Japan's exports to the ROK in 1989. This was a by-product of South Korea's continued dependence on the US for defence assistance, and it indicated a limitation placed by US military hegemony upon Japanese economic dominance in South Korea. [11]

10. Ibid. *FEA* 1981–82, 386; 1991, 342, 569. Steven, *Japan's New Imperialism* 132. Bill Emmott, *The Sun Also Sets: The Limits to Japan's Economic Power* (New York 1989) 192.

11. *FEA* 1991, 343, 570. Jiann-Jong Guo and Raymond Chung, 'Taiwan's Economic Relations with the United States of America' in Gary Klintworth (ed.), *Modern Taiwan in the 1990s* (Canberra 1991) 106–21. Paul W. Kuznests, 'Trade Policy, and Korea–U.S. Relations' in John P. Hardt and Young C. Kim (eds), *Economic Cooperation in the Asia-Pacific Region* (Boulder 1990) 69–81. Peter A. Petri, 'Korea's Export Niche: Origins and Prospects' and P.F. Alleigeier, 'Korean Trade Policy in the Next Decade: Dealing with Reciprocity' in Danny M. Leipziger (ed.), *Korea: Transition to Maturity* (New York 1988) 47–63, 85–97.

In Singapore in 1986, for the first time, Japanese investment in manufacturing exceeded the US input. Japan increased its proportional share of Singapore's overseas investments from 16 per cent in 1980 to 42 per cent in 1986, and by that year this little dragon had received 12 per cent of Japan's direct investment in Asia, second only to Hong Kong. Utilizing Singapore's well-educated population, the primary Japanese investment was in electronics, firms that were either wholly Japanese-owned or with the Singapore Government as a partner. In no other part of Asia was Japanese money more welcome, since it was seen as promoting the development of Singapore's role as the leading commercial and industrial centre in Southeast Asia. Consequently, electronics increased from 12 to 20 per cent of Singapore's exports from 1980 to 1989.[12]

The policies of a stable and interventionist government were major reasons for Singapore's economic success. Enforcing a puritanical discipline on its population based on traditional Chinese culture, Lee Kuan Yew's PAP government utilized the crisis of independence to impose curbs on trade unions as part of a strategy to open the republic to foreign investment. Its Economic Development Board was a major instrument in providing the financial catalyst for rapid industrialization. Government policies well equipped the island to take advantage of the trade boom generated by the Vietnam War and the growth of international trade in the late 1970s after a short recession induced by the 1973 oil shock. Along with political stability created by PAP electoral dominance, the island rapidly became Asia's leading financial centre. By 1975 its port had become the third busiest in the world, behind New York and Rotterdam – although later overtaken by Hong Kong – and its industries by the end of the 1970s were moving out of the labour intensive stage of development assisted by a government 'Second Industrial Revolution' strategy. There was an economic downturn in 1985 caused by wages outstripping productivity, but the strength of Singapore's economy was demonstrated in the way it bounced back in 1987 with the assistance of reductions in government charges for businesses. In 1990, when Lee Kuan Yew finally stepped down in favour of his deputy prime minister, Goh Chok Tong, the economy had been growing at rates of 11 and 9 per cent in the preceding two years,

12. *FEA* 1980, 1052; 1991, 978. Riedel, 'Intra-Asian Trade', 140. Steven, *Japan's New Imperialism*, 133–45.

fuelled by a continuing regional economic boom and despite a fall in electronics exports to the US.[13]

Hong Kong's 5,761,400 people in 1989 had been experiencing strong export-driven industrial growth. Exports of goods and non-factor services, including re-exports, contributed to 95 per cent of its GNP in 1983, giving Hong Kong's citizens a per capita income nearly as high as Singapore's. This economic growth resulted much less from government interventionist policies than in Singapore, Taiwan and South Korea. British government assistance was confined to the provision of economic infrastructure and educational and training resources, though there were less formal contacts between the government bureaucracy and the colony's business world. The educational and training resources were helpful in the growth of Hong Kong's industrial development and in the adaptability of the manufacturing labour force, but overall Hong Kong was an example of free market capitalism. American investment was still predominant in provision of overseas capital for the colony, though it was Japan's most prominent field of Asian investment. Hong Kong's role as a major trading door to the outside world for China was another source of the colony's prosperity. In the years 1987 to 1989 China contributed 25 per cent of Hong Kong's imports compared with 18 per cent from Japan. Much of the foreign investment and technological transfer traffic to China was routed through Hong Kong.[14]

However, there were problems facing the little dragon economies by the end of the 1980s. Rising wage rates were destroying the textile industries that were the original basis for export-oriented industrial expansion. The average cost in 1989 per operator hour in the NIC textile industry ranged from US$2.44 in Hong Kong to US$3.58 in Taiwan. The average cost in China was US$0.40 and in the Philippines US$0.64, with lower costs in Indonesia and Sri Lanka. Higher technology exports were the preferred new NIC

13. Turnbull, *A History of Singapore* ch. 9. Cheng Siok Hwa, 'Economic Change and Industrialization' in Chew and Lee (eds), *History of Singapore* 190–216. Garry Rodan, *The Political Economy of Singapore's Industrialization: National State and International Capital* (New York 1989) chs 3–5. Chong Li Choy, 'Business in the Development of Singapore: The Creation of an Environment' in Chong Li Choy, Tan Chwee Huat, Wong Kwei Cheong and Caroline Yeoh (eds), *Business, Society and Development in Singapore* (Singapore 1990) 2–11. *Asian Security 1990–91* 173–4.

14. Organization for Economic Co-operation and Development, *The Newly Industrialising Countries: Challenge and Opportunity for OECD Industries* (Paris 1988) 47–52. Patrikeeff, *Mouldering Pearl* chs 5–6. *FEA*, 1990, 365–8. T.K. Ghose, *The Banking System of China and the China-Hong Kong Nexus* (Perth 1990) 39.

option. But success in this area faced the strong reluctance of Japanese corporations, and also US companies, to part with their technology, using the little dragons for lower technology operations. South Korea and Taiwan have discovered this reality in attempts to establish their own fully controlled automobile industries, exemplified by the collapse of the Big Auto Plant project in Taiwan and by a comment by a Mitsubishi Motors representative that his company in the ROK 'does all the critical design work while Hyundai constructs the pieces and puts them together'. The same situation was facing the NICs in their attempts to break into high electronics technology beyond the level of the computer clones that Taiwanese companies became so adept at assembling.[15]

Elsewhere in the ASEAN states in the 1980s Japan was still concentrating on resource development, exploiting the rich raw materials of the region. These ASEAN nations were known as newly exporting countries to distinguish them from the NICs. Partial exceptions were Thailand and Malaysia, which by the late 1980s were experiencing significant industrial development; in both countries in 1988 manufacturing contributed to 24 per cent of GNP. Japan had become the dominant investor in Thailand, and in Malaysia Japanese investments were greater than those of Japan's two main competitors: Singapore and Britain. Much of the Japanese investment in Thailand was in joint ventures with Thai firms, such as the Siam Toyota Manufacturing Company, established in partnership with Siam Cement, Thailand's largest manufacturing firm. It contributed to an increase in the country's production of motor vehicles from 74,200 in 1986 to 157,600 in 1989. In Malaysia there was a significant linkage of Japanese investors with local Chinese capitalists and with the Malaysian elite. The largest Japanese ventures in Malaysia were still exploiting the country's rich natural resources, such as Malaysia LNG, a joint venture between Mitsubishi, the Dutch Shell company and the Malaysian state petroleum company. However, by the late 1980s Thailand and Malaysia were becoming a major target for relocation of Japanese industries, utilizing the cheap labour there. Consequently, in 1988 exports of machinery and transport equipment by Thailand and Malaysia, as a proportion of total exports, were respectively 18 and 28 per cent, compared with 8 per cent by the Philippines and 0.7 per cent by Indonesia. Malaysia and Thailand also by the late 1980s were becoming fields for Japanese electronics

---

15. Bello and Rosenfeld, *Dragons in Distress* 135 (quotation), chs 6, 15.

production, which was extending into the Philippines. There was a sharp jump in Japanese direct investment in Indonesia, from US$631 million in 1989 to US$1,105 million in 1990, which was only US$149 million less than Thailand, the biggest ASEAN destination of Japanese investment. This big increase was stimulating new industrial growth in Indonesia. However, raw materials, especially oil, rubber and metals, were still the top ASEAN exports to Japan.[16]

A new region for Japanese economic expansion in Asia was China. By the 1980s Japan had become China's leading supplier of high technology and manufactured consumer goods. The Japanese proportional contribution to China's imports increased from an average of 13 per cent in the three years 1977–79 to 20 per cent in 1987–89, though in 1988–89, Japanese imports were overtaken by goods from Hong Kong. Japanese government and business circles, however, were ambivalent about China. While they were seeking to promote prosperity there for increased reception of Japanese goods, there were Japanese predictions of future political and social instability after the architect of China's modernization, Deng Xiaoping, who was eighty-five years of age in 1989, died or stepped down. The little dragons were seen as more stable and profitable areas for Japanese investment in East Asia.[17]

The Pacific Islands were another region for increasing Japanese economic attention in the late 1980s. In December 1990 the skyline of Tuamon Bay in the US territory of Guam was punctured by cranes erecting Japanese hotels to add to those already dominating the shoreline. Local Chamorro people call their island 'Japan's Disneyland', where groups of young Japanese go on jungle river tours, have their photographs taken alongside blonde-haired Americans, and spend their money in glittering Japanese-owned department stores. The US was still dominant in the trade of Guam and of other North Pacific islands; and Australia was the leading supplier of imports for the independent states of the South Pacific. But Japan was either the second or third largest source of imports for those South Pacific states. Japan was also the most important purchaser of the agricultural and mineral production of Papua New Guinea and of the Solomon

16. Ibid. ch. 6, 250–4. *FEA*, 1990, 462–3, 631–2, 946, 1041–2. Richard Stubbs, 'US-Japanese Trade Relations: The ASEAN Dimension', *The Pacific Review*, vol. 5, 1992, 63.

17. *FEA* 1981–82, 363–4; 1991, 322. Gary Klintworth, *China's Modernisation: the Strategic Implications for the Asia-Pacific Region* (Canberra 1989) 92–3. For Japan's earlier economic involvement in China see Chae-Jin Lee, *China and Japan: New Economic Diplomacy* (Stanford 1984).

Islands. Furthermore, there was a notable increase in Japan's financial aid to Pacific States, from US$53.9 million in 1982 to US$251 million in 1988, part of a Japanese response to US pressure to spend some of the trade surplus on aid to poorer regions of the world of strategic importance. The new areas of aid provision were Polynesian and Micronesian islands. By far the biggest amount in 1988, US$114 million, went to Japan's former mandated islands in Micronesia, the Pacific Islands region of greatest Japanese economic activity and US strategic interest.[18]

Another Pacific Basin region of growing Japanese investment was Australia, a continent rich in mineral resources and agricultural and pastoral production. In the years 1983–88 Japanese capital inflows totalled A$16,861, which was 17 per cent of all incoming foreign capital in Australia, second only to Australia's traditional financial source, Britain (20 per cent) and outstripping the US (15 per cent). Only 22 per cent of the Japanese capital was direct investment, but this was just 1 per cent less than the direct investment proportion of Japanese worldwide capital outflow in 1989. In the 1970s the Japanese investment in Australia had concentrated on raw materials, especially mining, and on automobile manufacturing. In the 1980s, with liberalization of Australian capital markets, there was significant Japanese investment in the financial sector. There was also major investment in properties and tourism. In the year 1987–88 Japan was Australia's best customer, receiving 26 per cent of Australia's total exports, principally mining, agricultural and pastoral products. That year Japanese exports to Australia were 19 per cent of the total, 2 per cent less than those of the US.[19]

While Japanese investment was welcomed by Pacific Basin governments, there was popular apprehension about the new Japanese economic order. In Australia Japanese-financed land developments have aroused local community hostility in a country where bitter memories of Japanese mistreatment of Australian prisoners of war have largely, but not completely, died out. An Australian trade unionist, Abe David, has received strong support from groups of Australian unionists when addressing them about the threat of Japanese capitalism, which he expounded in the book he co-authored in 1989, *The Third Wave*. An opinion poll commissioned by the Australian

---

18. Personal observations. *FEA* 1991, 760–872. OECD, *Geographical Distribution of Financial Flows to Development Countries* (Paris 1989).
19. Ross Garnaut, *Australia and the Northeast Asian Ascendancy* (Canberra 1989) 94–6. *FEA* 1991, 191.

Department of Foreign Affairs and Trade in 1989 discovered that only 49 per cent of respondents supported the existing or any increased levels of Japanese investment. However, anti-Japanese rhetoric is not part of politics in Australia, which has traditionally relied on overseas sources of capital.[20]

In Guam, where there are some Chamorro memories of Japanese wartime brutality, there is broad acceptance, though also cynicism, amongst those people about the prominent Japanese economic presence. However, one American resident businessman aroused significant popular support in November 1990 when, under a Japanese nom de plume, Kenji Matsumoto, he wrote 'tongue in cheek' to a local newspaper. He thanked 'a passive but greedy administration' for permission 'to dispense with the formality of even using local businesses', so that 'our forays into operations, such as merchandising, autosales, charter boat operators etc., allow us to send a much larger percentage of the local dollar back to Japan'.[21]

The Japanese inroads into the American economy have aroused widespread public antipathy in the US towards Japan. The racism of the pre-Second World War era, which denigrated all things Japanese, has been transformed into a new fear of Japan provoked by apprehensions of a decline in US power. When in 1987 the British resident academic Paul Kennedy addressed that theme in his book, *The Rise and Fall of the Great Powers*, it became a bestseller as Americans avidly sought to discover why their country was in the process of decline compared with the rise of Japan. This combination of racism and fear has bred an American xenophobia about Japanese activities and intentions. Japanese scholar Kan Ito responded in 1990 that the Americans, who were nominating in opinion polls that 'the Japanese threat' was more dangerous to the US than the 'Soviet threat', should reflect that, while the Soviets had the capacity to kill most Americans, 'no Japanese put guns to Americans' heads to make them buy Toyotas or Sonys'.[22]

20. Personal information. Abe David and Ted Wheelwright, *The Third Wave: Australia and Asian Capitalism* (Sydney 1989). Garnaut, *Australia and the Northeast* 96–7.

21. Personal information. *Pacific Daily News* 27 Nov. 1990, 27; 29 Nov. 1990, 3.

22. Paul Kennedy, *The Rise and Fall of the Great Powers: Economic Change and Military Conflict from 1500 to 2000* (London 1987) ch. 8. David McLean, 'Symposium: the Decline of America? Paul Kennedy and his Critics', *Australian Journal of International Affairs* 45 (1991) 60–9. D. Eleanor Westney, 'U.S. Industrial Culture and the Japanese Competitive Challenge' in Alan D. Romberg and Tadashi Yamamoto (eds), *Same Bed, Different Dreams: America and Japan – Societies in Transition* (New York 1990) 67–82. Kan Ito, 'Trans-Pacific Anger', *Foreign Policy* no. 78, 1990, 132.

In Asia there was significant hostility in the 1980s towards the Japanese for past military expansionism and new financial dominance, as expressed in a Singapore cartoon that juxtaposed a Second World War Japanese soldier with a modern cigar-smoking Japanese capitalist. While the governments of the little dragons and ASEAN states have welcomed Japanese investment, many of their citizens resent Japanese economic dominance and fear a revived Japanese militarism. Koreans, who remember bitterly their four decades under Japanese rule, are the most hostile towards the Japanese. This antipathy was nourished by an outcry in the ROK at the LDP Government's move in 1982 to rewrite Japanese school textbooks, glossing over prewar oppression on the Asian mainland by substituting, for example, the word 'advance' for 'aggression'. Government protests from South Korea and China about the textbook changes were supported by Taiwan, by Southeast Asian countries and by North Korea. Only the fear that anti-Japanese agitations in South Korea could cause a breakdown in recently improved Japan-ROK relations caused the stubborn Japanese Government finally to offer to withdraw the offending books in two years' time, which did not mollify many Koreans. The textbook controversy served to reinforce Japan's negative image in Southeast Asia. When in 1987 people in ASEAN countries were asked in an opinion poll whether they believed that Japan might once more become a dangerous military power, affirmative answers were given by 53 per cent of Thais and 47 per cent of Filipinos. There were smaller affirmations in the other ASEAN states – 34 per cent of Malaysians, 29 per cent of Singaporeans and 21 per cent of Indonesians; a reflection of increasing geographic distances from Japan. While such opinion polls have limited value, the degree of fear revealed in them was expressed at a time when Japan was keeping low defence and foreign policy profiles.[23]

JAPAN AND THE AMERICAN DEFENCE NETWORK

Despite fears of future Japanese militarism in their own nation, US administrations started pressing Japan in 1980 to increase her defence

23. Chong-Sik Lee, *Japan and Korea: The Political Dimension* (Stanford 1985) ch. 6. Emmott, *Sun also Sets* 205.

expenditure, which that year was only 0.9 per cent of GNP, compared with 5.3 per cent in the US and 3.2 per cent in West Germany. Though the Japanese total expenditure of US$10 billion was eighth in the world, there was a strong feeling in the Carter Administration, matched by its successor, that the US was paying a high price to provide for Japan's defence. During the first half of the 1980s there were growing complaints in Washington that Japan was sheltering under this protection while profiting from the increasing American trade deficits. However, there was growing integration of the US and Japanese defence forces and industries, especially the exchange of electronics technology with military applications. Japan also accepted responsibility for defence of a 1,000 nautical mile zone around its shores. Furthermore, Japan remained a vital base for the US navy and air force for their watching brief over communist Asian powers.[24]

Guiding such US-Japan defence cooperation was Japan's prime minister from 1982 to 1987, Yasuhiro Nakasone, who promised Reagan in 1983 that Japan was 'an unsinkable aircraft carrier' in the 'alliance' between Japan and the US. He had served in the Japanese navy during the Second World War and in 1950 had joined the national Territory Defense Research Association, an anti-communist group formed to promote national security and overturn the unequal US-imposed peace treaty. As prime minister, Nakasone sought a military strength commensurate with his nation's economic power so that Japan could take an appropriate place among the great powers of the world and free itself from dependency on the US to become an equal partner in the Japan-US alliance. However, his LDP never had the two-thirds parliamentary majority necessary for amendments to the anti-war provisions of the Japanese constitution. Indeed, there were vocal critics in opposition political parties in Japan who argued that the existence of a 'self defence' force of 272,000 soldiers, sailors and airmen in 1986 already breached the constitution, and there were accusations that the Supreme Court was biased in constantly upholding the legality of these forces. The Japanese Socialist Party was advocating instead unarmed neutrality. Nakasone's government did breach in 1987 a previously established convention of 1 per cent of GNP as the ceiling on defence expenditure. In 1988 defence spending rose to 1.01 per cent of GNP, which pleased Washington. Japan also agreed in 1987 to pay some of the expenses of the US forces stationed there. However, the US was unable to achieve any fundamental

---

24. Malcolm McIntosh, *Japan Re-armed* (London 1986) 38–60.

change in the level of Japanese defence expenditure. Under the less hawkish Prime Minister Kaifu, the 1990 Japanese defence budget was again under 1 per cent: 0.99 of estimated GNP. The 1 per cent limit still has a big majority of public support in Japan, though even that degree of expenditure made Japan's defence budget in 1990 the sixth largest in the world.[25]

Nor to 1990 was the US able to persuade Japan to use its military power outside Japanese waters. In 1987 when the war between Iraq and Iran was causing missile attacks on oil tankers in the Persian Gulf, through which 55 per cent of Japan's oil was shipped, the Japanese Government rejected a call to share the cost of and provide naval assistance for the protective US naval action because of the anti-war provisions of the Japanese constitution. Nakasone could not persuade his Cabinet to support such a precedent. When in 1990 the US sent troops to Saudi Arabia after Iraq invaded Kuwait, there was renewed pressure on Japan to join other allies of the US in military and naval support. Because the Japanese constitution clearly forbade sending troops to the Gulf, the government considered providing naval ships, but public opinion explicitly opposed Japan sending SDF troops or ships to the Persian Gulf. Under strong US pressure Japan did agree to provide $4 billion to help pay for the military and naval forces protecting much of Japan's oil supply. Moreover, in April 1991, the Kaifu Government succeeded in dispatching four minesweepers to the Gulf, justifying this unprecedented move as protecting Japan's vital oil lifeline, but reflecting a new political climate since recent decisive electoral defeats of the Socialist Party. Conversely, the US has not been willing to concede major economic power to Japan. Washington opposed Japanese requests in 1984 and 1987 for increased voting power in the World Bank and the Asia Development Bank.[26]

Furthermore, at the end of the 1980s there was a controversy over development of a fighter support experimental (FS-X) aircraft to replace the F-1 used by the Japanese SDF. Initially the Japanese Defence Agency was led to understand that Japan could produce the

25. Nestor, *Japan's Growing Power* 78. 'Nakasone's Neo-Nationalism', *Far Eastern Economic Review* 19 Feb. 1987, 82–9. Kenneth B. Pyle, 'In Pursuit of a Grand Design: Nakasone Betwixt the Past and the Future', *Journal of Japanese Studies* 13, 1987, 243–70. Harries, *Sheathing the Sword* ch. 25. Hunter, *Modern Japan* 284–6. Defense Agency, *Defense of Japan 1990* (Tokyo 1990) 163.

26. Ibid. 238. Courtney Purrington, 'Tokyo's Policy Responses During the Gulf Crisis', *Asian Survey* XXXI, 1991, 307–23. Courtney Purrington, 'Tokyo's Policy Responses During the Gulf War and the Impact of the "Iraqi Shock" on Japan', *Pacific Affairs* 65, 1992, 161–81. Emmott, *Sun Also Sets* 231.

aircraft, but the US companies General Dynamics and McDonnell Douglas pushed for joint US-Japanese development of improvements to their F-16 or F-18 aircraft, and agreement was reached with Japan in November 1988 for joint development of the F-16 as the FS-X. However, many members of the US Congress opposed the deal as giving away aircraft technology to Japan. Despite the government's negotiation with Japan to restrict the transfer of such information, in May 1989 the Senate voted to reject the scheme unless there were more restrictions on technology transfer, to which the House of Representatives agreed. This congressional action and previous changes to the agreement damaged the faith of many Japanese in the efficacy of joint ventures with the US.[27]

Within Japan there has been significant public debate about the nation's acceptance of US military leadership, which was heightened by the FS-X affair. A leading advocate for change has been the publicist and LDP politician, Ishihara Shintarō, who argued that Japan's toadying to the US was encouraging a national moral malaise that portended social disintegration. Therefore it was imperative to restore Japan's military power and her national independence in a new form of partnership with the US. A book he co-authored in 1989 with the chairman of Sony Corporation, Morita Akio, entitled *'No' to ieru Nihon* (A Japan that can Say No) caused a big controversy in Japan, as well as hostile American reactions, over statements such as a speculation in the book about how the 'global military balance' could be overturned if 'Japan decided to sell its computer chips to the Soviet Union instead of the United States'. The authors used trade conflict issues, and Shintarō later added the MS-X affair, to demonstrate their argument that Japan should be prepared to refuse to give concessions to the US. One of his Japanese critics, university professor Nakanishi Terumasa, pointed out in 1990 that Japan had often said no to the US; for example, to the 1987 Persian Gulf plea. Also, he argued that Tokyo's ability to threaten Washington with high-technological blackmail was fast receding with growing rapprochement between the US and the USSR. So any major change to the present strategic balance in which the Japan-US alliance was set alongside 'confrontation between the two Koreas, animosity between China and Vietnam, and a delicate relationship between China and Taiwan' was fraught with danger. In Nakanishi's view, cooperation

---

27. Research Institute for Peace and Security, *Asian Security 1989–90* (London 1989) 28–33.

between Japan and the US was vital for the future of the Pacific Basin.[28]

THE US, THE USSR AND THE EAST ASIAN STRATEGIC BALANCE

During the 1980s a major change was taking place in the strategic balance in the East Asian sector of the Pacific Basin with a growing rapprochement between the US and China, which began in the 1970s. The four special economic zones in China for foreign capitalists, established to help promote the economic modernization sought by Deng Xiaoping, were utilized by American capitalists. China also sought technical assistance from the US, including American university places for students and the hiring of technical experts to go to China. One of them, E. E. Bauer, who arrived in 1980 to assist the Civil Aviation Administration to establish a modern airline, considered that Chinese assimilation of Western technology 'would take a full century' given the absence of technically trained people and other major impediments, such as poor transport and communication facilities. But by the time he left in 1984, he considered that an industrial 'take-off' had occurred. By 1985 China was producing 16,676,600 television receivers, compared with 517 in 1978, and there were similar huge increases in other low to middle technology manufacturing. The development was still controlled in mercantilistic fashion by the state, and import controls were used in 1984 to stop a surge in the country's trade deficit. Nevertheless, the benefit of the economic development for US exports to China rose from US$906 million in 1978 to US$7.9 billion in 1989, and the American contribution to China's imports had increased from 5 per cent to 13 per cent – in third place behind Hong Kong and Japan. By 1987 the US also had direct investments in China worth US$3.5 billion,

---

28. Ishihara Shintarō, 'A Nation Without Morality' in *The Silent Power: Japan's Identity and World Role* (Selected essays from *The Japan Interpreter* Tokyo, 1976) 76–95. Ishihara Shintarō, 'Learning to Say No to America' and Nakanishi Terumasa, 'Saying Yes to the Japan-U.S. Partnership', *Japan Echo* XVII, 1990, 29–42.

the largest of any of the nations taking advantage of China's search for foreign capital.[29]

The increasing warmth of the US-China relationship was marked by Washington's willingness to allow the sale of arms and military-related equipment to Beijing. A major example was the sale in 1983, for US$11 million, of a ground satellite-tracking station, which gave China the capacity to launch a communications satellite that would assist her nuclear targeting capabilities. The main American motive for such sales was to increase China's military power to counterbalance the USSR in East Asia. There was a wide range of US military assistance for improving the technological capacity of the Chinese army, air force and navy, such as anti-submarine sonars, fighter aircraft avionics and anti-tank missiles. US sales of military equipment reached a value of $106.2 million by 1989. However, this American defence support did not develop into any military alliance between China and the US. Beijing sought to maintain an independent foreign policy, and in the late 1980s was willing to respond positively to Soviet overtures. China also sold arms freely to Third World countries, much to US displeasure.[30]

New developments in USSR-China relations in the late 1980s were especially the work of Mikhail Gorbachev, who assumed the top position in the Kremlin in 1985. His concentration on economic development and reform in the USSR encouraged him to remove Sino-Soviet border tensions. In a major speech in the strategically vital Soviet Far Eastern port, Vladivostok, he said the 'USSR is prepared to discuss any measure aimed at creating an atmosphere of good neighbourliness in a most serious way'. He subsequently offered a readjustment of boundary disputes in China's favour and withdrew Soviet forces from Mongolia and from Afghanistan; and Vietnam agreed to remove its troops from Cambodia. Full normalization of

29. E.E. Bauer, *China Takes Off: Technology Transfer and Modernization* (Seattle 1986) chs 1, 21 (quotation, 25). *FEA* 1982–3, 362–4; 1990, 323. *YITS* 1988, 172. Gary Klintworth, *China's Modernisation: The Strategic Implications for the Asia-Pacific Region* (Canberra 1989) 11–28, 89. Richard Conroy, 'Technology and Economic Development' in Robert Benewick and Paul Wingrove (eds), *Reforming the Revolution: China in Transition* (Chicago 1988) ch. 9. See also Robert Kleinberg, *China's 'Opening' to the Outside World: The Experiment with Foreign Capitalism* (Boulder 1990). Harding, *Fragile Relationship* 94–100, 145–54.

30. Ibid. 87–94, 162–9, 371. Klintworth, *China's Modernisation* 87–91. A. James Gregor, *Arming the Dragon: U.S. Security Ties with the People's Republic of China* (Lanham 1987) ch. 5. Lillian Craig Harris and Robert L. Worden (eds) *China and the Third World: Champion or Challenger?* (London 1986) chs 7–8.

relations between the two nations was sealed at a summit meeting in Beijing between Gorbachev and Deng from 15 to 18 May 1989. A consequence of the improved relationship and economic reform in the USSR, which gave considerable freedom of trade to border regions, was an increase in Soviet Union exports to China from a mere one per cent of China's imports in 1979 to 4 per cent in 1989. China's exports to the USSR recorded the same increase.[31]

Gorbachev's USSR had a much harder task in establishing good relations with Japan as part of his *perestroika* doctrine of improving relations with the outside world. Soviet requirements were for foreign capital and technology to resuscitate a moribund economy; therefore capital rich, but resource poor Japan was a vital target. The major stumbling block was the Soviet occupation of the four islands at the southern end of the Kurile archipelago, which stretches between Japan and the Soviet Kamchatka Peninsula. These islands had been ceded to Japan in 1855 and 1875 by Czarist Russia in return for the cession to Russia of Japanese interests on Sakhalin, north of the Japanese archipelago. The four southern Kurile Islands had a land area of 4,996 square kilometres and a population of only about 17,000 when the USSR annexed them on 20 September 1945 in accordance with the Yalta Agreements. However, the islands were of major strategic importance. The only free Soviet naval access to the Pacific was through the Kuriles, since the other outlet, the Korea Strait, was dominated by Japan and by South Korea. While the Soviet navy used a route through the central Kurile Islands, it could easily be blocked in wartime with Japanese control of the bigger southern Kurile Islands. Japan also made the southern islands into a symbol of Japanese national aspirations, concentrating on them rather than on the other Soviet-occupied territory of southern Sakhalin, which Japan had seized in the Russo-Japanese War of 1904–05, and which had been reoccupied by the USSR in 1945. The Kurile Islands are also important to Japan for the rich fishing region around them. Tokyo has refused to sign a peace treaty with Moscow until the return of the southern Kuriles.[32]

31. Klintworth, *China's Modernisation* 85–6. See also Ramesh Thakur and Carl Thayer (eds), *The Soviet Union as an Asian Power* (Boulder 1987).

32. David Rees, *The Soviet Seizure of the Kuriles* (New York 1985) ix–xix (quotation xii) chs 6–8. For the background to Soviet-Japanese relations see M. Robertson, *Soviet Policy towards Japan: An Analysis of Trends in the 1970s and the 1980s* (Cambridge 1988). See also Gilbert Rozman, *Japan's Response to the Gorbachev Era* (Princeton 1991).

The southern Kurile Islands were known as the 'Northern Territories', and in January 1981 the Japanese Government decided to proclaim 7 February as 'The Day' of the Northern Territories, to start a week of official and unofficial protest meetings. The USSR reacted sharply, informing Japan's ambassador in Moscow that the protests bordered 'on enmity toward the Soviet Union' and declaring the islands non-negotiable. There the issue remained with consequent strained relations between Japan and the USSR, which encouraged the continuance of the Japan-US alliance and closer relations between Japan and China. Consequently, despite growing rapprochement between the USSR and the US, Kaifu firmly announced in July 1990 at a summit meeting of world leaders that there would be no Japanese aid for the ailing Soviet economy until the southern Kurile Islands were returned to Japan. A visit to Japan in September 1990 by the USSR foreign minister, Eduard Shevardnadze, though seen as a conciliatory Soviet move, produced no resolution to the issue. With the collapse of the Soviet Union at the end of 1991, the president of the Russian republic, Boris Yeltsin, suggested that Russia might trade the southern Kurile Islands for much needed Japanese capital; but nothing had been done a year later.[33]

A problem for the USSR was that Siberia was not seen as a major area for Japanese investment. By 1990, when many Soviet restrictions on foreign investment had been lifted, Japan's postindustrial economy had little need for the raw materials of the Soviet Far East. Of the 1,274 joint foreign-Soviet business ventures at the end of 1989, only twenty-one involved Japanese firms and all had a capital of less than US$1 million. The angry US reaction to Toshiba's venture into the Soviet market in 1987 also had deterred Japanese capitalists from contact with the USSR. Those who did venture into Siberia found the Soviet bureaucracy a great hindrance to adequate profits; and in 1990, with the lifting of many Soviet restrictions, a surviving barrier was the non-convertibility of the rouble.[34]

Gorbachev had an easier task in establishing closer relations with South Korea. Increasing contacts between the USSR and South Korea in the early 1980s suddenly halted when, on the night of 31 August 1983, Soviet fighters shot down a KAL 007, a ROK airliner, which

---

33. Rees, *The Soviet Seizure* chs 9–10. FEA 1991, 1076–7. Hoshira Kimura, 'Recent Japan-Soviet Relations: Gorbachev's Dilemma and his Choices' in Peter Drysdale (ed.), *The Soviets and the Pacific Challenge* (Sydney 1991) ch. 6.

34. Evgenii Kovrigin, 'Problems and Prospects for Japanese Investment in the Soviet Far East' in ibid. ch. 7.

had strayed into USSR airspace, with the loss of 269 lives. President Chun Doo Hwan declared it 'an utterly inhuman act', but the USSR refused to apologize. Foreign Minister Gromyko was convinced that 'the violation of Soviet airspace was carried out for purposes of [US] military intelligence', and one American scholar mounts a strong case for that hypothesis, though it cannot be proved.[35]

However, the ROK soon resumed a search for better relations with the USSR, though it had to wait for the advent of Gorbachev. On the eve of the Olympic Games in Seoul in 1988, he declared publicly that conditions on the Korean peninsular had greatly changed since the 1950s and suggested improving economic relations between the two countries. The reform-minded USSR Government was looking to this booming little dragon for economic advice and capital investment. While there was initial caution by South Korean capitalists because of the absence of diplomatic relations to protect their investments, the value of trade between the two nations increased from only US$36 million in 1980 to almost US$600 million in 1989. In April 1989 the ROK and the USSR agreed to establish trade offices, which eight months later became consulates. Further negotiations produced full diplomatic relations between the two nations on 30 September 1990. A sign of new Korean investor confidence was the investment in 1990 by Hyundai Construction Company of $1 million in a joint logging venture, and an announcement by the company of plans to participate in the development of natural gas in East Siberia. Unlike Japan, South Korea's economic development is at a stage where it can benefit from Siberian natural resources.[36]

The Soviet diplomatic recognition of South Korea occurred with the blessing of the US. When he came to power in 1981, Reagan damned the USSR as an 'evil empire' in a deepening of Cold War confrontations between the two superpowers in the early 1980s. But Reagan was stronger in rhetoric than in practice. Before Gorbachev came to power, the US was searching for nuclear arms limitation and other agreements with the USSR. A major stumbling block in the Asian sphere was the massive Soviet military action in Afghanistan against rebel opposition to the communist government there. But

35. Clough, *Embattled Korea* 334–5 (quotation 334). Gromyko, *Memories* 297. R.W. Johnson, *Shootdown: The Verdict on KAL 007* (London 1986) ch. 12.

36. Yu-Nam Kim, 'The Soviet Reforms and Relations with the Koreas' in Drysdale (ed.), *The Soviets and the Pacific* 98–101. Byung-Joon Ahn, 'Foreign Relations: An Expanded Diplomatic Agenda' in Lee (ed.), *Korea Briefing* 35–8.

Gorbachev made positive movements to improve relations with the US, driven by the huge strain that the war in Afghanistan and other defence expenditure was placing on his nation's faltering economy. Therefore he started withdrawing Soviet forces from Afghanistan in April 1988 and completed the withdrawal in February 1989. He announced in January 1989 that he would reduce by 200,000 the 597,600 Soviet armed forces personnel stationed east of the Ural Mountains that divide European Russia from Asia. In December 1989 he started winding down the Soviet naval base at Cam Ranh Bay in Vietnam. Such positive actions were helping significantly to smooth relations with Reagan's successor, the less ideologically conservative President Bush, who also was impelled by the need to reduce the US military expenditure that had contributed to a large budget deficit. There were constant exchanges of diplomatic and even, from 1988, military visits between the two nations. In 1990, with the Berlin Wall tumbling down in Germany, the emergence of non-communist states throughout Eastern Europe, and mutually observed Soviet and US destruction of weapons systems, the Cold War was over; a reality symbolized in East Asia by the Soviet recognition of the ROK that year.[37]

North Korea reacted angrily to Soviet diplomatic recognition of South Korea. Kim Il Sung, the longest surviving national leader in Asia, condemned it, with some accuracy, as 'diplomatic relations bargained for dollars'. There had been signs of improvement in relations between the North and South in 1980 with discussion between representatives of both countries, in which each side referred to the other for the first time by their DPRK and ROK titles. But this was still a long way from mutual diplomatic recognition. In September 1984 South Korea accepted food and other material aid from North Korea for flood victims, which prompted official talks between the two sides. A result in September 1984 was the reunion of fifty families separated by the Korean War. However, from 1985 to 1987 relations deteriorated with the North condemning joint ROK–US military exercises. A nadir for the decade was reached with the blowing up of a South Korean airliner in November 1987 by a DPRK agent, killing 115 people. Nevertheless, in 1988 Kim Il Sung took a major step by accepting the principle of coexistence. An ailing North Korean economy and the opening of trade and other relations between South Korea with China and the USSR were

37. *Asian Security* 1989–90 50, 65–6, 72–6.

probable motives for this major change in the DPRK's policy. Top-level negotiations from 1989 led in September 1990 to a visit to Seoul by the North Korean premier, Yon Hyong-Muk, a landmark occasion. His South Korean counterpart, Kang Young-Hoon, went to Pyonyang in the next month. Indeed, in December 1991 the text of an agreement between North and South Korea was made public. It aimed to promote reconciliation and non-aggression, and there was another agreement that month for mutual renunciation of nuclear weapons. These pacts were remarkable, especially in terms of North Korean concessions, which were probably influenced by a greater sense of diplomatic isolation marked by China's decision in 1991 not to block South Korea's application to join the UN. But concrete steps to implement the agreements were still needed in the face of North Korean delaying tactics.[38]

Nor was South Korea willing to abandon its alliance with the US. In 1980, despite the Carter Administration's concern for human rights, Washington was silent when ROK troops brutally crushed a popular uprising in the southwestern city of Kwangju, which killed at least 193 people. This insurrection developed from student demonstrations for more freedom during a time of unstable civilian government, exacerbated by a military coup, in which General Chun Doo Hwan seized the presidency. The failure of Washington to condemn the Kwangju massacre, and especially a Korean belief that ROK troops could not have been used without the permission of the US commander of the Combined Forces in the ROK, aroused significant public hostility towards the US. The US, however, exerted pressure on the South Korean army in 1986–87 not to intervene in a growing political crisis in the ROK. Inspired by the popular overthrow of President Marcos in the Philippines, Korean students were attempting, with some middle-class support, to depose Chun with widespread violent demonstrations. Though distancing themselves from the radical students, opposition parties pressed for major political reforms, which produced a stand-off with the ruling Democratic Justice Party. Chun's nominee as president, Roh Tae Woo, solved the impasse dramatically in June 1987 by accepting virtually all the opposition demands, with reforms including liberation of

38. Rhee Sang-Woo, 'North Korea in 1990: Lonesome Struggle to Keep Chuch'e', *Asian Survey* XXXI, 1991, 75. Chong-Sik Lee, 'North and South Korea: From Confrontation to Negotiation' in Lee (ed.), *Korea Briefing* 39–53. James Cotton, 'The Two Koreas and Rapprochement: Foundations for Progress?', *The Pacific Review*, vol. 5, 1992, 162–9.

political prisoners, freedom of the press and a promise of direct popular election for the presidency before February 1988. The South Korean opposition and the US Government welcomed the reforms, and a grateful ROK public elected Roh as president in December 1987. However, there was continued student unrest against the Roh Government, and in May 1990 students burnt down the US Information Center building in Seoul. Yet public opinion polls in South Korea revealed continued majorities favouring the maintenance of a military alliance with the US.[39]

In 1990–91 with the disappearance of former Communist friends in Europe and growing liberalization in the USSR, North Korea's foreign relations were changing. To assist an economy which was growing at less than 3 per cent per annum in the late 1980s, and which provided a GNP per person only one-fifth of the size of the GNP in South Korea, Kim Il Sung turned to his old enemy, Japan, for capital investment. He also moved to restore relations with China, which had cooled during the period of economic liberalization there.[40]

China was seeking better foreign relations in 1990 because of the international reverberations of the massacre of Chinese students and other citizens in Tiananmen Square in Beijing that started in the early morning hours of 4 June 1989. Over 1,000 people died as PLA tanks and soldiers moved into the square to arrest and disperse students camped there in a mass call for democratic reforms. The protests had started in April, centred on rising inflation and spreading corruption which had flowed from economic reforms. Exploiting the visit in May of the world's media to cover the summit between Gorbachev and Deng, the students had increased their demands to advocate the introduction of democracy. The newly free and often sympathetic Chinese media reported these calls, prompting widespread protests in other cities. The government was initially hamstrung in its approach to the dissent because of differences of opinion between reformers

---

39. Donald Stone Macdonald, *The Koreans: Contemporary Politics and Society* (Boulder 1988) 56–60, 233–8. Tae-Hwan Kwak and Wayne Patterson, 'The Security Relationship between Korea and the United States, 1960–1984' in Yur-Bok Lee and Wayne Patterson (eds), *One Hundred Years of Korean-American relations, 1882–1982* (University, Alabama 1986) 119–26. James Cotton, 'Conflict and Accommodation in the Two Koreas' in Stuart Harris and James Cotton (eds), *The End of the Cold War in Northeast Asia* (Melbourne 1991) 164–70. *Asian Security 1987–88* (London 1988) 13–17, 85–8. *Asian Security 1988–89* (London 1989) 3–4, 77–80. *Asian Security 1989–90* 131–40. *Asian Security 1990–91* 7–9, 132–5. See also Donald N. Clark (ed.), *The Kwangju Uprising: Shadows over the Regime in South Korea* (Boulder 1988).

40. Cotton, 'Conflict and Accommodation', 74–5.

and conservatives. However, by late May conservatives, including Deng and his premier Li Peng, gained the upper hand and ordered the military crackdown. Beside the deaths in Tiananmen square, during the next twelve months there were some 1,100 executions and tens of thousands of arrests across the country. The aged Beijing leadership succeeded in crushing what it saw as a serious rebellion against its authority that had arisen from the economic reform it had been promoting.[41]

A major diplomatic problem for China was that a recent opening of the country to Western media produced dramatic TV pictures and eyewitness reports of the massacre for the outside world. There was immediate and widespread condemnation. Only China's few remaining communist allies accepted Beijing's propaganda that the massacre was a repression of a 'counterrevolutionary revolt'. Concerned to maintain improved relations with China, Gorbachev described the massacre as 'clashes' between troops and 'participants in mass protests' and hoped that the Chinese would be able to 'turn this tragic page in their history . . . and surge ahead along the road of the construction of a strong, peaceful and free socialist China'. The US suspended all military and most economic aid to China and called successfully on international agencies to postpone new loans. EEC nations had already taken such a lead, and Japan suspended aid projects worth US$10 billion. Investors postponed new investments; some withdrew from China. A tourist industry worth US$2.2 billion in 1988 was under serious threat. Such economic punishment came in a year when Beijing already had predicted a US$2 billion budget deficit.[42]

The conservative leadership of China was reluctant to bow to the international pressure until it succeeded in placing the lid of repression on all dissidence and in purging reformers from the administration. Not until the end of June 1990 was a conciliatory gesture made to the Western World. This allowed Fang Lizhi, an eminent physicist and strong supporter of a Westernized China, who had been sheltering in

41. Lowell Dittmer, 'China in 1989: The Crisis of Incomplete Reform', *Asian Survey* XXX, 1990, 250–34. David Sambaugh, 'China in 1990: The Year of Damage Control', ibid. XXXI, 1991, 41–2. Yan Sun, 'The Chinese Protests of 1989: The Issue of Corruption', ibid. 762–82. Harrison E. Salisbury, *Tiananmen Diary: Thirteen Days in June* (London 1989). *Asian Security 1989–90* 5–6.

42. Dittmer, 'China in 1989', 34, 37–8. Alexander Lukin, 'The Initial Soviet Reaction to the Events in China in 1989 and the Prospects for Sino-Soviet Relations', *The China Quarterly* no. 125, 1991, 119–25. Harding, *Fragile Relationship* chs 7–8.

the US embassy in Beijing, to go into exile to Britain. A few other dissidents were released from prison with the lifting of martial law. However, these small concessions were enough for Western nations, with Japan in the lead, to begin the restoration of economic relations after Bush gave a green light at the meeting of the Group of Seven leading industrial powers of the world in Houston, Texas, in July 1990. Japan soon opened new lines of credit for China up to ¥810 billion for five years from 1990. Bush encountered stiff opposition in Congress to any relaxation of his government's hard line. However, China succeeded in restoring significant US economic assistance by cooperating in UN sanctions against Iraq. China also sent to the US in October 1990 a high-level trade mission which offered to purchase $700 million of US products, though this would be only a small reduction of the US trade deficit with China, which was $3.5 billion in 1989. By 1991 China had recovered much of the diplomatic ground lost at Tiananmen Square in June 1989.[43]

China also was able to improve relations with Asian countries by 1991. Progress towards re-establishing diplomatic relations with Indonesia, for the first time for twenty-four years, was suspended after the Tiananmen massacre but was revived and consummated in August 1990. Singapore, which was waiting for Indonesia, quickly followed suit.[44]

China's relations with Taiwan showed major improvements in the late 1980s. Representatives of the two estranged nations engaged in their first ever negotiations in May 1986 when they met in Hong Kong to discuss the return of a China Airlines plane and crew members to Taiwan after their captain had flown it to China. Trade between the two nations was increasing. In 1990 Taiwan capitalists, exploiting labour costs as low as one-twentieth of those in their home island, had invested US$1,300 million in China. Over 450,000 Taiwanese visited China between January and October 1989, using Hong Kong as the gateway, which was a 35 per cent rise on the same time period in the previous year, despite anger in Taiwan over the Tiananmen massacre. However that incident destroyed, at least in the short term, any hope of talks between China and Taiwan about reunification of their territories. Nevertheless, in 1990 the Kuomintang government allowed the first visits by mainlanders to Taiwan, and in April 1991 a Taiwanese delegation travelled to

---

43. *Asian Security 1990–91* 91–4, 90–101. Sambaugh, 'China in 1990' 36–49.
44. Ibid. 46–7.

Beijing to establish communication between the two countries. The new relations between Communist China and Taiwan were being demonstrated in the way Xiamen and Jinmen islands had become popular tourist spots rather than targets for Red Chinese artillery; and a booming trade between the two nations had increased in value from US$466 million in 1981 to US$5.8 billion in 1991. However, ripples on these newly calm waters were being created at the end of 1991 with Beijing's concern about political toleration of emerging indigenous Taiwanese advocates for an independent Taiwan.[45]

The Tiananmen massacre made many people in Hong Kong fearful for their future after 1997. That was the year of the expiration of the ninety-year lease on the New Territories, possession of which was vital for Hong Kong's existence. Britain, keen to divest itself of colonial remnants no longer of economic or strategic value, agreed with Beijing in 1984 to hand over on 1 July 1997 Hong Kong island as well as the New Territories. China agreed to allow the existence of a 'Hong Kong Special Administrative Region' which would 'enjoy a high degree of autonomy, except in foreign and defence affairs'. China promised that 'the current social and economic systems in Hong Kong will remain unchanged and so will their life style'. Freedom of speech, of assembly, of travel, the right to strike and the protection of private property would be preserved by law. The independence of the Hong Kong dollar, freedom from any Chinese taxation or tariffs and permission for 'Hong Kong China' to develop its own 'economic relations' with 'other countries' would be preserved. These Chinese promises reflected the value placed by the reform-minded government of Deng Xiaoping on the thriving economic performance of Hong Kong and its role as a capitalist doorway to the Western World. However, the ordering by that government of troops to massacre students in Tiananmen Square and the subsequent violent purges of dissidents throughout China made many citizens of Hong Kong, who had been publicly and vociferously protesting their opposition to the crushing of the Chinese pro-democracy movement, deeply suspicious of China's willingness to honour the commitments of 1984. This pessimism encouraged

45. Bello and Rosenfeld, *Dragons in Distress* 279–80. Martin L. Lasater, *Policy in Evolution: The U.S. Role in China's Reunification* (Boulder 1989) 141–3. Gary Klintworth, 'Taiwan: Evolution and Response' in Harris and Cotton (eds), *End of the Cold War* 115–18. *Asian Security 1990–91*, 96–102. Dennis Van Vranken Hickey, 'China's Threat to Taiwan', *The Pacific Review*, vol. 5, 1992, 255. Qingguo Jia, 'Changing Relations Across the Taiwan Strait: Beijing's Perceptions', *Asian Survey* XXXII, 1992, 277–89.

emigration from the colony of almost 50,000 people in 1988–89. Many of these were skilled people, whose departure had ominous implications for the future of the colony's economy. A growth rate in GDP of 7 per cent in 1988 dipped to an estimated 2.5 per cent in 1989, though a contraction in China's trade that year because of the Tiananmen massacre was a major reason for the decline.[46]

There was also significant public dissatisfaction in Hong Kong about Britain's role in the future transfer of power. Though approximately 3.2 million Hong Kong people carried British passports, a revised British nationality law in 1982 had limited their rights to move to Britain. Concern about the hostility in Hong Kong leading to economic and administrative collapse induced Britain in April 1990 to promise British nationality to 50,000 key civil servants and professionals in the private sector, plus their families, in order to keep them in the colony until 1987. This aroused displeasure in Beijing. Also in reaction to the strong criticism of the Tiananmen incident in Hong Kong, China sharply restricted the democratic content in the Basic Law, which provided a 'mini-constitution' for Hong Kong China. Whereas democrats in Hong Kong were pressing for sixty legislature seats, half of which would be filled by popular election by 1995 and all of them by 2003, Beijing allowed only 20 elective seats in 1995, 24 in 1999 and 30 in 2003, with a chief executive first appointed by China, an arrangement agreed to by London in February 1990. Britain was under criticism from human rights activists for refusing most people in Hong Kong citizenship and political rights.[47]

In October 1992 a new British governor of Hong Kong, a former influential Conservative Party politician, Chris Patten, attempted to improve British credibility. He proposed that more seats on the legislative council be elected by district boards and by industry groups to extend the number of elective seats in 1995 to thirty-nine. But he received a hostile reaction to that proposal from Beijing and opposition in Hong Kong from many businessmen and others who do not wish to rock the colony's shaky boat by offending China.[48]

There was also wider world humanitarian criticism of the British decision in December 1989 to forcibly return fifty-one of the many people who had fled by boat from Vietnam to Hong Kong. There

46. Y.C. Jao, Leung Chi-Keung, Peter Wesley-Smith and Won Siu-Lun (eds), *Hong Kong and 1997: Strategies for the Future* (Hong Kong 1985) 551–3, 1990–1. *FEA* 367. Richard Y.C. Wong and Joseph Y.S. Cheng (eds), *The Other Hong Kong Report 1990* (Hong Kong 1990), ch. 11.

47. Ibid., ix–xv, ch. 2. *Asian Security 1990–1991* 104–5.

48. *The Economist*, 14–20 Nov. 1992, 25.

were 54,341 of them in the colony in June 1990, of whom less than one fifth had been classified as genuine refugees awaiting overseas resettlement. However, the forcible repatriation was a single event designed to send a signal to Vietnam. It seemed to work, there being an 87 per cent reduction in the number of boat people arriving in the first six months of 1990 compared with the first half of the previous year. Nor has there been any international criticism of the return of 320,740 illegal immigrants from China since 1979 who have been caught by Ghurka soldiers and guard dogs who patrol Hong Kong's land border.[49]

By 1990 the strategic balance in East Asia had dramatically altered. Gorbachev's concern to concentrate on economic reform at home had encouraged an end to the hostility between China and the USSR that had dominated East Asian affairs since the 1960s. The consequent major reduction in Soviet forces in Asia and the growing warmth of relations between Moscow and Washington created a climate by 1990 for reductions in US defence expenditure, which had grown by 35 per cent in real terms during the 1980s. In 1990 US defence expenditure was reduced by 2.7 per cent in real terms with a budget request for a 2.6 per cent cut in 1991. East Asia was an obvious target area for reduced military expenditure with the retreat of the Soviet threat and China's search for international goodwill. In July 1989 the US and South Korea agreed about increased ROK financial contributions to the US defence umbrella and the handing over of full command of the ROKA to a South Korean general. Washington's objective was to increase ROKA capacity so that the US could start reducing its remaining forces. In January 1990 the US announced the beginnings of a phased withdrawal from South Korea, commencing with the evacuation that year of 2,000 of the 45,000 US troops stationed there. Developments in the USSR also in 1990–91 were reducing North Korea's ability to rely on the Soviet military assistance that had been maintaining what, by 1990, was probably only parity in military strength with South Korean forces. The one potential threat from North Korea was the nation's suspected development of atomic weapons; and the 1991 agreement for mutual North-South Korean renunciation of nuclear weapons has not yet been implemented.[50]

The improved US-Soviet relations had implications in 1990 for the Japan-US alliance. That year the Japanese minister of state and

---

49. Wong and Cheng (eds), *Other Hong Kong Report* ch.8.
50. *Asian Security 1990–1991*, 149–50. William W. Kaufmann, *Glasnost, Perestroika, and U.S. Defense Spending* (Washington 1990) 1–4. *The Defense of Japan* 21.

director general of the Defense Agency, Yozo Ishikawa, considered the Third World still vulnerable to conflict, as evidenced by the Iraqi invasion of Kuwait. Though there were also now greater possibilities of UN action to resolve such conflicts, his Defense Agency pointed to Japan's own region with the potentialities of conflict in Korea 'as well as the Northern territories issue between Japan and the Soviet Union'. This analysis presented the case for an actual increase of Japanese defence expenditure in 1990 of 6.1 per cent, despite the reduction in its proportion of GNP, and the ministry argued for a further 'modest' defence build-up. The withdrawal of US forces from Japan and any downgrading in the importance of the country in US defence plans could produce irresistible pressures within Japan for significantly greater defence expenditure on its armed forces.[51]

There were also portents of potential future economic conflict between the US and resource-starved Japan. That nation's surplus trade balance, on which its wealth depended, was declining. The percentage of imports in Japan's total trade increased from 37 per cent in 1986 to 44 per cent in 1990, though falling to 40 per cent in 1991, a year of recession and declining domestic demand. If the upward trend continues there will be a potential increase in efforts by Japan to push its products in overseas markets, of which the US was still by far the most important, receiving 31 per cent of Japan's exports in 1990 compared with 38 per cent in 1986. Such Japanese pressure could increase the anger of Americans, who in 1990 still suffered from the fact that US exports to Japan were only 37 per cent of the total trade between the two nations. This is a scenario which supports the argument presented by George Friedman and Meredith Lebard in their book, *The Coming War with Japan*. That book's predictions may well be false, but its publication in 1991 and the wide attention it received were indications of continued US mistrust of Japan.[52]

THE CAMBODIAN CONFLICT

By 1991 one conflict which had been poisoning diplomatic relations in Southeast Asia was heading towards a resolution. Since 1980, backed

51. Ibid. v, 4 (quotation), 167, 173.
52. *FEA* 1990, 497. *Japan: Country Report* 1991:2, 40. George Friedman and Meredith Lebard, *The Coming War with Japan* (New York 1991). *OECD Economic Outlook*, 51, June 1992, 54–9.

by 150,000 to 200,000 Vietnam troops, the PRK in Cambodia had been fighting an intermittent insurgency. In 1980 the Khmer Rouge had regrouped in the Thailand border region with some 25,000 to 30,000 soldiers. It was supported by Chinese military aid channelled through Thailand, which had concluded a secret agreement with Beijing in January 1979 for this purpose. Away from the Thai border the Khmer Rouge only had the capacity to operate in small groups, employing guerilla tactics such as ambushes, night raids and planting of mines. Though hailed in the West as the beginning of 'Vietnam's Vietnam', this insurrection was very different from the NLF in South Vietnam because the murderous brutality of Pol Pot's regime had aroused much Cambodian hostility to the Khmer Rouge. Therefore, its army could operate openly only in a belt of territory some twenty-five kilometres wide along the Thai border.[53]

The Chinese-supported Khmer Rouge was an embarrassing force for the ASEAN nations who were determined to prevent the Vietnamese-backed PRK from claiming to be the legitimate government of Cambodia. So the ASEAN states supported the Khmer People's National Liberation Front (KPNLF), formed in Paris in March 1979 and led by Son Sann, a former Cambodian businessman and politician. This non-communist front was employing ex-officers of Lon Nol's army to organize refugees along the Thai border into an army and engaged in a violent struggle with other right wing groups to emerge as the dominant one by 1981. With about 8,000 troops in 1983, the KPNLF failed to win Cambodian peasant support. A third force on the Thai frontier was led by Sihanouk, who also was supported by ASEAN. He disbelieved that 'the Khmer Rouge wolves' were 'capable of transforming themselves into lambs'.[54]

Sihanouk, however, was willing to join with the KPNLF and the Khmer Rouge in a Coalition Government of Democratic Kampuchea (CDGK), which was formed in Kuala Lumpur in June 1982. This disparate coalition of monarchists, republicans, and communists was a marriage of convenience, the Khmer Rouge seeking diplomatic respectability and the weaker non-communist groups welcoming Khmer Rouge military strength. CDGK forces operated only at

53. Evans and Rowley, *Red Brotherhood at War* 201–4. Leifer, *ASEAN and Security* 91. Timothy Carney, 'The Heng Samrin Forces and the Military Balance in Cambodia' in David Ablin and Marlowe Hood (eds) *The Cambodian Agony* (Armonk 1987) 180–207.

54. Evans and Rowley, *Red Brotherhood at War* 205–8. Nair, *Words and Bayonets* 125–6, 141–50. Leifer, *ASEAN and Security* 110–13.

guerilla level, but with increasing boldness with the flow of Chinese and Western arms. The insurgent border camps also were protected by Thai artillery fire against Vietnamese attacks, which from 1980 included forays across the Thai border in hot pursuit of insurgents. Hanoi concentrated on a military defeat of the coalition, claiming that once this was achieved, and if the PRK were internationally recognized as the government of Cambodia, then Vietnamese troops would be withdrawn. In a big dry season offensive in 1984–85 the Vietnamese army succeeded in smashing the border camps. However, in a reverse situation from its experience in South Vietnam, the PAVN's opponents retreated across the border, where they could regroup and refit in safety. The Khmer Rouge response was to avoid fighting and to infiltrate men and Chinese military supplies back into Cambodia for an uprising after the Vietnamese troops left the country. The KPNLF was crippled by faction fights, with some of its men indulging in robbing and raping refugees. Sihanouk concentrated on a diplomatic offensive much more than a military one.[55]

The diplomatic arena was the area of greatest success for the CDGK and its international supporters. Under Reagan's anti-Soviet crusade, USSR-supported Vietnam became a prime target. Washington swung its diplomatic and financial support of about $5 million per annum behind the two non-communist groups in Cambodia; the financial aid was doubled in 1986. The Administration was also accused in the US Congress of secretly channelling funds to the Khmer Rouge, but no trails leading that way have been discovered to prove the charge. China was regarded as an ally in the struggle, which included an ASEAN-supported US economic blockade of Vietnam.[56]

However, it was Beijing's moves to end Sino-Soviet hostility after 1985 which bore the most diplomatic fruit. A price asked of the USSR for rapprochement was not only withdrawal of troops from Afghanistan, Mongolia and the Chinese border but also an unconditional Vietnamese withdrawal from Cambodia. Gorbachev initially was unwilling to sacrifice Vietnam, but Beijing was able to make the evacuation of Vietnamese troops from Cambodia a precondition for the summit meeting between Gorbachev and Deng in May 1989. In January that year Hanoi announced that Vietnamese troops would be withdrawn by September. Soviet Foreign Minister

55. Nair, *Words and Bayonets* 181–5. Evans and Rowley, *Red Brotherhood at War*, 209–23.

56. Evans and Rowley, *Red Brotherhood at War* 231–3.

Shevardnadze later commented about USSR negotiations with China: 'The key problem was Cambodia . . . From the beginning of our talks with Deng Xiaoping on ways to normalize Soviet-Chinese relations, we invariably stumbled over this issue'.[57]

The Soviet Union, in fact, did not need to place great pressure on Vietnam to withdraw from Cambodia. Confident of its success in gaining control of all the country, apart from the Thai border region, Vietnam had offered in 1985 to pull its troops out of Cambodia by 1990 under a plan of 'national reconciliation'. The CDGK put forward its own reconciliation scheme for a coalition government in Cambodia, but major complications were the proposed relegation of the PRK to a minority of one among four equal partners and, especially, the inclusion of the Khmer Rouge. Khieu Kanhraith, editor of the *Kampuchea Weekly* and a member of the PRK parliament, explained that if the Khmer Rouge was given a place in an interim government it 'might then use its position to take up armed struggle to eliminate the other factions'. After the failure of conversations between Sihanouk and the PRK prime minister, Hun Sen, in Paris in December 1987 and January 1988, there was a round of low-key shuttle diplomacy between Phnom Penh and ASEAN capitals by the Soviet Union's Igor Rgachev, which produced an agreement by Hanoi in May 1988 to withdraw half of its troops by the end of the year. However, ASEAN and the US supported the continued CDGK demand for a quadripartite interim government, hoping to buy time for strengthening the non-communist groups in the anti-PRK coalition. Washington believed that the Khmer Rouge would be easily defeated in any election following a peace agreement. Thus a meeting between all Cambodian parties in Jakarta in July 1988 ended in failure. Hanoi, nevertheless, agreed in January 1989 to withdraw all troops by September that year, the agreement that set the wheels in motion for the USSR-China summit. Accusing Vietnam of leaving 130,000 soldiers behind in disguise, China delivered a large shipment of arms to the Khmer Rouge, and a meeting of ASEAN foreign ministers considered sending further military aid to the non-communist groups. This was calculated military pressure on the PRK to meet CDGK demands. In reality, Vietnam, having lost 55,000 soldiers in Cambodia since 1979 and suffering diplomatic and economic isolation, was keen for a settlement, but not one that would include Pol Pot's Khmer

---

57. Ibid. 233–42. Eduard Shevardnadze, *The Future Belongs to Freedom* (New York 1991) 159.

Rouge. An international conference in Paris in July-August 1989 – chaired by Indonesia's foreign minister, Ali Alatas, and attended by the four Cambodian parties, Vietnam, the ASEAN countries, the US, the USSR, China and other UN members – failed to reach a settlement. With Vietnamese troops gone, the Khmer Rouge went on the offensive, having pressed refugees into military service. Civil war again broke out in Cambodia, with the Khmer Rouge succoured by a flow of Chinese arms and Vietnam supporting the PRK.[58]

However, in 1990 a diplomatic solution to the Cambodian imbroglio was emerging. Australia, a nation with clean hands in the recent Indochina past, but also bearing a sense of responsibility for its role in the Vietnam War, led the way for a UN-sponsored settlement. The plan was for an interim Cambodian council of twelve representatives without full government powers and containing only two Khmer Rouge members. UN peace-keeping troops would monitor a cease-fire, and there would be national elections employing a secret ballot and on a proportional representative basis to minimize Khmer Rouge pressure on voters in areas under its control. Negotiations in the UN and at a conference in Jakarta in September 1990 produced a peace plan based on the Australian proposal. The US swung its weight behind this move in a belated realization that the PRK was vital to prevent a Khmer Rouge takeover in Cambodia, and the US Congress passed in October $20 million in aid to the Hun Sen Government. However, from November 1990 objections from the PRK, supported by Hanoi, about demobilization and other procedures were delaying a settlement of the conflict. An international peace agreement about Cambodia was not signed in Paris until 23 October 1991. Moreover, by the end of the next year the agreement, which scheduled UN-supervised elections in 1993, was being severely challenged by Khmer Rouge military action to extend the movement's influence in the nation.[59]

---

58. Evans and Rowley, *Red Brotherhood at War* 278–98. Khieu Kanhraith, 'What Future for Cambodia?' in Gary Klintworth (ed.), *Vietnam's Withdrawal from Cambodia: Regional Issues and Realignments* (Canberra 1990) 95. Gary Klintworth, *Vietnam's Strategic Outlook* (Canberra 1990) 1–12.

59. Gareth Evans and Bruce Grant, *Australia's Foreign Relations in the World of the 1990s* (Melbourne 1991) 210–8. Justus M. van der Kroef, 'Cambodia in 1990', *Asian Survey* XXXI, 1991, 94–102. United States Information Service, 'Cambodia Conference calls for Perpetual Neutrality', 23 October 1991.

THE ASEAN STATES

The Cambodian conflict was a major test for the cohesion of ASEAN and a proving ground for its diplomatic strength. The organization achieved a coup on the world stage by successfully lobbying for and running a UN-sponsored international conference on Cambodia in New York in July 1981. Attended by ninety-two nations, but not by Vietnam which objected to UN acceptance of Democratic Kampuchea as the representative of Cambodia, the conference called for a cease-fire and UN-organized elections in Cambodia. This resolution provided the imprimatur for ASEAN's opposition to Vietnam's occupation of Cambodia and for its support of the CDGK. ASEAN also kept up a continued dialogue with Vietnam, which elicited no positive response until after the successful Vietnamese offensive in 1984–85.[60]

In its approach to the Cambodian conflict, ASEAN retained a united front even though the interests of its members continued to diverge. Thailand remained the country most concerned about the Vietnamese occupation because of the potential threat to its security, though there is no evidence that Vietnam harboured any expansionist designs on its territory. Singapore, as a small vulnerable state, took a lead in maintaining a hard line against Vietnam because of the view that the war was a proxy one between the USSR and China, and that the Soviet Union was the greater threat with air and naval bases in Vietnam and Vietnamese troops dominating the whole of Indochina. Malaysia preferred a strong Vietnam as a buffer between China and the rest of Southeast Asia but regarded the invasion of Kampuchea as a violation of the principle of territorial sovereignty. The Philippines, facing a communist insurgency in its own backyard, saw a Soviet-backed Vietnam as the major threat to the region. Indonesia continued to be the ASEAN nation most ambivalent about the issue, given its desire to see a strong Vietnam as a bulwark to China. However, Jakarta supported ASEAN initiatives for the sake of regional unity. The leadership Indonesia displayed in seeking a

---

60. Carlyle A. Thayer, 'ASEAN and Indochina: The Dialogue' in Alison Broinowski (ed.), *ASEAN into the 1990s* (New York 1990) 138–61. Leifer, *ASEAN and Security* chs 4–5. Nair, *Words and Bayonets* chs 5–6.

negotiated peace demonstrated its concern to resolve the conflict and encourage the international rehabilitation of Vietnam.[61]

Another of ASEAN's achievements was the maintenance of peaceful relations between its members. Their association in the organization had encouraged cooperation between Malaysia and Thailand in managing border problems, such as a rebel Thai Muslim movement and remnants of the Malaysian Communist Party. At the ASEAN summit meeting in 1976 Marcos formally buried the claim of the Philippines to Sabah, despite some attempts by Filipino congressmen in 1986 to revive it. Disputes between Malaysia and Singapore have not been allowed to get out of hand. The Muslim ASEAN nations also supported the Philippines Government in its suppression of the Muslim insurgency by the Moro National Liberation Front on the island of Mindanao, which aroused the hostility of Islamic states in the Arab world. Indonesia also had its own reasons to refuse to encourage any Muslim separatist movement in neighbouring countries.[62]

The security of ASEAN was assisted by the military hegemony of the US. The closest US link with an ASEAN state was with the Philippines. When Marcos declared a state of emergency in September 1972, blaming communists for bomb blasts organized by his own henchmen, the US ambassador gave his support. Nixon and Kissinger were diverted by the problems of Vietnam, but Marcos's seizure of dictatorial power was sanctioned by Washington's silence. Marcos's firm anti-communist stance earned him continued US support, though there was haggling over the financial compensation and other details in the late 1970s for continued US leasing of the Clark Air Base and the Subic Naval base in the Philippines. These bases had become more important to the US after North Vietnam's conquest of South Vietnam. Carter was concerned about abuses of human rights in the Philippines but applied little pressure on Marcos lest he be accused of abandoning a staunch ally. Reagan particularly warmed to Marcos, praising him on a state visit to Washington in September 1982 as 'a respected voice of reason and moderation'. This was at a time when underpaid and ill-trained troops were engaging

61. Ibid. ch. 8. Clark D. Neher, 'The Foreign Policy of Thailand' in David Wurfel and Bruce Burton (eds), *The Political Economy of Foreign Policy in Southeast Asia* (London 1990) 194–6. Richard Stubbs, 'The Foreign Policy of Malaysia' in ibid. 111–14. Juwono Sudarsno, 'Global Political Trends: An Overview', *Indonesian Quarterly* 13, 1985, 169–75.

62. Stubbs, 'The Foreign Policy of Malaysia' 106–8. David Wurfel, 'Philippine Foreign Policy' in Wurfel and Burton (eds), *Political Economy of Foreign Policy* 166. Wurfel, *Filipino Politics* 155–65.

in murder and plunder in the Philippines countryside, which daily added recruits to the communist New People's Army. Reagan's support for Marcos was not even disturbed by the assassination of opposition leader Benigno Aquino, on a return from exile in the US, at Manila airport on 21 August 1983 while under military 'protection'. Reagan even resisted, for a time, information flooding to the US about ballot rigging and fraud in an election which Marcos called in February 1986 to paper over his rapidly diminishing popularity in the Philippines. But when, on 25 February, popular support for Benigno Aquino's widow, Corazon (Cory) – aided by the desertion of Marcos by his minister for defence, Juan Enrile – became irresistible, Washington recognized reality and offered Marcos and Imelda asylum in Hawaii. The Aquino movement had received some assistance from US officials in the Philippines, but many Filipinos were galled to hear Americans claim that the overthrow of Marcos was 'a triumph of Reagan's foreign policy'. A significant background cause of the Aquino uprising was an economic crisis created by a flight of capital from the country after the assassination of Cory's husband, a loss of confidence in the Marcos regime by the World Bank, by the International Monetary Fund group and by foreign investors, and a world trade slump.[63]

The other ASEAN states retained good relations with the US through the 1980s. Thailand valued continued US economic and military support. The Reagan Administration increased financial aid to Thailand from $63 million in 1980 to $133 million in 1983. US military equipment also flowed into Thailand to counter Vietnamese attacks on insurgent border camps in Cambodia. Singapore was prepared to throw out a US diplomat in 1988, who was accused of consorting with opposition members, which followed American criticisms of violations of press freedom in Singapore. However, the expulsion probably had more to do with the government's wish to discredit the political opposition. The incident was a ripple on the surface of basically good relations between a nation which valued American investment and overall military protection and the US, which saw the island state as a valuable anti-communist hub of

63. Ibid. ch. 10. Kurnow, *In Our Image* 356–60, 388 (quotation) 397–400. William E. Berry, Jr., *U.S. Bases in the Philippines: The Evolution of a Special Relationship* (Boulder 1989) chs 4–5. Raymond Bonner, *Waltzing with a Dictator: The Marcoses and the Making of American Foreign Policy* (New York 1987) *passim*. Vivencio R. Jose, 'Philippine External Debt Problem: the Marcos Years', *Journal of Contemporary Asia* 21, 1991, 222–45. For the New People's Army see Richard J. Kessler, *Rebellion and Repression in the Philippines* (New Haven 1989).

the Southeast Asian region. Malaysia's relations with the US were closer in the 1980s than previously. With the cutting of defence ties with Britain, Malaysia was buying military supplies from the US and engaged in joint exercises with US forces. Suharto's Indonesia remained firmly allied to the US, with Washington providing military aid in the late 1980s of between $35 million and $50 million a year. The US also turned a blind eye to human rights abuses in Indonesia including continued brutal oppression of irrepressible rebels in East Timor, though there was a shift in the late 1980s towards more emphasis on economic development as a means of integrating that region into Indonesia. Even in November 1991, when over 100 unarmed Timorese in a funeral march in Dili were massacred by trigger-happy Indonesian soldiers, the US Administration issued a public condemnation but made no indication of joining Canada and the Netherlands which suspended aid to Indonesia.[64]

However, with the end of the Cold War in the Pacific Basin there were signs that ASEAN nations will have to attend more to their own security. Rising nationalism in the Philippines was reflected in a decision by the nation's Senate in September 1991 to reject by one vote a new treaty for the US leases of military bases in the Philippines, resisting strong pressure from President Aquino and the US. The consequent American decision to withdraw US forces speedily from the Philippines and other signs of a lower American profile in Asia have prompted moves for more security cooperation. This is particularly evident between Malaysia, Singapore and Indonesia in the face of potential threats such as the continued dispute over the Spratly Islands, all of which are being claimed by China, the growth of the Chinese navy, and a potentially more assertive Japan. But this movement between the 'core' ASEAN states, as they have been called, has tended to separate them from Thailand and the Philippines.[65]

---

64. R. Sean Randolph, *The United States and Thailand: Alliance Dynamics, 1950–1985* 223–31. Linda Y.C. Lim, 'The Foreign Policy of Singapore' in Wurfel and Burton (eds), *The Political Economy of Foreign Policy* 140. Stubbs, 'The Foreign Policy of Malaysia' in ibid., 110. Dwight King, 'Indonesia's Foreign Policy' in ibid. 88. Taylor, *Indonesia's Forgotten War* ch. 12. Prof Dr Mubyarto et al, *East Timor: the Impact of Integration: An Indonesian Socio-Anthropological Study* (Northcote, Australia 1991), *passim*. Australian Department of Foreign Affairs and Trade, 'East Timor – 12 November 1991 Killings: Composite Chronology of Events', 26 Nov. 1991.

65. Alex B. Brillantes, Jr., 'The Philippines in 1991: Disasters and Decisions', *Asian Survey* XXXII, 1992, 141–3; Richard Stubbs, 'Subregional Security Cooperation in ASEAN: Military and Economic Imperatives and Political Obstacles', ibid, 397–401; Leszek Buszynski, 'Southeast Asia in the Post-Cold War Era: Regionalism and Security' ibid, 815–29.

Nor has ASEAN's greater unity in foreign policy in the 1980s been matched by economic union. Using tariff rates, ranging on average from 25 per cent in Malaysia to 33 per cent in Indonesia, for their own developing economies, the ASEAN states reduced tariffs only in the least threatening areas. Except for Singapore, which was an entrepôt for regional commerce, the complementary nature of the ASEAN economies provided little incentive for freer trade. Even with Singapore's imports that were re-exported, outside the regions, such as refined oil products from Indonesian crude oil, inter-ASEAN trade from 1984 to 1991 hovered around 20 per cent of all ASEAN exports. The end result, however, has probably been to the advantage of the economic development of countries which have been called 'new little dragons'. Despite falling prices for their agricultural and mineral exports, the yearly growth rates in GNP from 1981 to 1989 averaged 7 per cent in Thailand, 5 per cent in Malaysia and Indonesia, though only 1.7 per cent in the Philippines. One prosperous new member also joined ASEAN in February 1984: oil-rich Brunei, where in 1985 one in three people owned a motor car, though about 40 per cent of the 249,000 people were less than twenty years of age. However, in the face of the growing influence of the EEC and the development of the North American free trade zone, at their fourth Summit meeting in Singapore in January 1992 the ASEAN states resolved to move their organization 'towards a higher plane of political and economic cooperation to ensure regional peace and prosperity'.[66]

CONCLUSIONS

Along the Asian rim of the Pacific Basin there was great strategic change after 1980. By 1991 the Cold War between the US and the USSR was well over; China had restored good relations with the

---

66. Riedel, 'Intra-Asian Trade' 122–36. *FEA* 1991, 263. Amina Tyabji, 'The Six ASEAN Economies: 1980–88' in Broinowski (ed.), *ASEAN into the 1990s* 32–57. Srikanta Chatterjee, 'ASEAN Economic Co-operation in the 1980s and 1990s' in ibid. 58–82. Gerald Segal, *Rethinking the Pacific* (Oxford 1990) 357–60. *The Economist* 24 Oct. 1992, 25. C.P.F. Luhulima, 'ASEAN, the South Pacific Forum and the Changing Strategic Environment', *The Indonesian Quarterly*, XX (1992) 211.

Soviet Union; even the two Koreas were beginning to negotiate with each other. Chinese relations with the US had shown continued improvement and, after the hiatus created by the Tiananmen Square massacre, were being restored. The Cambodian conflict had also achieved diplomatic resolution because of the new spirit of co-operation between the three superpowers and especially because of Vietnam's desire to break out of economic and diplomatic isolation, though the Khmer Rouge was still a potential threat to a lasting peace in Cambodia. In Southeast Asia ASEAN had emerged as a new diplomatic force and a harbinger of international peace in its region, though there were still weaknesses in its unity.

The 1980s also saw the continuing spread of the tentacles of Japanese economic supremacy throughout Eastern and Southeastern Asia and into the wider Pacific Basin. Feeding off increasing flows of Japanese investment, the economies of the four little dragons were booming. However, changes in the Japanese trade balance and the degree of Japanese control over technological transfers portended future trade problems for Japan and for the little dragons. The 1980s also had seen greater trade conflict between the the US and Japan as well as US impatience with protectionism in the little dragons. The growth of the other ASEAN economies, with the exception of the Philippines, was creating potential new little dragons, though much of the development depended on Japanese investment and trade.

CHAPTER EIGHT

Conflicts and Coups in the Islands since 1980

The Pacific Islands, which had been relatively peaceful since 1945, experienced much more internal conflict and international confrontation in the 1980s, which is the main theme of this chapter. It ranges from violent independence movements in New Caledonia, Irian Jaya and Bougainville, violence in Palau and in New Zealand associated with opposition to nuclear weapons and testing, and military coups in Fiji. The chapter also considers the involvement in the islands of the greater Pacific rim powers, including Australia and New Zealand, and reactions by Pacific Islands states.

THE COUPS IN FIJI AND THEIR CONSEQUENCES

Despite the decline in support for the Fiji National Party in the second 1977 election, racist attitudes among Fijians simmered below the political surface. During the 1982 election campaign the Great Council of Chiefs called for a new constitution that would reserve two-thirds of House of Representatives seats and the offices of prime minister and governor-general for ethnic Fijians. In a racially charged campaign the Alliance Party won a four seat victory. But its hold on the Fiji Government was to disappear in the next election in 1987.[1]

A backdrop to the political change was economic decline in Fiji

---

1. Brij V. Lal, 'The Fiji General Election of 1982', *Journal of Pacific History* 18, 1983, 134–57. Lal, *Fiji Coups* ch. 5.

in the 1980s. Its economy suffered from falls in world commodity prices. The price received for Fiji's sugar, which in 1985 earned 65 per cent of export income, fell from F$35.19 per ton in 1980 to F$23.6 in 1985. Consequently, the balance of trade had worsened significantly, with imports worth F$507.993 million compared with a F$271.427 million export income; and the growth rate of gross domestic product had slipped into reverse, to minus 1.5 per cent.[2]

This depressed economic climate encouraged the emergence of the Fiji Labour Party in July 1985 with the backing of trade unions. It was a multi-racial party combining Fijian and Indian workers, some radical Indian intellectuals and young well-educated Fijians. It also attracted Fijian support from the Western region of Viti Levu. In particular the party objected to a wage freeze imposed by the Alliance Government in the previous year to cope with the economic problems.[3]

Just before the election in March 1987 the Labour Party formed a coalition with the Indian NFP, a marriage of convenience that succeeded in defeating the government. The Alliance Party suffered from a record low Fijian voter participation of 71 per cent, a reflection of the disillusionment with Ratu Mara's government on the part of many Fijians, who had no wish to vote for an Indian-dominated coalition. The Coalition also increased its Fijian vote from the NFP's 0.8 per cent of Fijian voters in 1982 to 9.6 per cent in 1987. This swing was not dramatic, but along with the smaller total Fijian vote, was sufficient to provide a twenty-eight to twenty-four seat majority to the Coalition, whose members were nineteen Indians, seven Fijians and two general electors. However, they received 46.2 per cent of the vote compared with Alliance's 48.6 per cent because the Coalition won some seats by small margins, especially in Suva, compared with big Alliance majorities in Fijian rural areas.[4]

Some Fijians started protesting against a government with an Indian majority, despite the fact that the Prime Minister was a Fijian medical doctor, Timoci Bavadra. The Taukei movement, a militant Fijian pressure group which had emerged in the last week of the election campaign to protest against the prospect of an Indian dominated government, organized mass marches in the streets of Suva and Lautoka to protest against threats to Fijian rights. Land rights

2. *PIYB* 16th edit., 91–118.
3. Norton, *Race and Politics in Fiji* 128–32. Lal, *Fiji Coups* ch. 12.
4. Ibid. 131–6. Brij V. Lal, *Power and Prejudice: The Making of the Fiji Crisis* (Honolulu 1988) ch. 3.

were a major concern of the demonstrators, despite the iron-clad constitutional protection for Fijian land. Some Taukei leaders openly expressed a preference for the deportation of Indians.[5]

Then, on 10 May, Lieutenant-Colonel Sitiveni Rabuka, leading ten armed and masked soldiers, marched into the Fiji parliament. Announcing 'This is a takeover', Rabuka ordered Bavadra and all members of his party to leave the chamber, where more soldiers were waiting to pile them into trucks which transported them to temporary detention. The governor-general, Ratu Sir Penai Ganilau, refused to sanction the coup. However, Rabuka organized an interim government containing Mara and most other members of the Alliance Cabinet.[6]

On Suva's streets the Taukei movement started a chain of violence when, on 20 May, its bully boys punched and kicked Indians at a protest prayer vigil. The intense phase of this violence was short-lived, but it instilled widespread fear in the Indian community, as the author discovered when speaking five weeks later with a number of Indians, ranging from a senior public servant to a hotel cook. Furthermore, the almost entirely ethnically Fijian army began exerting its new-found power with a series of arbitrary arrests of political opponents, foreign journalists and anybody else deemed to be acting suspiciously. Their interrogation methods, which had been learned from extensive UN peace-keeping experience in the Middle East, ranged from torture to short periods of detention. The only person killed, however, was an Indian whose car was blown up by a bomb he was conveying.[7]

The coup had devastating economic effects. Australian and New Zealand unions placed bans on ships travelling to Fiji, and numerous Indians with professional and other skilled qualifications fled the country. New foreign investment dried up. Tourism, one of the mainstays of Fiji's economy, collapsed. The author had the unique experience of being the only visitor on the last Saturday morning in June to Coral Gardens, a major tourist attraction, which was closed down when he travelled back to Suva with the Fijian manager, who spoke of his opposition to the coup.[8]

5. Ibid. 70–6. Robert T. Robertson and Akosita Tamanisau, *Fiji Shattered Coups* (Sydney 1988) 64–8. Deryck Scarr, *Fiji Politics of Illusion: The Military Coups in Fiji* (Sydney 1988) ch. 11.

6. Ibid. chs 17–20. Lal, *Fiji Coups* ch. 14. Robertson and Tamanisau, *Fiji: Shattered Coups* ch. 4.

7. Ibid. 123–5.

8. Ibid. 172–9.

The Indian community also tried to use economic pressure against the military regime. Indian sugar cane farmers maintained a two-month-long harvest-strike. But economic realities and army coercion, including threats of sequestration of property, drove them back to work.[9]

The military regime was not concerned about the economic consequences of the coup. The army became a de facto unemployment relief agency for Fijians as it grew from about 2,500 troops to 6,000. Other unemployed youths became useful street thugs for the Taukei movement. Some Taukei leaders even welcomed publicly the prospect of economic collapse as a means to revive traditional village life, reflecting a reactionary communalism which motivated many Taukei supporters.[10]

The governor-general worked hard for a compromise solution, and church leaders were prominent in trying to restore constitutional government. Indeed, Ganilau reached an agreement by September 1987 between the members of the Coalition and the Alliance Party, for a united caretaker government until new elections could be held.[11]

Such a solution was not what Rabuka or his Taukei supporters were seeking. On Friday 25 September soldiers stormed into radio and newspaper officers and seized public buildings in a well-organized second coup. When Ganilau protested, Rabuka declared Fiji a republic.[12]

The causes of the coups were complex and have been the subject of significant debate.[13] At least some of Fiji's Council of Chiefs were involved in plotting the first coup. There were disturbing features about the 1987 election result for many chiefs. The Labour Party, led for the most part by young educated Fijians, threatened the hegemony of the chiefs, who received disproportionately high incomes from Fijian landholdings and still tried to assert their traditional social control over the Fijian community. The Labour Party also represented a revival of regional antagonism within the Fijian community. Western Viti Levu, the home area of Bavadra, has been traditionally subservient to the eastern region of the islands, but Fijians in the west, though many did not vote for the Labour Party, had now deserted the chiefs and turned the tables of power. Some of the chiefs involved in the Alliance Party also faced a threat from the exposure of corruption.

9. Scarr, *Politics of Illusion* ch. 22

10. Lal, *Power and Prejudice* ch. 7.

11. Scarr, *Politics of Illusion* ch. 29. *Fiji Times*, 27 June 1987.

12. Lal, *Power and Prejudice* ch. 8.

13. For a summary of the debate see Michael C. Howard. 'State Power and Political Change in Fiji', *Journal of Contemporary Asia* 21, 1991, 78–9.

Charges that Alliance politicians had been milking the public purse were rife in the election campaign, and Mara's manifest wealth was linked to those accusations in a newspaper article by Josefa Nata, secretary of the Journalist's Association of Fiji. His view was: 'It is well known in Fiji that certain people in the Mara Government have accumulated much wealth for themselves during 16 years in power'.[14]

The chiefs showed their hand after the first coup. On 28 July the Great Council of Chiefs called for constitutional change that would guarantee to Fijians forty-one seats in a seventy-one seat parliament. In addition the positions of governor-general, prime minister and the ministries of Finance, Foreign Affairs, Home Affairs and Fijian Affairs would be reserved for indigenous Fijians.

The thirty-six-year-old Rabuka, however, was a significant play-maker in the political events. It is clear that the coup's timing was influenced by the absence in Australia of army commander Brigadier Epeli Nailatikau who spoke out against Rabuka's action. An anonymous major at the Queen Elizabeth barracks on the day of the coup admitted unguardedly to a Radio Australia reporter that neither he nor most of the other senior army officers had any forewarning of it. Rabuka had long been fascinated with coups, making a deliberate study of how they were carried out in other countries, and he confessed his willingness to organize one in 1977 in the event of a NFP government being formed. He was described by a friend of the author in Fiji as 'a rather self-centred and showy man with a taste for theatre', who had married into a chiefly family. He also was known to have been disappointed in being passed over for the top army position with the appointment of Nailatikau.[15]

Furthermore, the second coup showed lines of division among the chiefs. Some, such as Mara and Ganilau, were prepared to compromise with the Coalition, but others involved with the Taukei movement were insisting on entrenching Fijian control. A strong influence on the latter group was religious fundamentalism, which had been growing within the Methodist religion dominant among Fijians. Indeed, after the coup the Methodist Church became divided between the fundamentalists who supported Rabuka and broader churchmen.

The influence of this religious fundamentalism was indicated in one of Rabuka's early edicts after the second coup. On 25 September 1987

14. Interview with Josefa Nata, "International Report", Radio Australia, 19 May 1987.
15. Eddie Dean and Stan Ritova, *Rabuka: No Other Way* (Sydney 1988) chs 2–4.

all work, sport and public transport on Sundays were banned, a rigid sabbatarianism that even forced people who did not own cars to walk to church. The claim was that this law would help to establish a more religious and faithful community so that God would bless Fiji, but its effect was socially divisive. Soldiers even arrested people milking cows, until that essential activity was approved. Those arrested for breaking the Sunday observance laws often received rough treatment, including a group of seventeen children between the ages of five and twelve who were stripped, beaten until they could no longer stand up, and then forced to rub their faces on a concrete floor until their noses bled. When the Sunday law was lifted in November 1988 on the return of a civilian government led by Mara, Methodist militants set up Sunday road blocks and were arbitrarily released by Rabuka after they had been arrested. The opposition of some church leaders to the militants caused a split in the Methodist Church that reflected divisions in the Fijian community since the second coup.[16]

Fiji's return to democratic life was only partially completed by 1991. A new constitution discriminated against Indians by giving them only 27 of 70 parliamentary seats, and it loaded the electoral dice against urban Fijians. In the elections held in May 1992 a split in Fijian ranks resulted in the Fijian Political Party, led by Rabuka, winning 30 of the 37 Fijian seats and needing the support of 13 Fijian Labour Party members from Indian ethnic seats to govern. This was an ironic development which resulted in Rabuka becoming president at the cost of promised reforms to satisfy his new allies.[17]

By 1989 Fiji's economy was recovering from the effects of the coups, assisted by the granting of tax concessions to foreign investors and by the revival of the tourist trade. A decline of 6.3 per cent in gross domestic product in 1987 became a growth rate of 12.6 per cent in 1989. However, suppression of trade unionists and sweatshop working conditions were features of the new economic order. The effects of wider world recession also slowed down the annual growth rate to only 1.5 per cent in 1991.[18]

16. Howard, 'State Power and Political Change', 99–100. John Garrett, 'Uncertain Sequel: the Social and Religious Scene in Fiji since the Coups', *The Contemporary Pacific* 2, 1990, 100–4.

17. *Keesing's Record of World Events* vol. 38, 38917.

18. *FEA* 1991, 763. Satendra Prasad, 'Tax Free Zones and National Development'; Wadam Nasey, 'Privatization and the Poor' in Satendra Prasad (ed.), *Coup and Crisis: Fiji – A Year Later* (Melbourne 1988) chs 6–7. Shireen Lateef, 'Current and Future Implications of the Coups for Women in Fiji', *The Contemporary Pacific* 2, 1990, 113–19. Brij V. Lal, 'Fiji', *The Contemporary Pacific* 4, 1992, 390–1.

The first coup in Fiji received worldwide condemnation. Australia and New Zealand denounced it vehemently as a blow to democratic values. The anger of the Australian and New Zealand prime ministers was sharpened by the overthrow of a government led by a fellow Labour Party premier. Governments in Canberra and Wellington had been taken completely by surprise. People in the Australian Department of Foreign Affairs 'ran round like headless chooks', said one of them to the author. A later charge by Mara that Australia planned using a naval ship, which was on a normal visit to Suva at the time, to launch a military operation for the rescue of the detained Bavadra has been denied by the director of Australian military operations at the time.[19] However, Australia and New Zealand suspended all military and some economic aid to Fiji.

Australia and New Zealand were criticized by the Melanesian group in the Pacific Forum for not consulting with other Pacific Islands states. The Melanesian states, whose premiers sympathized with the desire of their fellow Melanesians in Fiji to protect their interests, achieved the addition of the words 'recognising the complexity of the problems' to the resolution expressing 'deep concern and anguish' about Fiji passed by the May 1987 meeting of the South Pacific Forum. There was little support in the forum for the diplomatic attempts by Australia and New Zealand to ensure a return to constitutional rule in Fiji.[20]

After the second coup, Australia and New Zealand further reduced economic aid to Fiji and refused to recognize the Republic of Fiji. However, France started fishing in the troubled waters, offering AUS$16 million in aid, which was eagerly accepted by Rabuka's regime. The prospect of France's supplanting Australia as the provider of most aid and as the main trading partner of Fiji encouraged Canberra to recognize the new Fiji state and restore economic, but not military, aid. However, a promise of future constitutional reform won for Prime Minister Rabuka, on a visit to Australia in September 1992, a resumption of Australian military assistance.[21]

19. *Age* (Melbourne) 13 Dec. 1991.
20. Roderic Alley, 'The 1987 Military Coups in Fiji: The Regional Implications', *The Contemporary Pacific* 2, 1990, 37–46.
21. Ibid. 46–56. Henningham, *France and the South Pacific* 216–17. *Pacific Islands Monthly* October 1992, 10–11.

PAPUA NEW GUINEA

Papua New Guinea faced its own violent problems during the 1980s. On its western border the OPM guerillas in Irian Jaya were still active. In 1984, as the result of a wave of Indonesian oppression, some 11,000 refugees crossed the border into New Guinea. Though the Papua New Guinea Government insisted that most were local people who traditionally wandered back and forth across the arbitrary boundary line drawn up in colonial days, many of them were genuine political refugees. However, there was great resistance from Port Moresby to call for UN assistance, a mark of the government's concern to appease Indonesia. Only reluctantly, after protests from churches and non-government aid agencies about deaths and disease in the refugee camps, was the UN High Commissioner for Refugees allowed to distribute aid to the people there. The government's policy had been influenced by the diplomatic necessity of a country with a small population facing a very populous neighbour with an aggressive reputation. The policy was certainly not in response to public opinion, as the author found out in 1984 when he raised the question with a large class of first-year students at the University of Papua New Guinea who unanimously supported their Melanesian cousins in Irian Jaya and expressed vociferous dislike of Indonesia. The Papua New Guinea Government of that time, led by Michael Somare, did protest about Indonesian hot pursuit of OPM guerillas across the border and was reluctant to send any refugees back. But when a split in the Pangu Parti resulted in a change of government led by Pius Wingti, a former Pangu member of a highlands constituency, Port Moresby became more accommodating to Indonesia. A friendship treaty was signed with Indonesia in 1986, and the Papua New Guinea army was instructed to cooperate with Indonesian troops in apprehending OPM guerillas. In 1991 that resistance movement was still active in Irian Jaya, though many of its warriors were armed only with bows and arrows.[22]

---

22. Personal knowledge (the author participated in the church pressure on the Papua New Guinea Government). May, 'East of the Border' and Alan Smith and Kevin Hewison, '1984: Refugees, "Holiday Camps" and Deaths' in May (ed.) *Between Two Nations* 100–59, 200–17. Beverley Blaskett and Loong Wong, 'Papua New Guinea Under Wingti: Accommodating Indonesia', *Australian Outlook* 43, 1989, 44–60. 'Rebels of a Forgotten World', Australian Broadcasting Commission television programme, 15 March 1992.

The Papua New Guinea Government also faced a rebellion on its own islands of Buka and Bougainville. Despite the concessions of higher copper mining royalties and a provincial government achieved after independence, popular resentment at the much larger profits being derived from the Panguna copper mine by the central government and by the Australia-based mining company, Bougainville Copper, was bubbling away under a surface tranquility in the islands.

The company had made efforts to conciliate the islanders by employing the American anthropologist, Douglas Oliver, from 1968 to 1979 to advise on how 'to shield Bougainvillians as much as possible from the harms that inevitably accompany such mining'. But neither he nor the company could stop the inevitable impact of the money that was generated for the provincial government, for Bougainvillians who worked at the mine and for landowners in a formerly 'sleepy, economically backward and culturally non-Westernized human setting'. The result was increased islander demands, not for the tinned food, knives and tobacco that were prized in pre-mine days, but now for refrigerators, video players and automobiles. Western education combined with the cargo cult flavour of traditional islander thinking contributed to such aspirations. Growing population also was placing pressures on land-use, which provoked anger about the area being appropriated by the ever-growing open pit and slag heaps of the mine. Furthermore, the company failed to check river pollution, which was believed by islanders to cause crop failure and human sickness. The islander clergy of the dominant Catholic Church supported Bougainvillian complaints about the copper mine. Fundamentally, the problem which had encouraged earlier moves for secession remained: the cultural and racial divisions between black Buka-Bougainvillians and brown-skinned Papua New Guineans. The sense of being 'Bougainvillian' had grown with improvements in transport facilities and geographical mobility provided by education, resulting in intermingling of islanders previously living in isolated small hamlets. The presence of 'red-skin' Papua New Guineans as employees at the mine, many holding higher paid jobs than Bougainvillians, was an additional resentment.[23]

There were also political developments encouraging opposition to the mine. Bougainville had been a neglected area for economic

---

23. Douglas Oliver, *Black Islanders: A Personal Perspective on Bougainville* (Melbourne 1991) xi–xviii, 199–200

development and, despite the revenue generated by the mine for the central and provincial governments, not enough money was being spent in the eyes of many Bougainvillians to improve roads, the distribution of electric power and other improvements. This political discontent was exploited by the Melanesian Alliance led by a Catholic priest, Father John Momis, who actually disliked the rush for westernized development in Papua New Guinea and had long opposed the copper mine. A result was the election of Joseph Kabui as provincial premier. His electorate covered the mine area and he had been an industrial relations officer for the Bougainville Mining Workers' Union, but he was no friend of the company. In the 1987 national election Momis pushed 'the Bougainville Initiative', which demanded a three per cent royalty from the gross income of the mine to the North Solomons Provincial Government. The company, bound by an agreement with the Papua New Guinea Government, was unable to comply. Into this confrontation stepped Francis Ona, a neighbour of Kabui, who started dynamiting mining company property. Described by one of his teachers as a mystic who was the most difficult of his students to get to know or like, Ona worked at the company as a mine-pit surveyor and haul-truck operator from 1973 until he resigned in 1988. He now demanded the closing of the mine and ten billion kina from the mining company as compensation for environmental damage. He obviously knew they were impossible demands for the company to meet, because his ultimate aim, as expressed in a letter to the landowners' association, was to 'break away from PNG'.[24]

Such demands were a recipe for confrontation. Four hundred police were sent to Bougainville to stop the sabotage and to arrest Ona and his companions, without success. Charges of police brutality, such as house burnings, looting and rape started to spread among Bougainvillians and whipped up hostility towards the Papua New Guinea Government. It offered to raise payments to the landowners and to the provincial government in a peace package. However, continued acts of sabotage against the mine, especially destruction of electricity transmission lines and attacks on personnel, caused it to cease operations in May 1989 and to close permanently in September. The mood of Ona and his followers was clearly indicated

---

24. Information from Dr Garry Trompf, Sydney. Ona to members of the Panguna Landowners' Association n.d. [1989] in Peter Polomka (ed.), *Bougainville: Perspectives on a Crisis* (Canberra 1990) 7. Oliver, *Black Islanders*, ch. 10.

on 11 September, two days before an agreement to implement the peace plan was signed by the provincial government, when the minister who had led the peace initiative, John Bika, was assassinated. The militants also gained the services of some military-trained Bougain-villians, especially Sam Kuona. He had been trained in jungle warfare in Australia and became the commander of the Bougainville Revolu-tionary Army (BRA). Using guerilla warfare tactics and armed with weapons preserved since the Second World War, the BRA was able to evade capture by a Papua New Guinea force that had grown to 500 soldiers and 200 police by July 1989. In the mountainous jungle of Bougainville it proved impossible for the nation's army, which was only 3,350 strong in 1989, to defeat the BRA in a bloody struggle, in which atrocities against the local population were committed by both sides. Indeed, the brutality of Papua New Guinea soldiers further alienated Buka-Bougainvillians who gave the BRA widespread support.[25]

To give into the BRA's secessionist demand was considered im-possible by Port Moresby because of the potential domino effect on other regions in the culturally and linguistically diverse country – although Buka-Bougainvillians were a more distinct group in the nation than any other region. Indonesia also was pressing Papua New Guinea to maintain control of the island because of Jakarta's constant fear of secessions within its own nation. Likewise other Pacific Island states were supporting Papua New Guinea – even the Solomon Islands Government, where there was public sympathy for the BRA, particularly in the ethnically-related Western Islands.

The government in Port Moresby launched on 12 January 1990 a final unsuccessful military campaign, 'Operation Footloose', to conquer the island. Its failure prompted a cease-fire agreement with the BRA on 28 February and evacuation of Papua New Guinea military and special police forces from Buka and Bougainville. An international observation team led by a Ghanian diplomat was assembled hastily to supervise the agreement, which included the surrender of BRA arms. This policy was by no means agreed to by all members of the Cabinet. Indeed, it was a major victory to the BRA in achieving official recognition and the withdrawal of PNG forces. Disenchanted with the agreement, the government controller of the state of emergency on Bougainville, Police Commissioner Paul Tohian, withdrew all police and prison guards, allowing the BRA to

25. Ibid., ch. 11.

take de facto control and providing no means to force the surrender of its arms. It declared the independence of Buka and Bougainville on 17 May 1990.[26]

Port Moresby's response was to withdraw all government services and to impose an economic blockade, resulting in major economic dislocation on Buka and Bougainville. While traditional bush gardening maintained basic food resources, the drying-up of medical supplies led to a dramatic rise in infant mortality and other deaths estimated to number more than 2,000 above the normal death rate by the end of the year. But one member of the Port Moresby Government, Bernard Narakobi, was maintaining radio contact with Kabui, the minister for justice in the BRA Government. Consequently, a peace initiative was launched from 29 July to 5 August 1990, assisted by the Government of New Zealand which supplied two frigates supporting its supply ship, *Endeavour*, as a neutral meeting ground for representatives of the BRA and the Port Moresby Government. They agreed to an accord which would restore Papua New Guinea Government services to Bougainville and postpone the political issue to a later meeting. But significantly Ona was not present at the talks, and some members of the Port Moresby Government led by Defence Minister Ted Diro opposed the accord. After one consignment of medical aid was landed from the *Endeavour*, further assistance was rejected by the BRA when, in breach of the spirit of the accord, Papua New Guinea troops landed on Buka in response to requests from the local people. With further fighting between BRA guerillas and government soldiers, Papua New Guinea troops had established by the end of 1990 tenuous control of Buka and an enclave on the northern coast of Bougainville. A further conference in January 1991 between BRA representatives and Papua New Guinea government members in Honiara, the capital of the Solomon Islands, failed to achieve any long-lasting peace. After an election brought Wingti back into power in Port Moresby in July 1992, there was an extension of military action to win back areas of land on the main island. A peaceful solution to the crisis was not in sight. The BRA remained in control of much of Bougainville, which continued to suffer from the blockade. It was broken only by some supplies organized by sympathizers in the Solomon Islands across the narrow seaway between the Shortland Islands and south

26. Terence Wesley-Smith, 'Papua New Guinea' in 'Political Review-Melanesia', *The Contemporary Pacific*, 2, 1991, 407–9.

Bougainville, to which the Solomon Islands Government was turning a blind eye.[27]

The Australian Government supported Port Moresby's attempts to suppress the rebellion. This was not primarily because Bougainville Copper was Australian. Canberra was concerned to maintain the political stability of Papua New Guinea as a traditional defence shield for Australia. Revenue from the mine also reduced the high degree of Australian financial support for the budget of its former colony which, though it had decreased since independence, was still 19 per cent of total revenue in 1989. The most tangible Australian military support was provision of four helicopters, ostensibly for transport purposes only, but used as gunships by PNG forces. In 1992 relations between Australia and the Solomon Islands became strained after incursions of Papua New Guinea troops into the Shortland Islands bent on destroying sources of supply to the BRA, especially a raid on 12 September which resulted in the deaths of two civilian Shortland Islanders. A serious crisis in Papua New Guinea-Solomons relations was defused by a promise from Port Moresby to put the offending troops on trial and to pay financial compensation.[28]

The Bougainville crisis increased economic and political instability in Papua New Guinea. The Panguna mine had been contributing 45 per cent of the country's exports and 17 per cent of its national revenue. After increasing by 4.8 per cent in 1988, Papua New Guinea's GDP declined by 3 per cent in 1989. Resulting government austerity measures increased internal disorder in a country with a rising crime rate. There was a failed coup in March 1990 led by Police Commissioner Tohian, smarting from his reprimand for exceeding government instructions on Bougainville. The Pangu Parti Government led by Rabbie Namaliu, a former foreign minister, faced instability in its parliamentary support, depending on Momis's Melanesian Alliance and other small parties because after the 1987 election Pangu had only 27 seats in the 107 member House of

27. Ibid., 409–10. Oliver, *Black Islanders*, chs 12–13. Yaw Saffu. 'The Bougainville Crisis and Politics in Papua New Guinea', *The Contemporary Pacific*, 4, 1992, 325–43. Warren Paia, 'An Island Between Two Nations: The Impact of the Bougainville Crisis on Solomon Islands/New Guinea Relations as well as on the Region', paper read at the 9th Pacific History Association Conference, Christchurch, New Zealand, 4 December 1992.

28. Oliver, *Black Islanders*, 124, 230–1. *FEA*, 1991, 812. *Pacific Islands Monthly*, October 1992, 6–7, November 1992, 6–7.

Assembly. The government succeeded in staving off no-confidence motions but was defeated in the national elections of July 1992.[29]

NEW CALEDONIA

The return of the Socialist Party to power in France in May 1981, for the first time since 1958, resulted in a more concerted French attempt to reach an accord with the Kanak community in New Caledonia. However, though party spokesmen acknowledged past injustices and the desirability of eventual independence, the Socialist Government under President Francois Mitterand did not abandon France's middle-power pretensions. So the CEP was retained, and a worldwide chain of small departments and territories, including New Caledonia, continued under French rule. Furthermore, there was an appreciation in Paris that a majority of people in New Caledonia were not supporting independence and that some of them were violently opposed to it. Indeed, in September 1981 UC Secretary-General Pierre Declerq, a French-born former school teacher, was murdered. This first political assassination in the South Pacific provoked Kanak road blocks, shots fired at European farmhouses, killing of cattle and rioting in Noumea.[30]

The French Government, however, was still determined to implement a reform programme in New Caledonia. In December 1981 a prominent Socialist politician, Christian Nucci, arrived in Noumea as high commissioner. Three new administrative offices were established to acquire land for Kanaks, to implement economic development for the interior and the Loyalty Islands, and to foster and preserve traditional Melanesian culture. Tjibaou was made director of the cultural office. Furthermore, provision was made for advisers experienced in customary Kanak law to be present in court proceedings involving Kanaks. The Socialist Government attempted further to

29. James Griffin, 'The Papua New Guinea Elections of 1987', *Journal of Pacific History*, 23, 1988, 106–16. Wesley-Smith, 'Papua New Guinea', 411–14. Hank Nelson. 'Papua New Guinea (November 1990–October 1991): Crises and Continuity', *Journal of Pacific History* 26:3, 1991, 74–9.

30. Henningham, *France and the South Pacific* 71–2. Connell, *New Caledonia or Kanaky* 286–95.

promote moderate political groups in New Caledonia at the expense of extremists on both sides. For a time this strategy worked. In June 1982 the FNSC broke with the RPCR on the issue of the introduction of income tax and helped the FI to pass that legislation. The RPCR then supported the FI to achieve a majority in the Government Council, headed by the front's leader, Tjibaou. However, in the embittered racial climate right wing elements reacted with violence to this Kanak majority government, such as an invasion of the Assembly by sixty masked men wielding clubs and assaulting FI and FNSC members. Riot police, tear gas and gaol sentences were necessary to quell such disturbances, though there were continuing brawls between Europeans and Melanesians. The land reform programme was a particular object of European anger, and Kanak counter-violence grew during 1983. Two gendarmes were killed in a violent struggle over a Kanak blockade of a saw mill, and the post office and five houses in the west coast village of Temala were firebombed in revenge for the death of a young Kanak.[31]

This poisonous racial climate destroyed the French Socialist Government's attempt to reach an agreement between Europeans and Kanaks about the future of the territory. At a conference of representatives of the main New Caledonian political parties in Paris in July 1983, Secretary of State Georges Lemoine recognized the Kanaks' innate right to independence, but he also acknowledged the right of Europeans to live in New Caledonia. However, the RPCR delegation refused to sign such a statement, and radical Kanaks had reservations. Nevertheless, the French Government implemented the Lemoine statute, which called for new elections in 1984, more internal autonomy and a referendum on independence in 1989. The RPCR and other right wing groups denounced the concessions to the FI, whereas it demanded an earlier referendum date and restrictions on the franchise to people with at least one parent born in New Caledonia.[32]

To place pressure on the French Government, the FI re-formed itself in September 1984 into the *Front de Libération Nationale Kanak et Socialiste* (FLNKS). The name expressed the front's major aims: to liberate Kanaks from capitalist and colonialist exploitation in a socialist republic in which only second generation Europeans would have the right to vote. To express its rejection of the Lemoine statute,

31. Ibid. 299–307. Henningham, *France and the South Pacific* 72–4.
32. Ibid. 74–6. Connell, *New Caledonia or Kanaky* 306–20.

the FLNKS boycotted the November 1984 assembly election, using road blocks and other pressure to stop Kanaks from voting. Some ballot boxes were destroyed and many polling stations in the Kanak strongholds on the east coast and in the Loyalty Islands did not open or closed early. However, elsewhere some Kanaks voted, though only 50 per cent of the whole electorate participated compared with the normal 70 to 80 per cent. After the election Kanak militants in some districts maintained the road blocks and kept European settlers, including the whole town of Thio, under siege. The FLNKS strategy was to use violence against property rather than people, though the distinction was not always maintained. A typical right wing press misrepresentation of the situation was the comment by a visiting *Le Figaro* journalist, who lamented that 40,000 whites in New Caledonia were 'at the mercy of a handful of savages who are ready for a massacre'.[33]

The French Government sought negotiation to resolve the escalating conflict. Edgard Pisani, a Socialist deputy in the EEC Parliament, arrived as a new High Commissioner and made an agreement on 5 December with Tjibaou for the lifting of the blockades. But that evening, two of Tjibaou's brothers and eight other Kanaks returning from a UC meeting, which agreed to the peace proposal, to their village in the Hienghene district on the east coast were ambushed and massacred by local mixed-race farmers who feared Kanak claims on their land. Tjibaou demonstrated his statesmanship by continuing to support the peace agreement. Pisani responded with a plan which sought to reconcile Kanak and European interests by promising a referendum in July 1985 which would offer a choice between the status quo and 'independence in association' with France. Under the latter choice people could become citizens of the new nation or retain French nationality, non-Kanak land would become leasehold with rents to traditional Kanak owners, special provisions would be made for Noumea, and France would provide for defence and support the territorial budget.

The main problem with the Pisani Plan was that it was too late. Though FLNKS leaders were willing to consider it, some members, embittered by the violent conflict, denounced it as neo-colonialist. The RPCR and its conservative allies condemned the plan out of hand,

---

33. Ibid. 321–34 (quotation, 332). Aliane Chanter, 'The Media and Politics in New Caledonia in the 1980s', *Journal of Pacific History* 26, 1991, 316–19. Henningham, *France and the South Pacific* 82–4.

though agreeing to support the referendum if there was no change to the existing franchise which allowed all French citizens to vote no matter how recently they had arrived in New Caledonia. A peaceful implementation of the plan was shattered in January 1985 when one of the FLNKS militants, Eloi Machoro, took a band of armed supporters to settle a score with a right wing opponent, Roger Galliot, which led to the killing of one of his relatives. In protest at this murder, European opponents of independence rioted in Noumea's streets, firebombing buildings owned by FLNKS supporters. The violence ended only with the news that Machoro and his wife had been killed by police sniper fire. Leading the European militancy were French immigrants, especially ex-army officers. An influx of French troops reduced, but did not eliminate, further violence. Despite the collapse of Pisani's compromise plan, the Socialist French prime minister, Laurent Fabius, went ahead with another scheme for the election of four regional councils, which would have significant local powers including economic development. The independence referendum was postponed until 1987. With only one of the new regions embracing Noumea, the FLNKS won control of the other three, with less than 40 per cent of the total vote.[34]

This partial Kanak victory in New Caledonia collapsed with the defeat of the French Socialist Party in the parliamentary election of March 1986. The new prime minister, Jacques Chirac, leader of the neo-Gaullist *Rassemblement Pour La République*, had visited New Caledonia in 1978 when he made contact with the newly formed RPCR. Since then he had cooperated closely with the RPCR leader, the millionaire Jacques Lafleur, who gave donations to Chirac's party and was one of the two New Caledonian members of the French Parliament. Unsurprisingly, Chirac and his minister for overseas territories, Bernard Pons, moved to weaken the power of the FLNKS. The Pons statute reduced the powers of the regional councils and rearranged boundaries to give Europeans control over the west coast. The land reform office was merged with the development office and purchases of properties for Kanaks ceased. More funds were spent in loyalist regions than in FLNKS strongholds. A government propaganda campaign denounced the FLNKS as terrorists who re-presented only a small minority of Kanaks. Chirac honoured the

34. Ibid. 84–90. Connell, *New Caledonia or Kanaky* 335–68. Frédéric Bobin, 'Caldoches, Metropolitans and the Mother Country', *Journal of Pacific History* 26, 1991, 310–11.

referendum proposal of the Fabius Plan, but prescribed only three years' residence in New Caledonia as the voting qualification, which effectively ensured an anti-independence majority. Appreciating this reality, the FLNKS called for a boycott of the vote, though the presence of over 8,000 French troops and riot police prevented most of the methods employed in 1984. This time 59 per cent of the electorate voted, with only two per cent supporting independence; but more than 70 per cent of Kanaks, who formed 43 per cent of the 1983 population, refused to vote. This referendum showed the continuing political polarization in New Caledonia.[35]

In early 1988 violence escalated in New Caledonia. Despite the spreading out of soldiers round the islands, Kanaks employed local knowledge to erect road barricades, to kill one of the perpetrators of the Hienghene massacre, and to harass other opponents of independence. The most serious foray occurred on the almost entirely Kanak populated island of Ouvea, one of the Loyalty Islands. In a dawn raid on 22 April, two days before the first round vote in the French presidential election, a group of armed Kanaks raided the local gendarmerie, killing four gendarmes and transferring twenty-seven French hostages to a cave hidden in the mountainous northern section of the island. The captors demanded the revocation of the Pons statute, the cancellation of regional elections, which were to be held in conjunction with the first round of the French election, and the withdrawal of all French military forces from the territory. Tjibaou, who was not involved in this local FLNKS action, declared that the violence on Ouvea was the consequence 'of the partisan, cynical and despicable policy of the RPCR'. The Kanak commandos, however, made the fatal mistake of releasing some of their hostages, who helped guide army special forces to the location. This was successfully raided two days before the second round of votes in the French presidential election. Twenty-three hostages were released unharmed, eighteen Kanak militants were killed, some after they were taken prisoner, at the expense of two dead French soldiers. There is little doubt that Chirac ordered the raid in the hope that a decisive victory over Kanak 'terrorists' would assist him in the election against President Mitterand. However, though the Ouvea drama brought

---

35. Henningham, *France and the South Pacific* 98–103. Helen Fraser, *New Caledonia: Anti-Colonialism in a Pacific Territory* (Parliament of the Commonwealth of Australia, Legislative Research Service, Discussion Paper no. 2, 1987–88) 28–38. John Connell, *New Caledonia: The Matignon Accord and the Colonial Future* (Sydney 1988) 9–13.

New Caledonia to prominence in the French media, Mitterand won easily.[36]

The Socialists also regained control of the French Parliament. Once more a change of government in Paris had a major influence on French policies in New Caledonia. The new Socialist prime minister, Michel Rocard, sought an accord to break the cycle of violence. Such was the concern in New Caledonia about the way the colony was lurching towards civil war, he received agreement to participate in talks in Paris from the FLNKS and from loyalist political groups. Exceptions were the extreme right *Front Calédonien* and the *Front National*, whose leader, Guy George, declared: 'In New Caledonia our roots have been irrigated with the blood of our dead . . . and we will not let the FLNKS pull them out'.[37] The result was the Matignon accord, signed on 26 June 1988 by Lafleur on behalf of the RPCR and by Tjibaou for the FLNKS. This momentous agreement repealed the Pons statute, placed New Caledonia under direct French rule for a year until new elections for three regions, consisting of the northern and southern portions of the main island and the Loyalty Islands, and promised a referendum in 1998 on a franchise restricted to those living in New Caledonia ten years earlier. Rocard also promised massive financial assistance to the underdeveloped northern and Loyalty Islands regions, in which the Kanak population was respectively 74 and 98 per cent.

The Matignon accord met with widespread approval in New Caledonia except from extremists on both sides. In November 1988 the accord received an 80 per cent affirmative vote in a referendum in France, though only 37 per cent of the population voted. In New Caledonia the affirmative vote was 57 per cent of the 64 per cent who voted, which reflected extremist dissension. Kanak militants expressed their frustration by assassinating Tjibaou and his deputy in May 1989, leaving a leadership gap in the FLNKS which was not filled until March 1990 when Paul Néaoutyine, the PALIKA president and an economics graduate, was elected as president. The 1989 regional elections displayed broad acceptance of the accord with the RPCR winning power easily in the southern region and the FLNKS in the other two. Assisting this development was a new moderation displayed by the major New Caledonian newspaper, *Les Nouvelles Calédoniennes*, under new French ownership, and by Radio France

36. Ibid. 13–15.
37. Quoted in ibid. 17.

Outremer. Also some European support for the Matignon accord can be viewed as an assertion of Caldoche people identifying with New Caledonia rather than with metropolitan France. However, the new-found peace was brittle, given the racial hatreds lurking under the surface.[38]

FRENCH POLYNESIA

There was no violent independence movement in French Polynesia in the 1980s. The conservative *Tahoeraa Huiraatira* (Rally for the People) party, which received 30 per cent of the vote in the 1982 election, had switched in 1980 to support for autonomy under French rule, a policy supported by its leader, a part-European former school teacher, Gaston Flosse. Therefore the *Tahoeraa* party, which assumed government in 1982 with the support of independents, welcomed the offer in 1983 of an increase in local autonomy by the French Socialist Government. However the autonomy statute retained French control over economic, immigration, defence and foreign policy. Many Polynesians in the territory were happy with restricted self-government and continued economic benefits flowing from the CEP. Flosse's party was able to increase its vote to 40 per cent in the 1986 election, and with the help of weighted electorates in the outer islands, gained twenty-two of the forty-one seats in the legislature. Chirac enhanced Flosse's prestige in 1986 by making him minister for the South Pacific, the first such devolution of political responsibility in French imperial history. However, allegations started circulating about corruption in his government which, though not unusual in a society with strong family ties and personal patronage, appeared to be on a large scale.

The *Tahoeraa* party also ran into trouble in October 1987 when striking dock workers, protesting at labour reductions and at the intervention against peaceful pickets by riot police sent from France, went on a rampage in central Papeete, causing widespread looting and destruction. Flosse, in Paris at the time, returned to a split in the

---

38. Henningham, *France and the South Pacific* 105–16. Chanter, 'The Media' 313–39. Bobin, 'Caldoches' 303–12.

party. Defectors objected to Flosse's authoritarian style and the use by the government of metropolitan police in the dock strike. A new governing coalition included the three members of the socialist pro-independence *Ia Mana* party. Though covering a broad ideological spectrum, this government remained in office until elections in March 1991 brought Flosse back to power heading an alternative coalition.[39]

The dock strike riot in 1987 was a reflection of declining economic and social conditions in French Polynesia in the late 1980s. Unemployed youths gave muscle to the rioters. There were also wide gaps in personal income. Polynesians, many of them seduced from traditional village life by the allure of Western culture, formed the least advantaged class. Nevertheless, French spending by the 1980s was double that in New Caledonia, despite the fact that New Caledonia's 1989 population of 188,814 was only 24,641 greater than in French Polynesia. The CEP was a major reason for the difference, and it contributed to a higher GNP per head in French Polynesia than in New Zealand. The result was that the *Tahoeraa* party, though expressing moral opposition to atomic weapons, supported the CEP as vital for French Polynesia's economy. Only the small *Ia Mana* and *Tavini Huiraatira No Te Ao Maohi* parties were staunchly opposed to the CEP and were advocates of independence. In 1986 they gained only 15 per cent of the vote and five seats, which was reduced to four seats, all for *Tavini*, in the 1991 election. However, personality and parochial factors influenced elections, and territory-wide support depended on more financial resources than the pro-independence parties possessed. Also the main Protestant church, the Evangelical Church of French Polynesia, which attracts the allegiance of half of the territory's population, was urging 'an end to the nuclear tests' and has been promoting the rights of the Maohi people, which has a nationalist ring. A proposal to integrate French Polynesia with the EEC aroused popular fears of being swamped by European immigrants, which caused a 90 per cent boycott of the European Parliament election in the territory in June 1990. But the prospect of an imminent ending of nuclear testing, with the announcement by the French Government in April 1992 of the suspension of tests, sent shock waves through the territory. This by-product of the ending of the Cold War and spreading nuclear test bans presaged

---

39. Henningham, *France and the South Pacific* 140–1, 148–55, 242. Karin von Strokirch, 'The Impact of Nuclear Testing on Politics in French Polynesia', *Journal of Pacific History* 26, 1991, 330–2.

sharp reductions of French expenditure in the territory, on which its economy almost wholly depended.[40]

OTHER PACIFIC NATIONS AND THE FRENCH PRESENCE IN THE PACIFIC

The CEP aroused widespread opposition from French Polynesia's Pacific neighbours in the 1980s. The election of Labour Party governments in Australia in 1983 and in New Zealand in 1984 increased the vehemence of those countries' opposition to French nuclear tests. These governments were unimpressed by the French claim that the tests contributed to nuclear deterrence in Europe and have argued that if underground testing was as safe at Moruroa as Paris has claimed, it could be conducted in France. Particularly galling to those Pacific nations has been France's rejection of an offer by the US Government to use its nuclear testing facilities in Nevada. The CEP had become a symbol of French military independence.[41]

New Zealand's relations with France nose-dived after the sinking in Auckland harbour, on 10 July 1985, of the *Rainbow Warrior*. That Greenpeace ship, which was on its way to monitor nuclear testing at Moruroa, was ripped apart by two explosions which killed its Spanish photographer. An anti-French furore broke out in New Zealand with the arrest of two French agents, Alain Mafart and Dominique Prieur, who were convicted and jailed for planting the bombs. The French Government retaliated with commercial pressure against New Zealand exports of wool to France and of lamb to New Caledonia and threatened to pressure the EEC to reduce the quota for New Zealand butter. New Zealand, which depended on an increasingly vulnerable agricultural economy, was forced to accept a deal of US$7 million

---

40. Ibid., 332–46. 'Memorandum of the 1986 Synod of the Evangelical Church in French Polynesia', *Pacific Conference of Churches News* January 1987, 4. Bruno Saura, 'The Tahitian Churches and the Problem of the French Presence in 1991', *Journal of Pacific History* 26, 1991, 347–57. Karin von Strokirch, 'Suspension of Nuclear Testing: The Implications for French Polynesia', paper read at the 9th Pacific History Association Conference, Christchurch, New Zealand, 4 December 1992. Henningham, *France and the South Pacific* 158–62.

41. Ibid., 169–70, 223. Firth, *Nuclear Playground* 116–19.

compensation and the release of Mafart and Prieur to serve detention for three years on Hao Atoll in French Polynesia. But within two years the Chirac Government brought the two agents back to France to resume military duties. New Zealand took this broken agreement to international arbitration and received a favourable judgement in April 1990. France was directed to pay a further US$2 million to New Zealand citizens, which France honoured.[42]

Australian relations with France declined also when Prime Minister Robert Hawke criticized the Chirac Government's confrontationist policies in New Caledonia, though not supporting the Kanak independence movement. The Australian consul in Noumea was expelled. Relations between the two countries remained at a low ebb until the advent of the Rocard Socialist Government, which promoted mutual prime ministerial visits between France and Australia in 1989. Rocard also repaired French relations with New Zealand with a public apology for the *Rainbow Warrior* affair. The ironical sequel was France's permission for *Rainbow Warrior II* to carry out the snooping in French Polynesia which France had sought to end with the bombing of its predecessor.[43]

AUSTRALASIA AND THE US

New Zealand also was involved in diplomatic conflict with the US in the 1980s. In 1984 the New Zealand Labour Party won office with a platform including opposition to visits of nuclear-armed ships to New Zealand. Effectively this policy banned US warships from New Zealand since the US policy was 'neither to confirm nor to deny' the nuclear arming of its warships. The new prime minister in Wellington, David Lange, was 'puzzled' by the way the New Zealand policy so upset the US. 'Whatever the Russians might be up to in the South Pacific', he wrote, 'it wasn't very much', therefore 'the presence in South Pacific harbours of American nuclear vessels wasn't going to make the least difference. New Zealand itself, a thousand miles distant from its neighbour, was not going to become the focus of Soviet strategic planning'. Yet he found hostile US officials 'unable

42. Henningham, *France and the South Pacific* 224–6.
43. Ibid., 226–9. Connell, *New Caledonia or Kanaky* 394–5.

to talk about events in the South Pacific without framing them in terms of a global struggle between the United States and the Soviet Union'.[44]

With the refusal in January 1985 by Lange's government to allow port-access to USS *Buchanan*, the first test case of the anti-nuclear policy, the US cancelled most of the military cooperation with New Zealand that had been part of the Australia, New Zealand, United States Security Treaty (ANZUS). With New Zealand's refusal to submit to this diplomatic pressure, the American Secretary of State, George Schulz, announced in July 1986 that the US would suspend its ANZUS obligations to defend New Zealand. While that country was of minimal strategic importance, Washington was deeply concerned about the precedent that New Zealand was creating, which might encourage more strategically important Pacific Islands to deny entry to US warships. The New Zealand Government's response was to emphasize a self-reliant defence policy. Opponents pointed to the incapacity of the nation's small industrial base and limited financial resources to maintain the stated Labour policy of defending not only New Zealand but also its dependent Pacific Islands states: the Cook Islands, Niue and Tokelau.[45]

Australia, the other partner in ANZUS, also opposed the New Zealand nuclear ship policy. In Lange's view, his Australian Labor colleague, Hawke, 'was just the man to encourage his country's infatuation with America'. Occupying a vast underpopulated continent, Australians have traditionally looked to great world powers to guarantee their defence, first to Great Britain and, with the British retreat from Asia by the 1960s, to the US. Left wing members of the Australian Labor Party had advocated banning US warships from Australian ports, but they were a minority within the party, which on assuming office in 1983 conducted a review of the ANZUS policy and fully endorsed the alliance. Whereas New Zealand's geographic isolation encouraged majority popular support for nuclear-free policies, the longstanding public nervousness about potential designs on Australia by foreign powers, which had been reinforced by threatened Japanese invasion in 1942 and postwar fears of Chinese communist expansionism, restricted opponents of the US alliance to a

44. David Lange, *Nuclear Free – The New Zealand Way* (Auckland 1990) 40.

45. Peter Jennings, *The Armed Forces of New Zealand and the ANZUS Split: Costs and Consequences* (Wellington 1988) chs 2–3. Ewan Jamieson, *Friend or Ally: New Zealand at Odds with its Past* (Sydney 1990) chs 2–3. Michael McKinley, 'The New Zealand Perspective on ANZUS and Nuclear Weapons' in John Ravenhill (ed.), *No Longer an American Lake?* (Sydney 1989) ch. 2.

small minority of the Australian community. Australia was willing to continue the traditional close defence cooperation with New Zealand. Australia's Foreign Secretary, Bill Hayden, reminded his parliament that 'Blood is thicker than water. Australia and New Zealand have certainly spilled enough of it together'. Also, since 1983 these two nations have been pursuing a programme to achieve complete free trade between them by 1995. However, on the nuclear ships issue, while suggesting to Washington a less condemnatory policy towards New Zealand, the Australian Labor Government was concerned not to upset in any way its treaty relationship with the US. As a major contribution to the alliance Australia hosted a wide range of communication, command, control and intelligence installations supporting wider world US naval operations and military space surveillance.[46]

The US did extend half an olive branch to New Zealand in 1990, offering to renew high-level diplomatic contacts between the two nations. However, there was no revival of the defence alliance. The dying of the Cold War had not thawed US concern to isolate the New Zealand anti-nuclear ship disease. In New Zealand the strength of public support for the policy was such that the Opposition National Party, which won a sweeping victory in the October 1990 election, did not promise to abandon the nuclear ships policy. However, in the new strategic environment of 1992 that resolve had dissipated, and New Zealand's relations with the US had markedly improved.[47]

THE US AND THE PACIFIC ISLANDS

The US use of the Pacific for nuclear ships and weapons engendered diplomatic tension with other Pacific islands in the 1980s, especially

---

46. Lange, *Nuclear Free* 46. Stuart McMillan, *Neither Confirm nor Deny: The Nuclear Ships Dispute between New Zealand and the United States* (Wellington 1987) ch. 13. Andrew Mack, 'Australian Defence Policy and the ANZUS Alliance' in Ravenhill, *American Lake* ch. 6. P.J. Lloyd, 'Australia-New Zealand Trade Relations: NAFTA to CER' in Sinclair (ed.), *Tasman Relations* 142–63. P.J. Lloyd, *The Future of CER: A Single Market for Australia and New Zealand* (Wellington 1991) 40. Desmond Ball, *A Suitable Piece of Real Estate: American Installations in Australia* (Sydney 1980) chs 4–10.

47. Jamieson, *Friend or Ally* chs 11, 13.

Palau. The constitutional ban on the presence of any nuclear weapons in this territory required a 75 per cent vote in a popular referendum to amend it. However, the US Administration and its supporters in Palau placed strong pressure on other Palauans to throw out the anti-nuclear clause. From 1983 to 1990 Palauans were subjected to seven such referenda in attempts to secure the requisite majority. It was never reached despite strong American economic cajolery with promises of $430 million in aid if Palau entered a compact of free association with the US without the anti-nuclear clause, as well as violent intimidation against Palauan supporters of the constitution. The chairman of the 1979 constitutional convention and Palauan president, Haruo Remeliik, was murdered on 1 July 1985, the first assassination of a Pacific Islands head of state. Four Palauans belonging to the anti-nuclear cause were charged with the murder but not convicted because of the absence of any strong motive and inadequate evidence. Many pro-constitution Palauans believe he was murdered by the CIA, alleging that he was about to reveal details of a financial scandal associated with the purchase of a 15 megawatt power generating plant from a British firm, International Power Systems Inc, which was too big for Palau's need and had imposed a crippling debt burden on its budget. US officials deny the charge. Remeliik's successor, Lazarus Salii, who was facing corruption allegations, committed suicide in 1988. The relentless pressure from the US and its Palauan supporters did achieve a 73 per cent vote in favour of changing the constitution in August 1987, and the same majority was given for a compact agreement with the US without the anti-nuclear provisions, which the American Congress moved to ratify. But in a climate of personal intimidation, including murder and firebombings, the Palau Supreme Court declared the compact vote unconstitutional. By February 1990 only 61 per cent of voters approved a compact with the US.[48]

The strong US interest in Palau devolved principally from its strategic location. This island group is 800 kilometres east of the Philippines where major American bases faced the threat of future prohibition. Palau is a southern anchor for a fallback defensive arc of islands going north through Guam to Tinian in the North Marianas. Palau's good harbours prompted the US to demand of Palauans

48. Firth, *Nuclear Playground* 62–4. Richard J. Pamentier, 'The Rhetoric of Free Association and Palau's Political Struggle', *The Contemporary Pacific* 3, 1991, 146–58. Robie, *Blood on their Banner* ch. 9.

the reservation of about a third of the biggest island in the group, Babeldaop, for potential base facilities. The other main points of the defensive arc were safely under US control. Guam remained US territory, without any major independence movement; and the North Marianas continued to succumb to the economic attractions of a compact of free association with the US which gave America full defence rights.[49]

Elsewhere in the Pacific the US was opposing a push by island states for a nuclear free Pacific. In 1985 there was an agreement to implement a Pacific Nuclear Free Zone Treaty at a meeting of the South Pacific Forum at Rarotonga in the Cook Islands. It was the culmination of a gradual development since the 1960s, which had received a fillip from a New Zealand Labour government initiative in 1975 to request UN support for a South Pacific nuclear free zone, which had been granted by a vote of 110 to nil with 20 abstentions, though vigorously opposed by the US. The Rarotonga treaty was pushed by the Australian Labor Government, supported by New Zealand and by the Polynesian states except Tonga. In reality it was an Australian move to preserve the Pacific from a more radical proposal being proposed by Vanuatu and supported by the other two Melanesian independent states. The Rarotonga treaty opposed nuclear testing, the dumping of nuclear waste and land-based nuclear weapons. It did not prohibit the transporting of nuclear weapons by air or sea across the Pacific or missile testing. Nauru and the Melanesian states argued that this freedom did not really make the Pacific a nuclear free zone. Australia rejected their attempt to include missile testing in the treaty's prohibitions. New Zealand's support for the Rarotonga treaty reflected its concern to limit diplomatic fallout with the US. Yet the Reagan Administration in Washington, lobbied vigorously by France, refused to endorse even this Australian attempt to protect US nuclear activities in the Pacific, arguing that 'a proliferation of such [nuclear free] zones in the free world, unmatched by disarmament in the Soviet bloc, is clearly detrimental to Western security'.[50]

49. Ibid. 163. Firth, *Nuclear Playground*, 60–4.
50. Quoted in Michael Hamel-Green, *The South Pacific Nuclear Free Zone Treaty: A Critical Assessment* (Canberra 1990) 114. For the nuclear free zone see ibid., *passim* and Robie, *Blood on their Banner* ch. 8.

AUSTRALIA, INDONESIA AND THE ISLANDS

Australia remained the main metropolitan power in the South Pacific during the 1980s. In 1989 its armed forces numbered 69,600, far more than the rest of the South Pacific, including New Zealand, combined. After using its military transport capacities to support Papua New Guinea's intervention in Vanuatu in 1980, Australia maintained a generally low profile and pursued a policy of 'constructive commitment'. As an Australian high commissioner to Papua New Guinea confessed, one of his main policies was to ensure that Australia was not seen to be dictating to its former colony. However, while giving equipment and army training support to Papua New Guinea's attempts to suppress the Bougainville rebellion, the Australian Government did protest about abuses of human rights by Papua New Guinea defence forces in that region. Australia also provided military aid to other South Pacific nations, such as riot-control equipment to Vanuatu when the government there in 1988 faced internal disturbances following a split in the ruling Vanua'aku Party. The Australian Government was concerned to keep communist influence out of the South Pacific, and there was a brief scare in 1987 about Libyan intervention to support Kanak and other potential Pacific Islands rebels. But Australia relied on its substantial financial aid, which in the financial year 1988–89 amounted to AUS$1 billion for island states, and retention of good relations with island governments to maintain political stability in the South Pacific. The financial aid was a vital ingredient for the budgets of Papua New Guinea and also was important for micro states such as Tuvalu, which in 1988–89 received from Australia AUS$1.3 million for developmental aid, which was more than 20 per cent of the island group's annual revenue.[51]

The economic vicissitudes of the 1980s had made many of the island economies more vulnerable than before. Even the wealthiest Pacific state, Nauru, was feeling the effects of declining phosphate production, which was due to die out in 1995. This problem was sharpening the republic's case, being prepared at the end of 1990, for a hearing before the International Court of Justice for AUS$72 million

---

51. Henningham, *France and the South Pacific* 221. Information from Mr Michael Wilson. John Connell, 'Vanuatu' in 'Political Review: Melanesia', *The Contemporary Pacific* 1, 1989, 163–4. Greg Fry (ed.), *Australia's Regional Security* (Sydney 1991) ch. 11. The Parliament of the Commonwealth of Australia, *Australia's Relations with the South Pacific* (Canberra 1989) 57–8. FEA 1991, 833.

compensation for damages caused by phosphate mining during the period of Australian administration. Australia was marshalling its case to resist the claim.[52]

Australia tried to retain good relations with its potentially powerful Southeast Asian neighbour, Indonesia. Canberra was careful to refrain from any support for guerillas in East Timor and Irian Jaya by muting criticisms of human rights abuses in those territories and other parts of Indonesia. However, the Australian Government could not stop a sharp cooling of relations in 1986 when the *Sydney Morning Herald* published an article exposing corruption and nepotism in the ruling Suharto family in Indonesia. However, by 1991 good relations between Australia and Indonesia had been restored to the extent that Australia was able to express to Jakarta its 'deep concern over the killings' in the Dili massacre in East Timor in November that year without any diplomatic downturn. Also, while there were some differences in Indonesian-Australian policies in the South Pacific, such as Indonesia's quick establishment of good relations with the post-coup government of Fiji, there has been a recent common concern to preserve the stability of island governments, especially with regard to the secessionist movement in Bougainville.[53]

CONCLUSIONS

The greater violence in the Pacific Islands in the 1980s was due principally to the continuation and the legacy of Euro-American imperialism in the Pacific. The British Empire had bequeathed to Fiji the racial tensions which underlay the Fiji coups. Moreover, the power of pro-coup eastern Fijian chiefs, which had been threatened by political change, had been entrenched by British colonial policy.

52. Stuart Inder, 'Nauru' in 'Political Reviews', *The Contemporary Pacific* 4. 1982, 188–90. For economic problems of other states see Christopher Browne and Douglas A. Scott, *Economic Development in Seven Pacific Island Countries* (Washington 1989).

53. David Jenkins, 'The Quiet, Bald Moneymaker of Jakarta's Elite', *Sydney Morning Herald* 19 April 1986. Desmond Ball and Helen Wilson (eds), *Strange Neighbours: The Australia-Indonesia Relationship* (Sydney 1991) chs 1–2, 5–6, 11–16. Australian Department of Foreign Affairs and Trade, 'Briefing for Meeting with Non-Government Organisations' 28 November 1991.

France's world power pretensions, which imposed the CEP in the Pacific, and the presence of a large French community in New Caledonia were the principal causes of the violence inflamed by Kanak aspirations for independence. The US concern to preserve the North Pacific Islands as a wide-ranging security zone created a climate of violence in Palau. The US demand for free passage of nuclear ships caused diplomatic conflict with New Zealand, where there was also an outbreak of violence caused by the presence there of a ship representing wider world opposition to French nuclear testing. France also pressed the US to oppose even the moderate nuclear free Pacific proposal suggested in American interests by the US's firm ally, Australia. Australia needed to provide additional defence assistance to Papua New Guinea to cope with the violent legacy of Australian and German colonialism which had separated Buka and Bougainville from the rest of the Solomon Islands. Consequently, during the 1980s the Pacific Islands had become a less peaceful region whereas other conflicts in the Pacific Basin were moving towards peaceful resolutions. The ending of the Cold War, though, may well remove some of the Pacific Islands tensions, as was happening in 1992 in US-New Zealand relations.

CHAPTER NINE

War and Cooperation in the Western Hemisphere since 1980

In the Eastern Pacific Basin in the 1980s the US Administration, especially under President Reagan, was still strongly opposed to revolutionary movements with any Marxist flavour. That is the main theme of this chapter, concentrating on the surrogate war fought by the US against the Sandinista Government of Nicaragua and support for Latin American governments combatting Marxist insurgencies. It demonstrates how the Cold War dominated the Latin American policies of the Reagan Administration at the same time as there were improving relations with China and the Soviet Union in the West Pacific Basin. Another theme is the degree to which, in the Cold War cause, the American administrations from 1980 to 1991 were willing to tolerate violations of human rights by anti-democratic governments. Another theme is US economic relations with nations of the Western Hemisphere. Also the interrelations of Latin American governments are discussed. The chapter ends with a consideration of relations between the Americas and the rest of the Pacific Basin.

THE US CRUSADE AGAINST NICARAGUA

Whereas Carter's Administration had accepted the coming to power of the Sandinista Government in Nicaragua in 1979, the Republican Party National Platform for the 1980 presidential election campaign declared: 'We abhor the Marxist-Sandinista takeover of Nicaragua'. Consequently, this small Central American republic became one of

Reagan's prime targets in his worldwide anti-communist crusade. An intense propaganda campaign was launched to convince the US public that Nicaragua was a second Cuba, another domino in the Soviet plot to impose communist dictatorship on the whole of Central America. The Sandinistas were presented as a symptom of a disease spreading in America's own 'backyard' and a threat in America's 'strategic rear'. The issue was also linked to America's championship of world freedom against the colossus of Soviet communism. Reagan exclaimed: 'If Central America were to fall, what would the consequence be for our position in Asia, Europe, and the alliances such as NATO? If the United States cannot respond to a threat near our own borders, why should Europeans or Asians believe that we are seriously concerned about threats to them?'. [1]

The Sandinista regime was not blameless in the confrontation with the US that developed in 1981. Concerned about potential threats from right wing neighbouring countries, the decision was made in 1979 to build up the Nicaraguan army, which was small under Somoza. Distrust of the US and ideological factors turned the Sandinista Government to Cuba and the USSR for arms, a move which was literally a red rag to wave at the American bull. The Nicaraguan army's size by 1981 was still small – 6,700 troops and another 8,000 paramilitary forces – and it was certainly not overwhelming compared with the 11,200 strong Honduras army and El Salvador's 17,000 troops. In addition the only confirmed delivery of Soviet heavy equipment to Nicaragua had been three light tanks. But because of its military ties with Cuba and the USSR, Nicaragua was already a concern to its neighbours and to the US. The most damaging Sandinista policy, in American eyes, was to provide a conduit for Cuban arms for Marxist guerillas who were pressing to overthrow the anti-communist regime in El Salvador. This was the excuse used by Reagan to suspend on 1 April 1981 the $15 million remaining from a $75 million aid package for Nicaragua provided by Carter. The Sandinistas, however, expected Reagan to condemn them whatever they did and therefore had no intention of abandoning the rebels in El Salvador, despite denying sending any weapons. [2]

1. Thomas W. Walker (ed.), *Nicaragua: The First Five Years* (New York 1985) 22–4. Edward Best, *US Policy and Regional Security in Central America* (London 1987) 51. Viron Vaky, 'Reagan's Central American Policy: An Isthmus Restored' in Robert S. Leiken (ed.) *Central America: Anatomy of a Conflict* (New York 1984) 233–57.

2. William M. LeoGrande, 'The United States and Nicaragua' in Walker, *Nicaragua* 425–29. Best. *US Policy and Regional Security* 51–3.

The US did offer a deal to the Sandinista Government. If it stopped supporting the El Salvadorian rebels and ceased its military expansion, Washington would be prepared to offer a non-aggression pact with Nicaragua, paramilitary training camps in the US for Cuban and Nicaraguan refugees would be closed, and Congress would be asked to restore economic aid. The deeply suspicious Sandinistas were not prepared to barter the El Salvadorian rebels or cuts in military expenditure for Washington's promises to abide by its own Neutrality Act and the Inter-American Treaty of Reciprocal Assistance of 1947, in which the principle of non-intervention in the affairs of other Latin American states had been established.[3]

With the failure of diplomacy, hardliners within the Washington Administration, supported by Reagan, gained the ascendancy over those who still sought to negotiate with the Sandinistas. A strong rebel offensive in El Salvador strengthened the case for military action. Secretary of State Alexander Haig, an ex-army general, sought to block the sources of supplies to the rebels without addressing the social conditions inside El Salvador which had spawned the rebellion. Direct US military action in El Salvador and Nicaragua was ruled out in these post Vietnam War days, when US foreign policy makers feared the political consequences of embroilment in potentially protracted and unpopular warfare. But, as well as a policy of imposing on Nicaragua economic isolation, it was decided to launch covert paramilitary action inside that nation, ostensibly to interdict arms flows but with the ultimate intention of overthrowing the Sandinista Government. Reagan signed in December 1981 an authorization for the CIA to spend $19.8 million to create a paramilitary force in Honduras for operations inside Nicaragua.[4]

These rebels, made up of ex-National Guardsmen, other former supporters of Somoza and opponents of the Sandinistas, were known as 'contras', who from May 1982 were receiving direct training by the CIA. But though 10,000 strong by 1983, the contras did not have sufficient power or popular support to challenge the Sandinistas in urban areas. The rebels restricted their activities to rural regions, especially in the northwest of the country, and utilized safe havens across the Honduras border. Their operations were mostly attacks on bridges, power generators, state farms, rural health clinics and small

---

3. Ibid. 52–3. LeoGrande, 'The United States and Nicaragua', 429–30.
4. Ibid. 431–4. Best, *US Policy and Regional Security* 55–7. William I. Robinson and Kent Norsworthy, *David and Goliath: Washington's War Against Nicaragua* (London 1987) 41–5. Pastor, *Condemned to Repetition* 230–6.

villages. The human rights agency Americas Watch reported in 1985 that contras 'systematically engaged in the killing of prisoners and the unarmed, including medical relief personnel; selective targets on civilians, and indiscriminate attacks; torture and other outrages against personal dignity'. Against rapidly expanding Sandinista armed forces, which by mid-1984 were estimated to number 61,800, and which clearly had the support of the majority of the population, the contras could gain no permanent base inside the country.[5]

Realizing that the covert war against Nicaragua was not being won, the CIA in mid-1983 assumed direct command. Using its own people and specially trained Latin Americans, US planes bombed selected targets. Fast speedboats, supplied by the US Drugs Enforcement Agency, launched attacks on harbour facilities and oil storages. In January 1984 CIA operatives started to lay mines in Nicaragua's harbours, which by April had sunk or damaged ten commercial ships, one of them Russian. When the USSR delivered a sharp protest, Washington simply replied that the mines and all other attacks were the work of the contras.[6]

However, the CIA was unable to keep secret its involvement in the undeclared war against Nicaragua. The revelation that American-planted mines were sinking ships in Nicaragua's harbours created a public uproar in the US. Even the Republican-controlled Senate passed a resolution in April 1984 calling for an end to the mining by eighty-four votes to twelve. More seriously for the Administration, the Democrat-controlled House of Representatives, members of which were becoming suspicious about the misuse of funds that were restricted officially to interdiction of arms supplies, voted to cut off all aid to the contras.[7]

The Administration did not accept this House decision. A surrogate network was established to distribute to the contras funds solicited from overseas allies of the US like Saudi Arabia, from private donations, and from the proceeds of arms sales, in violation of US

---

5. R. Pardo-Maurer, *The Contras, 1980–1989: A Special Kind of Politics* (London 1990) 2–3. Peter Kornbluh, 'The Covert War' in Thomas W. Walker (ed.), *Reagan Versus the Sandinistas: The Undeclared War on Nicaragua* (Boulder 1987) 21–8. Best, *US Policy and Regional Security* 56–60. Janus Bugajski, *Sandinista Communism and Rural Nicaragua* (New York 1990) ch. 5.

6. Kornbluh, 'The Covert War' 28–31. Robinson and Norsworthy, *David and Goliath* chs 3–4.

7. William M. LeoGrande, 'The Contras and Congress' in Walker (ed.), *Reagan Versus the Sandinistas* 202–13. Cynthia J. Arnson, *Crossroads: Congress, the Reagan Administration, and Central America* (New York 1989) 154–68.

neutrality laws, to Iran for its war against Iraq in exchange for the release of American hostages in Lebanon. Over \$60 million was raised by these efforts during the eighteen months of the congressional arms ban for the secret delivery of arms and equipment to the contras.[8]

This covert funding effort kept the contras going, their operations depending almost entirely on American money. Meanwhile, the Administration launched a massive propaganda campaign to reverse the congressional decision. Frank McNeil, a senior member of the State Department's Bureau of Intelligence and Research, commented: 'the intelligence process was prostituted to a desire to convince Congress to renew assistance to the Contras'. The contras were 'freedom fighters' opposing a Marxist 'tyranny', despite the fact that in 1984 the Sandinistas had held elections in which they received 63 per cent of the vote, in polls which were declared open and fair by international observers. To gain the support of Democrats in Congress, the Administration falsely claimed that pressure from the contras was the only way to get the Sandinista Government to negotiate for the restoration of democracy. Indeed, the US Administration pressured opposition candidates in Nicaragua to withdraw from the 1984 election in order to discredit it as a one horse race. Contras also took military action to prevent people from voting, though 75 per cent of registered voters participated. Washington harped on Sandinista human rights abuses, which ignored more serious violations by the contras. The Nicaragua Government was even charged with smuggling drugs to poison the youth of America. This unprovable charge was made while the US was using a known drug runner, General Manuel Antonio Noriega, the dictator of Panama, to provide the contras with information via the Panamanian embassy in Managua and as a source of financial aid.[9]

This intense pressure from Reagan, to whom the downfall of the Sandinistas had become an obsession, reversed the congressional ban. Congressmen had been worn down by the barrage of propaganda about the evils of the Sandinistas and the virtues of the contras. In vain did liberal Democrats legitimately claim that Nicaragua's closeness to Cuba and the USSR was a consequence of the undeclared

8. Kornbluh, 'The Covert War', 31–3.

9. Frank McNeil, *War and Peace in Central America* (New York 1988) 218. Eldon Kenworthy, 'Selling the Policy' in Walker (ed.), *Reagan Versus the Sandinistas* 159–77. Susanne Jonas, 'Elections and Transitions: The Guatemala and Nicaragua Cases' in John A. Booth and Mitchell A. Seligson (eds), *Elections and Democracy in Central America* (Chapel Hill 1989) 141–50. Frederick Kempe, *Divorcing the Dictator: America's Bungled Affair with Noriega* (New York 1990) ch. 11.

war which the US was waging. In reality the overstretched Soviet Union was unable to extend major financial support to Nicaragua in a region of no strategic importance to the USSR. Nor could Democrats gain mileage from the brutality and corruption of the contras against administration denials of the accuracy of the relevant reports. Political threats from party leaders helped switch the votes of Republican opponents of contra aid. In June 1986 a bill providing $100 million aid to the contras was approved in the House of Representatives by 221 votes to 209.[10]

Renewed American financial aid, however, did not save the contras. In the mid-term congressional election in November 1986 the Republicans lost control of the Senate. This defeat rendered the Reagan Administration vulnerable to the disclosure, which emerged within the next month, of information concerning the use of money from armaments sales to Iran to fund the contras. The Democrats were able to use their numbers in the Senate to launch a full investigation of the deals, which quickly became known as the Irangate affair, a reference to the Watergate cover-up of illegal government activity. The contras, however, gained significant publicity from the testimonies about the 'glorious' cause they represented. Flush with the money voted to them, they had been carrying out destructive raids deeper into Nicaragua, causing further damage to the badly faltering Nicaraguan economy. But Irangate had raised, for the first time since the last years of the Vietnam War, the issue of presidential control of foreign policy. The Administration's flouting of congress tipped the balance in the House of Representatives. In February 1988 the Administration's request for renewed aid for the contras was defeated. Deprived of vital financial assistance and wracked by internal disputes and poor leadership, the contra movement in 1988 rapidly lost effectiveness.[11]

Furthermore, there had been in 1987 a peace agreement between Nicaragua and its Central American neighbours. As early as 1984 a peace plan had been advanced by Mexico, Venezuela, Colombia and Panama, frontline states to the region of Central American conflict. In 1983 they had formed the Contadora group, named after the Panamanian Island where they met, to establish a common approach

---

10. LeoGrande, 'The Contras and Congress' 219–23. Bruce D. Larkin (ed.), *Vital Interests: The Soviet Issue in U.S. Central American Policy* (Boulder 1988) parts 2 and 3. Nicola Miller, *Soviet Relations with Latin America* (Cambridge 1989) ch. 7. Arnson, *Crossroads* 175–98.

11. Leslie Cockburn, *Out of Control: The Story of the Reagan Administration's Secret War in Nicaragua, the Illegal Arms Pipeline, and the Contra Drug Connection* (New York 1987) 247–9. Pardo-Maurer, *The Contras* ch. 5. Arnson, *Crossroads*, 201–9, 212–20.

to regional security. In the next year they forwarded a plan for ending the Nicaraguan conflict. Its major features were: respect for the sovereign rights of all states, mutual demilitarization, reduction in foreign military advisers and no support for insurgencies in other states. Nicaragua assented to the plan if the other Central American states would agree. But the US, alarmed by this move which would spell the end to its covert war against Nicaragua, placed pressure on the other Central American countries not to sign the treaty.

By 1987 these republics were willing to revive a peace plan put forward by Costa Rica's premier, Oscar Arias. A reason for this change was that the neighbouring countries no longer believed that Nicaragua was a threat to them, despite Reagan's propaganda about the alleged menace of the Soviet-supported military build-up there. The actual military balance was much more even. In 1985 Nicaragua had the largest army of the Central American republics, but also, with US assistance, neighbouring states had been strengthening their own armies. The Arias plan called for a cessation of aid to all insurgent groups and for domestic reconciliation based upon a cease-fire. This time the Central American republics resisted the pressure from the US, Irangate having created, in their view, a 'lame duck' Administration there. These states were keen to rid their region of insurgency violence, and in August 1987 in Guatemala City Nicaragua signed with them an accord which protected the Nicaraguan Government in return for a pledge from the Sandinistas not to support insurgency, to work towards national reconciliation with political opponents, and to hold elections in 1990.[12]

Despite this accord, the US did not relax economic sanctions against Nicaragua. In May 1988 Congress also voted for strictly controlled humanitarian aid for the contras, which prevented their dissipation. However, in March 1988 the Sandinista Government had signed an agreement with the contras for a sixty-day cease-fire, which was given monthly extensions, though some contra raids recommenced before the end of the year.

The Sandinistas called an election to be held on 26 February 1990. Most of the opposition parties combined in a National Opposition

12. Dunkerley, *Power in the Isthmus* 317–8, 324–6. Raúl Benítez Manaut et al., 'Armed Forces, Society, and the People: Cuba and Nicaragua' in Augusto Varas (ed.), *Democracy Under Siege: New Military Power in Latin America* (New York 1989) 152–4. Rico F. Carlos, 'The Contradora Experience and the Future of Collective Security' in Richard J. Bloomfield and Gregory F. Treverton (eds), *Alternative to Intervention: A New U.S.-Latin American Security Relationship* (Boulder 1990) 93–114.

Union, the *Unión Nacional de Opositora* (UNO). Its presidential candidate was Violeta Barrios de Chamorro, the owner of the *La Prensa* newspaper, who had a national status as an unflinching opponent of the Sandinistas. She had a Cory Aquino-style stature as the sixty-year-old smiling-eyed and matronly widow of the country's most famous martyr, Pedro Joaquín Chamorro, the leader of the bourgeois opposition to Somoza, who had been murdered by the dictator's National Guard in 1978. The Bush Administration persuaded Congress to vote $9 million in financial aid to UNO so as 'to level the playing field' in the contest with the governing Sandinistas, who were fielding as their candidate President Ortega. More effectively for the US cause, the economic blockade and the contra war had produced grave shortages of consumer goods and hyperinflation, and there was a popular belief that the US restrictions would be lifted only if Ortega were defeated. Consequently, Chamorro won with 55 per cent of the vote; and UNO gained 52 seats in the 90–seat National Assembly. The US had finally achieved the demise of the Sandinistas and promptly restored economic ties as well as supplying financial aid to the Chamorro Government. But by trying to conciliate the Sandinistas this government had earned right wing criticism and was facing incipient violence between elements of the left and the right.[13]

THE US AND THE LONG WAR IN EL SALVADOR

During the Republican Administrations in the 1980s El Salvador was a reverse case of major US support for anti-communist regimes, no matter what kind of government they were; it was a continuation of the former style of US policies in the Western Pacific Basin. As in Nicaragua, these were also more reactionary than Carter's El Salvador policies. The El Salavadorian Government, which had emerged after the coup of October 1979, was a combined military/civilian regime, and in May 1980 it joined in a coalition with the middle-class Christian Democratic Party. A major problem was that the new government had insufficient control over the security services, which continued to

---

13. Penny O'Donnell, *Death Dreams & Dancing in Nicaragua* (Sydney 1991) 195–223. *Keesing's Record of World Events* vol. 36, 37236–7, 37272; vol. 37, 38236.

carry out acts of violence against perceived enemies of the oligarchy. In January police opened fire on a peaceful march by a working-class opposition group, killing twenty-four marchers. The influential Catholic archbishop of San Salvador, Oscar Romero, urged Christian Democrats to leave the government and wrote to Carter requesting the withdrawal of an offer of $50 million aid to El Salvador. On 24 March Romero was assassinated while saying mass; and police opened fire on a crowd of about 80,000 gathering for his funeral. The government's legitimacy was rapidly disintegrating but, supported by the US, the Christian Democrats stayed in the coalition, thus destroying any hope of gaining popular support for a confrontation with the oligarchy and its murderous servants. The party's leader, Joseph Napoleón Duarte, later explained: 'The Christian Democrats were too afraid of violent attacks from the Right and the Left'.[14]

The Carter Administration was concerned about the possibility of a right wing coup. Its ambassador in San Salvador warned the coup plotters that the US would not tolerate such a move. Washington was placing its faith in the Christian Democrats to carry out meaningful reform. However, Carter's patience ran out when continuing right wing violence struck down three American Catholic nuns and a female lay-worker, whose bullet ridden bodies were found in a shallow grave. On 5 December 1980 US military aid to El Salvador was suspended. Two weeks later, however, the aid was restored after Duarte took control of the government and announced that the murders were being thoroughly investigated. Only four National Guard scapegoats were ultimately charged with the crime, which certainly involved higher military officers.[15]

With the advent of the Reagan Administration, the emphasis of US policy towards El Salvador changed. This shift was associated with a major offensive launched by Marxist insurgents in mid-January. During 1980 separate insurgent groups had combined into a National Liberation Front, the *Farabundo Martí Frente de Libearción Nacional* (FMLN). Assisted by arms from Cuba via Nicaragua, the FMLN was hoping for a general popular uprising, Nicaragua-style, provoked by the unpopularity of the government. This was the offensive creating the alarm in Washington that drove Reagan to launch his campaign against Nicaragua as well as to provide large-scale military aid to Duarte's regime in El Salvador.

14. Max G. Manwaring and Court Prisk, *El Salvador at War: An Oral History of Conflict from the 1979 Insurrection to the Present* (Washington 1988) 49–58. Balora, *El Salvador in Transition* 86–101.

15. Ibid. 105–16. McClintock, *American Connection* vol. 1, 257–83.

The FMLN's 1981 offensive did not inspire the anticipated popular uprising. The country was not being governed by an avaricious dictator like Somoza, and the Christian Democratic Party had church support and popularity going back to the days when it led the political opposition to the oligarchy. In addition the government had tried to implement reform, especially a decree in March 1980 for the expropriation of all properties of over 500 hectares in size for the formation of farm cooperatives. The reforms were to face trenchant oligarchic opposition, but initially they preserved the Christian Democratic Party's popular image.[16]

While the FMLN could not overthrow the government, it did attract significant popular support. The government's land reform programme did not assist the 60 per cent of peasants who were landless. Declining economic conditions following the Fútbal War, the oligarchy's emphasis on commercial farming, and rising prices for oil and manufactured goods, coupled with falling agricultural prices had greatly reduced the average standard of living. Thus, despite operating in a country far smaller than Nicaragua, with fewer mountainous retreats and with no cross-border havens as were enjoyed by the contras, the FMLN with some 8,000 insurgents, maintained an effective guerilla war. They were aided by the government's repressive counter-insurgency policies. The FMLN practice of releasing prisoners of war encouraged many of the press-ganged recruits in the army, which grew to 50,000, to surrender. But US military aid, which increased from $5.9 million in 1980 to $236.5 million in 1984, was a crucial factor in preventing a guerilla victory in the long-running war. Building on false claims of physical Nicaraguan involvement in the opening offensive of the war, Reagan nominated El Salvador as one of the dominoes that would fall into Soviet hands should the guerillas achieve victory. In fact the Soviet Union had no intention of aiding a guerilla movement which it did not see as having much chance of success; also, such aid would jeopardize its relations with other Latin American countries.[17]

Reagan also tolerated the return of the oligarchy to power, in the form of a new party, the *Alianza Republicana Nacionalista* (ARENA), in an election in 1982 boycotted by left wing parties. Washington was more comfortable when Duarte again became president in 1984. His close ties with the US were demonstrated when he refused to sign the Arias peace plan in 1987, though eventually he succumbed to regional

16. Dunkerley, *Power in the Isthmus* 367–8, 392–4, 399–400.
17. Ibid. 393–404. Miller, *Soviet Relations* 190–1.

pressure. In elections in March 1989, ARENA came back into power and continued to receive military aid from the Bush Administration. In the continuing civil war that year 1,079 soldiers and an army-estimated 3,697 guerillas died; and the US Congress voted $85 million in military aid for El Salvador for the next year. However, with the encouragement of other Central American states, peace talks between the government and the FMLN under UN auspices had commenced in Costa Rica in October 1989. Right wing terrorist groups were still active and achieved international notoriety on 16 November 1989 when soldiers murdered six Jesuit priests, their housekeeper and her daughter. Failure to convict any culprits prompted the US Congress in October 1990 to freeze military aid to El Salvador. This action produced results. On 28 September 1991 Colonel Guilermo Alfredo Benavides was found guilty of ordering the murders, the first case in the long history of the 'dirty war' in El Salvador of a senior officer being convicted of such a crime. In September 1991 a peace accord under UN auspices was signed in New York between the FMLN and the government, though given the continued economic and political control of the oligarchy there is doubt about the efficacy of its implementation.[18]

US RELATIONS WITH OTHER CENTRAL AMERICAN STATES AND PANAMA

In the case of Guatemala the government there had become so vicious that in 1981 the US Congress refused to sanction a decision by Reagan to rescind the Carter Administration's prohibitions on military aid and arms sales to that regime. An internationally scandalous example of its style was when in January 1980 the Spanish embassy in Guatemala City was invaded by troops bent on killing thirty-nine Indian peasants sheltering there. Also, unlike El Salvador, there were no accusations of supplies of Cuban or Soviet arms to the insurgents in Guatemala. However, the Guatemalan military had no real need for US assistance.

18. Dunkerley, *Power in the Isthmus* 405–12. José Z. Garcia, 'Recent Elections in El Salvador' in Booth and Selgison (eds), *Elections and Democracy* 70–89. *Power in the Isthmus: The Report of the President's National Bipartisan Commission on Central America* (New York 1984) 33, 49–50. *Keesing's Record of World Events* vol. 36, 37270. vol. 37, 38231, 38414.

It had turned to Israel and Argentina for arms and training and expanded from 15,000 in 1980 to 51,600 in 1985. The guerillas also made a strategic mistake, like the FMLN in El Salvador, of launching in 1981 a major military offensive in a vain search for a popular uprising. Weakened by a subsequent war of attrition, the guerillas were unable to prevent the Guatemalan army, with the assistance of civilian defence forces, launching a campaign against the Indian peasant population, which comprised about 650,000 in the total population in 1984 of 7.7 million. Based on Malayan Emergency and Vietnam War precedents, peasants, who were not willing to be herded into strategic hamlets, were targets in free fire zones. The grisly nature of the campaign ensured that not even Reagan was willing to restore aid to the Guatemalan army while it remained in control of the country.[19]

However, in 1986 the Guatemalan army handed power back to civilian control, with the election of the government of Mario Vinicio Cerezo Arvalo, leader of the Christian Democratic Party. Washington seized the chance to restore relations with the Guatemalan army, and by 1989 had become its leading arms supplier. The army and the right wing in turn ensured that radicalism did not get out of hand. In the first six months of 1989, 1,598 Guatemalans were murdered and 906 disappeared. Cerezo admitted that security forces, over which he had no control, were 'creating a climate of terror'. This was a situation which the Bush Administration, now no longer ideologically committed to the Cold War, could not tolerate, though it gave the Guatemalan military plenty of warning when in March 1990 the US Ambassador was withdrawn from Guatemala. On 22 December 1990 Washington suspended all military aid because of a failure of the government 'to criticize or exhaustively investigate' continued incidents, such as the massacre by soldiers of sixteen peasants that month who were engaged in a peaceful demonstration about army abuses of human rights. However, the Guatemalan army had also made an error. Most attention in the US official statement about the aid suspension was devoted to the murder of a US citizen and the torturing and rape of an American Catholic nun.[20]

19. Dunkerley, *Power in the Isthmus* 480–504. McClintock, *The American Connection* vol. 2, chs 8–9. Cesar D. Sereseres, 'The Highlands War in Guatemala' in Georges Fauriol (ed.), *Latin American Insurgencies* (Washington 1985) 97–130. World of Information, *The Americas Review* 1990 (London 1990) 65.

20. Dunkerley, *Power in the Isthmus* 427–8. Robert H. Trudeau, 'The Guatemalan Election of 1985' in Booth and Selgison (eds), *Elections and Democracy* ch. 4. *Keesing's Record of World Events* vol. 36, 37276, 37311, 37912.

Even Costa Rica, which was proud of its tradition of an independent foreign policy and had no need for an army, was driven into the arms of the US in the early 1980s. The conservative democratic government in Costa Rica was alarmed by the Sandinista regime in neighbouring Nicaragua and by the rapid growth of its army. Consequently, with the assistance of $26 million in US aid, the Costa Rica Civil Guard was expanded to 19,500 men, and US advisers arrived to train its members in counter-insurgency tactics. Costa Rica also provided sanctuary for an independent contra force operating in southeastern Nicaragua. By 1984–85 the US paid for 36 per cent of the republic's budget, a rich reward for the government's toeing of Washington's Nicaragua line. However, there was a political backlash in Costa Rica. In 1986 the pro-US premier, Luis Monge, was replaced by Arias, who switched back to a more independent foreign policy as demonstrated by his advocacy in 1987 of the Nicaragua peace plan.[21]

Honduras in the 1980s was known by such names as 'state for sale', 'Pentagon republic' and 'US aircraft carrier'. Its role as the main base for the contra war against Nicaragua was invaluable to Washington. Nicaragua assisted in locking Honduras into this system in August 1983 by sending there a guerilla band of about 100 men, who were quickly rounded up by US troops engaged in military exercises. This 'invasion' was excellent US propaganda material, which was reinforced by subsequent Nicaraguan incursions across the frontier in hot pursuit of contras who were free to use Honduran soil for their murderous raids in the other direction. The unruly contras were uncomfortable guests. One contra leader was expelled in January 1985 for giving a press conference in Tegucigalpa which exposed the lie about no training camps for contras in Honduras. There were complaints about clashes between contras and farmers, and in October 1985 three contras were arrested for murder. However, in late 1989 Nicaragua was still complaining about contra bands, which had renewed violent attacks across the border from bases in Honduras. In 1989 there were also Honduran complaints of Salvadorian violations of airspace and border lines, a continuance of the old enmity between those two republics.[22]

One of the Reagan Administration's most valuable Latin American supporters, Noriega of Panama, had a less enduring relationship with

21. Dunkerley, *Power in the Isthmus* 622–48.
22. Ibid. 519–21, 577–8. *Keesing's Record of World Events* vol. 36, 37275.

the US. He was an army officer who had been employed by the CIA in the 1960s and who had become the intelligence chief and right hand man of Panama's dictator, General Omar Torrijos, who seized power from the Panamanian oligarchy in 1968. In that position Noriega had profited from Mafia money-laundering, gunrunning and drug-trafficking, for which Panama became a centre after Cuba was sanitized by Castro. After Torrijos's death and a struggle for power, Noriega in 1983 became dictator and was used by Reagan as a source of intelligence, a conduit for arms and a supplier of money for the contras. A Panamanian political opponent, Hugo Spadafora, also accused him of selling arms to the Sandinistas plus other crimes, for which he was beheaded. The Reagan Administration ignored shootings and beatings of Noriega's opponents in Panama, though its intelligence knew much about them – they tapped a satellite phone line they had provided for him. Panamanian business people and other middle-class citizens, who had no history of such repression in easygoing Panama, started a public agitation in 1987 in the form of a Civic Crusade. The handkerchief-waving, horn-honking crowds of this agitation were no real threat to Noriega. But the publicity provided an opportunity for one of his Panamanian opponents to attract the attention of Senator Edward Kennedy. He organized a Senate resolution, passed by 75 votes to 13, calling for a public investigation of charges that Noriega was responsible for Spadafora's murder, for corrupting the 1984 Panamanian election, for drug-trafficking and for money-laundering. Noriega responded with public demonstrations against the US embassy, which provoked the Ambassador to cut off all aid. The CIA reluctantly dropped Noriega from its payroll, a saving of $200,000 per annum. Noriega thought he could count on his friends in the CIA, but the exposure of its secret deals in the Irangate affair and the death of William Casey, its director, had introduced a new regime unprepared to save him. Nevertheless, Reagan was uninterested in doing more. However, US Drug Enforcement Administration officials busily prepared a case for Noriega's indictment in February 1988 by a grand jury for having conspired with the Medellin cartel of Colombia to traffic drugs into the US.[23]

This unprecedented indictment of the head of a foreign power locked the US into a struggle to depose Noriega. In April 1988 Washington imposed partial economic sanctions on Panama, but they

23. Kempe, *Divorcing the Dictator* chs 4–14.

hurt the population much more than the dictator. The Panamanian president, Eric Aruro Delvalle, whom Noriega had shunted aside, was recognized as the head of the Panama Government so that its assets in the US could be seized. An attempt to bargain for Noriega's resignation in return for dropping the drug indictments collapsed when news of it leaked to the American press so that it was considered dangerous for George Bush's election campaign. The Bush Administration placed hope on a national election in Panama in May 1989, which was required by the Panama Canal Treaty, and for which Washington spent $10 million to boost opposition candidates. They won easily, but Noriega used military force to overturn the result before it was declared. Bush responded by sending extra troops to the Canal Zone, and ordered US military exercises to be held there. But this military pressure was applied to a dictator who believed the US would not dare use military force. The Bush Administration lost patience after Panamanian soldiers on 16 December 1989 mortally wounded a US serviceman, who with three friends had lost his way, and tortured an American naval officer and his wife who witnessed the shooting. On 20 December 24,000 US troops, who had been making preparations for two months, invaded Panama to depose one man. He fled to the Papal Embassy but was pressured by the Papal Nunciate to leave and was taken as a prisoner to Miami. Though claiming he was an unlawfully-seized political prisoner, he was convicted and imprisoned in 1992 for drug-trafficking. However, the US invasion of Panama was condemned by the UN and the OAS, though some governments sympathized with Bush's dilemma, and raised fears of continued US military interventionism in Latin America.[24]

THE US AND OTHER AMERICAN NATIONS

There were no American invasions, covert wars or even involvements in coup attempts elsewhere in the Pacific Basin states of Latin America. However, in the Cold War cause, the US was giving

24. Ibid. chs 15–22. Conniff, *Panama and the United States* ch. 9. Ivan Musicant, *A History of United States Military Intervention in Latin America from the Spanish-American War to the Invasion of Panama* (New York 1990) ch. 10. Bruce W. Watson and Peter G. Tsouras (eds), *Operation Just Cause: The U.S. Intervention in Panama* (Boulder 1991). *Keesing's Record of World Events* vol. 36, 37179.

financial assistance to regimes fighting Marxist insurgencies. One of the most vicious was the *Sendero Luminoso* (Shining Path) movement in Peru. It evolved in the 1960s from the ideas and teaching of Marxist staff members at the University of Huamanga in the city of Ayacucho, who regularly took students to Cuba and who formed a tightly organized Maoist faction. In 1980 it launched a guerilla war against the bourgeois state. *Sendero*'s first appearance in May that year was in the burning of presidential election ballot boxes and the appearance of dead dogs hanging from lamp-posts in Ayacucho and Lima bearing signs that read: 'Deng Xiaoping, Son of a Bitch'. From late that year *Sendero* carried out bombings of public buildings and private companies and assassinations of public figures in the area of its greatest strength, around Ayacucho. It fed on the deprived nature of the mostly Indian province of Ayacucho, long neglected by governments. In the 1960s the province had benefited from some economic development, which passed by the Indian peasants but gave them an inkling of a better life.[25]

By 1983 the Peruvian Government realized it was facing a serious revolt of a movement with as many as 3,000 armed members. Subsequent strong military pressure drove *Sendero* largely out of its home base area. But there were enough other depressed rural areas in a nationwide environment of serious economic decline, producing hyperinflation and government austerity measures. Furthermore, the Peruvian army implemented a US Vietnam-style strategic hamlets programme to isolate the groups with similar socio-economic dislocation, which aided *Sendero*. By 1989 it was credited with 5,000 active members and was carrying out bombings and assassinations, including ambushing two army lorries in October, killing thirteen of their occupants. The US approach to the guerilla problem in 1990 was to promise $35 million to build a US military base in Peru and to train soldiers to fight *Sendero* rather than to offer money to improve the social and economic conditions on which the guerillas thrived. A new Peruvian president elected in 1990, Alberto Fujimori, achieved a major success after suspending the constitution in April 1992, by capturing in September *Sendero*'s supreme leader Professor Abimael

---

25. David Scott Palmer, 'The Sendero Luminoso Rebellion in Rural Peru' in Fauriol (ed.), *Latin American Insurgencies* 67–96. Carlos Iván Degregori, 'Return to the Past' in David Scott Palmer, *The Shining Path of Peru* (New York 1992) ch. 3.

Guzmán Reynoso. But *Sendero*'s violent response did not bode well for the future stability of Peru.[26]

Neighbouring Chile had peaceful political change when in 1988 Pinochet finally bowed to popular and international pressure and offered to hold in the next year a plebiscite on the continuance of his regime, as he had promised in 1980. When making this decision, the divided nature of the opposition and some economic progress in the 1980s encouraged Pinochet to believe he would win, especially as the plebiscite offered voters the choice of saying only 'yes' to Pinochet or 'no', the latter representing an uncertain future that Pinochet could paint as a threat of returning to the Allende years. Fed by false opinion polls, he received a shock when, in October 1989, 55 per cent of Chilean voters turned him down. To his credit, Pinochet's government accepted the popular decision and called for elections for a president and a new congress. But in the deal he made with his opponents, he was guaranteed command of the armed forces for the next eight years. The Bush Administration was delighted with the result, for while Pinochet was a staunch anti-communist, his regime was an embarrassment to the cause of democracy which Washington likes to promote.[27]

The US was also pleased when Ecuador also returned to democracy in the 1980s after a period of military rule. Democratic government, however, was plagued by political contests between the President and a congress controlled by his political opponents, which did not help a badly faltering economy. That year the conservative president of Ecuador, León Febres Cordero, was praised on a visit to Washington by Reagan as 'an articulate champion of free enterprise' who had pursued a free market economy. Reagan promised that Ecuador would be high on the list of nations qualifying for new US loans to be given to developing countries. But with the world trade slump of the mid-1980s, Ecuador did not benefit from being opened to the vicissitudes of free trade; and Febres' economic policies and strong support of the US were attacked in the Ecuadorian congress in which he did not have a majority. The Democratic

26. Michael Radu and Vladimir Tismaneanu, *Latin American Revolutionaries: Groups, Goals, Methods* (Washington 1990) 323–45. Masterson, *Militarism and Politics* 275–86. Palmer, *The Shining Path of Peru, passim.* The World Bank, *Peru: Policies to Stop Hyperinflation and Initiate Economic Recovery* (Washington 1989) 1–22, 120–9. *Keesing's Record of World Events* vol. 36, 37485–6, vol. 38, 38846, 39091, 39138. Young, *The Vietnam Wars* 317.

27. Falcoff, *Modern Chile* 310–12. *Keesing's Record of World Events* vol. 37, 38244.

Left's Rodrigo Borja Cevallos was elected president in 1988 and pursued a more independent foreign policy, especially in cooperation with other Andean republics. In 1990 Reagan's favourite son, Febres, was arrested and charged with embezzling US$150,000 of public funds while he was in office, though he was able to return in May 1992 as a local politician.[28]

Cooperation between Ecuador and other Andean nations was leading towards the establishment of free trade among the Andean Pact nations. Meetings in Caracas in Venezuela, in the late 1980s revived the flagging organization, and in 1991 the Andean Pact nations – Bolivia, Colombia, Ecuador, Peru and Venezuela – agreed to create free trade between them by 1992.

Ecuador also was cooperating with Colombia in 1989–90 in a vicious war which the Colombian Government was waging against the Medellin drug cartels, with which Noriega had been involved. An agreement in 1979 to extradite drug bosses to the US had not been enforced until the Colombian minister of justice was murdered in 1984, and even then only a small number of extraditable traffickers were sent to the US. In Colombia many drug bosses went free because of bribery and intimidation. Police officers, judges, government officials, journalists and any others thought to be in the way of Medellin operations were assassinated, and public buildings were bombed. Colombians were unaware of the extent of the Medellin operations until the publication in 1987 in the *Miami Herald* of details about the cartel, which reputedly earned $8 billion and was the source of 80 per cent of the cocaine imported into the US. Washington poured financial aid into a Colombian army campaign to crush the cartel, which had become a state within a state. The appointment of a government of national unity under President César Gavria Trujilo in August 1990, resulted in halting the military offensive against the cartel, waiving extradition to the US and offering reduced prison sentences. In 1991 the main cartel boss Pablo Ezcobar Gavira and some other drug leaders surrendered, but they were given special privileges as prisoners; and early in 1992 Gavira was reported to be still running his drug cartel from prison.[29]

---

28. Ibid. vol. 36, 37482; vol. 37, 38246; vol. 38, 38908. David Corkill and David Cubitt, *Ecuador: Fragile Democracy* (London 1988) chs 3–5.

29. Jorge P. Osterling, *Democracy in Colombia: Clientalist Politics and Guerilla Warfare* (New Brunswick 1989) ch. 7. Bruce Michael Bagley, 'The New Hundred Years War? U.S. National Security and the War on Drugs in Latin America' in Donald J. Mabry, *The Latin American Narcotics Trade and U.S. National Security* (New York 1989) ch. 4. *Keesing's Record of World Events* vol. 36, 37482–4; vol. 37, 38245; vol. 38, 38717. .

The common market movement in the Andean Pact states was matched by negotiations for a free trade agreement between the US and Canada, which was implemented on 1 January 1989. The aim was to improve bilateral trade between the two nations, which exceeded US$129 billion in 1987, the most valuable commerce between any two nations in the world. The agreement was initially a Canadian move supported by a Conservative Party government elected in 1984, by economists wedded to market forces and by a business community enthused by visions of freer access to the huge American market. Significant latterday fear was generated by the opposition parties in Canada about an American takeover of the country. But though Canada already enjoyed a healthy trade balance with the US that was worth US$12.38 billion in 1988, this concern was not strong enough to sweep the Conservatives from office at the November 1988 election. It is too early to assess the net benefits to Canada of free trade with the US. However, initially, as Canadian industries suffered and the Canadian dollar appreciated against American currency, the Canadian economy slumped into recession. However, a wider-world economic downturn in 1990–91 influenced this slump, especially a weakening of demand in the US, Canada's main export market.[30]

The US had a different kind of economic problem with its southern neighbour, Mexico, the Latin American nation most dominated by American commerce and investment. The US controlled about two-thirds of Mexico's foreign trade and direct foreign investment there. In 1982 Mexico shocked the financial world by freezing all its US dollar accounts, closing its foreign exchange market and declaring a moratorium on repayments of its US$100 billion external debt, the largest in the world except for Brazil's. The Mexican economy had been booming in the late 1970s, driven by rising prices for oil which earned about 70 per cent of the country's foreign exchange and 45 per cent of government revenue. But the boom masked deep structural inadequacies in the Mexican economy, which had relied for too long on increasing injections of foreign capital. Hence there was a crisis when oil prices fell in the early 1980s.[31]

At least Reagan did not take the attitude of the conservative

30. Robert Bothwell, *Canada and the United States: The Politics of Partnership* (New York 1992) 142–53. Dorothy Robinson-Mowry, *Canada-U.S. Relations: Perceptions and Misconceptions* (Latham, MD 1988) chs 2, 5. *YITS* 1988, 140. *OECD Economic Outlook*, 51, June 1992, 83–7.

31. Miguel D. Ramírez, *Mexico's Economic Crisis: Its Origins and Consequences* (New York 1989) *passim*.

Republican US Senator Jesse Helms, who opened a Senate enquiry into Mexico's problems and declared: 'If Mexico wants United States help, the Mexican people have no choice, it seems to me, but to bring about fundamental political reform'. Reagan and his advisers knew how sensitive Mexican citizens were. The Helms enquiry threw them into a frenzy, with public demonstrations against the US embassy and formal protests to the State Department. So Reagan did not press the ruling party to open up the Mexican political system. He also was willing to discard his free trade ideology sufficiently to provide Mexico with a US$9.45 billion financial aid and credit package, a case of pragmatic necessity to assist a country of vital interest to the US. But in the rescheduling of its debt repayments, Mexico was subjected to an austerity programme imposed by the International Monetary Fund, which produced only cosmetic improvements and decreased wages and the general standard of living of the Mexican people. The economy also was bleeding from a flight abroad of Mexican capital. This was an example, repeated elsewhere in Latin America, of neoconservative economic ideology being applied to an economy with problems too deep to be solved only by emphases on free trade, financial deregulation and reductions in government spending. A renegotiated International Monetary Fund plan, which provided US$7.7 billion from the fund and US$6 billion in commercial bank loans, was applied in 1986 to a still sick economy. However, the economy was improving because of more efficient taxation, trade liberalization, the selling of unproductive state enterprises and other economic reforms which were partly a result of American pressure. A US-assisted debt scheduling programme, known as the Brady Plan, was implemented in April 1990. It greatly assisted in restoring overseas investor confidence in Mexico and assisted an average annual growth rate in GDP of 4 per cent in the years 1989–1991, compared with an average of only 0.6 per cent from 1982 to 1988. Furthermore, Mexico started negotiations in June 1991 for a free trade agreement with the US and Canada, a North American Free Trade Agreement, to which many Mexicans were looking forward. However, Mexico still suffered from grossly uneven distributions of income and widespread poverty, exacerbated by a devastating earthquake in 1985.[32]

During the 1980s the Reagan Administration also had problems

32. Robert A. Pastor and Jorge G. Casatañeda, *Limits to Friendship: The United States and Mexico* (New York 1988) chs 4–7 (quotation 119). Riordan Roett (ed.), *Mexico and the United States: Managing the Relationship* (Boulder 1988) chs 2–6, 12–13. *OECD Economic Surveys: Mexico*, 1991/1992, 14, 36–43.

with Mexico's refusal to join his campaigns against Nicaragua and the rebels in El Salvador. The Mexican Government considered that revolutionary change in Central America was inevitable and that to support the US policies to stem the tide would prevent its ability to mediate in disputes there and would provoke denunciations from left wing Mexicans. Another source of tension in US-Mexico relations was the growth of the country as a source of drugs and illegal immigrants entering the US, which resulted in tightening of American border controls.[33]

The economic problems of the 1980s did not assist Latin American republics to escape from US economic dominance. The spread of neoconservative economic policies served to facilitate American and other overseas direct investment. The US was still the principal source of imports for each of the Pacific Basin Latin American states and their principal market, except Nicaragua, on which there was a US trade ban. By 1988 the average standard of living in Latin America was 6.6 per cent below the level of 1980 and the American-imposed debt rescheduling programmes had contributed to an even greater debt burden with a net transfer of capital out of Latin America from 1982 to 1988 of $178.7 billion plus an estimated flight from the region of at least another $100 billion. This was an export of twenty-eight times the value of the US's Alliance for Progress aid in the 1960s. The only comfort to Latin Americans was that from 1982 to the end of 1986 the US national debt had trebled to $2,217 billion, with about 11 per cent of it owed to foreigners, especially Japanese.[34]

THE AMERICAS AND THE PACIFIC BASIN

Japanese trade to Latin America had its vicissitudes in the 1980s reflecting the economic downturn in Latin American republics in the 1980s. US$10.5 billion worth of Japanese exports to that region

33. Langley, *Mexico and the United States* chs 6–7.
34. Bailey, 'Foreign Investment in Mexico' in ibid. ch. 2. Joseph Ramos, *Neoconservative Economics in the Southern Cone of Latin America, 1973–1983* (Baltimore 1986) chs 7–9. *YITS* 1981, 1989 *passim.* Ronald A. Pastor, 'The Centrality of Central America' in Larry Berman (ed.), *Looking Back on the Reagan Presidency* (Baltimore 1990) 43–4. Akira Iriye, 'U.S.-Asian Relations in the 1980s' in David E. Kyvig (ed.), *Reagan and the World* (New York 1990) 144–5.

in 1981 fell to US$6.4 billion in 1983 and did not pass the 1981 level until 1991, when Japan earned US$12.8 billion from exports to Latin America. That amount was only 4 per cent of Japan's total trade. It was also US$3 billion higher than Latin American exports to Japan, a gap which had grown in the previous two years. The big increase in Japanese imports from Latin America in the 1970s had slackened with a shift in Japanese raw materials purchasing to Asia. But Japan remained the second most important market and source of supply for Latin America after the US, though only at a level of 6 per cent for imports and 7.5 per cent for exports and not far ahead of Germany. However, the Pacific Basin nations Chile and Peru depended on Japan in 1991 for 21 and 12 per cent respectively of their exports, principally base metals. Also, some US exports to Latin America by 1991 were from Japanese subsidiary companies in the US.[35]

Japanese direct foreign investment declined in Latin America in the 1980s as Japanese capitalists sought more profitable regions. Pacific Basin exceptions were Chile and especially Mexico. The nature of Japanese investment was changing from mining developments to financial and commercial enterprises, but with little attention to manufacturing, with the exception of Mexico, which was second only to Brazil as a Latin American location for Japanese capital. Mexico was offering incentives for foreign capitalists in bonded industrial zones along the US-Mexican border, called *maquiladoras*. Only ten Japanese firms had taken advantage of these opportunities by 1986, mostly electrical companies such as Sanyo and Sony. But by late 1987 twenty-one other Japanese firms had joined them or were planning to do so. For example, in 1988 Mitsubishi was making in Mexico parts for assembling forklifts in the US in order to escape American penalty duties and to exploit Mexican wage rates that were only ten per cent of those in the US. This investment helped increase the contribution of manufactured goods to Mexico's imports from 30 per cent in 1983 to 56 per cent in 1989. Japan's proportional contribution to Mexico's imports increased from 5 to 7 per cent from 1980 to 1991. Direct Japanese investment in Mexico jumped much more sharply from US$87 million in 1988–89 to $168 million in 1990–91. Still, in March 1991 Mexico's share of Japanese worldwide accumulated direct investment since 1951 was only 0.5 per cent. Latin America's share was 13 per cent, including 5 per cent in Panama,

35. A. Blake Friscia, 'Japanese Economic Relations with Latin America: An Overview' in Purcell and Immerman, *Japan and Latin America* 8–16.

which was mainly in ships of flag-convenience. By comparison the US had absorbed 42 per cent of Japanese direct investments.[36]

The Government of Japan did not see Latin America as a major field for trade and investment. It was recognized in Tokyo that this was a region of primary US strategic and economic interest and therefore that there should be minimal economic friction there, particularly in view of the emerging trade conflicts between these two economic superpowers. Consequently, Japan had acknowledged American diplomatic leadership in the region, which continued in the 1980s, for example by refusing any government aid to Nicaragua in the 1980s and by not ostracizing Pinochet's Chile. But there were limitations to this support. No attempts were made to ban private sector Japanese trade with Cuba or Nicaragua. American-Japanese cooperation in Latin America continued in the post-Cold War era when the Bush Administration exhibited more keenness to promote economic growth in Latin America in 'A New Partnership for Trade, Investment and Growth'. At a time of huge budget deficits this American policy could not be carried out by government aid as in the Alliance for Progress in the 1960s. The emphasis was on free trade and foreign investment, which the debt crises of the 1980s had forced most Latin American governments to accept. In this process the Bush Administration looked to Japan to play a role, and received a ready response in Tokyo. Japan has also cooperated with the US in debt rescheduling strategies in Latin America. A result was that from 1987 to 1991 the proportion of the Latin American debt owed to Japanese banks increased from 17 to 26 per cent, compared with a decline in the debt to the US from 29 to 20 per cent.[37]

To 1991 in the Latin American region of the Pacific Basin, Japan was willing to concede the importance of US political and economic hegemony. Indeed, the US empire in the region was a much more paternalist one than Japan's economic empire in the Western Pacific Basin which had not to this stage sought, or indeed needed, any assertions of even informal Japanese political control. However, the difference has been significantly influenced by the Cold War, which on the one hand allowed Japan to shelter under the American defence

36. Ibid. 18–26. *YITS* 1980, 578; 1989, 572. A. Blake Friscia, 'Japanese Economic Relations with Latin America: An Overview' and Luis Rubio, 'Japan in Mexico: A Changing Pattern' in Susan Kaufman Purcell and Robert M. Immerman (eds), *Japan and Latin America in the New Global Order* (Boulder 1992) 15, 20, 69–100.

37. Friscia, 'Japanese Economic Relations' and Susan Kaufman Purcell and Robert M. Immerman, 'Japan, Latin America, and the United States: Prospects for Cooperation and Conflict' in ibid. 34, 122–32.

umbrella and on the other provoked US governments to oppose radical political movements in Latin America. The post-Cold War era could well see changes, in particular a possible US retreat from political interference in Latin American affairs. However, with the likelihood of Japanese economic interests in Latin America further expanding in the future and other potential tensions in US-Japanese relations, it is questionable whether Japan will continue to defer to US leadership in Latin America. Indeed, in the post-Cold War era there have been numerous statements by Japanese leaders that they are looking for a more equal partnership between Japan and the US in the whole of the Pacific Basin.

Latin American countries bordering the Pacific Ocean also looked to the wider Pacific Basin for economic benefits. In 1991 Chile, Mexico and Peru joined the Pacific Economic Cooperation Conference (PECC) – an unofficial body to provide economic advice – which originally consisted of the US, Canada, Japan, Australia, New Zealand, South Korea and the ASEAN nations, and which in 1991 was widened also to include China, Taiwan and Hong Kong. Mexico, Chile and Ecuador also applied without success to join a more high-powered government organization to discuss trade cooperation, the Asia-Pacific Economic Conference (APEC), founded at Canberra in November 1989 by the original PECC members. But APEC has not yet looked anything like an alternative Pacific Basin trade block as feared by the EEC.[38]

Diplomatically, Chile's Pinochet had more success in the 1980s with his 'Pacific drive'. After breaking off relations with the Philippines after Marcos refused him entry, he received an apology from Manila and established good relations with that ASEAN nation. A result was that only the Philippines supported the application by Chile, Mexico and Ecuador to join APEC. Pinochet's Chile also established good relations with an Asian nation in the opposite ideological camp, Communist China, demonstrating his pragmatic attempts to increase Chile's influence in the Pacific. Such initiatives contributed to an increase from 1980 to 1988 in the non-Soviet Asian proportion of Chile's export trade from 18.8 to 23.1 per cent. Peru was more inward-looking in the 1980s with its serious economic problems and the *Sendero* insurgency. But another left-leaning government elected in 1985 looked across the Pacific to the Soviet Union for support. Not to be outdone by the USSR, China maintained in the 1980s good

38. Donald Crone, 'The Politics of Emerging Pacific Cooperation', *Pacific Affairs* 65, 1992, 68–83.

relations with Peru, despite accusations there about Chinese support for Peruvian insurgents. Mexico had an ambition to play a greater role in the Pacific Basin, which lay behind its applications to join PECC and APEC. With its new free market economy, Mexico was starting to look for more Pacific Basin trading opportunities and to model its future development on the East Asian NICs.[39]

But the Latin American nations had not contributed greatly to the growing economic importance of the Pacific Basin in the 1980s. By 1986 Pacific Basin economies constituted just under 50 per cent of world GNP compared with under 35 per cent in 1965. In 1986 Mexico, the largest Pacific rim Latin American economy, contributed only 2.1 per cent of Pacific Basin GNP and the Pacific rim nations of Latin America as a whole only 4 per cent, compared with Australia's 3.1 per cent and Japan's 34 per cent, which had almost caught up with the US's 36 per cent. Nor were Latin American countries much involved in the growth of trade across the North Pacific, which during the 1980s became more extensive in volume and value than trade across the North Atlantic. Furthermore, the Latin American states south of Panama were not strategically important since only local shipping used the sea lanes down the west coast of South America. Nor did Latin American countries seek to become involved in the nuclear free Pacific campaign, they having established an earlier nuclear free zone in Latin America – the Tlatelolco Treaty – signed by all Pacific rim states except Chile. That treaty in fact was one of the inspirations for the nuclear free movement in the South Pacific.[40]

The US contribution to economic growth in the Pacific Basin was much greater. During the 1980s Japan, the East Asian NICs and the newer developing ASEAN economies benefited from relative peace under an American strategic umbrella. Also Japan and the East Asian 'little dragons', in particular, benefited from trade with the US which swung increasingly in their favour during the 1980s. Moreover, US investments helped give kick-starts to their economic growth. Reagan – though not, like the Californian-born Nixon,

39. Gamba-Stonehouse, *Strategy in Southern Oceans* 40, 54, 62–3. *YITS*, 1989, 162. Rubio, 'Japan in Mexico' in Purcell and Immerman, *Japan and Latin America* 87–8. Teritomo Ozawa, 'The Dynamics Of Pacific Rim Industrialization: How Mexico Can Join the Asian Flock of "Flying Geese"' in Riordan Roett (ed.), *Mexico's External Relations in the 1990s* (Boulder 1991) 129–54.

40. Segal, *Rethinking the Pacific* 286–8. Gavin Boyd, *Pacific Trade, Investment and Politics* (New York 1989) ch. 1. Gamba-Stonehouse, *Strategy in Southern Oceans* 64–5. Hamel-Green, *South Pacific Nuclear Free Zone* ch. 2.

the first US President to be born in an American Pacific Basin state – spent most of his adult years and all his political life in California and showed appreciation of the growing importance of the Pacific Basin. In 1984 he publicized the fact that the Pacific region had become more important than Europe for American trade. He and other members of his Administration often spoke of the coming Pacific age. This was certainly an improvement on the relative lack of interest paid by the Carter Administration to Pacific and East Asian affairs except for failed human rights campaigns, normalizing relations with China and a retreat from dismantling US military support for South Korea. However, Reagan's initial primary foreign policy interest was to strengthen the US crusade against Soviet Union-backed communism. This created his obsession with combatting alleged communist threats in Nicaragua and El Salvador, and with pursuing an arms build-up which greatly increased the US public debt. One of the main emphases in Reagan's East Asia policies was pressure on Japan and other allies to spend more on their own defence to make their trading policies more acceptable to the US. However, he also presided over the growing détente with China and with the USSR. Even if the reform governments of those countries took more initiatives, Reagan responded positively to those opportunities. Reagan's East Asian and Soviet Union policies were generally continued by the Bush Administration. However, with the end of the Cold War and with other pressures from deficit budgets and Philippine nationalists, the Bush Administration was starting the final process of military withdrawal from East Asia, which the new Democratic Party president, Bill Clinton, is likely to continue. His Administration's main interest in East Asia may well be meeting the economic challenge from Japan.[41]

---

41. David E. Kyvig, 'The Foreign Relations of the Reagan Administration'; Iriye, 'U.S.-Asian Relations in the 1980s' and 'Reagan and the World: A Roundtable Discussion' in Kyvig, *Reagan and the World* chs 1, 7, 8. John Lewis Gaddis, *The United States and the End of the Cold War: Implications, Reconsiderations, Provocations* (New York 1992) ch. 7. Samuel P. Huntington, 'America's Changing Strategic Interests', *Survival* XXIII (1991) 3–17.

CONCLUSIONS

The US Government demonstrated in the 1980s its strong opposition to any Marxist expansion in Latin America. The consequence was continued support for oligarchic control in El Salvador, compromising the demilitarization of Costa Rica, maintenance of a military regime in Honduras, and support for a drug-trafficking dictator in Panama until his oppressive reign gained the attention of American senators and drug enforcement administrators. Only military governments in Guatemala, where human rights abuses were notorious, were abandoned by the Reagan and Bush Administrations.

The overthrow of the Sandinista Government of Nicaragua became an obsession for Reagan. It justified any means, including gross violations of human rights by contra guerillas, direct CIA acts of war, and the use of a known drug-trafficker, Noriega. Despite the winding down of the Cold War, the Bush Administration still imposed economic sanctions on Nicaragua and provided financial aid to political opponents of the Sandinistas in a final successful attempt to depose that government.

The attention placed by the US on military opposition to insurgencies in Central and South America ignored even the advice of a bipartisan commission of enquiry on Central America headed by Henry Kissinger. Its report recognized that: 'Widespread hunger and malnutrition, illiteracy, poor educational and training opportunities, poor health conditions, and inadequate housing are unstable foundations on which to encourage the growth of viable democratic institutions'.[42] Furthermore, the neoconservative economic policies favoured by the US Administration and the International Monetary Fund did not take into account structural weaknesses, such as inequitable distributions of income and widespread poverty in Latin America. A consequence was the persistence of guerilla movements in many Latin American countries and the threat of new social disruption in Mexico. The US economic dominance of the region also is likely to be preserved or increased with the free trade agreement that was achieved with Canada and the one being negotiated with Mexico. US free trade policies always have been a reflection of American economic strength, and even though the US economy has weakened, it is still dominant in Latin America. However, in the post-Cold War era of the 1990s there

---

42. *Report of the President's National Bipartisan Commission* 81.

was a new concern by the Bush Administration to promote private investment-generated economic growth in Latin America, which even led to Japan being invited to contribute to this development. This will increase Japanese economic involvement in Latin America, which has been the most important force in breaking down Latin America's isolation from the Island and Asian regions of the Pacific Basin.

Conclusion

The Pacific Basin in 1991 had undergone a dramatic transformation since 1945. From a region devastated by the Pacific War, with European powers attempting to revive colonial empires, and with Japan crushed by defeat and under military occupation, the Pacific Basin in 1991 had become the region of the greatest economic activity in the world. Japan had recovered more than its prewar economic dominance to become a feared economic rival of the US, which had been the world's dominant economic power in 1945. Two of Japan's former colonies, South Korea and Taiwan, and two island states of the old British Empire, Singapore and Hong Kong, had become 'little dragons' with booming industrialized economies. Other Southeast Asian countries, especially Malaysia and Thailand, were following their industrializing path. Indonesia, China and Mexico on the other side of the Pacific Basin were showing signs of future great potential economic growth. By contrast, the US was suffering economic decline with a burgeoning foreign debt, unfavourable trade balance and symptoms of industrial decay. However, a new potentially powerful area of free trade was being created in North America between the US and Canada with the prospect of Mexico joining it; and there was a new drive for more economic unity in the ASEAN states in the face of this development and success of the economic union in Europe. But wider economic unity in the Pacific Basin was still a vision to be worked out. A new era of peace had broken out with the end of the Cold War, a tenuous agreement in Cambodia and even the potential end of two of the worst Latin American conflicts in El Salvador and Nicaragua. But there were continuing violent conflicts in the island Pacific and in Latin America.

Many of the events in the Pacific Basin in the intervening years were influenced by the contest between the superpowers, the US and the USSR. Important consequences of the Cold War were the restructuring of Japan to serve US interests, the freezing of relations between the US and China, the partition of Korea and the Korean War, the division of Vietnam and the long Vietnam War, the survival of US and French colonialism in the Pacific Islands and US support for right wing governments in Latin America. The Cold War also induced Russian support for North Korea, froze relations between the USSR and Japan and encouraged Soviet support for newly independent nations in Southeast Asia, especially North Vietnam.

However, the growing split between the Soviet Union and China caused a competition between those powers for influence in Indochina, which in turn encouraged further warfare in that region after the US withdrawal. The Soviet-China split, as well as the experience of the Korean War, removed the danger of any new war between the US and China and encouraged a search for détente between those major Pacific Basin powers by the end of the 1960s. Similarly the USSR had no interest in provoking a war with the US, so postwar Pacific Basin conflicts never grew into wider wars. Also the ending of the Cold War has resulted in the movements for peace in Cambodia and in Central America, though with doubts about how successful they may be.

Another major force shaping the destinies of postwar Pacific Basin nations was indigenous nationalism. French and Dutch pretensions to restore their colonial empires in Southeast Asia unleashed nationalist revolutions, whose outcomes were influenced by the Cold War. The defeat of communism in Indonesia gained US support for the revolution there, while the spectre of communism sucked the US into opposing nationalism in Vietnam. The easy postwar achievement of independence in the Philippines assisted the defeat of a communist revolution, but the dominance of the socio-economic elite bequeathed further revolutionary violence to that republic. Malay nationalism was a factor in the defeat of the Chinese-based revolution in Malaya. Conversely, the earlier British colonial policy of importing immigrant labour forces to protect indigenous communities created conditions for the Malayan Emergency and also for the later military coups in Fiji.

In the Pacific the cultural diversity of islanders and prewar paternalistic colonialism delayed independence movements in most island groups. The absence of major economic resources in the islands also encouraged a generally non-violent transference of colonial power in the British and Australasian territories. There was even significant British and Australian pressure on islanders, in the interests of shedding economic burdens and avoiding UN criticism, to become independent. Conversely, the strategic interests of the US in the North Pacific and France's world power pretensions by the 1980s were provoking violence in territories still under their control. Furthermore, the legacy of colonial boundaries has produced violent conflict in regions of ethnic diversity, as Indonesia discovered after seizing power in East Timor and Irian Jaya, and as Papua New Guinea has experienced recently in Bougainville.

The Cold War in the Pacific Basin also encouraged the revival of the Japanese economic empire which lay in ashes in 1945. Stimulated by 'reverse course' American policies and its use as an arsenal during the Korean War, the trade-driven Japanese economy was booming by the 1960s. Ripples of Japanese trade and investment in East Asia were becoming rolling waves in the Pacific Basin by the 1970s. In East and Southeast Asia the little dragons received a major boost from Japanese investment and trade, and more recently Japan has been financing emerging industrial countries of Southeast Asia and Latin America. However, there are potential problems for the future in Japanese reluctance to share high technology. More seriously, the growing trade imbalance with the US has engendered commercial conflict between the two strategic allies, which could lead to future serious conflicts between the US and Japan with the loosening of the Cold War glue that had held those two nations together since the Second World War. The US economic hegemony in Latin America was preserving inequitable social systems which provoked continuing violent conflicts in that region. This study has demonstrated, in fact, that though much of the conflict in the Pacific Basin was influenced by the Cold War, there are economic and nationalist forces at work which might create future violent struggles in the region.

Indeed, the Pacific Basin world is not nearly as united as is the North Atlantic community. Religious, cultural and linguistic diversities in the Pacific are much greater. The Christian background of the North Atlantic nations is shared in the Pacific Basin with the other great religions of Islam and Buddhism, the philosophy of Confucianism and a host of lesser non-Christian religions. The Asian and Pacific Island languages have far less common roots than those of Western Europe. Political ideology is also more diverse in the Pacific Basin. Communism was a greater and more growing force than in Europe, though it also displayed less unity with communists killing each other, especially in the post Vietnam conflicts in Indochina. Even with the collapse of communism in the former

Soviet Union, it has survived a democratic challenge in China, is defiantly alive in North Korea and remains dominant in Indochina. Also there were still in 1991 surviving major Marxist insurrections in the Philippines, Peru and Guatemala. The democratic ideology, so promoted by the US, had spread to more Latin American states by 1991 with Chile and Panama returning to the democratic fold, but it was having a shaky time in Peru, Guatemala and Colombia. Fiji's experience demonstrated the frailty of democracy in the island Pacific, where cultural influences have mutated democratic institutions, as in West Samoa and Tonga. Democracy is strongly entrenched in Australasia. In Asia, Malaysia, Singapore and Japan are democracies that have been dominated, like Mexico, by one political party, and in Singapore and Malaysia there have been restrictions on free speech. In South Korea there have been new trends to a more open political system. Democracy has revived in the Philippines, though threatened by military coup attempts. In Thailand military rule is being compromised by democratic pressures. In Taiwan and Hong Kong there were developments towards more democracy, which were not pleasing China. The military regime in Indonesia has shown no signs of relaxing its political control.

Economically, the NICs and ASEAN states compete much more with each other than do the states of Western Europe, as demonstrated by the smallness of inter-ASEAN trade. By 1991 another source of unity in the Pacific, the US-led defence alliance system, was starting to crumble with the end of the Cold War. This gave Philippine nationalists the courage to evict US military bases, and has caused ASEAN countries to become more concerned about their own defence. This new strategic environment is likely to make Taiwan, South Korea and Japan less valuable allies of the US. The nations of the Pacific Basin may well be more disunited in the future.

Further Reading

This is a guide to major publications for readers who wish to delve more deeply into topic areas of this book. For further publications consult the footnotes for each chapter.

THE RECONSTRUCTION OF JAPAN

A valuable book on the American occupation of Japan is Robert E. Ward and Sakamoto Yoshikazu (eds), *Democratizing Japan: The Allied Occupation* (Honolulu 1987). An earlier good survey of the literature, including theses that later became books, is Carol Gluck, 'Entangling Illusions – Japanese and American Views of the Occupation' in Warren I. Cohen (ed.), *New Frontiers in American East Asian Relations: Essays Presented to Dorothy Borg* (New York 1983). The best book by a participant is Theodore Cohen, *Remaking Japan: The American Occupation As New Deal* (New York 1987). For a Japanese view see Masumi Junnosuke, *Postwar Politics in Japan, 1945–1955* (Berkeley 1985). A recent discussion of the era is contained in a whole issue of *Daedalus* Summer 1990. A more recent valuable study using some Japanese sources and covering the whole occupation era is Richard B. Finn, *Winners in Peace: MacArthur, Yoshida, and Postwar Japan* (Berkeley 1992).

CHINA AND THE COLD WAR

A new interpretation of the Cold War in Asia is Marc S. Gallicchio, *The Cold War Begins in Asia: American Policy and the Fall of the Japanese Empire* (New York 1988), and there is a useful historiographical essay by Robert L. Messer in Akira Iriye and Warren Cohen (eds), *American, Chinese and Japanese Perspectives on Wartime Asia 1931–1949* (Wilmington 1990). For an overview of US policy towards China that is very critical of US policies see Bevin Alexander, *The Strange Connection: U.S. Intervention in China, 1944–1972* (New York 1992). For detailed scholarly studies of aspects of the 1945–49 period, see especially William Stueck, *The Wedemeyer Mission: American Politics and Foreign Policy During the Cold War* (Athens, Ga 1984); June M. Grasso, *Truman's Two-China Policy 1948–1950* (Armonk 1987); and Nancy Bernkof Tucker, *Patterns in the Dust: Chinese-American Relations and the Recognition Controversy 1949–1950* (New York 1983). For a good study of early Soviet-Chinese relations see John W. Garver, *Chinese-Soviet Relations 1937–1945: The Diplomacy of Chinese Nationalism* (New York 1988). A new book with a good bibliography on the Chinese Civil War is E.R. Hooton, *The Greatest Tumult: The Chinese Civil War 1936–49* (London 1991).

THE DIVISION OF KOREA AND THE KOREAN WAR

For the division of Korea and the causes of the Korean war, an influential, detailed and revisionist book is Bruce Cumings, *The Origins of the Korean War*, 2 vols (Princeton 1981, 1990). A good shorter overview is Peter Lowe, *The Origins of the Korean War* (London 1986). Useful, more specialized monographs on American policy towards Korea, with a range of interpretations, are Charles Dobb, *The Unwanted Symbol: American Foreign Policy, the Cold War, and Korea, 1945–1950* (Kent 1981); William Whitney Stueck, Jr., *The Road to Confrontation: American Policy toward China and Korea, 1947–1950* (Chapel Hill 1981) and James Irving Matray, *The Reluctant Crusade: American Foreign Policy in Korea, 1941–1950* (Honolulu 1985). An analysis of the Korean origins of the war is John Merrill, *Korea: The Peninsular Origins of the War* (Newark 1989).

The Korean War has become a new historiographical growth area. The best short history of the war is Burton I. Kaufman, *The Korean War: Challenges in Crisis, Credibility and Command* (Philadelphia 1986). A recent collection of readings on causes and the politics of the war is James Cotton and Ian Neary (eds), *The Korean War in History* (Atlantic Heights 1989). A good diplomatic history of the war is Rosemary Foot, *The Wrong War: American Policy and the Dimensions of the Korean Conflict, 1950–1953* (Ithaca 1985). Also valuable is Richard Whelan, *Drawing the Line: The Korean War, 1950–1953* (Boston 1990). An account of Chinese intervention based on conversations with Chinese officials is Russell Spurr, *Enter the Dragon: China's Undeclared War Against the U.S. in Korea, 1950–51* (New York 1988). A valuable recent discussion of relevant literature is Rosemary Foot, 'Making Known the Unknown War: Policy Analysis of the Korean Conflict in the Last Decade', *Diplomatic History* 15, 1991, 411–31. There is a good recent bibliography by James Matray, *A Bibliography of the Korean War* (Boulder 1991).

THE INDONESIAN REVOLUTION

The best overall survey of the Indonesian revolution is still Anthony Reid, *The Indonesian National Revolution 1945–50* (Melbourne 1974). More recent good studies of aspects of the revolution are William H. Frederick, *Visions and Heat: The Making of the Indonesian Revolution* (Athens, Ohio 1988); Theodore Friend, *The Blue-Eyed Enemy: Japan Against the West in Java and Luzon, 1942–1945* (Princeton 1988); and Robert Cribb, *Gangsters and Revolutionaries: The Jakarta People's Militia and the Indonesian Revolution 1945–1949* (Sydney 1991). For Britain and the origins of the revolution see Peter Dennis, *Troubled Days of Peace: Mountbatten and South East Asia Command, 1945–46* (Manchester 1987). For US policy towards Indonesia, see Robert J. McMahon, *Colonialism and Cold War: The United States and the Struggle for Indonesian Independence, 1945–49* (Ithaca 1981). For postwar US involvement in Southeast Asia, see Andrew J. Rotter, *The Path to Vietnam: Origins of the American Commitment to Southeast Asia* (Ithaca 1987).

THE MALAYAN EMERGENCY

The authoritative study of the Malayan Emergency is Anthony Short, *The Communist Insurrection in Malaya 1848–1960* (London 1975). A recent military study is Robert Jackson, *The Malayan Emergency: The Commonwealth's Wars 1948–1966* (London 1991). The impact of the emergency on the peoples of Malaya is analyzed well in Richard Stubbs, *Hearts and Minds in Guerilla Warfare: The Malayan Emergency 1948–1960* (Singapore 1989), which has a good bibliography. For the Malayan background, with a good bibliography, see Albert Lau, *The Malayan Union Controversy 1942–1948* (Singapore 1991).

THE HUK REBELLION, THE US AND THE PHILIPPINES

The best study of the Huk rebellion and its origins is Benedict J. Kerkvliet, *The Huk Rebellion: A Study of Peasant Revolt in the Philippines* (Berkeley 1977). Lawrence M. Greenberg, *The Hukbalahap Insurrection: A Case Study of a Successful Anti-Insurgency Operation in the Philippines, 1946–1955* (Washington 1987) provides an analysis of the defeat of the rebellion. US policy towards the Philippines in the era is covered by Stanley Karnow, *In Our Image: America's Empire in the Philippines* (New York 1989), which has good bibliographical essays for this and later periods of Philippines history. For a critical survey of later US-Philippines relations see Raymond Bonner, *Waltzing with a Dictator: The Marcoses and the Making of American Foreign Policy* (New York 1987).

THE VIETNAM WARS

Jaques Dalloz, *The War in Indo-China 1945–54* (Dublin 1990) provides a good survey from the French viewpoint of the first Vietnam War. For US involvement in this war see Lloyd C. Gardiner, *Approaching*

Vietnam: From World War II Through Dienbienphu 1941–1954 (New York 1988). A good study, using Vietnamese language sources, of the evolution of the Vietminh army is Greg Lockhart, *Nation in Arms: The Origins of the People's Army of Vietnam* (Sydney 1989). Carl Thayer, *War by Other Means: National Liberation and Revolution in Viet-Nam 1954–1960* (Sydney 1989) is another valuable study based on Vietnamese sources.

A good survey of the causes of the war is Anthony Short, *The Origins of the Vietnam War* (London 1989). A very good more extensive study of causation that pays attention to the Vietnamese side is George McT. Kahin, *Intervention: How America Became Involved in Vietnam* (New York 1986). A recent collection of readings is Jeffrey P. Kimball, *The Debate About the Causes of U.S. Involvement in the Vietnam War* (New York 1990).

The best short history of the whole war from the American perspective is George C. Herring, *America's Longest War: the United States and Vietnam, 1950–1975* (2nd edit., Philadelphia 1986). William S. Turley, *A Short Political and Military History, 1964–1975* (Boulder 1986) is the best short military history, which examines the war from the Vietnamese as well as the American side. The best of the more recent general histories of the war is Marylin Young, *The Vietnam Wars 1945–1990* (New York 1991).

It is invidious to single out the many good specialized studies of the war, but ones especially useful for the writing of this book were Thomas C. Thayer, *War Without Fronts: The American Experience in Vietnam* (Boulder 1985) which is full of carefully compiled statistics; Eric M. Bergerud, *The Dynamics of Defeat: The Vietnam War in Hau Nghia Province* (Boulder 1991) which admirably complements Jeffrey Race's much earlier local study, *War Comes to Long An: Revolutionary Conflict in a Vietnam Province* (Berkeley 1972); Larry E. Cable, *Conflict of Myths: The Development of American Counterinsurgency Doctrine and the Vietnam War* (New York 1986), which places the war in the context of preceding guerilla wars; Neil Sheehan, *A Bright Shining Lie: John Paul Vann and America in Vietnam* (New York 1988), which is the best of the many recent biographies of Americans in the war; and Douglas Pike's recent studies of the war from the Vietnamese perspective: *PAVN: People's Army of Vietnam* (Novato 1986) and *Vietnam and the Soviet Union* (Boulder 1987).

A recent bibliography on the war is in James S. Olson and Randy Roberts, *Where the Domino Fell: America and Vietnam, 1945 to 1990* (New York 1991), which also has a useful chronology. James S. Olson (ed.), *Dictionary of the Vietnam War* (New York 1988) is a compendium of much useful information, though it is limited in analytical depth. A new bibliography is Lester H. Brune and Richard Dean Burns, *America and the Indochina Wars, 1945–1990: A Bibliographical Guide* (Claremont, CA 1991).

INDONESIA, MALAYSIA AND CONFRONTATION

The best study of the origins and course of Confrontation is still J.A.C. Mackie, *Konfrontasi: the Indonesia-Malaysia Dispute 1963–1966* (Kuala Lumpur 1974). A more recent study of Australia's involvement in Confrontation and the Irian Jaya dispute is Gregory Pemberton, *All the Way: Australia's Road to Vietnam* (Sydney 1987), which has a good bibliography. Christopher J. McMullen, *Mediation of the West New Guinea Dispute, 1962: A Case Study* (Washington 1981) provides a comprehensive account of the international negotiations. Franklin B. Weinstein, *Indonesia's Foreign Policy and the Dilemma of Dependence: From Sukarno to Suharto* (Ithaca 1976) is a study of the making of Indonesian foreign policy in the period. Pamela Sodhy, 'Malaysian-American Relations during Indonesia's Confrontation against Malaysia, 1963–66', *Journal of Southeast Asian Studies* XIX, 1988, 111–36 is a good study of US policy towards Confrontation. The most comprehensive English language account of the attempted coup and fall of Sukarno is Harold Crouch, *The Army and Politics in Indonesia* (2nd edit., Ithaca 1988). Another study of these events is Nawaz B. Mody, *Indonesia under Suharto* (New York 1987), which has a comprehensive bibliography.

For the Indonesian invasion of Timor and its aftermath see John G. Taylor, *Indonesia's Forgotten War: The Hidden History of East Timor* (London 1991). A good introduction to Indonesia's problems in Irian Jaya is Robin Osborne, *Indonesia's Secret War: The Guerilla Struggle in Irian Jaya* (Sydney 1985). For Australia's relations with Indonesia see Desmond Ball and Helen Wilson (eds), *Strange Neighbours: The Australian-Indonesia Relationship* (Sydney 1991), which has a useful bibliography.

THE US, USSR AND CHINA

A good recent overview of this topic to 1972 with a good bibliography is Gordon H. Chang, *Friends and Enemies: The United States, China, and the Soviet Union* (Stanford 1990). A recent competent overview of US Chinese relations from 1972 to 1990 is Harry Harding, *A Fragile Relationship: The United States and China Since 1972* (Washington 1992). A revisionist study of early US-Communist China relations is David Allan Mayers, *Cracking the Monolith: U.S. Policy Against the Sino-Soviet Alliance, 1949–1955* (Baton Rouge 1986). R.K.I. Quested, *Sino-Russian Relations: A Short History* (Sydney 1984) provides a brief overview with good bibliographical essays. A comprehensive bibliography is the ABC Clio Information Services, *Sino-Soviet Conflict: A Historical Bibliography* (Santa Barbara 1985). Other more specialized studies are: Michael R. Beschloss, *The Crisis Years: Kennedy and Kruschev 1960–1963* (New York 1991) and John W. Lewis and Xue Lital, *China Builds the Bomb* (Stanford 1988).

ASEAN AND INDOCHINA

For the development of ASEAN see Alison Broinowski (ed.), *Understanding ASEAN* (London 1983), which has a useful 'further reading' section, and Michael Leifer, *ASEAN and the Security of South-East Asia* (London 1989). A very good study of conflict in Indochina after the conquest of South Vietnam is Grant Evans and Kelvin Rowley, *Red Brotherhood at War: Vietnam, Cambodia and Laos since 1975* (revised edit. London 1990), which has a useful bibliography. For Pol Pot's Kampuchea see especially Elizabeth Becker, *When the War was Over: Cambodia's Revolution and the Voices of its People* (New York 1986). For the Sino-Vietnamese War of 1979 see King C. Chen, *China's War with Vietnam, 1979* (Stanford 1987). For ASEAN and Vietnam's occupation of Cambodia see K.K. Nair, *Words and Bayonets: ASEAN and Indochina* (Selangor 1986). For recent developments in ASEAN see Alison Broinowski (ed.), *ASEAN into the 1990s* (New York 1990).

THE NEW JAPANESE ECONOMIC ORDER

A Marxist, but well researched study of Japanese economic expansionism is Rob Steven, *Japan's New Imperialism* (London 1990). See also William R, Nestor, *Japan's Growing Power over East Asia and the World Economy* (London 1990). For a Japanese view see Masataka Kosaka (ed.), *Japan's Choices: New Globalism and Cultural Orientations in an Industrial State* (London 1989). For a critical analysis of where the Japanese economic empire is heading see Bill Emmott, *The Sun Also Sets: The Limits to Japan's Economic Power* (New York 1989). For economic conflict between the US and Japan see Edward J. Lincoln, *Japan's Unequal Trade* (Washington 1990) and Chris C. Carvounis, *The United States Trade Deficit in the 1980s: Origins, Meanings and Policy Responses* (Westport 1987). For a scenario about where such conflict is heading see George Friedman and Meredith Lebard, *The Coming War with Japan* (New York 1991).

EAST ASIAN LITTLE DRAGONS

A critical overview of the economic progress of South Korea, Taiwan and Singapore is Walden Bello and Stephanie Rosenfeld, *Dragons in Distress: Asia's Miracle Economies in Crisis* (San Francisco 1990). For the economic development of South Korea see Danny M. Leipziger, *Korea: Transition to Maturity* (New York 1988) and Alice H. Amsden, *Asia's Next Giant: South Korea and Late Industrialization* (New York 1989). For a recent overview of economic and political developments in Korea see Chong-Sik Lee (ed.), *Korea Briefing, 1990* (Boulder 1991). For Taiwan's economic performance and diplomatic relations see Gary Klintworth (ed.), *Modern Taiwan in the 1990s* (Canberra 1991) and Martin L. Lasater, *Policy in Evolution: The U.S. Role in China's Reunification* (Boulder 1989). A readable and analytical account of Hong Kong's development is Felix Patrikeeff, *Mouldering Pearl: Hong Kong at the Crossroads* (London 1989). A good history of Singapore is C.M. Turnbull, *A History of Singapore 1819–1980* (Singapore 1989).

LATIN AMERICA

There is a comprehensive bibliography relating to Central America up to 1983 in Thomas M. Leonard, *Central America & United States Policies, 1820s–1980s: A Guide to Issues & References* (Claremont, California 1985). An excellent survey of recent history and the nature of the political systems in Central America is James Dunkerley, *Power in the Isthmus: A Political History of Modern Central America* (London 1988). A useful set of readings is John A. Booth and Mitchell A. Seligson (eds), *Elections and Democracy in Central America* (Chapel Hill 1989). For Panama see Michael L. Conniff, *Panama and the United States: The Forced Alliance* (Athens 1992).

Valuable studies of the Eisenhower era are Stephen G. Rabe, *Eisenhower and Latin America: The Foreign Policy of Anticommunism* (Chapel Hill 1988) and Richard H. Immerman, *The CIA in Guatemala: The Foreign Policy of Intervention* (Austin 1982). For a survey of the Alliance for Progress see Stephen Rabe's chapter in Thomas G. Paterson (ed.), *Kennedy's Quest for Victory: American Foreign Policy, 1961–1963* (New York 1989).

A good analysis of US policy towards Nicaragua is Robert A. Pastor, *Condemned to Repetition: The United States and Nicaragua* (Princeton 1987). For the Sandinista era see especially Dennis Gilbert, *Sandinistas: The Party and the Revolution* (New York 1988), which has a good bibliography, and Thomas W. Walker (ed.), *Reagan Versus the Sandinistas: The Undeclared War on Nicaragua* (Boulder 1987). A more sympathetic but critical analysis of the Contras is R. Pardo-Maurer, *The Contras, 1980–1989: A Special Kind of Politics* (London 1990).

For other good books on the Pacific Basin states of Latin America see Lester D. Langley, *Mexico and the United States: A Fragile Relationship* (Boston 1991), which has a good bibliographical essay; Jorge P. Osterling, *Democracy in Colombia: Clientalist Politics and Guerilla Warfare* (New Brunswick 1989); Daniel M. Masterson, *Militarism and Politics in Latin America: Peru from Sánchez Cerro to Sendero Luminoso* (Westport 1991); David Corkill and David Cubitt, *Ecuador: Fragile Democracy* (London 1988); Mark Falcoff, *Modern Chile 1970–1989: A Critical History* (New Brunswick 1989); Augusto Varas (ed.), *Democracy Under Siege: New Military Power in Latin America* (New York 1989). For an analysis of Japanese economic interests in Latin America see Susan Kaufman Purcell and Robert M. Immerman (eds), *Japan and Latin America in the New Global Order* (Boulder 1992).

THE PACIFIC ISLANDS

The best general history of the islands is Deryck Scarr, *The History of the Pacific Islands: Kingdoms of the Reefs* (Canberra 1990), which has a good bibliography. A new history of the Pacific in the twentieth century with a historiographical bent, Robert Kiste, Kerry Howe and Brij Lal (eds), *Waves of History: The Pacific Islands in the Twentieth Century*, will be published by the University of Hawaii Press in 1993. For a good history of France in the Pacific since 1945 see Stephen Henningham, *France and the South Pacific: A Contemporary History* (Sydney 1992). For specific island groups there are shortages of good modern histories but some that are valuable are: Ian Downs, *The Australian Trusteeship, Papua New Guinea 1945–75* (Canberra 1980); Judith Bennett, *Wealth of the Solomons: A History of a Pacific Archipelago* (Honolulu 1987); Howard Van Trease, *The Politics of Land in Vanuatu: From Colony to Independence* (Suva 1987); Robert Norton, *Race and Politics in Fiji* (2nd edit., St Lucia 1990); Malama Meleisea, *The Making of Modern Samoa: Traditional Authority and Colonial Administration in the Modern History of Western Samoa* (Suva 1987); Barrie Macdonald, *In Pursuit of Sacred Trust: Trusteeship and Independence in Nauru* (Wellington 1988); and Barrie Macdonald, *Cinderallas of the Empire: Towards a History of Kiribati and Tuvalu* (Canberra 1982).

For recent history of the islands the journals *Journal of Pacific History* and *The Contemporary Pacific* are invaluable. For islanders' struggles for independence and a nuclear free Pacific see Stewart Firth, *Nuclear Playground* (Sydney 1987) and David Robie, *Blood on their Banner: Nationalist Struggles in the South Pacific* (London 1989). A competent historical analysis of the rebellion on Bougainville with a good bibliography is Douglas Oliver, *Black Islanders: A Personal Perspective of Bougainville 1937–1991* (Melbourne 1991). For the Fiji coups see especially Brij V. Lal, *Power and Prejudice: The Making of the Fiji Crisis* (Honolulu 1988).

THE PACIFIC BASIN

A new book analyzing the concept of the Pacific Basin is Gerald Segal, *Rethinking the Pacific* (Oxford 1990). It provides a valuable background to political, ideological, cultural, strategic and economic aspects of the Pacific Basin in the mid–1980s, with some more general consideration of historical developments since the beginnings of its human habitation. For two other useful and recent books discussing contemporary aspects of the Pacific Basin see Gavin Boyd, *Pacific Trade, Investment and Politics* (London 1989); and Janos Radvanji (ed.), *The Pacific in the 1990s: Economic and Strategic Change* (Lanham, Maryland 1990).

Maps

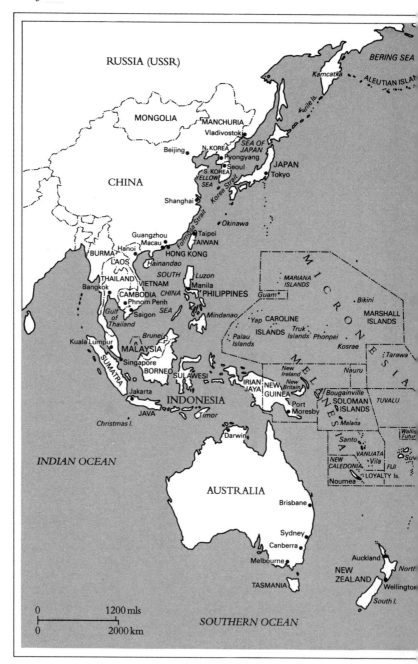

Map 1 The Pacific Basin

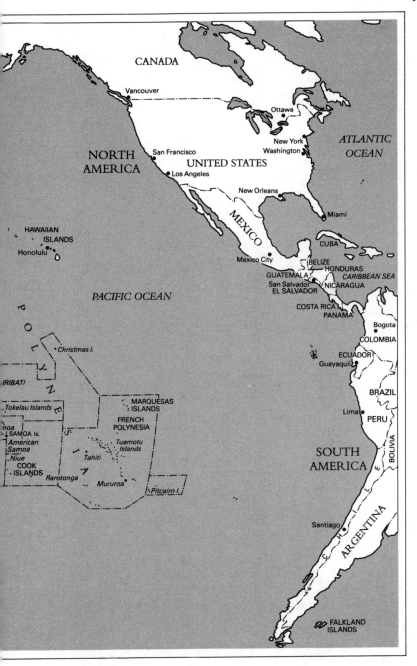

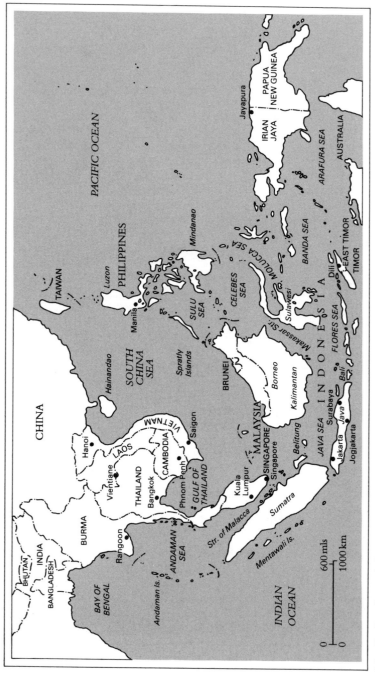

Map 2 Southeast Asia

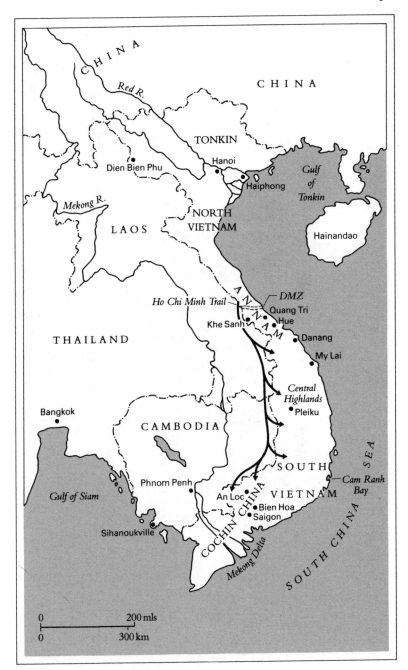

Map 3 North and South Vietnam

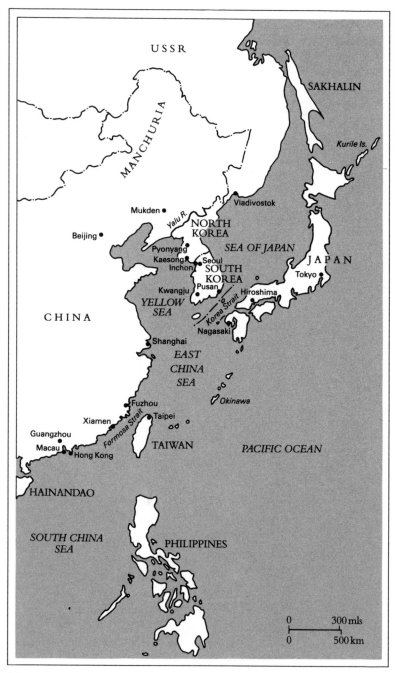

Map 4 Eastern China, Korea and Japan

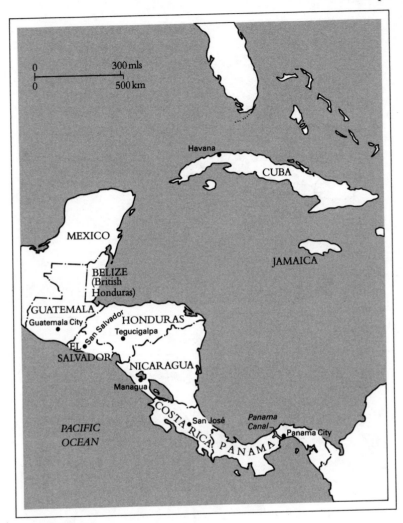

Map 5 Central America

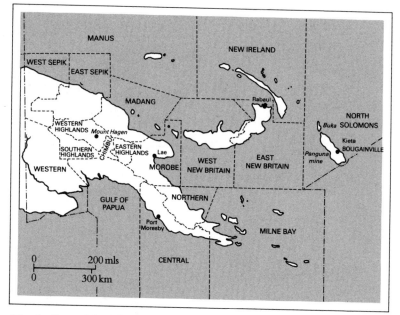

Map 6 Papua New Guinea

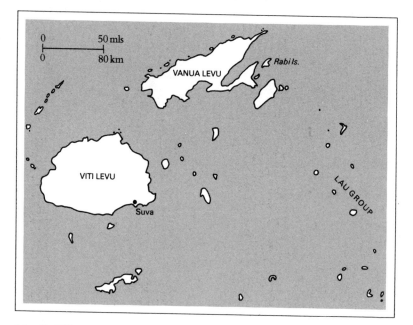

Map 7 Fiji

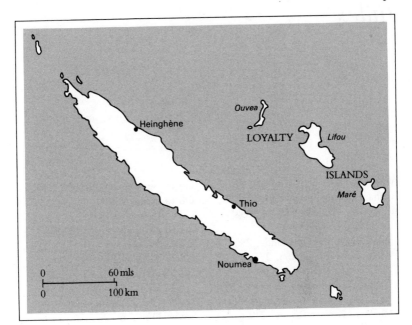

Map 8　New Caledonia

Index